MEDIA/READER

Perspectives on Mass Media Industries, Effects, and Issues

Media/ Reader

Perspectives on Mass Media
Industries, Effects, and Issues

SHIRLEY BIAGI

California State University, Sacramento

Wadsworth Publishing Company / Belmont, California /
A Division of Wadsworth, Inc.

Communications Editor: Kris Clerkin
Editorial Assistant: Tamiko Verkler
Production Editor: Michael G. Oates
Designer: MaryEllen Podgorski
Print Buyer: Barbara Britton
Copy Editor: Alan Titche
Compositor: Omegatype Typography, Inc.
Signing Representative: Robin Levy

Printed in the United States of America   19

2   3   4   5   6   7   8   9   10—93   92   91   90   89

Library of Congress Cataloging in Publication Data

Media/reader : perspectives on mass media industries, effects, and
   issues / [edited by] Shirley Biagi.
      p.   cm.
   Includes bibliographies and index.
   ISBN 0-534-08955-0
   1. Mass media—Social aspects.   2. Mass media—Social aspects—
United States.   I. Biagi, Shirley.
   HM258.M3745   1989
   302.2'34—dc19

88-34366
CIP

Thank you, Michael Oates

Preface

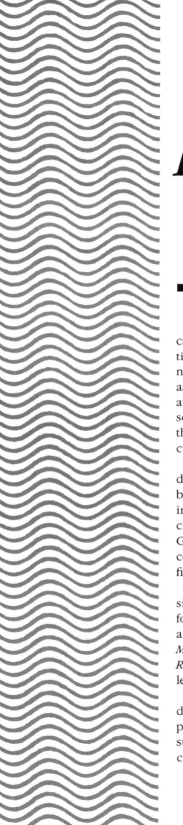

Trying to keep up with media issues is like chasing a speeding train in a car—every once in a while you catch the train at the station, but most of the time you miss it. You can corner an issue one day and then the events of the next day transform the arguments. Yet there is much value in staying as current as possible with the changes—as cable operators battle broadcasters for the audience, as the Supreme Court decides who will have the final word on high school newspaper content, and as critics charge that television causes everything from low school achievement to sexual promiscuity to a vapid American culture.

Media/Reader is designed to help you slow down the speeding train of media issues long enough to take a thoughtful look at how some of the nation's best media observers analyze what is happening. Collected here are 89 readings on classic media topics as well as today's most timely media issues, including insights from journalists Edna Buchanan, Bob Greene, and Ellen Goodman; media scholars L. John Martin, John Hulteng, and George Gerbner; commentators Jeff Greenfield, Dorothy Thompson, and Lewis H. Lapham; and filmmakers George Lucas and Steven Spielberg.

The text, divided into 16 chapters, can be used as a stand-alone reader designed for Introduction to Mass Media and Mass Media and Society classes and for Media Issues seminars. *Media/Reader* also can be used as a companion to any introductory mass media text, including *Media/Impact: An Introduction to Mass Media*. The chapter organization is the same as *Media/Impact*, but *Media/Reader* also covers international media issues to prepare students for the challenges of global media.

Chapter 1 (Understanding the Mass Media Industries) offers an overview discussion. Chapters 2–10 cover the specific American media industries (newspapers, magazines, radio, television, movies, recordings, and books) and their support industries (advertising and public relations). Chapters 11–14 present current media topics (ownership and news gathering, media effects, legal and regulatory issues, and ethical practices). Chapters 15 and 16 introduce students to world media systems and issues, including discussions about how the media operate in other countries and how technology has transformed the world into a single media marketplace.

Each article is preceded by a *Perspective*—a summary of major points in the form of questions for discussion and contemplation. Each chapter ends with a brief list of selected readings as guidelines for further research.

Media/Reader includes articles from journals (*Columbia Journalism Review* and *National Forum,* for example); trade magazines (*Advertising Age* and *Publishers Weekly,* for example); and the popular press (*The New York Times, Harper's, The Wall Street Journal,* and the *Washington Post,* for example). Also included are book excerpts on timely media topics.

I selected topical articles from the popular press to keep readers current with the dynamics of today's media industries and issues. I included readings from journals and books to highlight the literature of the media and to reflect the richness of research available. Several articles are appearing here in print for the first time. I hope you will find these selections provocative, timely, and readable.

Acknowledgments

This text could not have been compiled without each of the voices represented here. Their constant and productive analysis, criticism, and praise of the world's media are what make the study of mass media so challenging.

In addition, thanks go to my colleagues at universities and colleges throughout the country for reviewing this text, especially Thomas Beell, Iowa State University; Kenneth Harwood, University of Houston—University Park; Seong Lee, Appalachian State University; and Maclyn McClary, Humboldt State University.

Please send your comments, criticisms, and suggestions to me at California State University, 6000 J Street, Sacramento, California 95819. Thank you.

Shirley Biagi

Contents

Chapter Fourteen

Ethical Practices   283

PART V

International Media   313

Chapter Fifteen

World Media Systems   314

Chapter Sixteen

World Media Issues   334

MEDIA/READER

Perspectives on Mass Media Industries, Effects, and Issues

Overview

PART I

Understanding the Mass Media Industries

CHAPTER ONE

How Does the Communications Revolution Affect Society?

Every day you are affected by the mass media in some way—when you study a textbook for school, when you turn on the radio in your car, when you rent a movie at the video store to watch at home. The collective effects on society of all these media choices are what Ray Newton talks about in this essay.

Consider:

1. In what terms did Harold Lasswell describe the media's roles?

2. Which of the six press systems described in this article best defines the way the mass media actually work in the United States?

3. What roles should the media play in a democratic society?

4. Does the special privilege afforded the press under the First Amendment carry special responsibilities? Explain.

Roles, Rights, and Responsibilities: Whom Should the Media Serve?

RAY NEWTON

Slightly more than 550 years ago, a German craftsman invented a machine which introduced to the then-civilized world what is now known as mass media. Johannes Gutenberg and his colleagues little realized that moveable type and the printing press would initiate what ultimately became the "communications revolution"—a revolution which has affected virtually everyone throughout the world. . . .

Revolution it has been. It is impossible to tell how many millions of words and pictures have been disseminated in just the past 100 years, let alone since the invention of the printing press. But in that 100 years, we have shifted from the primitive, hand-operated printing presses, which changed little from those of the fifteenth century, to sophisticated, technologically superior systems and devices which permit almost instantaneous transmission of media messages to any locale in the world. Only the most naive among us would say we are not affected by those messages, particularly here in the United States. From the moment people tumble out of bed in the morning until they crawl under the covers at night, they are in some way subjected to the influences of mass media. The

Ray Newton is Dean of the College of Creative and Communication Arts at Northern Arizona University.

extent and effects of that media influence are examined [here].

Consider this: Just today, some 63 million copies of almost 1,700 daily newspapers are being circulated. Just this week, more than 50 million copies of some 7,500 weekly newspapers will be distributed. Just this month, approximately 10,000 magazine titles will reach the media marketplace. And just this year, some 45,000 new book titles will compete for readers.

The extent of influence of the electronic media is even more difficult to assess. Some 1,450 television stations will send signals to an estimated 98 percent of American households. Additionally, cable television signals will reach an estimated 33 million homes. Radio—who honestly knows the extent of its listenership? Approximately 8,500 stations, AM and FM, are picked up by more than 500 million radio receivers. No one really knows how many radio sets are operative in this country, given the millions of inexpensive transistorized personal receivers that the public uses while jogging, working, or relaxing.

It is also true that no one really knows the extent of the distribution of films. An estimated 400 to 500 feature films are released annually. They are viewed on the big screen in some 21,000 movie theatres across the country by millions of movie-goers (mostly teenagers and young adults). How many millions more watch the same films on VCRs in the privacy of their residences? How many students watch films in classrooms? How many organizations and corporations use films of various types for training?

The above media are the most prominent and publicly conspicuous. Others, though, are so much a part of our lives that we often forget to consider them as mass media—billboards, posters and brochures, matchbook covers, specialty advertising gimmicks such as embossed keychains and golf balls—myriad other forms of messages that compete for our attention and interests.

Media influence is pervasive and persuasive. It surrounds us, engulfs us. Mass media are such an integral part of our educational, social, political, and economic systems today that if they were to disappear, our society would suffer serious consequences.

Developing as they have into perhaps the most significant social influences in the nation today, the media have taken unto themselves—or in some cases, been assigned—several different roles. Forty years ago, Harold Lasswell, a prominent social scientist, developed the concept in *Communication of Ideas* that media have three major roles in society. The first is surveillance—reporting to society the threats, changes, and dangers to the well-being of the greater community. This function has been popularly labeled as the "watchdog role."

The second role, Lasswell suggests, is the interpretation of current events in the social environment: evaluating and analyzing the impact of contemporary events.

The third role the media play, Lasswell says, is communicating to future generations the social heritage which characterizes that particular culture: media provide a means for transmitting the events of the past to the future. Thus, the media form a unique system whereby values within the social system are perpetuated and give the continuity and consistency which endow a culture with its distinct qualities of identity. Generations ago, this role was often taken by parents and grandparents who transmitted verbally to their children what had happened in the past. Now this transmission of heritage is more often accomplished through some form of media.

The consequences of the roles the media play in our lives are staggering. In fact, it has been speculated that the mass media set the agenda for much of what we do. The media are often telling us what should and should not be important to us socially, culturally, educationally, politically, and economically.

The major events in the nation and the world, about which most of us have strong beliefs and attitudes, undoubtedly have been brought to our awareness, interpreted, and assigned value through media, not personal experience. Nuclear power, AIDS, the energy crisis, the Middle East, famine and drought in Africa, space exploration, education reform, science and religion, minority rights—these and dozens of other topics about which we have vigorous opinions are likely the result of our having been exposed to media transmission of messages.

Sorting out these messages is perhaps one of the most difficult tasks we face. Because of the almost exponential explosion of information, we cannot possibly sift through and assimilate all that surrounds us. We are compelled to let others assess and compress information for us. We are, in a sense, victims of our own inability to handle such large quantities of information without confusion.

We must of necessity let those who are presumably trained and skilled make those decisions about what is important for us—set the agenda, so to speak.

That becomes a critical issue. . . . Can we trust the watchdogs who tell us what has happened or is likely to happen and what the effects of those happenings will be? Have the three roles which Lasswell described been sustained, or have they been misused and corrupted by contemporary media? To be sure, misuse or corruption is not necessarily by design. But is it possible that the media messengers, the information brokers, and the agenda setters have neglected what might possibly be the most critical component of mass media—social responsibility to an audience?

More than thirty years ago, three noted media scholars and critics examined the development and growth of media in a book called *Four Theories of the Press*. In brief, Theodore Peterson, Fred S. Siebert, and Wilbur Schramm examined the different roles which media seemed to play in several forms of government. They suggested that four dominant press sytems were in place: *authoritarian,* where a dictator controls and regulates the press (even though the press might be privately owned) so that the dictatorship will be sustained; *libertarian,* which is in opposition to the authoritarian concept in that it is assumed that the individual rather than

the government is superior, and hence, that no governmental control at all is preferable; *Soviet-communist,* where the media are owned and controlled by the government (not necessarily an individual) and are to protect the status quo of the government; and *social responsibility,* where the media are charged with providing the public with meaningful news and information, free from governmental control and yet responsive to societal and sometimes governmental pressures.

A fifth theory of the press was proposed in 1981, when scholar William Hachten suggested a *developmental* model, where the press is viewed as a collaborator with government, especially in Third World and underdeveloped nations, in urging positive social, economic, and political improvements.

In 1983, yet another theory was suggested by Robert G. Picard, when he envisioned a *democratic socialist* system wherein media ownership is public, non-profit, and intended to permit the citizens to debate what they consider important societal concerns.

Still other variants of the above-noted theories exist, and none is totally comprehensive. The theories do, however, point up that differences exist among governments and peoples regarding what they view as the role of media in the social system.

Most Americans would agree that the social responsibility theory is perhaps the ideal toward which the press should aspire, for contained within it is the concept that if the press takes liberties or becomes too excessive in its zeal, the government has the right and responsibility to curb those excesses to protect its citizens. Yet a conflict seems to be growing in the United States between the media and the government, with the frequent complaint that the freedom of the press guaranteed in the First Amendment to the Constitution is being ignored and violated, both legally and ethically.

Ironically, articulate and vocal proponents from both sides of the issue, those who advocate freedom of the press from any governmental restraint and those who support governmental limitations upon alleged abuses by the press (libel, invasion of privacy, and the like), more and more frequently use the media to express their points of view. One of them, Jean Kirkpatrick, in a syndicated column in the *Los Angeles Times* this past May, questioned the right of the media to inquire into the private life of former Democratic presidential candidate Gary Hart and his relationship with Donna Rice. She wrote:

The fact that no further revelations concerning Hart's sex life followed his withdrawal from the presidential race (although we are told the Washington Post *has in hand affidavits concerning these matters), tacitly suggests a corollary to the principle: presidential candidates have no right to privacy, but ex-candidates do.*

She also notes that public opinion polls indicate that most Americans believe that presidential candidates do in fact have rights to privacy and that they did not approve of the *Miami Herald*'s investigation and consequent stories.

Nationally known columnist Mike Royko of the *Chicago Tribune* discussed the same issue in a recent column. In an extended anecdote, he tells of telephoning the public relations department at the *New York Times* to ask some personal questions about the top management of the newspaper. Royko reported that he asked the following: "What I want to know is if they are married. And if they have ever been divorced. And if they have been divorced, when did it happen?"

Royko says the woman who answered responded, "I'm not going to give out that information," and she hung up.

Royko continues his anecdote by commenting that he found it ironic that one of the world's major newspapers, which had asked extremely personal questions of presidential candidates—questions about their medical records and psychiatric backgrounds—refused to reveal what, in fact, was a matter of public record about its own executives.

Royko comments that he does not think it unreasonable to ask personal questions about

editors of a newspaper which shapes domestic and foreign policy and examines critically the political and public figures of the world. He wrote: " . . . it seems only fair that we should have some insight into the character and judgment and stability of these people."

The point of his anecdote is clear.

A third nationally known writer-columnist looked at the same situation in still another fashion. Ellen Goodman for the *Boston Globe* asked exactly how far the media should go in probing into the personal lives of presidential candidates, citing both the *Miami Herald* stories about Gary Hart and the *New York Times* inquiries of presidential candidates about their private lives. Goodman defends the right of the press to ask any question it wants of candidates—but she also defends the right of the candidates to say, "I do not have to answer that question." She additionally says that the right to ask questions does not belong exclusively to the press; it also belongs to every citizen. But so does the right to say, "I don't have to answer."

She suggests that often the press is on a fishing expedition—and it wants to fish without licenses in private ponds.

Kirkpatrick and Royko and Goodman certainly are not the only respected opinion leaders who have complained about the media's "going too far." They represent a goodly number of respected professional writers and reporters and editors who know down deep the differences between the public's right to know and an individual's right to privacy. They also represent a substantial number of media professionals who do try to present accurate, balanced, and complete information about significant issues to the public. Among them is Tom Wicker of the *New York Times*.

A recent detailed interview with political columnist Wicker in the Spring 1987 issue of *American Thought Leader* (published by the BB&T Center for Leadership Development at East Carolina University) focuses upon Wicker's observations of the strengths, weaknesses, and influences of mass media as he perceives them today. For several decades, Wicker has covered regional and national political events and has won dozens of awards for his in-depth analysis of what he observes (the interpretive role of the press). During his interview, he responded to a question about ethics and ethical behavior among media practitioners.

No question about it. Journalistic ethics is, I think, a real matter, a real subject, one that at least used to be scanted by the journalism schools. I think they ought to put more emphasis on it; but then again, it is very difficult. I wouldn't want to sit down myself, for example, and try to write a code of ethics for reporters. It is very difficult. . . .

What you have to inculcate in journalists—the editors should, and the journalism schools really should—is a sense of responsibility toward generally sound human values. There are times when journalistic values override what might normally be considered human values. There are other times when they don't. I hear a lot of my colleagues say, "Oh, yes, I'd commit a crime right away in order to inform the public." Then you should say to your colleague right away, "Well, are you prepared to go to jail for doing that?" "Oh, no," he will say, "Why should I go to jail? I am serving the public's right to know." But I don't think you have any right to commit crimes to serve the public's right to know. If you commit a crime, you commit a crime. There's no way you can go to the judge and plead some extenuating circumstance.

Wicker also comments extensively about the roles the media must play in a democratic nation, and he frequently is critical of what he perceives as abuses which occur through media. Like many of us, he questions whether or not the media are motivated by the social responsibility which has been ascribed to them or by the profit motive and the desire to become power brokers. He decries the influence which television has in shaping public opinion, saying that the networks perhaps have turned their news into trivia and entertainment because of their concern for ratings and profit. Wicker also sug-

gests that the print media have not fulfilled their social responsibility, either. He cites the growth of newspaper chains and the disappearance of local ownership as weaknesses, suggesting the local ownership has more of a stake in a community than do outside owners.

Despite the criticisms of the mass media—and only a few have been noted above—most thoughtful persons will agree that mass media in America in the main do a superior job in reporting the news and informing the public.

Granted, there are those who will claim that the media are controlled by a few—that the content of the media is controlled and manipulated by a cabal of powerful editors and publishers and network executives and station managers. This is simply not true. The competitive nature of the individual reporters and the media themselves mandate against such collusion. The reality is that the tradition and training of most of the professional media personnel in this country are such that they tend to be similar in isolating key ideas and facts. They are taught to put the most critical elements of news—the traditional who, what, when, where, why, and how—at the beginning. Hence, the similarities are not the result of any conspiracy but rather the quest for significant details.

Walter Mears, a Pulitzer Prize-winning newspaperman who is now a vice president with Associated Press, the world's largest news-gathering organization, recently collaborated with John Chancellor, longtime TV anchorman for the NBC news network. In their book, *The News Business,* they talk about the competitive scramble for stories. They describe vividly the daily race to meet deadlines in both print and electronic media, all in an effort to beat the opposition. They analyze how and why newspaper content and news broadcasts often seem similar and yet are distinctly different from one another. And they conclude that the criticism accusing the press of "pack journalism" is simply not true. Rather, they claim that most professional news personnel have as both short- and long-range goals the objective of beating the competition and having more and better information and details than anyone else. The ultimate result of this objective, of course, is increased circulation or better ratings—which translates into more money for the ownership. . . .

It is not coincidental that the First Amendment to the Constitution is the one which focuses upon freedoms of speech and of the press. Those freedoms, if seriously contemplated and responsibly practiced by media personnel in relationship to the roles, rights, and responsibilities of their profession, define the obligation of the media to the public.

Thomas Jefferson, a primary architect of the Constitution, was certainly aware of the significance of the document and the consequent First Amendment and the power it gave to the press. He addressed this very issue when he wrote in a letter in 1787, "The basis of our government being the opinion of the people, the very first objective should be to keep that right; and were it left to me to decide whether we should have a government without newspapers, or newspapers without a government, I should not hesitate a moment to prefer the latter."

Jefferson, of course, had no way of knowing that newspapers, then the dominant medium, would evolve and expand into what they are today. He certainly had no idea of the likelihood of development of electronic media which would evolve some 140 years later. But he did have the wisdom and the insight to recognize that despite all the flaws and warts and wrinkles, the press (now more broadly defined as the mass media) should and would become the most significant and influential force in the nation. What remains is for the mass media to continue evaluating and assessing their social obligations with respect to their roles, rights, and responsibilities. ■

PERSPECTIVE 2

Understanding Mass Communication

Mass communication is the process by which we receive messages from the mass media. In this excerpt from their book *Understanding Mass Communication,* Jay Black and Frederick C. Whitney describe that process.

Consider:

1. How do the four functions that mass communication serves in society differ from one another?

2. Describe the part that symbology plays in the transmission of culture.

3. How important is the role of advertising as an economic support for the American mass media?

4. What roles do the mass media play in communicating stereotypes and myths?

An Introduction to Mass Communication

JAY BLACK and FREDERICK C. WHITNEY

Functions of Mass Communication

The mass media can be described as having four primary functions: (1) information, (2) entertainment, (3) persuasion, and (4) transmission of the culture. We refer to them here as the primary or most important functions, but there are, of course, others. For instance, the media serve an adversary/symbiotic function with government; they serve to help people cope with or escape from their environment; they create new values and channel old ones; and they serve an important economic function by keeping the wheels of commerce turning. For each of these positive and intended functions, there may be an opposing or negative "dysfunction." Some examples of this are war nerves or unrest among citizens who are constantly told of crises among governments, or anti-social, greedy, or self-destructive behavior among some who have experienced entertainment programming or commercial messages originally intended to bring diversion or pleasure.

In individual communication, functional gears can be shifted at will. We plead, assert, instruct, joke, question—moving from one mode to another as situation and inclination demand. In mass communication, altering the primary functional thrust of a medium is somewhat more difficult. This is because the highly organized, institutionalized nature of the mass media cre-

ates a ponderous inertia resistant to change. Like living organisms, the systems making up the media are in delicate balance, and even slight adjustments can have quite an impact.

Audiences have grown to expect one format—or a certain combination of formats—from each medium, and a departure deceives audience expectations and threatens profit. The thrust of the *National Enquirer* is basically entertainment, providing sensation, spice, and escapism. The concern of the *New York Times* is information, to be "the newspaper of record." Drastic changes in these—or any—media's basic functional mix are seen as indications of serious identity crises. In such cases, the death of such a medium is more likely than metamorphosis or transmutation.

We will take up each basic function in turn, pointing out some overlapping of the functions and problems that arise when the functions are confused in the minds of the gatekeepers and media consumers.

Information

When we think of the various functions of the mass media, the information function frequently comes to mind first. Information is the easiest of the functions to identify, because it comprises a part of each, and the most prominent form of information is news.

The emphasis on news has camouflaged the fact that 60 percent of the average newspaper is advertising and that a considerable portion of

Jay Black is Chair of the School of Journalism at the University of Alabama. Frederick C. Whitney is Professor Emeritus, Department of Journalism, San Diego State University.

what is left over after the ads have been inserted is entertainment of one sort or another, starting with the comics and ranging from selected features, editorials, and columnists to a variety of sensational and human-interest stories. However, the basic thrust of the newspaper remains informational. That is what the audience expects of it. The *New York Daily News* satisfies its information function, for example, by finding a high quotient of sensational material—such as violence and sex—and presenting it with proper news leads, written in a punchy style.

As adjuncts to mass media, the wire services (particularly the Associated Press [AP] and United Press International [UPI]) have the highest information content. Their business is selling information, specifically news of current events gathered worldwide. Further, their customers or clients—the newspapers, television networks, and individual television and radio stations across the nation—represent such a broad spectrum of approaches, interests, formats, and editorial policies that the wire services tend to rely on straight news—an objective, unadulterated informational approach that avoids all attempts to color the news. The wire services leave it to their clients to choose specific items from those offered and to season those items as they see fit.

Textbooks, making up about half of the book publishing industry, are expected by their publishers and readers to consist primarily of information. Their voluntary readership is slight, and they are generally read at the direction of an instructor. For this reason publishers frequently attempt to interject humor (entertainment) as a relief from the heavy dose of information. Not incidentally, publishers also hope to sell a lot of books in order to make a profit. The other branches of book publishing—trade books, fiction, and nonfiction—are freer to depart from pure information as their thrust, but their information function is still relatively high, covering a wide variety of topics from which readers select and choose at their own discretion.

Although television's primary function is entertainment, it does include some information.

There are regularly scheduled newscasts that tend to take on entertainment overtones. News commentators are not so much in competition with each other as they are with other prime-time personalities. Their formats are doctored to move quickly and dramatically regardless of the significance of the information they are presenting.

Documentaries also take on a dramatic quality and sometimes, but not always, develop a point of view that: (1) is designed to appeal to the presumed taste of their massive audience, and (2) is not necessarily objective in its analysis. Award-winning and highly rated "60 Minutes" is probably the most obvious example. The CBS team uses such dubious techniques as that of accosting unsuspecting news sources in the street with cameras rolling and choosing controversial story topics that are intended to raise ratings.

Television cannot be entirely blamed for cursory treatment of serious topics. Profit is the motivating force. Television's ratings indicate massive regular departures of viewers whenever a documentary appears. For instance, would you be more interested in watching an hour-long program on industrial waste or a network showing of a Hollywood blockbuster?

Entertainment

The broadcast media—radio, television, and film—have a basic, although by no means exclusive, entertainment thrust. Film is included in this category because, although there are differences, film is such a large part of contemporary television that one cannot realistically be considered without the other.

That the broadcast media are intensely, purposefully, and enthusiastically entertainment oriented is fairly obvious. Also apparent is the persuasive, commercial aspect of television. Anyone who has had the misfortune of being hospitalized for a week or so can testify to the unremitting and highly imaginative diet of entertainment and persuasive fare that daytime television offers, with its fantasies of soap operas, game shows, old movies, and reruns. Prime time (during the evening) is a wonderland of scheduled police situations, private eyes, hospitals, situation comedies, personalities, serials, and premiere movies that move inexorably in the direction of sex, violence, and deviance.

The Public Broadcasting Service (PBS) is confirmation of broadcast's need to entertain. PBS—supported by government funding, private donations, and corporate underwriting—has no commercial requirements to make money or show a profit. Devoid of these commercial pressures, it is also free to offer programs of consequence (culture, education, documentaries), and it presents these to almost always smaller audiences·than the commercial networks would tolerate. There is a serious question about how much incentive exists either to produce or to watch a non-commercial medium in a commercial society.

The largest portion of radio is the same mixture of entertainment and commercials that television offers. Lacking television's video quality, radio must concentrate on what it does best—appeal to the ear—and this generally means music. The spectrum of music offered by radio is impressive. Station by station, radio has selectively carved out a segment of the audience to which it appeals, and station by station, it continues to move goods to these audiences: components to stereo enthusiasts, blemish ointments to teenagers, and annuities to the affluent. Radio's audiences are far more diversified than television's, and its production costs are far less. This permits it to specialize toward selective audiences, and such specialization may take a form other than music. Some radio stations have found their niche in broadcasting a series of constantly updated news bulletins, emphasizing information in a largely entertainment medium.

Film has shown a gradual metamorphosis in recent years. In its heyday during the 1930s and early 1940s, it was essentially a mass entertainment medium, playing in baroque palaces to large audiences. Now it has moved under television's competitive pressure to be a more expressive medium, freed from the tyranny of appealing to the tastes of the lowest common denominator. Further changes are starting to occur with the growth of the home video market.

Although most of film still has a basic entertainment thrust, particularly that portion serving the television industry, two other facets of filmmaking are becoming evident: (1) a distinctly persuasive-informative orientation in industrial or commercial films, and (2) a self-conscious role as social critic in the so-called popular movies that typically play to smaller, more selective audiences.

While the broadcast media and film have been identified as the basic purveyors of entertainment, this function is always intermixed with others. A high degree of entertainment pervades all mass media, often serving as the vehicle for more serious functions.

The entertainment function of the media requires an extraordinarily affluent society to support the level inherent in American mass communication. When considering that mass communication is time-consuming, and that a substantial portion of it is pure entertainment, as evidenced by television, we become aware of the prerequisite leisure and affluence of our society that enables us to spend so much of our time unproductively. But this makes a certain amount of sense in our democratic society when we figure that the average consumer of mass media is consciously seeking to fulfill personal needs and interests.

Persuasion

The persuasive function of the media in contemporary society is as significant as the information and entertainment functions. Advertising, of course, is its most apparent form, but there are other more subtle manifestations of persuasion that are likely to have lasting effects on the future of mass communication. The one-hundred billion dollars spent annually on advertising is only a portion of the amount spent on American mass media persuasion. Public-relations activities, special promotional events, and blatant as well as subtle efforts at image manipulation and public-opinion formation pervade the media environment. Editorials, letters to the editor, and opinion columns are obvious examples of overt persuasion; the subtle ways in which individual, social, and economic values are reflected in news columns, cartoons, music videos and other entertainment programs are something else. Because we recognize advertisements and editorials for what they are—blatant persuasion—we give them their proper due. But how do we cope with subtly implanted commercial products such as brand name beer, candy, cereal, or household products in our Hollywood films? And do we tell our children that their favorite Saturday morning cartoons are nothing but lures to bring them into the stores to buy the commercial products those cartoon characters represent?

Much of the persuasion in mass communications is concealed. Any public-relations practitioner can testify to the fact that a considerable portion of what passes for news in the media has a persuasive origin and an ulterior purpose. Much of what the public reads, hears, or watches in all the media is designed to influence in one way or another.

Political campaigns, which periodically command vast attention in the mass media, are almost pure persuasion. Much of governmental news at all levels has a propaganda base as government seeks to declare or justify its actions in a democratic society. A good part of business and financial news is advocacy. In today's environmental and consumer-conscious society, business is increasingly under attack and seeks to utilize the mass media in defense.

The doses of persuasion masquerading as information in mass communication are huge, and inevitably the functions have tended to merge, obliterating distinctions. This in turn leads to a credibility gap, because what appears to be bona fide news repeatedly turns out to be political or commercial advocacy, or is flavored by newspaper bias or television distortion.

Most of American mass media are supported by advertising in one way or another; commercial radio and television are 100 percent so. Newspapers and magazines in varying degrees rely heavily upon advertising revenues. The price of a newspaper does little more than cover distribution costs, leaving all editorial costs, all production costs, and all profit to be borne by paid advertising. Magazines vary widely in their use of advertising, but generally at least half their revenue, and hence, all their profit, comes from advertising.

It is obvious that television is not all entertainment. The schedule is regularly interspersed during daytime and evening hours with a mosaic of commercials touting used cars, beers, cosmetics, household sprays, fast-food restaurants, intimate hygiene products, major appliances, and ballpoint pens. Some of the commercials, we might note subjectively, appear better than the surrounding programming. That advertising should conform to or even surpass the format of the medium is not at all surprising.

In fact, a good case can be made that the role of advertising agencies in mass communication industries is to inject entertainment into commercial persuasion, lest the public's attention, subjected to unrelenting exposure to so many sales pitches, begins to wane and thus defeat the advertiser's purpose. In any event, it becomes apparent that the purpose of television programming is to provide a vehicle for the commercials, to deliver customers to the advertisers.

It is also significant that, although only 10 percent or less of the information or news that is available to media reporters and editors eventually appears in the news medium or newscast, nearly all of the available advertising is published or broadcast (with only minor exceptions, such as ads that are obscene, for illegal or overly controversial products, or that simply cannot be squeezed into the available time and space). This may offer a commentary on the relative values placed on advertising and information in a commercial society.

We generally think of entertaining feature movies when we consider films, but of the sixteen thousand films produced each year in the United States, only 150 or so are for theater distribution.

A highly profitable aspect of filmmaking is concerned with persuasion and information. Commercials are an obvious example. In addition, there are training, educational, and institutional films: travelogues, and driver-training, how-to-do-it, and sales-orientation films. Like textbooks, these films have limited appeal and are shown for specific reasons before captive audiences. They constitute a large portion of filmmaking, easily the greatest number of new films each year. But they lack the public exposure of either paid-admission films or television's "nights at the movies."

Film today shows considerable persuasive and informational content. It begins to lay serious claim as a prime medium of cultural transmission, recording and playing for inspection the triumphs, failures, and foibles of society. A good deal of social concern has proven profitable, and movies appear to have capitalized on this.

Transmission of the Culture

Cultural transmission is one of the most widespread but least understood functions of mass communication. Cultural transmission is inevitable, always present, for any communication has an effect on the individual recipient. Thus, any communication becomes, if ever so slightly, a part of the individual's experience, knowledge, and accumulated learning. Through individuals, communication becomes a part of the collective experience of groups, publics, audiences of all kinds, and the masses of which each individual is a part. It is this collective experience reflected back through communications forms, not merely in the mass media, but also in the arts and sciences, that paints a picture of the culture, of an age, of a society. Heritage, then, is the cumulative effect of previous cultures and societies that have become a part of humanity's birthright and being. It is transmitted by individuals, parents, peers, primary and secondary groups, and the educational process. This cultural communication is constantly modified by new experience.

Thus, cultural transmission takes place at two levels: the contemporary and the historical.

These two levels are unseparated and constantly interweaving. Furthermore, the mass media are major tools in the transmission of the culture on both levels. On the contemporary level, media constantly reinforce the consensus of society's values, while continually introducing the seeds of change. It is this factor that leads to the enigma surrounding the mass media; they are simultaneously the conservator of the status quo and the vehicle of change. Television, for instance, is both mirror and molder of the times. As television programs and original movies increasingly show previously taboo themes, such as nudity and sex, they reflect a change in the social structure—a change that television itself may be partially responsible for causing. The process is no less true of other media messages, even those primarily informational or persuasive.

Some records left by the mass media are conscious and intentional; others seem incidental but are nevertheless important. The market ads, for example, and white goods sales in daily newspapers are good indicators of contemporary living standards and of the tastes and values of society. Anthropologists of the twenty-second century, in searching for a full record of twentieth-century culture, would do well to study the cultural records transmitted in the catalogs issued by Sears, J. C. Penney, and Montgomery Ward. Although some may question the accuracy of television's portrayals of everyday life, this medium too collates and transmits today's cultural values. It must, because it is a commercial medium.

To understand the process of cultural transmission, indeed of communication itself, it is worthwhile to peer back as far back as possible into prehistory.

Two things about human communication are unique. The first is what, in his theory of general semantics from *Science and Sanity,* Alfred Korzybski called humans' "time-binding" ability based in memory. *Homo sapiens* alone, of all the creatures on earth, has been able to consciously store its experiences and pass them along from one generation to the next. Thus, the progress of the species has been more or less constant. This ability has led to cultural transmission as a function of the media, and to the entire institution of education, so much a part of this function. Nor should it be forgotten, particularly in today's deafening competition for attention, that only a part of this education is a formal, in-the-classroom, from-the-textbook education; an enormous amount of it is acquired willy-nilly from the mass media (most often, television) as they transmit their version of contemporary culture.

Historically the human race has been able to continually draw on the past and add new experience from the present to guide the future. Not only have humans been able to accumulate experience, but they have proven themselves able to sort and sift among these memories, discarding the unneeded and ordering the rest for ease in transmission both to their fellows and to posterity. It is this process that prunes knowledge from raw experience. With other species that lack the time-binding ability, each new generation starts more or less where its predecessor did and finishes at roughly the same state of development that all previous generations did, subject only to the ponderous process of biological evolution. In other words, all other species are somewhat static in time, whereas humans collectively and consciously determine their own future. Elephants of the twenty-first century, for all their intelligence and longevity, will be about the same as they are presently. However, it is safe to predict that humans will be substantially changed—socially, politically, economically, and technologically—and that the mass communications network serving the third-millenium culture as its central nervous system will be radically different both in cause and effect from that of today.

Related to all this, possibly a cause of it, is humanity's other unique distinction—its ability to deal in abstractions, to let symbols stand for things, thoughts, events, states of mind, and even for emotions, for very complex processes indeed. For example, human communication itself is an abstraction, requiring tools for the transfer of meaning. Sets of symbols, called "codes," or more simply, "languages," are employed. Most familiar to us are verbal symbols, such as the spo-

ken language. However, they probably are no more important to successful communication than are the entire range of nonverbal symbols such as body English, eye contact, mime, music, art, and graphics.

Words are symbols of things, thoughts, and emotions. No symbol is exact; it is, after all, only the attempted portrayal of reality, and "the map is not the territory," as general semanticists say. We all know what "flower" stands for—or do we? Since people's experiences with them differ, which flower does "flower" bring to mind—a rose, a violet, daisies in the field? Even narrowing the categories, does "rose" bring to mind the flower picked by young lovers, the one sent by an individual seeking forgiveness, or the one on a casket?

People think in words, verbally, and words mean special things to different people. But some words are more distinctive than others. To describe this relative difference, consider denotative and connotative words. Denotative words mean pretty much what they say they do. They are fairly explicit and have a general commonality, with little variation in meaning from person to person. "Bookcase" is a good example; "blackboard" is another. Wars are not likely to start over different interpretations of such words.

Connotative words, on the other hand, are less explicit; they imply rather than denote. They are far more abstract, referring rarely to things but rather to thoughts and abstract concepts such as justice, patriotism, love, beauty, truth, freedom, and courage. There is little commonality of acceptance in the meaning of these words. What is strategic defense? What is a peacekeeper missile? What is equal opportunity? What is the right to life? What is newer than new, whiter than white, fresher than fresh? The answers to these questions depend not only upon whom we ask, but the way in which we ask and the conditions under which we ask. Yet this is the stuff of which mass communication and public opinion are made, and, as we well know, the stuff over which battles are fought. Language and abstractions— the uniquely human tools mankind has designed to separate itself from other species—divide individuals and societies just as readily as they bind them together. As noted earlier, this semantic noise is an inevitable component of the mass communication process, just as it is a prime ingredient in cultural transmission.

Manipulation of language—verbal and non-verbal—in transmitting culture is the media's stock-in-trade. Such manipulation is not limited to the persuasive arts of advertising and public relations. It may be more readily observed in persuasion, but is no less influential when employed in informational and entertainment contexts. Two prime ways media use to bind culture together is through use of stereotypes and myths.

Stereotypes and Myths In this complex society, with its mounting competition for attention, rising decibels of noise, confusion, and accelerating pace, individuals live vicariously and, for the most part, experience their world only indirectly through the mass media. Reality, in large part, is what the media say reality is. In this situation stereotypes and myths provide some perceptual shortcuts to understanding. They are an economic means of ordering confusion, saving both time and labor; they are a useful mental filing system permitting an individual to sort and store experience with minimal effort.

Consider the nature of stereotypes. When some people hear "yuppies," it immediately invokes media-enhanced images of upwardly mobile baby-boomer professionals who dress casually but expensively, eat at fine restaurants, drink vintage wines, and talk about little other than work, money, leisure, and people. The stereotype also works in reverse. When those people see an under-forty man or woman driving a sporty car or engaging in any of the leisure time activities typically enjoyed by "yuppies," they automatically think "yuppy," and rightly or wrongly, that individual has been tucked into a pigeonhole of understanding. People carry all sorts of stereotypes around with them pertaining to politicians, absentminded professors, hookers, bankers, ditchdiggers, and rednecks.

One of the problems with stereotypes is that they may be in error. For decades, Stepin Fetchit was the stereotype in white America of the black male: a shiftless, subservient, comically ignorant black man of uncertain age. It was wrong, but it was convenient and it fitted well with the prevalent racial viewpoint. Thus, stereotypes, for all their usefulness and economy, must be used with great caution lest they help paint an erroneous picture of the world, and inhibit rather than assist understanding.

Myths are related to stereotypes; indeed, they are institutionalized stereotypes. They generally refer to beliefs and situations rather than to people. There is the myth of the power of the press, or the myth of women's superior intuition, both still prevalent. One thing noteworthy about stereotypes and myths is that generally there is a sufficient modicum of truth in them to make them believable. This credibility, once established, holds them over long after the original model passes away.

Like language itself, stereotypes and myths exist by consensus because a sufficiently large portion of society finds them to be a convenient shortcut to deeper, more analytical thought that also suits its particular world view. For the same reason, mass communication is replete with myths and stereotypes. In a thirty-second commercial, the little pictures of the good life in a viewer's head are invaluable aids in creating wants and desires. Network television and popular movies are full of white hats and black hats, good and bad personified for the audience in the quaint morality plays that compose most television series and many popular films. In a sociological and psychological sense, there really is little difference between the stereotyping and mythmaking of "Dallas," "Falcon Crest," "Days of Our Lives," "The Cosby Show," "Miami Vice," *Rambo,* or *Rocky.*

News reporters similarly use stereotypes and myths as a kind of shorthand for their readers. The headline "Yuppies Influence Election" creates a legend of impressions in only three words without saying much at all about what happened. Yet somehow people are deceived into thinking that they know all about it, enough at least to repeat it to a neighbor ("Say, did you see in the paper where the yuppies have had a major effect on the outcome of elections all over the country?"), and the stereotype passes on through cultural transmission.

As shortcuts to emotion, as well as shortcuts to understanding, myths and stereotypes are put in the hands of mass media gatekeepers for exploitation, whether to further a cause, to attract attention, or to appeal to the known prejudices of their particular audiences. Most likely, the use of stereotypes and myths may simply reflect the subconscious attitudes of a particular gatekeeper, or reflect the gatekeeper's views of audience orientation. They are not used perniciously to manipulate the unsuspecting public. A successful media system in a democratic society depends upon audiences' selection of media fare that is consistent with their own values, beliefs, needs, interests—and, indeed, stereotypes and myths.

A good case can be made for the fact that it is the degree to which the mass media fulfill the mythology of their particular audiences that determines the media's relative success in the marketplace. Cumulatively, the process results in cultural transmission, the most generic function of mass communication. ∎

PERSPECTIVE 3

Media as Entertainment

In this excerpt from his book *Trivializing America,* Norman Corwin discusses the easy availability of various entertainments in the United States and his belief about how they have transformed our society.

Consider:

1. Is entertainment as necessary to our society as Corwin claims? Why? Why not?

2. How does the U.S. system of media encourage and promote entertainment?

3. Why does Corwin believe that Americans have become "bored, spoiled children" seeking sensational experiences?

4. What is Corwin's antidote? Do you agree or disagree? Why? Why not?

Trivializing America: Entertainment

NORMAN CORWIN

Where Life becomes a Spasm
And history a Whiz
If that is not Sensation
I don't know what it is.
LEWIS CARROLL

There is a joke that goes, Why are ten pall-bearers needed at a rock funeral? Answer: Eight to carry the coffin, and two to carry the radio. It is not much of a joke, but it illustrates a phenomenon of the times—the inundation of America by a rising flood of entertainment, to such an extent that millions have become water-logged. So pressing is the need for distractions that hikers, amblers, joggers on the street and at the beach and in the country, and shoppers at the supermarket cover their ears with headset radios and listen as they ambulate. It is not enough for some spectators to be present at baseball and football games, watching the action; they listen to other games going on at the same time.

But sports, already a massive industry both *in loco* and on the air, are only a fragment of the universe of entertainment. Every day of the year, in every major city of the country and in many minor ones, attractions are heaped on attractions: movies, plays, concerts, dancing, galleries, museums, night clubs, cabarets, fashion shows, massage parlors, zoos, Disneylands, Sea Worlds, Woodstocks, festivals, pageants, touring, horse racing, dog racing, car racing, drag racing, roller-skating derbies, mudwrestlers, circuses, amusement parks, arcades, recordings—and on top of all that, around-the-clock programs on radio and television, ramified at home by ancillary tapes, discs, cartridges and cables.

And then come private and semi-private entertainments—hobbies, puzzles, partying, swap meets, sociables, smokers, bees, balls, picnics, clambakes, fishing, bowling, skiing, tennis, golf, card games, bingo, gambling. So pervasive is the concept of entertainment as daily necessity that home furnishings now include wall units known as entertainment centers, consisting of modular cabinets and shelves accommodating stereo, phonograph, tape decks and other performing hardware.

Such mass absorption in glomerations of entertainment could signify a lively, curious, fun-loving populace, affluent enough to afford the costs and fees entailed, rewarding itself for hard work well done, enjoying the benefits of a sound, salubrious culture. And while this is to some extent true, most of our amusements, recreations, regalements and revels represent avenues of escape, and not always from the harsh realities of life, from intimations of mortality, from a sense of void, but often from boredom. Sheer boredom.

"The average man," wrote Mencken, "gets his living by such depressing devices that boredom becomes a natural state to him"—a variation of Thoreau's better known observation that most men live lives of quiet desperation. But entertainment itself can become boring through sameness

Norman Corwin is the author of 17 books and he writes frequently about the media.

and surfeit. This happens when escapist fare like TV westerns and hospital dramas dominate the listings for a few seasons and then fade away. Stars burn out on earth as they do in heaven.

So here we have the paradox of the most entertained country in the world seeking still more entertainment in an apparently unslakable thirst for sensation. And the exploitation of sensation as style, device and marketable product ranges all the way from home games to art forms to vandalism.

Sensation is everywhere. Special effects of destruction fill the screen; sensational car chases careen across the tube nightly; sensational stuntists like Evel Knievel, and the nutty exhibitionists who scale skyscrapers, enthrall the media; Guinness-record-seekers strain to make the next edition; rock bands whose very names are sensational (The Bangs, The Pits, Cheap Trick, Rat Scabies, Burning Sensation, Social Distortion, Fear, Bad Religion, The Criminals, Jack Mack & The Heart Attack, Cheri & The Hit Men, Huge Killer Bats, Vultures, The Stilettos, The Grenades, Vicious Fish) put on sensational concerts featuring destruction of musical instruments, TV sets, and on-stage Cadillacs.

The Plasmatics smash autos. Less discriminating musicians of punk rock persuasion bite the heads off pigeons. They are masters of programmed vandalism. Far from being unique excrescences of the culture of sensationalism, they are merely the loudest and least respected. Higher on the scale of respectability, to the point of being displayed in great museums of America and abroad, are sensationalists, like Arman (Armand Pierre Fernandez) who smashes pianos, burns violins and blows up automobiles. An admiring article in *Horizon* recounts that

At one points he furnished an entire art gallery exactly like a middle-class suburban living room, right down to the minutest details, and then axed the place. He called it "Conscious Vandalism."

Arman is quoted as believing there is no fundamental difference between accumulating objects and smashing them. If you break a fiddle, for ex-

ample, "you get something romantic." Because he is "especially fond of strings"—violins, cellos, basses—"he broke them and burned them and put them in Plexiglass, cut up or chipped or charred or smashed to smithereens. The results were so universally romantic that Arman attracted a great deal of notice. From gallery and museum shows he moved up into major museum collections".....

Sensation is not only fed to the masses, it is force-fed. Not long after the motion pictures *Star Trek, Star Wars* and *The Empire Strikes Back* (all of which dealt heavily in the destruction of populated planets) had swept the country, one of the largest department stores in California advertised the Atari Defender Game cartridge:

Alien forces have invaded the Earth bringing with them their death machines. Launch your attack rocket . . . then fire your laser cannons! Only you can prevent the aliens from kidnapping your fellow humanoids and transforming them into treacherous mutants.

Most of the ad was taken up by a monstrous creature holding the Earth in his hands and looking at it hungrily as though it were an edible basketball. It can be argued that not even very young kids believe we are threatened by aliens with death machines. But it is not a question of belief, it is the persistent surfeit of sensation to the point where it begins to jade. Joyce Maynard, in *Looking Back: A Chronicle of Growing Up Old in the Sixties,* tells of taking a four-year-old child to a circus:

. . . she leaned back on her padded seat . . . toughly, smartly, sadly, wisely, agedly unenthralled. . . . We had seen greater spectacles, unmoved, our whole world was a visual glut, a ten-ring circus even Ringling Brothers couldn't compete with. A man stuck his head into a tiger's mouth and I pointed it out . . . to my cool, unfazed friend, and when she failed to look [I] turned her head for her, forced her to take the sight in. The tiger could have bitten the tamer's head off, I think, swallowed him whole . . . and she wouldn't have blinked.

But a man's head in a tiger's mouth is nothing compared to an inhabited planet in the sights of a weapon that will blow it to shivereens. George Plimpton, author, actor, salesman, made the boast in a commercial for Atari, that a certain TV game was the only one which offered "total destruction of a planet." What circus can offer that?

George F. Will, castigating the movie *Indiana Jones* for scenes in which characters are flogged, roasted and eviscerated, and the menu of an opulent meal includes live snakes, beetles, eyeball soup and monkey brains, called it "an example of the upward ratchet effect of shocking extremism in popular entertainment," and concluded that "This march toward the shocking is producing a generation that would yawn through the parting of the Red Sea."

In the motion picture *My Dinner with Andre*, Wally asks, "Are we just like bored, spoiled children who've been lying in the bathtub all day, playing with their plastic duck, and now they're thinking, What can I do?"

"Yes," says Andre. "We're bored, now. We're all bored." This comes after Andre has spent half the picture telling Wally how he had gone around the world seeking far-out sensations—to Poland, the Sahara, India, Scotland, Yugoslavia, China, Tibet, Israel—"experiencing a lot of synchronicity... hallucinating nonstop... things were exploding. . . ." But after all that, he concludes

the truth is, Wally, that in retrospect those things I was involved in are all, in a way, disgusting to me. . . .

Andre, a director in the theater, at one point echoes Joyce Maynard's allusion to "visual glut" by recalling an impulse he entertained while staging a production of *The Bacchae* at Yale:

. . . when Pentheus has been killed . . . and they rip him to shreds and I guess cut off his head—my impulse was . . . to get a head from the New Haven morgue and pass it around the audience—so that the people somehow could realize that the stuff was real, see.

The actress who played Agawe refused to carry a head from the morgue and so it was not used, but Andre clings to the idea:

I still think it would be wonderful if the perceptions of the audience could be brought to life.

Though light years separate the art of Andre Gregory from that of Herschell Gordon Lewis, producer of gory horror movies, they are disconcertingly close in their views of the need for, and means of, bringing the perceptions of an audience to life. No movie before Lewis's *Blood Feast* showed a tongue being ripped out. No play before Andre's *Bacchae* came close to passing a dead head around. Had this been done, no doubt some of the audience would have fainted, vomited, turned green, and left the theater, just as they did at Lewis's *Blood Orgy*.

Spectators who have been exposed to gristle and gore, to the feel and smell of a cadaver's head, may find lesser sensations so tame they fall asleep in the theater. Wally, himself a playwright, tells Andre that people today have "redefined the theater in a trivial way . . . they are deeply asleep. . . . I began to feel that there was nothing [he or the actors] could do to reach those people." Thus the theater audience could no more be impressed by lines in the mouths of his characters than the four-year-old girl at the circus could be impressed by the man with his head in the mouth of a tiger. . . .

There are any number of ways to measure America's development from the time when Jefferson, still seeking entertainment in 1786, paid a shilling to see "a learn'd pig" perform, but one of the most enlightening ways is in terms of the things that people find amusing. There was no Pac-Man in the days of Monticello, no discos, no all-night movies, no DJ's, no walkmans, no porno parlors, no drag racing, no *Saturday Night Live,* no divisional playoffs, no comic books, no horror pix, no Mrs. America beauty contests. On the other hand, there was time to read a book. ∎

The Mass Media's Future

The future of the United States and the future of the mass media are so inter-related that they are difficult to separate. In this speech, Everette E. Dennis de-scribes how he believes the mass media will adapt to our changing society.
   Consider:

1. How do technological changes in the media affect the economics of the media?

2. What effects do mergers and acquisitions have on the delivery of media in-formation and entertainment?

3. Define what Dennis means when he talks about the media's "law of right numbers."

4. How do today's new styles and standards of journalism differ from earlier styles and standards?

A Coming of Age: Sea Changes for the Mass Media

EVERETTE E. DENNIS

Three great converging forces—all interre-lated—are changing the shape of media in America. They are: (1) the technological revolution; (2) the economic upheaval and re-configuration of media ownership; and (3) the resulting impact of both on the information en-vironment and on new journalistic styles and standards.

The Communication Revolution

What was once in the realm of futurist forecasting is now with us. We have moved from the rhetoric

Everette E. Dennis directs the Gannett Center for Media Studies in New York.

of such cliches as "the age of information" and "the communication revolution" into a period when we are transmitting, processing and receiv-ing information with the help of microchips, satellites and computers. We use VCRs, video discs and on-line databases. We do our work on personal computers and subscribe to videotext services as we cope with various broadband com-munication activities, including cable, subscrip-tion television and direct-broadcast satellites.

   As we monitor the development of new tech-nologies and services, their market penetration and, in some instances, their glacial growth, we also need to consider the impact that these new delivery systems are having on old media. For example, the competition for advertising dollars that these new media represent has given newspapers a much greater concern for their audiences. Indeed, as one critic said, newspapers have at last discovered the need to view their readers in a self-conscious way, something that broadcasters have done since the beginning. Newspapers now engage in research and have pioneered a marketing approach to news. They are concerned more and more with market segmentation and the precise nature of their audiences. Newspaper editors now speak not just of "the paper," but of "the product" and of "packaging," as well as the "upscale" audiences they hope to attract. Broadcasting has just completed its first decade with electronic news gathering (ENG), during which there as been a continued blurring of the distinction between news and entertainment. We are now experiencing a regionalization of television, in which power is no longer centralized in the networks and local stations are becoming less reliant on them. We've seen the virtual death of the documentary and the rise of mini-series and docu-dramas.

In the world of magazines, there is continued specialization. Indeed, more than any other medium the magazine anticipated the age of information and emphasized discrete audience segments that were identified and planned for on the basis of market research. Though they were ahead of the game, magazines now face stiff competition from other media and, in many instances, are struggling to survive. Still, magazines have always had somewhat cyclical histories; they are born, they grow up and they die.

My point is that we may want to spend more time assessing the impact of new technology—such as satellites—on old delivery systems and established media—such as newspapers—than assessing its impact on the emergence of genuinely new communication industries. Remember that the time lag between the invention of a new technology and its popularization and widespread use may be considerable. I think of this when I hear carping critics writing off cable television, remembering that it took 70 years for the

telephone to become a truly national medium that reached 50 percent of the population. I know that technological change is rarely dramatic, but is instead subtle and incremental. As you know, the promise that cable seemed to offer in the 1960s and 1970s has not yet been fully realized. What was technologically feasible then met market and governmental resistance, and the result has been a much slower movement in that new and promising industry than we might have expected. Technological determinism is not the whole story. . . .

The Economic Upheaval

This is a time for mergers and acquisitions, for concentration and reorganization of much of the corporate sector. This has affected the media industries profoundly. As one commentator said recently, there have been more dramatic changes in broadcasting in the last two years than in the previous 30 or 40, at least as far as ownership goes. The ABC-Capital Cities merger, General Electric's purchase of RCA (and thus NBC), and CBS' attempt to thwart a hostile takeover bid are dramatic indicators of what is happening in the communication industry, what some have called "merger mania."

We're also seeing newspaper companies making continued acquisitions, such as Gannett's "Triple Crown" (Des Moines, Detroit and Louisville) during the last 18 months, and bullish moves by Times Mirror and other media companies. It is a turbulent and complex picture. Media companies are growing, acquiring both print and broadcast properties, blurring the distinction between the print and electronic media. This is especially evident in the national editions of various newspapers, among them *The Wall Street Journal, The New York Times, The Christian Science Monitor* and, most visibly, *USA Today.* The old print and electronic distinctions are rapidly disappearing, as witnessed by the joint venture of Hearst-ABC and the recent agreement between Conus and the Associated Press.

What's behind the economic upheaval? I believe it is a new and more sophisticated concept of marketing in the midst of great competition. It is a discovery of audience, a recognition that there might not be a great undifferentiated national audience, or not much of one. Instead there are distinct demographic and special-interest audiences that need to be coddled and courted. This is leading to what some critics call "the death of mass communication." They argue that there is not mass communication but only segmented communication serving only parts of the total population. In local terms this means that there is a difference between "the community" a newspaper or broadcast station serves and its "actual audience," those people who plight their troth with a given medium by subscribing, viewing or buying advertising.

We have moved from media governed by a law of large numbers, in which the gathering together of large heterogeneous audiences served the interests of the mass media, to a law of right numbers, in which media seek smaller and more target audiences. What this may mean for the decline of democratization and the rise of elitism and class consciousness is a matter of much speculation. I believe there is nothing to fear, because the changes that occur in media audiences only reflect the changing nature of society and its natural segmentation into what Anne Wells Branscomb calls "teletribes and telecommunities," new publics made possible by modern telecommunication. Beyond the traditional mass media, there are heretofore unknown audiences conversing with each other through "citizen-band" services on interactive databases.

Newspapers, still a vital force in the media community, have responded to the changing environment and economy with vigor. Faced with declining circulations and a diminished market penetration, partly because of electronic media competition, they have commissioned market research to better understand who their audiences are. They have repackaged themselves in special sections, restructured their operations and even encouraged new writing styles and reporting strategies. Traditional journalists decried all this, but it is very much a reality today, and not, I think, in the least harmful to freedom of expression. We

have little social memory for similar upheavals in the past, including the one that brought us the mass press in the 1880s and 1890s. Then the press became more egalitarian and less elitist as it attempted to lure a new mass audience, and journalists and other critics decried that as the debasing of information. Today just the opposite is occurring, and critics are making similar charges.

The New Information Environment and Journalism

The economic pressures affecting the distribution and marketing of information have also given rise to new styles and standards of journalism. These are driven by a new definition of news that is audience-oriented and characterized by pertinence to the individual. This has led to the so-called "use paper" and to service journalism in print and broadcasting. The emphasis is on useful information in a no-nonsense age. This new definition of news has been called soft-and-sexy, humanistic, process- rather than event-oriented and many other things. It is marked by spare, lean prose that delivers useful information.

Beyond a new definition of news, there is also more descriptive, analytic reporting. Today reporters place more emphasis on the consequences of a story than on its bare facts alone. Well beyond simple description, news today is most often in the realm of analysis and forward-looking, speculative stories. A story about a new tax bill, for example, will focus more on the effects the legislation will have on individuals than on the details of how Congress passed the bill.

Amid these substantive changes in news there seems to be a decline of investigative reporting. Perhaps this is because investigative reporting tends to run in cycles. Nevertheless there is less of it than there once was, due, many people think, to libel suits and press credibility issues. While there are still a good many investigative reports, such as journalistic accounts of Mrs. Marcos' fortune, there is less attention given to penny ante local political corruption, less treatment of matters involving sex and violence.

As old-fashioned, blood-and-guts investigative reporting is on the downswing, service journalism, aimed at solving people's problems and looking at the quality of life, is on the rise.

We are an information society. People care about the ownership of information because more than ever before information is valuable. ■

CHAPTER ONE

For Further Reading

Books

Everette E. Dennis and John C. Merrill, *Basic Issues in Mass Communication* (New York: Macmillan, 1984).

Shearon A. Lowery and Melvin L. DeFleur, *Milestones in Mass Communication Research,* 2nd ed. (New York: Longman, 1988).

Dennis McQuail, *Mass Communication Theory: An Introduction,* 2nd ed. (Beverly Hills: Sage, 1987).

Werner J. Severin with James W. Tankard, Jr., *Communication Theories,* 2nd ed. (New York: Longman, 1988).

Periodicals

Communication Abstracts
Communication Research
Journal of Communication
Journalism Quarterly
Mass Comm Review

Media
Industries

PART II

The Newspaper Industry

Covering Miami

Edna Buchanan has been covering the police beat for the *Miami Herald* since 1971. As an example of someone who works a difficult beat in a difficult city, no one describes it better. This excerpt is from Buchanan's book *The Corpse Had a Familiar Face.*

Consider:

1. What continues to fascinate Buchanan about her assignment?

2. Most reporters would be jaded by the continuous parade of grizzly stories. What seems to make Buchanan different?

3. Why does Buchanan feel that covering the "major murder" each day is not enough for a crime reporter to do?

4. In your opinion, what role does a reporter like Buchanan play in serving the public interest?

Miami, It's Murder

EDNA BUCHANAN

I'm not afraid to die. I just don't want to be there when it happens.
                                                                    WOODY ALLEN

The crime that inevitably intrigues me most is murder. It's so final.

At a fresh murder scene you can smell the blood and hear the screams; years later, they still echo in my mind. Unsolved murders are unfinished stories. The scenes of the crimes may change over the years; highways are built over them, buildings are torn down, houses are sold. I drive by and wonder if the new occupants, as they go about their daily lives, ever sense what happened there. Do they know, or am I the only one who still remembers?

The face of Miami changes so quickly, but the dead stay that way. I feel haunted by the restless souls of those whose killers walk free.

Somebody owes them.

And nobody is trying to collect. Detectives divert their energies to new cases with hot leads. It is only natural.

But I can't forget.

The first homicide victim I ever wrote about was sixty-seven years old and from New Jersey,

---

Edna Buchanan won a Pulitzer Prize in 1986 for her crime reporting in the *Miami Herald.*

a retired dealer in religious books. Somebody beat him to death with a strange object resembling an elephant-sized Q-Tip. The killer dropped the weapon. Police found it, but they could never figure out what it was, much less who used it.

His last night on earth began pleasantly for Edward Becher; he escorted his wife to the theater. The vacationing couple returned afterward to their oceanfront hotel. He left his wife at the front door and drove off alone to park the car in a lot two blocks away.

He failed to return and his wife became concerned. Eventually she went to look for him. In the parking lot, she found the police with a shaken motorist who had discovered her husband unconscious on the pavement. He had already been taken to a hospital, where he died.

The murder weapon was the only clue: an iron pipe, thirty inches long, swaddled at each end with burlap. Everyone who saw it said the same thing: it looks like a giant Q-Tip. Baffled police created duplicates and displayed them to the public hoping for a link to the killer.

The weapon was not, as some citizens suggested, a tool to lubricate machinery or a torch used by fire dancers at a local nightspot.

The circus was in town at the time of the attack; it moved on a day or so later. I always suspected that perhaps the weapon was a tool used in some way by roustabouts or animal tenders. We will never know. Like most whodunits in Dade County, the case remains unsolved. The detectives who investigated it have all since retired or quit. Five police chiefs have come and gone since somebody smashed the skull of the man who dealt in religious books. I doubt that anyone now connected with the department even remembers that homicide.

But I do.

What the heck was that thing? It is still a perplexing and troubling question, nagging along with all the others. I am uncomfortable with unsolved mysteries—and with the fact that whoever did it is still out there.

Somewhere.

The unsolved slaying of Edward Becher was the first of more than three thousand murders I have reported. Every crime, every victim is different. Some remain more vivid in memory than others, but none can really be forgotten. Each time, I want to know it all, everything. If I could just somehow piece it all together, perhaps the things that people do to each other might make some sense.

Years ago, murder was rare and unusual, and almost every killing was front-page news. Then homicide became more and more common and less and less newsworthy. When Miami broke all prior records for violence in the years 1980–81 and its murder rate skyrocketed to number one in the nation, I was often forced to squeeze six, seven, even a dozen slayings into a single story. City-desk editors listed it on their daily budget as the "Murder Round-up." Combining the most outrageous cases in the lead, I would report them in a reverse chronology with the most recent first. Each victim's last story had to be limited to just a paragraph or two.

Despite the constraints of space, I still felt a need to learn all I could about each case. I rushed from one murder scene to another and another, engaged in a daily struggle to cram as much detail as possible into those too-brief paragraphs.

Speeding back to the *Herald* on deadline one night, with my notes on several homicides, I heard the unmistakable echo of gunfire as I roared beneath a highway overpass near a housing project. Suddenly I felt crazed, uncertain whether to continue on back to the paper, or stop and investigate, perhaps finding another story there would be no room to print. The hesitation was just for an instant. The U-turn left rubber in the road behind me.

Looking back, I see now that for the better part of those two years, I was numb, shell-shocked, and operating strictly on instinct. I remember little of my personal life during that time, only the stories I wrote and the sense of being caught up in something totally out of control. The only reality was what I had to do. That paragraph or two devoted to each homicide was painstakingly put together.

I felt obliged. Often it was the first and last time the victim's name ever appeared in a newspaper. Even at that, I felt a sense of guilt for such a cursory send-off.

The woman left dead by the side of a desolate road in her yellow nightgown wanted to live just as much as you or I do. So did the illegal alien whose charred body was found in a cheap trunk in The Everglades. How dehumanizing to be regarded merely as numbers in the mounting statistics of death.

They deserved better.

Often assistant city editors, short on space and patience, would insist that I select and report only the "major murder" of the day. I knew what they meant, but I fought the premise. How can you choose?

Every murder is major to the victim.

Sure, it's simpler to write about only one case and go home. But some strange sense of obligation would not let me do it. The *Miami Herald* is South Florida's newspaper of record, and I felt compelled to report every murder, every death on its pages—names, dates, facts—to preserve them in our newspaper, in our files, in our consciousness, on record forever, in black and white. On my days off, or when I worked on other stories or projects, some murders went totally unreported. So I would carefully resurrect them, slipping them into the local section in round-ups, wrap-ups, and trend stories about possibly related cases. There was always a way, you could always find an angle. For instance: Victim number 141 in 1980 proved to be the widower of victim number 330 in 1979.

A bright young reporter I talked to recently casually referred to what he called dirt-bag murders: the cases and the victims not worth reporting. There is no dirt-bag murder. The story is always there waiting to be found if you just dig deep enough. ■

PERSPECTIVE 2

Tabloid Journalism

In the following article, Jon Nordheimer discusses the reasons tabloid journalism succeeds and the reasons tabloid journalism may be changing. Nordheimer explains why the tabloids may have to change their approach to keep their audience.

Consider:

1. How does tabloid journalism differ from mainstream journalism?

2. What factors are forcing changes in the tabloid approach, according to Nordheimer?

3. Are the tabloids, as one editor claims, "real down-home, like neighbors sharing gossip with neighbors in a small town"?

Tabloid Circulation Falls as the Rude Replaces the Lewd

JON NORDHEIMER

Now the shocking inside story can be told! The tabloids are going soft.

After years of rapid circulation growth based on a formula of sex, luridness, the occult and Hollywood gossip, the six major supermarket tabloid newspapers that reach an estimated 50 million readers a week in America have run into a weakening market, and circulation is drooping. Worse yet, in the view of several editors in the field, the unpardonable is happening: Blandness is replacing brashness, the merely rude is pushing out the lewd.

There is still a lot of glorious humbug to be found in such headlines as "A SPACE ALIEN MADE ME PREGNANT" (*Weekly World News*) or "CAT EATS PARROT—NOW IT TALKS (Says: 'Kittycat wants a cracker')" (*Sun*) on the rack in supermarkets and convenience stores across the nation.

But "sex" is a word rarely used on front pages. Nudity is taboo. Blood and human and animal deformities are nowhere to be seen. Instead, "miracle" diet plans, celebrity gossip, and inventful astrologists and psychics crowd the pages.

"The supermarket managers don't want us to upset their patrons," sighed Tony Miles, executive publisher of Globe Communications, which

produces the *Globe,* the *National Examiner* and the *Sun,* whose combined weekly circulation is 2.3 million.

He suggested the main reason the tabloids no longer deal with grisly murders, sex crimes or other disturbing subjects is because 90 percent of those buying the tabloids are women, chiefly white women of middle age or older.

"These women will not buy something that is too horrific or shocking," said Miles, an ebullient man who was formerly chairman of the London Daily Mirror Newspaper Group. "They don't want other shoppers to think they're interested in such things."

In the old days, tab editors say, most buyers were men, and they bought the tabloids at newsstands and tobacco shops: hence, the greater emphasis back then on sex, crime and gore. The *National Enquirer* led the tabloids' move to the supermarkets, toning down its content initially to appeal to more upscale advertisers as well as female shoppers.

Globe Communications relocated to Boca Raton three years ago from Montreal in an unabashed decision to be close to the king of the heap, *The Enquirer,* up the road in Lantana since 1971. The *Enquirer,* which also publishes the smaller (circulation 900,000) but spicier *Weekly World News,* is the market leader with 4.5 million

Jon Nordheimer is a reporter for *The New York Times.*

copies sold every week, down from more than 5 million a few years ago.

"The reason we moved to Boca Raton is because the *Enquirer* has attracted a vast pool of tabloid talent to this area," explained Mike Nevard, editorial director of all three Globe publications. "A lot of the free-lance talent used by the *Enquirer* came from Britain, and they liked Florida so much they would do almost anything to stay." It has also made it possible for the competitors to field cricket teams and play each other.

The only one of the major supermarket newspapers that is not published in the "Tabloid Valley" of southern Palm Beach County is Rupert Murdoch's 3.3 million-circulation *Star,* based in Tarrytown, N.Y.

Iain Calder, editor and publisher of the *Enquirer,* is a Scot who has been with the tabloid for 24 years and acidly resists comparison with any competitor.

"The *Enquirer* has changed dramatically from the old days, and it hurts us to be compared with these others," Calder said. "They design their covers to look like us," he added, dropping his accented voice an octave or two to register contempt for his opposite numbers, "so if one of them runs some headline saying 'Hitler Found Alive in Florida' we get tarred with the same brush by browsers who confuse it with an *Enquirer* headline."

Nevard, down the road at Globe Communications, chortled at what he considered the *Enquirer's* haughtiness. "Iain Calder's a dry stick who runs a very old-fashioned tabloid that looks very thrown together," he said the other day as he oversaw production of the *Globe*'s weekly edition, with a cover story headlined "ENJOY 2,000 CALORIES A DAY & STILL LOSE WEIGHT."

A former editor at the *Enquirer,* Nevard said its domination in sales has made a fortune for its owner, Generoso Pope Jr., a former Central Intelligence Agency officer and publisher of the Italian-language newspaper *Il Progresso* who purchased the *Enquirer* from the Hearst chain in the early 1950s. Pope declined to be interviewed, and his office said profit figures for the publication are confidential.

One thing the competitors could agree on was the absence of a blockbuster world figure whose photo on a tabloid cover could sell out an entire issue. Since most of the tabloids rely almost entirely on impulse buying from shoppers waiting at a supermarket checkout counter (hence the emphasis on bold and bizarre headlines), many more copies are usually circulated than are sold.

"There's no one star or world personality who's huge today," said Calder. "No one compares to Jackie Kennedy in her heyday. The deaths of Elvis Presley, Princess Grace and Natalie Wood carried us for a long time. There was a period when Farrah Fawcett was on every cover. Rock Hudson and Liberace dying of AIDS provided us with exclusives. Joan Collins was big but is fading. Vanna White turned out to be a flash in the pan."

It is widely acknowledged among the tabloids that the *Enquirer* spends the most money—and pays better than most standard American newspapers—to get out the product. Calder said his newsroom budget is $16 million a year, but he would not discuss how it is spent.

The *Sun,* with a circulation of 500,000, is put out by three editors piecing together items gleaned from news services or free-lancers, according to Nevard. "It's very whacky stuff, full of Big Foots, UFOs and the occult," he explained. "There's a competition among the editors to come up with the best shock headline."

The tabloids all pay money for stories, photographs and tips. The *Enquirer* boasts it scooped everyone [1988] by purchasing exclusive photos and accounts of Gary Hart with Donna Rice on their weekend in the Bahamas. "The *Star* sulked for a month," chortled Calder.

Off the record, staffers boast about acquiring exclusive interviews with celebrities by threatening to publish compromising photographs of them, usually of a sexual content.

"A star's agent is usually a great source for dirt about his own client, especially if the client is on the way down," said one tabloid writer. "He'll sell the star out to get space for his next client."

The celebrity gossip approach has been

known to backfire, most notably in the case of entertainer Carol Burnett. In 1981, a jury awarded her $1.6 million after deciding that she had been wrongly reported by the *Enquirer* to have been drunk in a restaurant. A trial judge reduced the verdict and Burnett settled her suit in 1984.

The bulk of the stories appearing in the three leading tabloids is fairly tame stuff compared to the "SON KILLS FATHER AND EATS HIM" screamers of the past.

"When our readers look at the tabloids, they can understand what they see," McLachan said. "The masses don't relate to confusion over Nicaragua or the Iran-Contra investigation. But when you get past our headlines, you find we are real down-home, like neighbors sharing gossip with neighbors in a small town—except we give them more glamorous gossip than what they get at the parish door." ∎

THE BORN LOSER® by Art & Chip Sansom

PERSPECTIVE 3

The Newspaper Owner as Media Entrepreneur

As a result of concentration of media ownership—when large corporations buy up small media companies—a local newspaper is one of the few places that individuals can enter the media business as owners. The following article describes the challenges that faced Julie Ardery and Bill Bishop when they decided to buy the *Bastrop County Times*. It is an important case study in the difficulties of first-time media ownership.

Consider:

1. Why does Bill Bishop say that the business of newspaper publishing has been taken out of the small-time, independent publisher's control?

2. What stories can a small-town newspaper cover differently from a larger newspaper?

3. What personal price must a small-town publisher be willing to pay, according to Bishop?

4. Do you agree with Bishop that the future winners in the newspaper business will be "the fellows who understand cash flow, marketing, and demographics"? Why? Why not?

Owning Your Own Weekly
A Warning from Smithville

BILL BISHOP

Slip a few beers into many a metropolitan reporter and he'll tell you he wants nothing more from life than his own smalltown weekly newspaper. No more editors, no more rush to meet the daily deadline, no more stuffy assignments. That conversation's good for another round (until the dreamer gets stuck with the tab).

It was my dream, too. So in the summer of 1983 my wife, Julie Ardery, and I bought the *Bastrop County Times*—a 3,000-circulation fact of life in Smithville, Texas, since 1892. During the next four years we published one of the better small weeklies in the state. We conducted an investigative series that changed a major state agency; we printed a short story, long reviews and editorials; we sponsored an ugly dog contest; we won awards for our news writing and features and for community service. We had fun and we made money.

But in August 1987 we sold the paper to our competitor in a town 12 miles away, and it was not exhaustion that convinced us to sell; we'd expected the long hours. What we didn't count on

was a new rural economy that takes the business of newspapering out of the small-time independent publisher's control.

Before we get into the business end of things, this introduction to rural newspaper publishing should carry a warning: weekly newspapering can be hazardous to your health. The terrors of small-business ownership are compounded by the pressures of news reporting. And everything is so, well, close up. A lost ad account isn't just a problem for somebody on the third floor. It means you have to skip paying yourself to cover the next printing bill. And imagine finishing your editorial excoriating Ed Meese only to meet him a half hour later, coming down a grocery aisle between the Little Debbie snack cakes and the Folgers coffee. There ain't no place to hide.

And even if there were, there wouldn't be time. In 1976 I worked at the *Mountain Eagle,* an award-winning weekly in the coalfields of eastern Kentucky. The paper was, and is, Tom and Pat Gish, a brilliant pair of journalists who passed the burnout stage of weekly newspapering sometime in the mid-1960s. Though he had done the heart bypass routine several years before I arrived in Whitesburg, Tom still spent every Tuesday night

Bill Bishop is a Texas writer.

(production night at most weeklies) at the newspaper office until dawn. He would sit ashen-faced at his desk, reading copy or tapping out an editorial. Then, about midnight, he would collapse on one of those narrow, nylon cots you get at K-Mart. Someone would throw a dust-covered blanket over the famous editor, and he would snore as we pasted up headlines and finished the grocery ad.

Pat was tougher, though I suspect the last time she felt well-rested was sometime during the Eisenhower administration. She would proof all the copy and finish the layout while the rest of us were club-handed with fatigue, and, as the sun came up, hustle off to her 9-to-5 job running a rural housing authority. I once asked Jim Branscome, who contributed articles on the Tennessee Valley Authority to the *Eagle,* if he would ever consider buying a weekly. ''Naw,'' muttered Branscome, now a McGraw-Hill editor. ''I think I'd rather go to prison.'' At least in prison you have a chance of parole.

By 1982, the memory of Tom snoozing away on that little aluminum cot had waned and the romance of the weekly returned. Julie and I had started and then sold a small newsletter, so we had some money to shop with. We felt that we had something to say and that, through a weekly newspaper, we might get it said. Moreover, we wanted to measure an American community; the weekly seemed a subtle and accurate thermometer. For the better part of a year we looked for just the right paper.

There are nearly 8,000 publications in this country that come out less often than daily and at least weekly, according to the National Newspaper Association, and each is occasionally for sale. If you have lots of money, you look for three things: the ideal paper is in a growing market, lacks significant competition, and has a gross income of nearly $500,000. Few papers of these standards ever come up for sale, and when they do, they'll cost $900,000, minimum, with a good third of that required in a cash down payment.

Got $300,000, plus enough in the bank to operate the paper through the first three months? Neither did we, so we found ourselves considering Smithville's newspaper, even though it violated two of the three cardinal rules: Smithville, located 50 miles east of Austin, is the smallest town in a county with three newspapers (competition writ large) and the *Bastrop County Times* was grossing only $160,000. We bought the *County Times* because it was for sale at a price we could afford and because we liked the town. Our decision to put $40,000 down on the paper was made over a Shiner beer at Charlie's Bar-b-que, a Main Street establishment that serves sausage and brisket sliced onto butcher paper, garnished with a package of saltines. We'd wanted romance. Well, this was it.

During the month before our move to Smithville, Julie and I had a chance to think about what kind of paper the *County Times* would be. Weekly newspaper editors become famous when they are assaulted or their headquarters are torched. The Gishes, in fact, received national recognition for their work after a policeman paid a teenager 50 bucks to burn down the *Mountain Eagle* office (bad things happen to smalltown publishers when they are critical of the local constabulary). That's a high price to pay for fame. Julie and I decided our move to Smithville was to be no exercise in self-immolation. We wanted a tough newspaper, but we wanted to survive.

At the same time, we believed that a weekly can achieve a style and form denied metropolitan dailies. They can become living, breathing creatures, complete with charms and foibles. The grand small papers, it seems, are built on human eccentricity. The Gishes brought an intensity to the *Mountain Eagle*; Sam Ragan's poetry imbues the Southern Pines, North Carolina, *Pilot*; the *Hungry Horse News* (Columbia Falls, Montana) is a weekly exhibit of Brian Kennedy's photography, and the *Vineyard Gazette* (Martha's Vineyard, Massachusetts) still rings with the elegance and clear thinking of its late publisher, Henry Beetle Hough. Our goal at the *County Times,* we decided, was to orchestrate a true community newspaper with a chorus of photos, art, and stories from a panorama of local contributors.

Before we get too far astray, hard-news enthusiasts should know that a weekly can contain—and readers enjoy—as much enterprising journalism as you can dish out. The weekly deadline demands that stories be written in a more explanatory way, since readers may pick up the paper at any time over the week between publications. But you'll find the same range and depth of stories in a rural county as in Metropolis.

News stories in a weekly can have substantial impact: our continuing reports on a regional power agency led to a $385,000 investigation by a former U.S. attorney. But crusading editors soon meet the test of the grocery aisle. Knowing the subjects of your reporting—taking pictures of their kids in school and their parents in the nursing home—makes you more understanding, and, I believe, fairer.

News gathering, while hard work, was the predictable part of our experience. What we'd hoped for, but could never have foreseen, was the vibrancy of Bastrop County's residents. We built up a corps of columnists, ranging from Homer (a former country music singer who divulged the county's night life) to Doris Laake (a proper Lutheran widow from the hamlet of Paige).

Doris turned out to be our best reporter, a fearless chronicler of her town's activities. When a person fell from a ladder, twisting an ankle, Doris was ready with the hospital report; an attack of bees was good for a headline; she enumerated the losses, down to the last sausage link, when fire took a smokehouse. She was also the first reporter to write about what became, in 1985, the most active oil play in the state. But Doris's first love was disaster. I remember when the state police called to ask about the gray-haired woman with the Polaroid who'd crossed their yellow barriers to snap a close-up of an automobile wreck. I could only imagine the police, slack-jawed, as they watched Doris bend over the carnage, her camera spitting out its little photo-squares.

We had an imaginative layout artist. For several weeks she changed the job titles in the staff box to fit her fancy. One week we became characters from "Star Trek," and for New Year's week we were all highballs. For a while, the *County Times'* staff box became the best read part of the paper.

Two fine artists in the county contributed editorial cartoons. One charged $25; the other expected two six-packs.

And then there was the Bird Lady, Melissa Bishop (no relation). Melissa was, and is, bird crazy. She ministers to sick birds, runs what appears to be a bird orphanage, and studies birds constantly, hiding under a pile of leaves or standing mannequin-still in the middle of a field. We met her one day on a country road as she walked her geese, and asked if she would write about birds for the paper. She did, and her "Bird Lady" column became an instant hit. (Particularly popular was the account of the Bird Lady's Thanksgiving Day ritual—serving her turkeys a cake in the shape of a pilgrim.)

In four years of running the paper, we published pictures of every unusual edible item grown, caught, or created in Bastrop County. There were eggs big enough to be a hen's worst nightmare, catfish of biblical proportion, two-handed pears, and turnips so large they would set a smile on the face of the grimmest Bohemian farmer. Our philosophical justification for this weekly horn of plenty was that we wanted people not only to read the paper, but to *be* the paper. Everyone was a potential contributor.

We wanted each issue to be a surprise. We ran an April Fool's page every year (some readers are still upset that Ferdinand and Imelda Marcos are moving to nearby Kirtley).

The bottom-line result of this combination of hard news, editorials, features, and a cornucopia of contributors was a 33 percent increase in subscribers in the first three years to more than 4,000. Revenues also jumped, from the $160,000 in the year before we bought the paper to $285,000 in 1986, a 78 percent increase.

What seemed a successful business venture, however, produced an intolerable way of life. There was always too much work and not enough money. Stories were dashed out Tuesday afternoons, between taking classified ads and fixing a typesetting machine.

Even when the paper was finished the job wasn't over. One morning, having been up until 3 a.m., putting the paper to bed, we were living the life of the righteous—drinking coffee, trading gossip—when word came from the press; the computer-generated list of our 2,000 mail subscribers was off center. The machine that sliced and pasted each address label was tirelessly separating city from state, first name from last. It was a disaster, and we spent our only off-day of the week (and every Glue Stic in Smithville) cutting and pasting those 2,000 labels by hand.

"You want your own voice, at least that's how I started 20 years ago," says Kentucky weekly publisher Albert Smith, in words that make more sense now than before we put out our first edition. "I had had it with writing for these people, had it writing for dull editors, had it with unresponsive, insensitive pieces about serious topics. I would do my own thing. So you start, and the first thing you find out is that you are preoccupied with just economic survival, and your voice begins to croak or fall mute in your desperate sweat to produce the paper, to get enough ads to pay the bills."

By early 1987 we were croaking. Every bit of creativity, the fun of the job, came *after* the full-time chore of putting out a paper. And there was never a break. Even our infrequent three-day-weekend vacations became traumatic. We returned one Monday morning to learn that an employee had taken the company car (a ten-year-old Pontiac station wagon) on a shopping trip with his family. The car had caught fire on the road and the driver had steered the smoldering heap into the parking lot of a restaurant holding a grand-opening celebration. The restaurant owner was on the phone first thing that Monday threatening us with a lawsuit. In 1983, we would have laughed; three years later it stopped us as cold as an oar in a set of wagon wheels.

We learned in 1987 why the day of the independent smalltown weekly is passing.

By early that year we had survived the collapse of the Texas economy (i.e., oil and real estate), but we didn't know if we could withstand prosperity in Bastrop County. Developers had announced that a large shopping center would open in Bastrop, the county seat 12 miles west of Smithville and the hometown of our large, twice-a-week competitor, the *Bastrop Advertiser.* The center would house a Wal-Mart department store and an H.E.B. grocery, both, at that time, big advertisers in small Texas newspapers.

Normally, this would have been good news. But we weren't in Bastrop, and we had seen that having a Wal-Mart in the area wasn't necessarily a good thing. For the uninitiated, Wal-Mart is the prodigy of a Bentonville, Arkansas, genius named Sam Walton. Walton realized that chain marketers had ignored small towns, so he began opening huge department stores in rural areas, first in Rogers, Arkansas, and now in 23 other states. In Texas, these stores are enormously popular. Families will spend the afternoon or evening at a Wal-Mart, checking the bargains, meeting friends, and, most of all, buying Mr. Walton's goods. Rural people have made Sam Walton the richest man in America.

Two Wal-Marts had already opened near Smithville; we had learned the effect these stores had on the local economy—and our newspaper. A new Wal-Mart takes away business from nearly every store on Main Street. In the two towns near us, Giddings and La Grange, several businesses closed. The rest saw their profits slip away.

Even though many merchants in Giddings and La Grange advertised with the *County Times,* the Wal-Mart did not. Moreover, since our regular customers, the ones still in business, were short of cash, they cut back on their advertising—or, as one soon finds out in the newspaper business, they just didn't pay.

What would happen, we asked ourselves, when the new stores opened in the Bastrop shopping center? Would they advertise with us? How many of our old Bastrop customers would still have the cash to spend with the *County Times?* And if we didn't get the new accounts, would we begin losing subscribers? Our content was good, we knew, but people buy newspapers also to see ads. What would happen if those ads weren't in the *County Times?*

We were, indeed, in Smith's "desperate sweat."

Press associations make several recommendations for how small newspapers can attract chain advertisers, and we tried them all. We cut our ad rates, showed off our healthy circulation in a market that would be served by their stores, and bragged about our growth and the quality of the paper. We did not get one written answer to our inquiries. When I would call the main corporate office, I would get vague admonitions that "we normally only advertise in the hometown paper."

Bad news. It seemed we were finally going to pay for violating Rule One: we'd bought a paper in the wrong town. The only business solution was to combine with our adversary in Bastrop and present a united front to the chains. We approached the owners of that paper about merging the two enterprises; they preferred to buy us out. In May we agreed on a price, $440,000. Selling was the only realistic thing to do. The dream was over.

As I look back, it is clear that we had experienced, in less than a year, the economic forces that have shaped newspaper ownership over the last generation: mass merchandisers consolidate advertising dollars and seek the biggest and cheapest print medium. The preferred medium becomes the monopoly newspaper. Smaller publications are bought up or go out of business. The monopoly becomes so profitable it can only be purchased by a corporation with access to huge amounts of capital. Hello, Mr. Neuharth.

We saw that this same process had shifted to rural towns. Mass merchandisers have invaded the countryside. Fifteen years ago, few small towns had a McDonald's; now they have the Golden Arches and a Hardee's and a Burger King and a Long John Silver's.

The cost for rural papers in growing small towns has increased as smaller newspaper chains, excluded from the cities by the Gannetts and Knight-Ridders, bid up the prices for the remaining independent print franchises. Singly, but inexorably, independent newspapers fall to the chains. The combination of the *County Times* and its new sister paper in Bastrop will go on the block some day for well over a million dollars. Only a chain will be able to swing that kind of deal.

Moreover, those weekly newspaper publishers who remain in the trade are finding that the invasion of chain merchandisers has changed their way of doing business. Advertising decisions once made at the front counter of a newspaper office are now fashioned at corporate headquarters. The flick of an MBA's pen in Dallas or Bentonville can put a healthy paper on the rocks overnight.

Indeed, two months after we sold our paper, the chain-owned grocery that opened in the new shopping center changed from run-of-paper ads to preprinted inserts. The result: most small newspapers in Texas lost between $10,000 and $40,000 of pure profit. To save money, many Texas weeklies did the only thing they could do to compensate for the lost revenues; they laid off reporters. This is not an isolated story. Several years ago, K-Mart dropped its newspaper advertising in several Midwestern states. The impact on small weeklies was "devastating," according to one publisher. Meanwhile, Wal-Mart has begun to move away from print advertising, shaving 10 to 15 percent off its advertising budget for community newspapers each year.

The winners in this game will be the sharp-pencil boys, the fellows who understand cash flow, marketing, and demographics. Those spending the long hours required to produce a great newspaper will be honored by their readers, but not by the gang at corporate headquarters.

This was not the kind of business we had bargained for when we came to Texas. Nor, I suspect, is it the stuff of a newsroom dreamer's fantasy. It is, however, the way the wind is blowing out here in the sticks. If you don't believe it, just wet a finger. ■

Minority Hiring at Newspapers

The American Society of Newspaper Editors reports that about 60 percent of all daily newspapers employ no minority newsroom professionals and, in a country with a minority population nearing 30 percent, the percentage of professional personnel that are minorities in American newsrooms is under 6 percent. The following article describes one editor's attempt to change those statistics.

Consider:

1. Does the solution that Mike Hengel suggests for minority hiring seem appropriate? Why? Why not?

2. What advantages are there to the type of hiring program Hengel used?

3. What hazards are there to the type of hiring program Hengel used?

4. If you were a newspaper editor at a paper like Hengel describes, would you take the same approach? Why? Why not?

How (and Why) One Small Daily Hired Five Minority Journalists in Just Six Months

MIKE HENGEL

Our city editor loves to pass along the best piece of advice she ever received as a journalist. It came from a crusty city editor she worked for years ago. It seems she was having an especially tough time on a story—sources weren't returning her phone calls, she couldn't get ahold of so-and-so. The story just wasn't coming together. His advice to her: "Just *do* it!"

Who can't relate to that? Anybody who has ever worked as a reporter can tell a similar story. And it's good advice.

It occurs to me that maybe if more editors would apply the same principle to hiring minorities there wouldn't be this universal *concern* about the lack of minorities in the nation's newsrooms.

The Pine Bluff (Ark.) *Commercial* is a small daily with a big reputation. I knew that before I came to work here a year ago. In fact, that's one of

---

Mike Hengel is editor of the Pine Bluff (Ark.) *Commercial.*

the reasons I wanted to move to Pine Bluff. In 1969, the *Commercial* won a Pulitzer Prize for the courageous stand it had taken on integration in the South—a stance that wasn't all that popular with its readers at the time.

I was surprised, however, to find upon my arrival here, that in this city of 65,000—half black, half white—there was only one black reporter in the newsroom. That tarnished my impression of the *Commercial.* Integration, though apparently a good thing for the town as a whole, wasn't all that important in the newsroom. I saw nothing to suggest that the management of the newspaper had ever confronted the issue seriously. In, fact, I saw nothing to suggest the issue had ever been recognized as a problem.

But that was the past. The paper had a new owner (the Donrey Media Group) and new management.

One black reporter out of 25. That's 4 percent—in a town that is 50 percent black in a nation that's 30 percent minority. It was an embarrassment. And it was *my* problem to solve. In my first staff meeting, I pointed out the obvious, and said we were going to do everything possible to change it.

Two days later, an organized boycott of the newspaper was launched in reaction to several stories we published on the black football coach at the local university. The *Commercial* revealed that he was collecting paychecks for teaching a class he wasn't attending. It was a good story.

But several influential people in town thought it was just another instance of the *Commercial* picking on blacks in general and the school in particular. We weren't, but at least 400 people in town saw it otherwise; they dropped their subscriptions. The organizers of the boycott weren't making an issue of our lily-white staff, but they did mention it to us in several meetings we had conducted with them.

Within a few weeks, the boycott began to fizzle, and the organizers called it off—apparently because they could see it wasn't getting them anywhere. A good story stands on its own merits.

But our credibility among the town's blacks was low and would continue to suffer if we did not have minorities covering and editing the news in Pine Bluff. It didn't take a genius to figure that out.

Boycott or not, we were going to change that. Now we no longer fill any vacancies in the newsroom until we have interviewed at least one qualified member of a minority group. At first, I didn't know where we were going to find them. I had just moved to Pine Bluff from the West Coast. I sure didn't have any connections in Arkansas.

I was confident, however, that—faced with the possibility of not filling openings for weeks or even months—we could find a way. We are in a business that puts a premium on resourcefulness. If we expect people to be creative and enterprising in putting out a newspaper, we can expect them to show the same qualities in filling staff positions.

It worked.

Within six months we had five black reporters and one black copy editor. That's almost 25 percent of our newsroom. We haven't reached our goal (50 percent of the staff) but we have come a long way in six months.

Like most dailies our size (22,000), we hire rookies to fill some of our openings. But of the five black journalists we hired, only one did not have previous experience in the field.

▲ One was the sports editor of a nearby small daily.
▲ One had worked as a radio reporter.
▲ Two had done internships on newspapers.

We only had to recruit two of the five from outside of Pine Bluff. The other three were working here and jumped at the opportunity to work for the paper. In a town with 33,000 black residents, including a predominantly black university, it's not that hard to find eager applicants who are willing to learn the craft.

We haven't had any turnover in the past six months, but our policy is still intact: We will not hire anyone to fill any position until we have interviewed at least one qualified minority applicant.

Whenever I get together with newspaper editors, I hear the same old whines about the lack of qualified applicants from minority groups. I'll admit I find it reassuring to hear that my colleagues have the same problem I do. It takes some of the guilt away and makes it easier not to do something about it. They—like me—too often wait for the openings to occur before they start looking for applicants. But that's too late. There's too much pressure to get the position filled.

There are plenty of qualified minority applicants who would love to work at our newspapers. They're not easy to find, but they are there. We have to stop making excuses, and like that old city editor said, "Just *do* it!" ∎

PERSPECTIVE 5

Women in Newsroom Management

In 1988, the American Society of Newspaper Editors published the following information about women as newsroom managers. Overall, women account for 5.2 percent of publishers/general managers at dailies, although at newspapers with circulations of less than 10,000, the percentage of women who are publishers/general managers is 6.1 percent. If the current trend continues, says ASNE, it will be 70 years until women attain editorship levels equal to their level in the general population (53 percent).

1987 Publishers/General Managers on all U.S. Daily and Sunday Newspapers by Gender

Circulation	Less than 10,000		10,001– 25,000		25,001– 50,000		50,001– 100,000		100,001– 250,000		Over 250,000		Grand Total	
	Men	Women	Men	Women	Men	Women	Men	Women	Men	Women	Men	Women	Men	Women
Numerical Total	553	36	428	20	213	14	122	4	78	3	60	2	1,454	79
Percentage of Total	93.9	6.1	95.5	4.5	93.8	6.2	96.8	3.2	96.3	3.7	96.8	3.2	94.9	5.2

Source: *ASNE Bulletin*, No. 701, January 1988, p. 14.   ∎

How Much Do Reporters Earn?

This is a survey, published in 1988, of starting salaries for newspapers that belong to The Newspaper Guild, which is the reporters' union.

Reporter-Start Rates Average $378 U.S., $472 Canada

Listed here are starting minimums for reporters and photographers in 125 Guild contracts in the United States, Canada and Puerto Rico on Dec. 1 [, 1987].

The table, compiled from data supplied by TNG's Collective Bargaining Dept., includes the starting reporter minimums at five news services along with those in 120 daily newspaper contracts.

Average of the starting minimums in 13 contracts with newspapers and news services in Canada was $472.35 a week; the average in 110 contracts with newspapers and news services in the United States was $378.34 a week.

The reporter starting minimum in 60 percent, or 76, of the contracts was $350 a week or more. In 47, or 38 percent, it was $400 a week or more.

A starting minimum of $500 a week or more was included in 14 of the contracts, while in 29 of them the starting minimum topped $450 a week.

Results of settlements effective after Dec. 1 and deferred increases effective in the interim are not included.

	Minimum		*Minimum*
New York Times	$900.16	Hamilton Spectator	518.00
New York Daily News	787.77	Canadian Press	492.99
New York Post	677.75	Reuters of Canada	490.36
Reuters	601.75	Royal Oak Tribune	480.80
Chicago Sun-Times	575.69	Wilkes-Barre Sunday Independent	478.90
Montreal Gazette	569.00	Seattle Times	475.25
Vancouver Sun and Province	549.43	Pittsburgh Post-Gazette	474.00
Victoria Times-Colonist	547.08	Toronto Globe & Mail	473.93
Ottawa Citizen	533.99	Seattle Post-Intelligencer	462.74
Honolulu Advertiser	523.50	St. Louis Post-Dispatch	462.27
Honolulu Star Bulletin	523.50	Maui News	457.69
Hilo: Hawaii Tribune-Herald	519.34	San Francisco Chronicle and Examiner	457.49
Toronto Star	518.18		*Continued*

	Minimum		Minimum
San Mateo Times	457.49	Milwaukee Journal and Sentinel	350.00
Windsor Star	455.06	Lynn Item	347.96
Denver Rocky Mountain News	454.00	Pawtucket Times	347.43
Manchester Union Leader	453.30	York Daily Record	344.69
Philadelphia Inquirer and Daily News	447.65	United Press Int'l.	343.21
Denver Post	447.00	Harrisburg Patriot and News	341.75
Boston Herald	443.36	Dayton News and Journal Herald	337.50
San Jose Mercury-News	443.27	Bellevue Journal-American	336.79
Santa Rosa Press Democrat	443.21	Bakersfield Californian	336.70
Eugene Register-Guard	429.45	Youngstown Vindicator	336.50
Oakland Tribune	429.34	Lowell Sun	334.41
Detroit News	428.84	Erie News and Times	331.52
Detroit Free Press	427.14	Canton Repository	329.63
Minneapolis Star & Tribune	423.25	Waterbury Republican and American	329.07
Toledo Blade	423.21	Tonawanda News	327.86
Mt. Clemens: Macomb Daily	420.48	Norristown Times Herald	320.79
Monterey Herald	410.00	Allentown Call	325.50
Cleveland Plain Dealer	408.52	Akron Beacon Journal	325.00
Modesto Bee	407.00	Baltimore Sun and Evening Sun	325.00
St. Paul Pioneer Press and Dispatch	405.89	Woonsocket Call	324.71
Tacoma News Tribune	405.60	Oshawa Times	322.54
Sacramento Bee	400.18	Norristown Times Herald	320.79
Fresno Bee	398.79	Gary Post-Tribune	320.39
Associated Press	396.00	Pottstown Mercury	316.13
Woodbridge News Tribune	395.95	Albany Times Union and Knickerbocker News	315.65
Malden News, Medford Mercury and Melrose News	392.46	Great Falls Tribune	315.00
Sheboygan Press	392.40	Sioux City Journal	314.38
Sacramento Union	391.45	Knoxville News-Sentinel	312.65
Delaware County Times (Primos, Pa.)	390.31	Kingston Daily Freeman	308.50
Portland Press Herald and Express	385.96	Sudbury Star	301.52
Providence Journal and Bulletin	383.67	Peoria Journal Star	300.00
San Diego Union and Tribune	380.00	Yakima Herald-Republic	299.00
New Brunswick Home News	380.50	Duluth News-Tribune and Herald	293.50
Salem News	374.17	Lexington Herald-Leader	290.00
Jersey City: Jersey Journal	374.03	Newport News Daily Press and Times-Herald	285.00
Fall River Herald-News	371.93	Brockton Enterprise	280.85
Memphis Commercial Appeal	371.45	Monessen Valley Independent	278.00
Long Beach Press-Telegram	370.00	Scranton Tribune	277.03
Buffalo News	369.93	Rochester Democrat & Chronicle and Times-Union	275.00
Brantford Expositor	368.52	Hazelton Standard-Speaker	272.32
Stockton Record	368.08	San Antonio Light	268.45
Kenosha News	367.00	Lansing State Journal	265.36
San Juan: El Vocero	365.00	Bristol Press	265.30
Waukegan News-Sun	364.33	Scranton Times	259.73
Joliet Herald-News	363.32	Massillon Independent	249.61
Indianapolis Star	362.15	Terre Haute Tribune-Star	247.54
Cincinnati and Kentucky Post	360.00	Utica Observer-Dispatch	245.00
San Juan Star	359.00	Pueblo Chieftain	244.79
York Dispatch	354.51	Battle Creek Enquirer	184.00
Washington Post	352.35	Chattanooga Times	180.00
		Glens Falls Post-Star	180.00

Editorial Cartoonist Paul Conrad

Paul Conrad continues a tradition that goes back to Thomas Nast's caricatures of the corruption of Tammany Hall in *Harper's Weekly* from 1869–1871. Boss Tweed reportedly shouted about Nast's drawings: "Let's stop them damn pictures!" Surely many of today's contemporary figures feel the same way about Paul Conrad, the acerbic, versatile editorial cartoonist at the *Los Angeles Times*. This *Wall Street Journal* profile describes Conrad's contributions to American journalism.

Consider:

1. What can an editorial cartoonist offer readers that print journalists cannot?

2. Which characteristics best describe Conrad's style?

3. What are the risks to a newspaper of continuing to publish biting editorial cartoons, such as Conrad's?

4. Would you be willing to defend Conrad's editorial freedom as strongly as did editor William F. Thomas? Why? Why not?

Paul Conrad's Work Uses Dramatic Images and Packs a Wallop
Liberal Has Depicted Reagan As King Kong and Dunce; Rehnquist's White Hood

EILEEN WHITE

One Paul Conrad cartoon depicts a fetus nailed to a cross labeled "abortion on demand." In another, dealing with gun control, Pope John Paul II is a Christ figure stumbling as he carries a giant handgun in the form of a cross. A Christmas plea for peace shows the Earth as an ornament hanging on a star by a cord frayed to a thread.

Such stark, dramatic images are the hallmark of the cartoonist who has for 22 years displayed his passions to readers of the *Los Angeles Times* and 100 other newspapers through syndication.

Eileen White is a staff reporter of *The Wall Street Journal*.

While the work of many political cartoonists is notable for its amusement, Mr. Conrad's art is notable for its bite.

"Conrad is an angry cartoonist," says Tony Auth, the political cartoonist of the *Philadelphia Inquirer.* "Things infuriate him. He would be a journalist if he weren't a cartoonist."

On the Op-Ed Page

The drawings of the three-time Pulitzer Prize winner are so hard-hitting that *Times* editors moved them to the op-ed page from the editorial page during the Watergate era, and have kept them there, to deflect criticism that he spoke for the paper. Nonetheless, his work—unabashedly liberal, except for his stand on abortion, and often anti-Republican—is considered a symbol of the *Times's* transformation from a conservative right-wing organ in the 1950s to a more liberal voice of national reputation today.

Much of Mr. Conrad's reputation has been gained through two decades of lampooning the two California politicians who gained the presidency during his tenure at the *Times.* Nixon cartoons during the 1970s, such as the unforgettable depiction of the president nailing himself to a cross, earned Mr. Conrad a place on the White House enemies list. He says that that is why his federal tax returns were audited in 1973.

More recently, the 62-year-old cartoonist has hammered unrelentingly at President Reagan. Such cartoons as one that showed President Reagan holding up a beaker of urine for drug testing and bore the caption "Uncle Sam wants yours" have drawn more letters to the *Times* than any other *Times* feature during the Reagan administration.

Libya and Apartheid

When Mr. Reagan sent Navy fighter planes into Libya, Mr. Conrad drew him defending the action as something he "had to do." In the next frame, South African Premier P. W. Botha, who had just ordered the bombing of neighboring African countries, says simply "Ditto."

The president has also appeared in Conrad cartoons as Col. Moammar Gadhafi, King Henry VIII, King Kong, Prof. Henry Higgins, Uncle Sam, a shogun warrior, a vulture, a concentration-camp inmate, an elephant's hind end, a scarecrow, a panhandler, a jailbird, a dunce, a clown, the warhead of a nuclear missile, and God.

Reagan's men haven't fared much better. [Recently] a Conrad cartoon showed Supreme Court Justice William Rehnquist being offered his judicial attire by an aide who asks, "Justice Rehnquist, will you be wearing your hooded white or your black robe today?"

"Lots of cartoonists are more subtle in their humor than Con," says William F. Thomas, the *Times's* editor and executive vice president. He describes Mr. Conrad's cartoons as "unfair by their very nature," although he has never refused to run one and describes himself as a strong defender of the cartoonist's right to speak out.

Mr. Thomas demonstrated this recently when he didn't hesitate to run a Conrad jab at the *Times's* decision to omit a week of Doonesbury cartoons. Mr. Thomas had objected to "inaccuracies" in cartoonist Garry Trudeau's long list of Reagan appointees who allegedly left office under pressure. Mr. Conrad's follow-up, imitating the Doonesbury style, chided the *Times* for "sleaze" in leaving out Doonesbury while tolerating Conrad cartoons.

The nose-thumbing to his own newspaper is typical of the Conrad style. A self-described bleeding heart, he says his mission is "to speak for the people who have no voice." His art often employs national or religious symbols—Mr. Conrad is a Catholic—to make absolute statements about right and wrong. It is created at a titled drawing table that holds a bronze sculpture of Sisyphus pushing the rock. Nearby, a giant poster photograph of Albert Einstein is captioned "Great spirits have always encountered violent opposition from mediocre minds."

Mr. Conrad, a tall, lean native of Iowa, was recruited to the *Times* personally by now-retired publisher Otis Chandler after Mr. Chandler began changing the paper's editorial voice in the 1960s. As the Denver *Post's* cartoonist, Mr. Conrad had already made a name for himself with his swipes at President Eisenhower and had won his first Pulitzer.

"Otis said you can have as much editorial freedom here as you had before. But he didn't know that I had total freedom," Mr. Conrad chortles. In reality, *Times* editors retain the right to censor or reject a Conrad cartoon, but Mr. Conrad recalls only one instance of censorship: Nicholas Williams, then the editor of the *Times,* made him remove a whiskey bottle he had drawn in the pocket of former Mayor Sam Yorty's coat.

Mr. Conrad has given *Times* editors plenty of uncomfortable moments. Edwin O. Guthman, the paper's national editor from 1965 to 1977, remembers frequent evenings when he would go out for dinner and spend "the entire evening defending . . . the paper for having Conrad."

Sinatra Among Critics

The *Times* was sued for libel by Fred Hartley for a Conrad cartoon depicting the Unocal Corp. chairman as Scroogelike during the 1970s oil crisis. (Mr. Hartley lost the suit.) Frank Sinatra lambasted the cartoonist in a 1983 letter to the *Times* for poking fun at Mr. Reagan's hearing aid. Mr. Conrad's cartoons even led to his rejection as a juror in a case. "When I said who I was," he recounts, "everyone said, 'You've got to be kidding,' including the judge." His objectivity suspect, Mr. Conrad was excused, although the judge asked for a cartoon of himself—and got one.

The criticism hasn't abated. But in recent years, the paper's editors have perceived a growing sophistication among readers and increasing openness to divergent views. The current publisher and chief executive officer, Thomas Johnson, says he receives praise for Mr. Conrad's brilliance as often as criticisms.

He cites businessman Walter Annenberg, one of Mr. Reagan's most ardent supporters, as one critic of Mr. Conrad who occasionally compli-ments his cartoons. (Mr. Conrad tells of writing a reply to one Annenberg note and asking to play on the tycoon's private golf course in Palm Springs, Calif. "I never heard back from the S.O.B.," he says.)

At least once, the cartoonist evidently pleased even Mr. Hartley. After the Unocal chairman stood up to takeover artist T. Boone Pickens, Mr. Conrad drew him as a one-man band. Mr. Hartley asked for, and received, the original.

The Uninvited

Some victims don't forgive easily. Mr. Conrad was omitted from the guest list for a recent White House luncheon for political cartoonists hosted by President Reagan. White House communications director Patrick J. Buchanan, challenged about it by Mr. Conrad during a meeting the following week, joked that "the invitation must have gotten lost in the mail." Publisher Johnson says that the slight was "small of the Reagan administration."

Mr. Conrad simply says that "it would have been nice to have been invited." But he doesn't seek detente with Reaganites. His own politics are decidedly Democratic, and his views are reflected in his cartoons, which were much easier on Jimmy Carter than on Republican presidents. He laments the death of Robert Kennedy, who he says "would have made a great president."

Although Mr. Conrad's cartoons aren't officially subject to editing until they are completed, he engages in voluntary pre-censorship. He spends mornings working on pencil sketches in his office near editorial writers. Then he circulates the sketches among them and to favorite reporters and editors. When a cartoon might be a real shocker, Mr. Conrad shows it to the *Times* editor or publisher.

This process recently resulted in Mr. Conrad's decision not to pursue a cartoon showing Mr. Reagan crawling out from under an outhouse, with the caption, "He always comes out smelling like a rose." The drawing, Mr. Conrad says, was considered "not in good taste."

Some Slip By

Still others of questionable taste have slipped by. Publisher Johnson says he would have objected to two recent cartoons if he had been consulted. In one, Lee Iacocca's contretemps over the Statue of Liberty foundation became a portrait of Lady Liberty with the Chrysler Corp. chairman's head and, in place of a torch, an upraised middle finger. The other, concerning Northern California's refusal to share its water resources with the parched south, was shown as a man standing in the northern part of the state and urinating southward. Both cartoons were approved by the editor, Mr. Thomas.

On the one day a week when Mr. Conrad isn't drawing political cartoons, he is an artist, creating bronze sculptures and watercolors at his beachside home, and a prize-winning, hot-air balloonist. He frequently donates cartoons to Democratic party fund-raisers and charities at the behest of his wife and four children, whom Mr. Conrad also describes as "bleeders."

Lately, he has been spending much spare time trying to persuade the American and Soviet governments to donate 41 old missiles to create "Missilehenge," a Stonehenge of the space age in California.

But the project hasn't distracted Mr. Conrad from stalking his favorite Republicans. When *Newsweek* magazine heralded Mr. Nixon's return to the public eye with a cover proclaiming "He's Back," Mr. Conrad drew the former president as a blood-sucker in a cartoon entitled "The Vampire Strikes Back."

"When you win three Pulitzer Prizes," he says, "you can do goddamn near anything you want to." ■

Paul Conrad's view of television.

CHAPTER TWO

For Further Reading

Books

Robert Gottlieb and Irene Wolt, *Thinking Big: The Story of the Los Angeles Times* (New York: G. P. Putnam's Sons, 1977).

Norman E. Isaacs, *Untended Gates: The Mismanaged Press* (New York: Columbia University Press, 1986).

Lauren Kessler, *The Dissident Press* (Beverly Hills: Sage, 1984).

Madelon Golden Schilpp and Sharon M. Murphy, *Great Women of the Press* (Carbondale: Southern Illinois University Press, 1983).

Anthony Smith, *Goodbye Gutenberg: The Newspaper Revolution of the 1980s* (New York: Oxford University Press, 1981).

W. A. Swanberg, *Citizen Hearst* (New York: Bantam Books, 1971).

Gay Talese, *The Kingdom and the Power* (New York: Anchor Books, 1978).

Periodicals

Editor & Publisher

Journalism Monographs

Newspaper Research Journal

Presstime

Quill

The Magazine Industry

How Magazines Work

Before radio and television, magazines were the best way to reach a large audience quickly; even the largest metropolitan newspapers circulated only in the regions where they originated. So magazines became the nation's educators and entertainers. Today, the magazine industry earns $13 billion a year. This Perspective concentrates on the structure of magazine publication.

Consider:

1. What are the three general categories of magazines and who are their audiences?

2. Why are magazines considered a targeted medium?

3. What is the proportion of advertising to copy in most consumer magazines?

4. What is the advantage of regional editions for large-circulation magazines?

Understanding Magazines

SHIRLEY BIAGI

Turn-of-the-century American muckraker Ida Tarbell, known for her exposure of the Standard Oil Company as a monopoly, began her writing career as a free-lancer, submitting articles purely on speculation to magazines in America while she paid her way through Europe. In Paris, American editor S. S. McClure ran up the eighty steps to Tarbell's apartment one day and knocked on her door. Her writing impressed him, he said, and would she write for his new magazine, *McClure's,* when she returned to the United States?

McClure's disheveled, disorganized manner made Tarbell doubt that he would ever start the

Shirley Biagi is Chair of the Department of Journalism at California State University, Sacramento.

magazine, yet she agreed to consider the idea. Tarbell grew even more doubtful about her future when, as McClure was leaving her apartment, he asked for a forty-dollar loan. She gave him the money, which she had been saving for a vacation.

Tarbell's doubts were misplaced, however, because for twenty-one years *McClure's* magazine was the very successful showcase for Tarbell, as well as Lincoln Steffens and Rudyard Kipling. And McClure returned the forty dollars.

Editors are as diverse as their magazines. Writer Dorothy Parker claimed that *New Yorker* magazine editor Harold Ross had a "profound ignorance." He admitted he could not spell and once asked a colleague whether Moby Dick in the novel was the man or the whale. Yet, he attracted and published the writings of Dorothy Parker,

Robert Benchley, James Thurber, Janet Flanner, and H. L. Mencken.

In *The Powers That Be,* author David Halberstam called *Time* founding editor Henry Luce "a curiously artless man, graceless and brusque and lonely, rude inevitably even to those whose favors and good will he coveted; he could only be what he was, he could never be facile or slick, though on frequent occasions his magazines were."

Esquire founding editor Arnold Gingrich liked to wake at dawn to fish in the trout stream near his home. Then he dressed in natty tweeds for work, where he arrived early so he could practice his violin. *Esquire* published Hemingway, Fitzgerald, and Steinbeck under his direction.

American magazines celebrate their 250th birthday in 1991. They have evolved from their polemical beginnings in 1741 with Ben Franklin's *General Magazine* and Andrew Bradford's *American Magazine* to the general interest magazines born in the 1930s, such as *Life* and *Look,* to today's proliferation of specialized publications, such as *International Musician* and *Dairy Herd Management.*

According to *Magazine Industry Market Place,* more than 350 magazines are created in the United States each year. Of these, only ten percent will survive the marketplace, which indicates the competitiveness of the magazine business.

Company, Trade, and Consumer Magazines

Magazines can be divided into three categories—company publications, trade publications, and consumer publications.

Company publications are produced by a specific company or industry mainly for its employees, stockholders, and customers. Trade publications are produced by businesses for professional retailers, manufacturers, and technical experts in a particular industry. Consumer publications are all those popularly marketed at newsstands, in supermarkets, and bookstores.

Employees of the Underwood Company, for example, may read *The Red Devil,* a company publication that emphasizes food products and the history of food, while your grocer reads the trade publication *Progressive Grocer* to learn how to create a more attractive canned meat display and you read the consumer publication *Family Circle* to learn how to use minced ham to stretch your food budget. Clearly each magazine has a different audience, which in turn dictates the magazine's content.

How Magazines Are Organized

Magazines, small and large, follow a predictable pattern of organization. The larger the magazine, the more elaborate the staff.

Overseeing both the business and the writing on a magazine is the publisher, who owns the publication. The publisher may sometimes also be the editor, but more often these functions are separate.

The business side must organize subscriptions, advertising, marketing, and production of the magazine. The editorial side worries about what goes inside the magazine and how the magazine looks.

Most magazines, except for those concerned with personalities (*People*) and news (*Time* and *Newsweek*), have a three-to-four month lead time from final copy to publication. So, editors celebrate Christmas in August or September and get ready for the Fourth of July in the winter.

Magazine editors use charts to track future magazines and their status in production. An editor of a monthly magazine may have three issues going at once, so each of these issues is assigned to an associate editor.

A magazine's size each month is decided by the size of the issue at the same time the year before and the number of advertisements sold for each issue. A consumer magazine usually runs about forty percent ads and sixty percent copy.

How Magazines Are Published

Most of today's magazines are published using computers. With desktop publishing, copy can be organized on-screen and then sent to computer typesetters to prepare the magazine for publication. Large-circulation national magazines that publish regional editions can send articles by satellite to printing plants sprinkled throughout the country, where regional copy and ads are inserted for each area. A national magazine that sells ads to Arizona advertisers who want to reach primarily the Arizona market, for example, can insert copy on Arizona subjects in its Southwest edition to cater to that audience and those advertisers.

Using market research, most magazine publishers target their audiences carefully—by sex, income, education, even zip code. In a magazine without advertising, the articles must entertain and inform the audience so the readers will return to the magazine. The articles in magazines that carry advertising must complement the ads.

Magazine staffs supervise cover design, organize and copyedit articles, select artwork and styles and sizes of type, and meet deadlines. Into all of this must fit the audience, for whom all magazines are created. This audience can be as specific as people who raise goats (*Dairy Herd Management*) or as broad as people who watch television (*TV Guide*).

Because magazines are delivered directly to subscribers, they are a very *targeted* medium. Their audiences are much easier to define than the audience for a TV program, for example. This makes magazines very efficient for advertisers. For example, the magazines owned by the Hearst Corporation (including *Good Housekeeping, Redbook,* and *Sports Afield*) earned $873 million in 1987. (See the article on the Hearst Corporation, pp. 195–201.) In an era saturated with visual media, the success of major magazine publishing firms like Hearst reaffirms the continuing power of print. ■

PERSPECTIVE 2

A Case Study in Magazine Journalism

Former *New York Times* reporter Gay Talese is a frequent magazine contributor, as well as a novelist. Talese was one of the pioneers in a type of magazine-style writing known as "New Journalism" that became popular in the 1960s. Here he describes the anatomy of New Journalism in a magazine article he wrote in 1965 for *Esquire* magazine about Frank Sinatra.

Consider:

1. How does Talese gather his material to write?

2. How does the focus of the Sinatra article change as Talese conducts his interviews and completes his research?

3. What characteristics describe New Journalism, and how did Talese use those elements in his profile of Sinatra?

4. According to Talese, how have magazine writers changed today from when he first began?

When Frank Sinatra Had a Cold

A Reflection on the Cause of Today's Common Journalism

GAY TALESE

As one who was identified in the 1960s with the popularization of a literary genre known best as the "New Journalism"—an innovation of uncertain origin that appeared prominently in *Esquire, Harper's, The New Yorker,* and other magazines and was practiced by such writers as Norman Mailer, Lillian Ross, John McPhee, Tom Wolfe, and the late Truman Capote—I now find myself cheerlessly conceding that those impressive pieces of the past (exhaustively researched, creatively organized, distinctive in style and attitude) are now increasingly rare, victimized in part by the reluctance of today's magazine editors to subsidize the escalating cost of such efforts and diminished also by the inclination of so many younger magazine writers to save time and energy by conducting interviews with the use of that expedient but somewhat benumbing literary device, the tape recorder.

I myself have been interviewed by writers carrying recorders; and as I sit answering their questions, I see them half-listening, nodding pleasantly, and relaxing in the knowledge that the little wheels are rolling. But what they are getting from me (and I assume from other people they talk to) is not the insight that comes from deep probing and perceptive analysis and old-fashioned legwork; it is rather the first-draft drift of my mind, a once-over-lightly dialogue that—while perhaps symptomatic of a society permeated by fast-food computerized bottomline

impersonalized workmanship—too frequently reduces the once-artful craft of magazine writing to the level of talk radio on paper.

Far from decrying this trend, most editors tacitly approve of it because a taped interview that is faithfully transcribed can protect the periodical from those interviewees who might later claim that they had been damagingly misquoted—accusations that, in these times of impulsive litigation and soaring legal fees, cause much anxiety, and sometimes timidity, among even the most independent and courageous of editors.

Another reason editors are accepting of the tape recorder is that it enables them to obtain publishable articles from the influx of facile freelancers at pay rates below what would be expected and deserved by writers of more deliberation and commitment. With one or two interviews, and a few hours of tape, a relatively inexperienced journalist today can produce a three-thousand-word article that relies heavily on direct quotation and (depending largely on the promotional value of the subject at the newsstand) will gain a writer's fee of anywhere from approximately $500 to slightly more than $2,000—which is fair payment, considering the time and skill involved; but it is less than what was being paid for articles of similar length and topicality when I began writing for some of these same magazines more than a quarter of a century ago.

In those days, however, the contemporary writers I admired usually devoted weeks and

Gay Talese is a frequent contributor to magazines as well as being a novelist.

months to research and organization, writing and rewriting, before the articles were considered worthy of occupying the magazine space that today is filled by many of our successors in one-tenth the time. And in the past, too, magazines seemed more liberal than now about research expenses.

During the winter of 1965 I recall being sent to Los Angeles by *Esquire* for an interview with Frank Sinatra, which the singer's publicist had arranged earlier with the magazine's editor. But after I had checked into the Beverly Wilshire, had reserved a rental car in the hotel garage, and had spent the evening of my arrival in a spacious room digesting a thick pack of background material on Sinatra, along with an equally thick steak accompanied by a fine bottle of California burgundy, I received a call from Sinatra's office informing me that my scheduled interview the next afternoon would not take place.

Mr. Sinatra was very upset by the latest headlines in the press about his alleged Mafia connections, the caller explained, adding that Mr. Sinatra was also suffering from a head cold that threatened to postpone a recording date later in the week at a studio where I had hoped to observe the singer at work. Perhaps when Mr. Sinatra was feeling better, and perhaps if I would also agree to submit my interview to the Sinatra office prior to its publication, the interview could be rescheduled.

After commiserating about Mr. Sinatra's cold and the news item about the Mafia, I politely explained that I was obliged to honor my editor's right to be the first judge of my work; but I did ask if I might telephone the Sinatra office later in the week on the chance that his health and spirits might then be so improved that he would grant me a brief visit. I could call, Sinatra's representative said, but he could promise me nothing.

For the rest of the week, after apprising my editor of the situation, I arranged to interview a few actors and musicians, studio executives and record producers, restaurant owners and female acquaintances who had known Sinatra in one way or another through the years. From most of these people I got something; a tiny nugget of information here, a bit of color there, small pieces for a large mosaic that I hoped would reflect the man who for decades had commanded the spotlight and had cast long shadows across the fickle industry of entertainment and the American consciousness.

As I proceeded with my interviews—taking people out each day to lunch and dinner while amassing expenses that, including my hotel room and car, exceeded $1,300 after the first week—I rarely, if ever, removed a pen and pad from my pocket, and I certainly would not have considered using a tape recorder had I owned one. To have done so would have possibly inhibited these individuals' candor, or would have otherwise altered the relaxed, trusting, and forthcoming atmosphere that I believe was encouraged by my seemingly less assiduous research manner and the promise that, however retentive I believe my memory to be, I would not identifiably attribute or quote anything told me without first checking back with the source for confirmation and clarification.

Quoting people verbatim, to be sure, has rarely blended well with my narrative style of writing, or my wish to observe and describe people actively engaged in ordinary but revealing situations rather than to confine them to a room and present them in the passive posture of a monologist. Since my earliest days in journalism, I was far less interested in the exact words that came out of people's mouths than in the essence of their meaning. More important than what people say is what they think, even though the latter may initially be difficult to articulate and may require much pondering and reworking within the interviewee's mind—which is what I gently try to prod and stimulate as I query, interrelate, and identify with my subjects, and personally accompany them whenever possible, be it on their errands, their appointments, their aimless peregrinations before dinner or after work. Wherever it is, I try to physically be there in my role as a curious confidant, a trustworthy fellow traveler searching into their interior, seeking to discover, to clarify, and finally to describe in words (my words) what they personify and how they think.

There are times, however, when I do take notes. Occasionally there is a remark that one hears—a turn of phrase, a special word, a personal revelation conveyed in an inimitable style—that should be put on paper at once, lest part of it be forgotten. That is when I may take out a note pad and say, "That's wonderful! Let me get that down just as you said it"; and the person, usually flattered, not only repeats it but expands upon it; and on such occasions there can emerge a heightened spirit of cooperation, almost of collaboration, as the person interviewed recognizes that he has contributed something that the writer appreciates to the point of wanting to preserve it in print.

At other times I make notes unobserved by the interviewee—such as during those interruptions in our talks when the person has temporarily left the room, thus allowing me moments in which to jot down what I believe to be the relevant parts of our conversation. I also occasionally make notes immediately after the interview is completed, when things are still very fresh in my mind. Then, later in the evening, before I go to bed, I sit at my typewriter and describe in detail (sometimes filling four or five pages, single-spaced) my recollections of what I had seen and heard that day—a chronicle to which I constantly add pages with each passing day of the entire period of research.

This chronicle is kept in an ever-expanding series of cardboard folders containing such data as the places where I, and my sources, had breakfast, lunch, and dinner (restaurant receipts enclosed to document my expenses); the exact time, length, locale, and subject matter of every interview, together with the agreed-upon conditions of each meeting (i.e., am I free to identify the source, or am I obliged to later contact that individual for clarification and/or clearance?). And the pages of the chronicle also include my personal impressions of the people I interviewed, their mannerisms and physical description, my assessment of their credibility, and much about my own private feelings and concerns as I work my way through each day—an intimate addendum that now, after nearly thirty years of habit, is of use for a somewhat autobiographical book I am writing; but the original intent of such admissive writing was self-clarification, reaffirming my own voice on paper after hours of concentrated listening to others, and also, not infrequently, venting some of the frustration I felt when my research appeared to be going badly, as it certainly did in the winter of 1965 when I was unable to meet face to face with Frank Sinatra.

After trying without success to reschedule the Sinatra interview during my second week in Los Angeles (I was told that he still had a cold), I continued to meet with people who were variously employed in some of Sinatra's many business enterprises—his record company, his film company, his real estate operation, his missile-parts firm, his airplane hangar; and I also saw people who were more personally associated with the singer, such as his overshadowed son, his favorite haberdasher in Beverly Hills, one of his bodyguards (a 300-pound former football lineman), and a little gray-haired lady who traveled with Sinatra around the country on concert tours, carrying in a satchel his sixty hairpieces.

From such people I collected an assortment of facts and comments, but what I gained at first from these interviews was no particular insight or eloquent summation of Sinatra's stature; it was rather the awareness that so many of these people—who lived and worked in so many separate places—were united in the knowledge that Frank Sinatra had a cold. When I would allude to this in conversations, citing this as the reason my interview with him was being postponed, they would nod and say, yes, they were aware of his cold and they also knew from their contacts within Sinatra's inner circle that he was a most difficult man to be around when his throat was sore and his nose was running. Some of the musicians and studio technicians were delayed from working in his recording studio because of the cold, while others among his personal staff of seventy-five were not only sensitive to the effects of his ailment but revealed examples of how volatile and short-tempered he had been all week because he was unable to meet his singing standards. And one evening in my hotel, I wrote in the chronicle:

. . . it is a few nights before Sinatra's recording session, but his voice is weak, sore, and uncertain. Sinatra is ill. He is a victim of an ailment so common that most people would consider it trivial. But when it gets to Sinatra it can plunge him into a state of anguish, deep depression, panic, even rage. Frank Sinatra has a cold.

Sinatra with a cold is Picasso without paint, Ferrari without fuel—only worse. For the common cold robs Sinatra of that uninsurable jewel, his voice, cutting into the core of his confidence, and it affects not only his own psyche but also seems to cause a kind of psychological nasal drip within dozens of people who work for him, drink with him, love him, depend on him for their own welfare and stability.

A Sinatra with a cold can, in a small way, send vibrations through the entertainment industry and beyond as surely as a President of the United States, suddenly sick, can shake the national economy. . . .

The next morning I received a call from Frank Sinatra's public relations director.

"I hear you're all over town seeing Frank's friends, taking Frank's friends to dinner," he began, almost accusingly.

"I'm working," I said. "How's Frank's cold?" (We were suddenly on a familiar basis.)

"Much better, but he still won't talk to you. But you can come with me tomorrow afternoon to a television taping, if you'd like. Frank's going to try to tape part of his NBC special. . . . Be outside your hotel at three. I'll pick you up."

I suspected that Sinatra's publicist wanted to keep a closer eye on me, but I was nonetheless pleased to be invited to the taping of the first segment of the one-hour special that NBC-TV was scheduled to air in two weeks, entitled "Sinatra—A Man and His Music."

On the following afternoon, promptly and politely, I was picked up in a Mercedes convertible driven by Sinatra's dapper publicist, a square-jawed man with reddish hair and a deep tan who wore a three-piece gabardine suit that I favorably commented upon soon after getting into the car—prompting him to acknowledge, with a certain satisfaction, that he had obtained it at a special price from Frank's favorite haberdasher. As we drove, our conversation remained amiably centered on such subjects as clothes, sports, and the weather until we arrived at the NBC building and pulled into a white concrete parking lot in which there were about thirty other Mercedes convertibles as well as a number of limousines in which were slumped black-capped drivers trying to sleep.

Entering the building, I followed the publicist through a corridor into an enormous studio dominated by a white stage and white walls, and dozens of lamps and lights dangling everywhere I looked—the place resembled a gigantic operating room. Gathered in one corner of the room behind the stage, awaiting the appearance of Sinatra, were about one hundred people—camera crews, technical advisers, Budweiser admen, attractive young women, Sinatra's bodyguards and hangers-on, and also the director of the show, a sandy-haired, cordial man named Dwight Hemion, whom I knew from New York because we had daughters who were preschool playmates. As I stood chatting with Hemion, and overhearing conversations all around me, and listening to the forty-three musicians sitting in tuxedoes on the bandstand, warming up their instruments, my mind was racing with ideas and impressions, and I would have liked to have taken out my note pad for a second or two. But I knew better.

And yet after two hours in the studio—during which time Sinatra's publicist never left my side, even when I went to the bathroom—I was able to recall later that night precise details about what I had seen and heard at the taping; and in my hotel I wrote in the chronicle:

Frank finally arrived on stage, wearing a high-necked yellow pullover, and even from my distant vantage point his face looked pale, his eyes seemed watery. He cleared his throat a few times.

Then the musicians, who had been sitting stiffly and silently in their seats ever since Frank had joined them on the platform, began to play the opening song, Don't Worry About Me. Then Frank sang through the whole song—a rehearsal prior to taping—and his voice sounded fine to me, and it apparently sounded fine to him, too, because after the rehearsal he suddenly wanted to get it on tape.

He looked up toward the director, Dwight Hemion, who sat in the glass-enclosed control booth overlooking the stage, and he yelled: "Why don't we tape this mother?"

Some people laughed in the background, and Frank stood there tapping a foot, waiting for some response from Hemion.

"Why don't we tape this mother?" Sinatra repeated, louder, but Hemion just sat up there with his headset around his ears, flanked by other men also wearing headsets, staring down at a table of knobs or something. Frank stood fidgeting on the white stage, glaring up at the booth, and finally the production stage manager—a man who stood to the left of Sinatra, and also wore a headset—repeated Frank's words exactly into his line to the control room: "Why don't we tape this mother?"

Maybe Hemion's switch was off up there. I don't know, and it was hard to see Hemion's face because of the obscuring reflections the lights made against the glass booth. But by this time Sinatra is clutching and stretching his yellow pullover out of shape, and screaming up at Hemion: "Why don't we put on a coat and tie, and tape this . . ."

"Okay, Frank," Hemion cut in calmly, having apparently not been plugged into Sinatra's tantrum, "would you mind going back over . . ."

"Yes I would mind going back!" Sinatra snapped. "When we stop doing things around here the way we did them in 1950, maybe we . . ."

. . . Although Dwight Hemion later managed to calm Sinatra down, and in time to successfully tape the first song and a few others, Sinatra's voice became increasingly raspy as the show progressed—and on two occasions, it cracked completely, causing Sinatra such anguish that in a fitful moment he decided to scrub the whole day's session. "Forget it, just forget it!" he told Hemion. "You're wasting your time. What you got there," he continued, nodding to the singing image of himself on the TV monitor, "is a man with a cold."

There was hardly a sound heard in the studio for a moment or two, except for the clacking heels of Sinatra as he left the stage and disappeared. Then the musicians put aside their instruments, and everybody else slowly turned toward the exit. . . . In the car coming back to the hotel, Frank's publicist said they'd try to retape the show within the week, he'd let me know when. He also said that in a few weeks he was going to Las Vegas for the Patterson-Clay heavyweight fight (Frank & friends would be there to watch it), and if I wanted to go he'd book me a room at the Sands and we could fly together. Sure, I said . . . but to myself I'm thinking: how long will Esquire continue to pay my expenses? By the end of this week, I'll have spent more than $3,000, have not yet talked to Sinatra, and at the rate we're going, it's possible I never will. . . .

Before going to bed that night, I telephoned my editor in New York, Harold Hayes, briefed him on all that was happening, and not happening, and expressed concern about the expenses.

"Don't worry about the expenses as long as you're getting something out there," he said. "Are you getting something?"

"I'm getting something," I said, "but I don't know exactly what it is."

"Then stay there until you find out."

I stayed there another three weeks, ran up expenses close to $5,000, and then took another six weeks to organize and write a fifty-five-page article that was largely drawn from a two-hundred-page chronicle that represented interviews with more than one hundred people and described Sinatra in such places as a bar in Beverly Hills (where he got into a fight), a casino in Las Vegas (where he lost a small fortune at blackjack), and the NBC studio in Burbank (where, after recovering from the cold, he retaped the show and sang beautifully).

The editors entitled the piece "Frank Sinatra Has A Cold," and it appeared in the April 1966 issue. It remains in print today in a collection of mine called *Fame and Obscurity*. While I was never given the opportunity to sit down and speak alone with Frank Sinatra, this fact is perhaps one of the strengths of the article. What could he or *would* he have said (being among the most guarded of public figures) that would have revealed him better than an observing writer watching him in action, seeing him in stressful situations, listening and lingering along the sidelines of his life?

This method of lingering and careful listening and describing scenes that offer insight into the individual's character and personality—a method that a generation ago came to be called the "New Journalism"—was, at its best, really fortified by the "Old" Journalism's principles of tireless legwork and fidelity to factual accuracy.

But examples of such pieces are, as I mentioned earlier, becoming more and more rare in the 1980s. Most of the best of the nonfiction writers today are either having their research expenses underwritten by the book industry (and are excerpting parts of their books in magazines); or they are best-selling writers who can afford to do a well-researched magazine piece if they fancy the subject; or they are writers whose financial support comes mainly from faculty salaries and foundation grants. And what this latter group of writers are publishing today, mainly in modestly remunerative literary periodicals, are pieces that tell us more about themselves than about other people—they are opinionated pieces of intellectual or cultural content, or articles that are decidedly reflective and personal, and not dependent on costly time and travel. They are works researched out of a writer's own recollections. They are close to a writer's heart and place of dwelling. The road has become too expensive. The writer is home. ∎

PERSPECTIVE 3

The Importance of Readership

To sell their audience to advertisers, magazines use readership information provided by various sources, such as Mediamark Research Inc. (MRI) and Simmons Market Research Bureau Inc. What happens when the sources disagree? Whom should advertisers believe? That is the subject of this article, which originally appeared in *The Wall Street Journal*.

Consider:

1. How important are readership figures to magazines? Why?

2. How do these two readership surveys differ?

3. Why are discrepancies among readership figures significant for advertisers?

Readership Figures for Periodicals Stir Debate in Publishing Industry

JOANNE LIPMAN

"Today, mama's got a lot more cooking than dinner," says the trade advertisement. "That's why she reads *Family Circle*. The magazine that's not written for old fashioned housewives, it's written for the newest, hottest mamas ever. Or at least 23,000,000 of them."

Or is it only 19,578,000 of them? Probably, neither figure is right. And therein lies the central issue of a long-simmering controversy.

The numbers come from the two major readership research firms: the first from Mediamark Research Inc., a unit of London-based MAI PLC; the second from Simmons Market Research Bureau Inc., a unit of WPP Group PLC, also in London. Besides measuring how many people read various magazines and national newspapers, the firms look at such demographic information as readers' ages and incomes. Based largely on these numbers, advertisers decide where to place more than $5 billion of print ads annually.

Yet Simmons and MRI, as Mediamark is known, rarely agree in their results. Sometimes they aren't even consistent with themselves, showing inexplicable readership swings.

The Need to Know

The question of which is closer to the truth is an urgent one. As the magazine and newspaper industries enter the third year of an advertising

Joanne Lipman is a staff reporter for *The Wall Street Journal*.

slump, ad-rate increases and new advertisers are ever harder to win. Poor numbers—accurate or not—can spell trouble. As a result, many publications, including *The Wall Street Journal*, have challenged the research firms' methods and results.

The readership figures "are life and death for individual publications," says Robert Coen, a senior vice president of the New York office of the advertising firm McCann-Erickson Worldwide. "If the readership figures shift just a hair, there's a big shift in the (number of) ad pages."

Executives at both Simmons and MRI stand by their research. "We're like the umpires at the ball game," says Frank Stanton, president and chief executive of Simmons. "Everybody boos the umpire."

Publishers say that it's difficult to tell which figures are more accurate, and complain that the differences between them are hard to reconcile. For example, MRI says that last year 20.9 people read each copy of *House and Garden;* Simmons says the figures was only about 9.2. This year, Simmons says, 37.5 million people read *Reader's Digest,* while MRI puts the figure at 50.9 million.

Nor do changes in a single firm's results always seem logical. Mal Ochs, a magazine consultant currently working with *Us* magazine, says Simmons reported a 21% drop in *Us* readership this year—despite a circulation gain. (Readership figures are usually higher than those for circulation because more than one person reads each copy.)

Simmons's Mr. Stanton notes *Us* has undergone editorial changes and says, "The techniques we use tend to be hypersensitive to changes the publisher makes."

The key to the quirks—and the controversy—lies in the two firms' research methods. Simmons shows specific issues of magazines to people, and counts as readers those who have read or glanced through those issues. MRI shows people flash cards with magazine logos printed on them, and counts as readers anyone who says they have read a weekly within the past seven days or a monthly within the past 30 days. While both firms interview about 20,000 people for each study, MRI's figures are generally higher—in 1987, about 10% higher for weeklies and 35% higher for monthlies, according to research by Simmons.

Problems can crop up for smaller-circulation magazines because the research samples for them are often small. For example, Simmons's latest study included responses from only 424 readers of *Esquire,* which has a circulation of more than 700,000. When the figures are broken down to look at certain income and age groups, "you're getting under 30 respondents, and the data is completely useless," contends Alan Lutrin, *Esquire*'s research director.

Still, adds W. Randall Jones, *Esquire*'s publisher, poor numbers "absolutely affect us economically. It takes a lot of selling" to woo advertisers put off by the figures.

MRI and Simmons respond that their reports flag numbers that are based on samples too small to be reliable, and that they list a margin of error for each magazine's results.

Critics have disputed other procedures as well. To prevent backaches among its researchers, who must lug 110 different magazines door to door, Simmons uses stripped-down issues that include only nine or so articles and no ads. But publishing executives say the stripped versions of certain magazines don't bear any resemblance to the originals.

Metropolitan Home, to illustrate the point, commissioned a study of women who said they read the magazine. When shown an actual issue, 42% said they were sure they had read it. When shown the same issue in the stripped version used by Simmons, only 28% said they were sure they had read it. "Simmons was remaking our magazine," says Stephen Burzon, the publisher of *Metropolitan Home,* which was measured by neither firm this year. (Simmons responds that it did a similar study in 1976 and that the results for actual and stripped copies were identical.)

Critics contend that MRI's technique, on the other hand, may overinflate readership figures in some cases. They argue that people get confused by similar names—such as *House and Garden* and *Better Homes and Gardens*—and are apt to say they read publications they really don't. In a study done several years ago, they note, Time Inc. asked people about four magazines that were either fictitious or defunct. It came up with 13.1 million people who claimed to read them, including 2.8 million for *Popular Sports* (fictitious) and 6.7 million for *Look* (defunct).

"Sure, there are errors," concedes Timothy Joyce, MRI's chairman and chief executive. "If

---

Study in Contrasts

Top five magazines based on total adult readership, in millions

The Simmons List

1 TV Guide	43.2
2 Reader's Digest	37.5
3 People	24.6
4 National Geographic	23.6
5 Time	23.2

The MRI List

1 Reader's Digest	50.9
2 TV Guide	46.8
3 Better Homes and Gardens	35.5
4 People	30.4
5 National Geographic	30.3

NOTE: Excludes Sunday magazines

you put in a plausible name, you'll get a few readers." However, he defends the validity of MRI's studies.

Considering Other Factors

In acknowledgment of the inconsistencies in the figures, big ad agencies often massage the raw data from the two firms, and they try to take into account other factors when deciding where ads should be placed. But the agencies' media planners often stick to the numbers anyway.

"I've seen magazines knocked off of lists when the data falls," says Phillip Bernstein, a media supervisor at the ad agency Backer Spielvogel Bates, a unit of Saatchi & Saatchi PLC. "Sometimes we'll adjust the data or come up with our own numbers. We try to give guidance (to the media buyers) and flag the numbers that aren't stable—but who knows? The bottom line is, you never know how a media planner deals with the data."

To help resolve the issue, a committee of advertising and research executives are trying to come up with absolutely accurate results by counting as readers only those people in study populations who say they read a publication the day before.

But the committee still needs $200,000 to finish its four-magazine trial. Measuring all 250-plus U.S. magazines, says Richard Lysaker, president of Audits and Surveys Inc. and committee chairman, "could be very expensive"—if possible at all. ■

PERSPECTIVE 4

Magazines Tell Their Cover Stories

Although most magazines are sold by subscription, editors also realize the importance of a magazine cover to sell copies off-the-rack. This article describes which magazine covers have succeeded while others failed and also gives an insight into the editorial debate over why people buy magazines.

Consider:

1. Do you agree with art director Bob Ciano who says, "No one knows what works"? Why? Why not?

2. What percentage of magazines are sold on newsstands? Are newsstand sales increasing or decreasing?

3. List the four steps that Ron Scott delineates as part of the magazine-buying decision. Explain.

4. List five factors that affect magazine newsstand sales. Explain.

Magazine Cover Roulette
What Sells, What Bombs

MARY W. QUIGLEY

Three to five seconds. That's the time the average reader spends scanning a magazine cover before deciding whether to buy the issue. All those carefully planned photo sessions, arguments with art directors, and clever cover lines are judged by a reader's brief glance at dozens of titles and by some imponderable image catching the eye.

Publishers, circulation managers, editors, and art directors spend hours trying to figure out what sells a magazine. Some have resorted to surreptitiously observing shoppers at supermarkets, others have sent surveyors to malls with cover mockups, and still others have hired research companies to measure the eye movements of readers scanning covers.

But no one has yet come up with a guaranteed method of making a magazine fly off the newsstand. Some editors and art directors argue that it's impossible to guess what will appeal to the average reader. "It's a crapshoot," says *Travel & Leisure* Art Director Bob Ciano. "No one knows what works."

Others counter that, despite uncontrollable variables and occasional surprises, a skillful editor can compile a track record of winning covers. "I see picking covers as a game like poker," says John Peter, a New York magazine consultant. "With practice, a player improves and wins over a period of time. But on an individual cover you may not do as well as expected. It's not a science

because of all the variables, ranging from having the right number of copies in the right number of outlets to placement on the newsstand to the cover image and cover lines."

Why are covers important? The vast majority of the 11,000 magazine titles published annually are sold by subscription rather than through single-copy sales. Whether readers plunk down $2.50 at a newsstand or receive a magazine mixed in with junk mail and bills, the cover is what lures them to discover what is new, interesting, entertaining, and informative in a particular issue. "Smart editors watch newsstand sales very carefully because they are a barometer for what interests all readers," Peter says.

"Newsstand sales" is itself a misnomer since only about 11 percent of magazines are actually sold on newsstands. Single-copy sales, the term circulation experts use, is a more accurate description for the approximately 3,000 different titles sold each month at retail outlets. Supermarkets are the point of purchase for almost 54 percent of those magazines, according to the Periodicals Institute, a magazine-marketing organization located in Fairfield, New Jersey. Ranking after supermarkets and newsstands are drugstores at 9 percent, bookstores at 8 percent, and convenience stores at 5 percent. Women buy more magazines because they shop more frequently than men.

A *Redbook* survey found that about 60 percent of magazine buyers had no specific title in mind before purchasing a magazine, nor did they have any previously made plans to buy one. And a

Mary W. Quigley teaches magazine journalism at New York University.

New York Times Company study determined that shoppers spend an average of three to five seconds deciding whether or not to buy a particular title.

Ron Scott, a single-copy sales consultant for a number of publications, has broken down the process of buying a magazine into four steps. "The first step is when the consumer scans the fixture and stops his eyes on a particular cover," Scott says. "Second, the cover is attractive enough that the consumer actually picks the magazine up and looks at the cover. Third, the consumer looks at the image and cover lines coming in at the top lefthand corner. If you can get the consumer to keep his eye on the cover for more than five seconds, you've increased his interest. Fourth, the consumer fans through the magazine looking for an image that attracts him. The buy-or-no-buy decision can be made at any one of these points."

Nonetheless, Scott says, "Magazines are one of the most difficult products to sell because the magazine has to be the same but different every month."

Peter agrees. Magazine editors, he says, face two conflicting factors when deciding on a cover: consistency and change. "One set of elements requires that a magazine is consistent in size, cover stock, logo, and format in every issue. You change them at your peril. The elements of consistency are very much like a package in a supermarket: That's 'Duz.' Boom! Buy it, based on package recognition. The elements of change include the date, which is often buried. The consumer has to know it's a new issue. The next element is color, which some people make a big deal of. Next important is blurbs. But probably the most dominant factor is the image. Most people remember the image and who was on the cover last time."

Most editors agree that the cover image, focusing on a particular topic, is what sells magazines. Obviously, the topics vary greatly from magazine to magazine. But there *are* some guidelines. Among editors, Time Inc.'s Richard Stolley is recognized as a cover guru, especially when it comes to predicting hot cover subjects. Stolley, now director of special projects for Time Inc., was managing editor of *People* from 1974 to 1982, of *Life* from 1982 to 1986, and of the ill-fated *Picture Week* from 1986 to 1987.

During his years at *People*, Stolley devised a set of cover laws: "Young is better than old, pretty is better than ugly, TV is better than music, music is better than movies, movies are better than sports, and anything is better than politics," Stolley recalls. Clearly, the basic ingredient for the cover of *People*, as well as many other magazines, is a recognizable face, usually a celebrity's. "It's an aphorism that, with a magazine's contents, sooner is usually better than later," Stolley says. "With the covers, later is better than sooner. There is a tendency to overestimate the extent to which a cover subject is known, admired, recognized, and loved. Part of that is being in New York City with its media blitz. You've got to remember that in other areas of the country the awareness of a celebrity might not be so great."

Life ran smack into that problem with its low-selling May 1987 cover of stars Warren Beatty and Dustin Hoffman, who were pitching their soon-to-be megaflop, "Ishtar." The movie received a lot of hype in the New York press, and Hoffman and Beatty were in Manhattan making a promotional video for the movie when *Life* arranged to photograph and interview the pair. According to Assistant Managing Editor Mary Youatt Steinbauer, "The cover came out just before the movie. People just weren't talking about it. There weren't enough people around interested in the movie to buy that issue."

Stolley warns, "You take a real chance when you close a cover on a movie in advance of the movie's release because if the movie dies then awareness across the country is zero."

US suffered a similar fate when it put "L.A. Law's" Harry Hamlin on the cover. "Harry Hamlin came to 'L.A. Law' with a well-known name, documented good looks, and a well-publicized love life, but he just didn't command the interest we thought he would," says Jay Gissen, former executive editor of *US* and current editor of the *Cable Guide*. Hamlin also had the distinction of bringing down a *People* cover, which touted him as "The Sexiest Man Alive, 1987." "This proves editors are not as smart as they think they are," says James R. Gaines, managing editor of *People*. "He looked like he would qualify as our sexiest man, but I guess judging the country's collective hormones is not an easy matter."

Ron Scott warns that celebrity covers are a double-edged sword. "If you're right you win big, but if you're wrong you lose big," he says. "Celebrities can affect sales negatively as well as positively. When you pick the wrong one, you pay."

Still, many editors seem willing to take their chances with celebrity or personality covers because of the instant recognition factor. *Advertising Age* runs a column called "Cover Story," which tracks celebrity appearances on magazine covers. The 1987 cover champion was none other than the slightly scandalous and endlessly fascinating Princess of Wales, Lady Di. *Advertising Age* estimates that Her Royal Highness was on no fewer than 30 separate magazine covers during the year. Lady Di was followed by, in descending order, Bruce Willis, Michael J. Fox, Cybill Shepherd, and Fergie a k a the Duchess of York.

Even within celebrity ranks there is a pecking order for a top-selling cover. Joseph Elm, director of single-copy sales for Murdoch Magazines, says, "At the *Star,* we have a saying that the best covers are about people hatched, matched, and dispatched—born, married, or died."

Stolley, only slightly less flippantly, terms the "dispatched" category as the "recently dead," citing cover stories on the deaths of John Lennon, John Belushi, Karen Carpenter, and Liberace as all-time best sellers. *People*'s Gaines adds, "Every cover ever done with someone deceased has done exceedingly well. When someone passes from the scene, people want one last look and feel of them. People want to own one last part of that person."

"Other people's problems" is another surefire topic, exemplified by one of *People*'s bestselling issues; the August 1987 cover story featured Joan Rivers, after her husband's suicide. "The best covers for us are people very much in the public eye who have something happen to them," said Gaines.

When celebrities or public figures cope with problems in front of packs of reporters and television crews, the stories can boost single-copy sales of newsweeklies by the hundreds of thousands. The troubles of TV evangelists Jim and Tammy Bakker and the Senate testimony of Oliver North sent sales skyrocketing.

"There was so much about the Bakkers on television and in the newspapers that the newsmagazine syndrome took over," says Richard Duncan, *Time*'s assistant managing editor. "People wanted to find out more about them."

But media attention doesn't guarantee good newsstand sales. *Esquire* Editor Lee Eisenberg learned that lesson in February 1987 with a cover story on Baseball Commissioner Peter Ueberroth's suggestions for solving the country's drug problems. It bombed on the newsstands. "The issue of drugs and society was very prominent in the daily newspapers," Eisenberg says. "If we misjudged anything it was how much the newsstand public was concerned about a solution to that problem."

Roberta MacDonald, *Newsweek*'s director of retail sales, agrees, citing the magazine's worst-selling cover for 1987, "Finally, An Arms Deal That *Can* Work." "Politics isn't real strong to begin with, and the arms deal—something people were hearing about on all the other media sources, including cable and radio—is real hard-core news that people don't want to take the extra time to read about," she says.

Nonetheless, *Newsweek* Editor-in-Chief Richard Smith never considered another cover story. "There was no doubt that the arms-deal story was going to be one of our lowest sellers," he says. "We know people find the topic difficult and complex, but we believed we had to lay out the landscape on arms control for our subscribers because they expect coverage of that kind of story."

The only topic that seems to sell worse than politics is *international* politics. A *Time* cover story on South Africa in May 1987 ranked near the bottom of newsstand sales. "Foreign news only sells if you're telling urgent news or a good yarn," Duncan says. "You can't go to your reader and say, 'You have to care about South Africa and read this.'" Foreign news doesn't even sell for the business magazines, despite an increasingly global economy. In the *Forbes* cellar last year was a cover story on "Zen and the Art of Japanese Stock Pricing." "International subjects are the kiss of death," says *Forbes* Circulation Director John Thornton. "People are not interested in knowing what goes on beyond their own back fence. Our worst cover ever was on German Chancellor Helmut Kohl."

If hard news doesn't sell unless it borders on celebrity (Oliver North) or scandal (the Bakkers), what does sell? "Soft news overall does well," says *Newsweek*'s MacDonald, referring to covers on staying married, twins, and the movie "The Untouchables." "It's really a matter of the lifestyle people are into. They don't have a tremendous amount of leisure time and when they do spend time reading they are often looking for pleasure-type reading. They can get the hard news on TV." A survey of the top-selling issues of a wide range of magazines confirms that soft news and service pieces do sell best, from *New York*'s "Second Thoughts on Having it All" to *Los Angeles*'s "20th Annual Restaurant Super Guide" to *Esquire*'s "The Passions of Men, 1987."

Other topics that intrigue readers include science and money. One of *Time*'s best sellers last year featured a cover story about an exploding star. The cover blurb? "BANG!" "Science covers . . . are good for us because they are both informative and escapist," says *Time*'s Duncan. At *Forbes,* topics such as "how to get more out of personal investments" or "how much other people earn" top the charts.

Another winning category is subjects that generate newspaper and television coverage. *Playboy* increased the press run—and the price—of the May 1987 issue with Vanna White on the cover, knowing her popularity would generate free publicity.

One key factor for newsstand success is a strong visual element on the cover. Most editors agree that photographs, especially of faces—women's not men's—sell better than illustrations. "Photography is generally looked at as reporting reality," says consultant John Peter. "If an editor must use an illustration it should be drawn as close to reality as possible, like a Norman Rockwell, so people think they are looking at a photograph. The more it becomes like Picasso the more controversy and questions you are going to have from readers."

An exception is all-type covers. "You can't do an all-type cover for every issue," Peter says. "But they do make sense for special issues because they provide a change of pace from regular issues." Both *Rolling Stone* and *Esquire* rank issues with all-type covers at the top of their best-seller lists. "Readers know from the all-type covers that this is a special issue," says *Esquire*'s Eisenberg. "We spend up to two and three years thinking about and executing the idea, and our hope is that specialness is apparent."

Glamour Editor-in-Chief Ruth Whitney pores over hundreds of slides each month for her cover photograph. "I bet on eyes rather than smiles," she says. "Eye contact between the model on the cover and the reader matters more than smiles. What makes me think I've got the right cover is when I begin smiling back at the face. That's a person who likes me and I like her back."

While the purpose of the image is to get the reader's attention, it's the cover lines, or billings, that clinch the sale. A debate rages at magazine offices, usually between art directors and editors, on the number of cover lines that are necessary—none, four, ten? No prescribed number works for every magazine, but the best sellers generally have a single, strong image with up to six cover lines. "We know from research that the reader will buy a magazine for a single cover line," says consultant Ron Scott. "Using cover lines effectively is like being a politician. You have a certain number of constituents and you must let each one of those constituents know in each issue there's something important in the magazine for him."

The best cover lines are short and simple, says Time Inc.'s Stolley, who adds, "Cover lines that are too clever delight your peers but confuse your readers. You've got to remember the mood people are in when they're buying your magazine. They've just been through this damn supermarket where everything is over-priced; they're tired; they may have a kid hanging on them. You want a cover line that's very appealing, very bold, and speaks its piece very simply. Cute just doesn't do it."

One recent trend is to place cover lines above the logo, in an effort to compensate for display in vertical racks where only the logo shows. But some experts argue that those cover lines have little effect. "We've done all kinds of research using laser scanners, and what it shows is that no one ever looks above the logo," says William Kerr, president of the New York Times Company Magazine Group. He adds, laughing, "I haven't found an editor yet who really believes that research."

Other magazines have also conducted tests to try to settle the more-versus-fewer cover-line controversy. *Better Homes and Gardens* split the run of its August and October issues, with half containing several cover lines and the other half with only one. "We did this test because we were alert to the fact that reader perceptions have changed," says Managing Editor Kate Greer. "They are exposed to so much more design, so much more visual stimuli, that we wondered, does the photo say more than words? Are we getting to be a less literal and more visual society? From our split run we found that words are still awfully important, at least on the newsstand. The issues with more cover lines pulled much better than other issues."

Still, that doesn't mean one should crowd the cover with blurbs. "Our test found that while it varies from cover to cover, the maximum number of cover lines should be the amount you can fit comfortably without crowding," Greer says. "You don't want to look junky or frazzled. And, above all, the cover lines must be readable."

Cover lines should be easy to read from ten paces. "When you walk into a newsstand today," Peter says, you'd be surprised how many wonderful blurbs on top magazines are not readable because of the background contrast or color that blends perfectly with the cover lines. It's almost like there's a ploy to lose the words." Peter adds that the conventional wisdom about bright colors being better than dark colors isn't as important as the contrast.

Placement of cover lines is generally on the left-hand side of the cover because magazines overlap on the newsstand. It's also important because research indicates that after looking at the image, the reader's eyes go to the top left and then come around the cover in a counterclockwise direction. The SAMI/Burke Co. in Cincinnati uses computers, fiber optics, and customized software to determine how readers react to a cover, where they look, and how much time they spend looking.

Other magazines rely on less exotic tests. Among other methods, *US* deploys testing teams armed with cover mock-ups to shopping malls to find out which covers the potential readers will respond to. *Family Circle* sends observers into supermarkets to watch readers purchase magazines, and follows up with exit interviews to ask why a particular choice was made.

All the research sometimes can't contend with the variables of seasonality, competition, and newsstand placement. Most magazines have peak periods. In the summer, *Rolling Stone* does well because it's good beach reading while *TV Guide* hits bottom because its readers aren't indoors watching reruns. Fall issues are best sellers for fashion magazines. "September will always sell well even if it's a terrible cover," says *Glamour*'s Ruth Whitney. For *Los Angeles* magazine, October and November are the worst months. "No matter what we put on the cover in those months, it doesn't seem to move," says Editor Geoff Miller.

Even when an editor correctly predicts what will attract readers, a magazine can be hurt by its competition. "The thing you can't isolate is that you are competing with 20 other covers," says Kerr of the New York Times Magazine Group. "If this spring four other magazines have fantastic flowers on the cover like we did for our best seller last spring, we will all probably kill each other."

Many magazines don't even get the chance to compete because they don't have front-row or flat positions on newsstands. Retailers give prominent play to the magazines that are the big sellers and those that pay a retail-display allowance, a percentage of the cover price over and above the usual cut. Back-of-the-rack magazines can still have good newsstand sales if they are displayed with other titles in a similar category, such as automotive, sports, or home decorating. But they must capitalize on the visible part of the cover. "That upper-left-hand corner can be a valuable piece of real estate because that's where sales start," Scott says. "It's amazing how a magazine can slowly track its way from the back of a fixture to the front simply because the sales are there."

Many editors face one common challenge over which they have no control: declining newsstand sales. Single-copy sales have dropped 15.6 percent over the last five years, according to *Capell's Circulation Report*. Dan Capell, a New York consultant, blames several factors, including competition from cable TV and VCRs, the increase in titles competing for the same amount of display space, significant price increases, and the big push for subscription sales. "There has been a tremendous increase in what I call gimmick offers on the subscription side, from premiums like cameras and calculators to sweepstakes to free issues," Capell says. "Magazines keep telling consumers so many times how foolish they are not to save money and get a subscription instead of buying at the newsstand." He notes that the top 100 consumer magazines have been successful in their efforts, with subscription sales up 47 percent over a five-year period—more than offsetting the drop in newsstand sales.

Also on the positive side, those newsstand-turned-subscription readers may turn out to be a magazine's loyal customers, renewing again and again.

Whether the magazine is sold by subscription or single copy, the cover is crucial. As Stolley says, "The packaging is the thing that sells your magazine, no matter how it's sold. What's on the cover is the determining factor on whether people are going to find out what's inside the magazine." ■

For Further Reading

Books

Russell N. Baird and J. William Click, *Magazine Editing and Production,* 4th Ed. (Dubuque, Iowa: Wm. C. Brown, 1986).

Otto Friedrich, *Decline and Fall* (New York: Harper & Row, 1969).

Leonard Mogel, *The Magazine,* 2nd ed. (Chester, Conn.: Globe Pequot Press, 1988).

Frank Luther Mott, *History of American Magazines* (New York: D. Appleton, 1930).

James Playsted Wood, *Magazines in the United States,* 3rd ed. (New York: Ronald Press, 1971).

Periodicals

COSMEP Newsletter, published by the Committee of Small Magazine Editors and Publishers

Folio: The Magazine for Magazine Management

Inside Print

Magazine Magazine, Vol. 1, No. 1, Fall 1985, published by Magazine Publishers Association

Writer's Digest

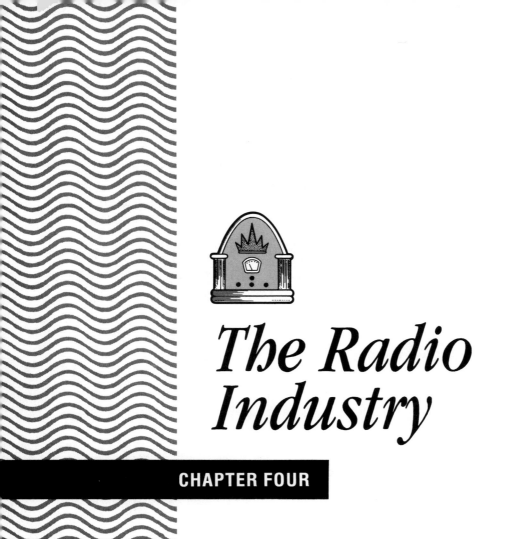

The Radio Industry

CHAPTER FOUR

The Role of Popular Music

Popular music forms the basis of most radio formats today. The radio industry estimates that the average adult listens to the radio three hours a day. Music's all-encompassing presence triggers emotions and evokes memories. In this short essay, novelist John Updike explains how important popular music on the radio has been in his life.

Consider:

1. What does John Updike mean when he says that radio is an "incessant and apparently inutile [useless] accompaniment to earthly lives"?

2. Do you agree that from music broadcasts we each extract an "emotional autobiography"? Why? Why not?

3. Do you agree that popular music "beckons us toward a fullness of which our lives are shadows"? Why? Why not?

4. What role do radio and popular music play in your life?

Radio Romance
A Man Has to Stay Tuned

JOHN UPDIKE

For many, popular music is more pain than pleasure, and any of us, trapped on a subway car with a ghetto blaster or in an elevator leaking old Mantovani, might admit there is much too much of it. That hypothetical visitor from Mars we used to talk about, before Mars was exposed as a spherical pink desert lightly frosted at the poles, would surely be struck by this incessant and apparently inutile [useless] accompaniment to earthly lives, as they move from musical alarm clock to car radio to a workplace insidiously saturated with psychologically programmed Muzak through a lunchtime stroll amid mendicant buskers and breakdancers and, after work, to a tinkling drink in a bar with an old-fashioned jukebox and, if not home to a suburban house where teenage children have their tapes turned way up, then on to a romantic rendezvous orchestrated by a gypsy band at the restaurant, a cocktail pianist with the nightcap, and sleepy old Sinatra records in the dimmed apartment. What do they mean, all these tunes, as miraculously as

Pulitzer-prize winning author John Updike has published 14 novels, including *Rabbit Run, Poorhouse Fair, The Witches of Eastwick,* and *S.*

snowdrops no two quite alike but again like snowdrops melting over the days into gray slush and then into air, thin air?

Hormones, the answer must be. Popular music, save for the small fraction designed to excite martial or religious ardor, has to do with mating and breakup, with love and its losses, with the anticipation of love reaching deep into childhood (Lollypop Pop) and its recollection extending far into senescence (Golden Oldies). We dance, we touch, we shut our eyes, we become the song. From the decades' massive flow of technologically broadcast songs we each extract an emotional autobiography. The first popular songs that memorably impinged upon my evolution were "Playmates," with its oddly thrilling invitation to "look down my rain barrel, slide down my cellar door," and, in 1939, "Oh, Johnny!" The little girls chanted "How you can love!" at me on the way to second grade and back, my ears and cheeks burning and all my conscious desires simply bent upon getting to my next balsa-wood model airplane.

Then came the Great Patriotic War and "Sleepy Lagoon" and "Paper Doll" and "That Old Black Magic" (icy fingers up and down my spine!), along with the relatively asexual "Mairzy Doats" (but what did it mean, to "kiddley-divey, too"?) and "Praise the Lord and Pass the Ammunition." Postwar, there was high school, and dances in the gym, and drooping crepe paper taped to the basketball backboard, and plump white strapless shoulders in the violet lights, and "Tenderly," and "They Say It's Wonderful," and six boys on the stage doing our local small-band version of the big-band sound, saving (what else?) "Star Dust" for last. The hormones had the tune down pat, though the lyrics still wondered why they spent the lonely nights dreaming of a song. The big-band sound was an erotic engine, a soft machine of sax-throb and phallic clarinet moving down its tracks as irresistibly as the Chattanooga choo-choo. That certain party at the station, in old satin and lace, that we used to call Funny Face, turned into Doris Day announcing a sentimental journey ("never knew my heart could be

so yearny") whose final prolonged "ho-o-o-ommmmme" opened a delicious abyss of sheer female power. On the jukebox at the Bluesmoke Luncheonette, the sly, laid-back melodiousness of Bing Crosby and the Ink Spots gave way to big, twanging voices: Frankie Laine and Patti Page, "That Lucky Old Sun" and "Tennessee Waltz." Laine was especially thrilling, hollering to his mules and his ghost riders in the sky and wanting to go where the wild goose went and mincing out the exact specifics of his "dee-zy-yuh" ("We'll sip a little glass of wine, I'll gaze into your eyes divine, I'll feel the touch of your lips, press-*sing* on mi-yun"). His voice was gutty; it rubbed the secret spots within.

The popular music of the late Forties and early Fifties, falling between the fading of the big bands and the beginning of rock, is generally forgotten; no jazzomaniacs or rock addicts or show-tune nuts visit its files, and Golden Oldie disc jockeys rarely touch it. But it has preempted millions of my neurons with half-remembered titles and lyrics. Girls' names: "Peg o' My Heart" and "Amy" and "Laura" and "Linda" ("When I go to sleep, I never count sheep, I count all the charms about Linda"). Strange little men: "The Old Lamplighter" and "Nature Boy" and that old master painter from the faraway hills whom we teenagers so inevitably recast as the old masturbator. Who could get moony over "Golden Earrings" or "Tree in the Meadow"? We could, that's who. In 1948, James C. Petrillo called every orthodox musician out on strike and left us to dream along with un-unionized sweet potatoes, banjos, bones, whistling choruses ("Heartaches"), and musical saws; and we dreamed on anyhow. "So Tired," made great in Russ Morgan's arrangement, was, with "Star Dust," the epitome of high school violet-spotlight chic, the draggy end of the dance, the fag end of our sophisticated, smoky days—"so tired, so tired of living" and all of seventeen.

Then came college and, for me, a kind of pop silence. There was no music in the libraries then, and little in the dorms—it was believed to interfere with thought processes, rather than (as now) to be essential to them. I do seem to recall, from those four lost years, incredulously auditing in a humble Cambridge eatery Johnnie Ray's "The Little White Cloud That Cried." I knew it was the end of something, but I didn't know of how very much. Rock 'n' roll began to shake the Eisenhower chapel; Elvis Presley suddenly achieved divinity—but all out of my earshot. The first song I remember distinctly getting to me, postgrad, was "Blueberry Hill," where Fats Domino claimed to have found his thrill. Was finding your thrill anything like kiddley-diveying? No matter: I knew in my hormones what he meant, and just why Chubby Checker wanted to twist again like we did last summer. We had become suburbanites and wage earners and parents, but our glands were less quiescent than they should have been: the sounds of revolution (Baez and Dylan; Peter, Paul, and Mary; Sonny and Cher) trickled through the Marimekko curtains, and our children taught us to frug. Oh, those glorious piping sugar-harmonied Supremes records before Diana Ross became a law unto herself! And of course the Beatles, who were intellectually ambitious even,

and kept going deeper, just like Beethoven. I suppose my heartfelt farewell to popular music came in England, at the end of the Sixties, crooning and thumping and blinking back tears through the endless chorus of "Hey Jude," in which the Beatles could be heard dissolving. Sing a sad song to make it better.

But you never really say farewell; popular music is always there, flavoring our American lives, keeping our mortal beat, a murmuring subconscious sneaking up out of the car radio with some abrupt sliding phrase that hooks us into jubilation, into aspiration. I like it when, say, Madonna's "True Blue" comes on: catchy. Long ago, driving to school with my father on cold winter mornings, I would lean into the feeble glow of the radio dial as if into warmth: this was me, this yearniness canned in New York and beamed from Philadelphia, beamed through the air to guide me, somehow, toward infinite possibilities. Popular music bathes us in echoes of emotion and beckons us toward a fullness of which our lives are shadows. ■

PERSPECTIVES 2 & 3

Orson Welles's "The War of the Worlds"

On October 30, 1938, Orson Welles's *Mercury Theater on the Air* broadcast over CBS a dramatization of an H. G. Wells story about an invasion from Mars. Although the announcer in New York interrupted three times to emphasize that it was a dramatization, many listeners believed it was a news story; some distraught people fled into the streets in terror. The uproar resulted in a reexamination of the responsibility of broadcasters to their audience.

Perspective 2 consists of several excerpts from the program, and Perspective 3 is a commentary by well-known columnist Dorothy Thompson about the implications of the audience's reaction. The column appeared on November 2, 1938 in the *New York Herald Tribune*. (Remember that Thompson's commentary was written against the backdrop of impending war in Europe.)

Consider:

1. Which events described in the script do you think would most frighten an audience?

2. Do you agree with Dorothy Thompson that the event proves how easy it is to start a "mass delusion"?

3. How is Thompson's commentary a criticism of the use of propaganda techniques? What evidence does she use to support her assertion?

4. Is it possible today for the media to create what Thompson calls "mass prejudices and mass divisions and schisms"? Why? Why not?

The War of the Worlds

ORSON WELLES

ANNOUNCER

Ladies and gentlemen, here is the latest bulletin from the Intercontinental Radio News, Toronto, Canada: Professor Morse of Macmillan University reports observing a total of three explosions on the planet Mars, between the hours of 7:45 p.m. and 9:20 p.m., eastern standard time. This confirms earlier reports received from American observatories. Now, nearer home, comes a special announcement from Trenton, New Jersey. It is reported that at 8:50 p.m. a huge, flaming object, believed to be a meteorite, fell on a farm in the neighborhood of Grovers Mill, New Jersey, twenty-two miles from Trenton. The flash in the sky was visible within a radius of several hundred miles and the noise of the impact was heard as far north as Elizabeth.

We have dispatched a special mobile unit to the scene, and we will have our commentator, Mr. Phillips, give you a word description as soon as he can reach there from Princeton. In the meantime, we take you to the Hotel Martinet in Brook-

lyn, where Bobby Millette and his orchestra are offering a program of dance music. (SWING BAND FOR 20 SECONDS . . . THEN CUT)

ANNOUNCER

We take you now to Grovers Mill, New Jersey.
(CROWD NOISES . . . POLICE SIRENS)

PHILLIPS

Ladies and gentlemen, this is Carl Phillips again, at the Wilmuth farm, Grovers Mill, New Jersey. Professor Pierson and myself made the eleven miles from Princeton in ten minutes. Well, I . . . I hardly know where to begin, to paint for you a word picture of the strange scene before my eyes, like something out of a modern Arabian Nights. Well, I just got here. I haven't had a chance to look around yet. I guess that's *it*. Yes, I guess that's the . . . *thing,* directly in front of me, half buried in a vast pit. Must have struck with terrific force. The ground is covered with splinters of a tree it must have struck on the way down. What I can see of the . . . object itself doesn't look very much like

After a brief career in radio, Orson Welles wrote, directed, and appeared in several movies, including "Citizen Kane."

a meteor, at least not the meteors I've seen. It looks more like a huge cylinder. It has a diameter of . . . what would you say, Professor Pierson? . . .

ANNOUNCER

Ladies and gentlemen, I have a grave announcement to make. Incredible as it may seem, both the observations of science and the evidence of our eyes lead to the inescapable assumption that those strange beings who landed in the Jersey farmlands tonight are the vanguard of an invading army from the planet Mars. The battle which took place tonight at Grovers Mill has ended in one of the most startling defeats ever suffered by an army in modern times; seven thousand men armed with rifles and machine guns pitted against a single fighting machine of the invaders from Mars. One hundred and twenty known survivors. The rest strewn over the battle area from Grovers Mill to Plainsboro crushed and trampled to death under the metal feet of the monster, or burned to cinders by its heat-ray. The monster is now in control of the middle section of New Jersey and has effectively cut the state through its center. Communication lines are down from Pennsylvania to the Atlantic Ocean. Railroad tracks are torn and service from New York to Philadelphia discontinued except routing some of the trains through Allentown and Phoenixville. Highways to the north, south, and west are clogged with frantic human traffic. Police and army reserves are unable to control the mad flight. By morning the fugitives will have swelled Philadelphia, Camden and Trenton, it is estimated, to twice their normal population.

At this time martial law prevails throughout New Jersey and eastern Pennsylvania. We take you now to Washington for a special broadcast on the National Emergency . . . the Secretary of the Interior. . . . [pause]

ANNOUNCER

I'm speaking from the roof of Broadcasting Building, New York City. The bells you hear are ringing to warn the people to evacuate the city as the Martians approach. Estimated in last two hours three million people have moved out along the roads to the north, Hutchison River Parkway still kept open for motor traffic. Avoid bridges to Long Island . . . hopelessly jammed. All communication with Jersey shore closed ten minutes ago. No more defenses. Our army wiped out . . . artillery, air force, everything wiped out. This may be the last broadcast. We'll stay here to the end. . . . People are holding service below us . . . in the cathedral. (VOICES SINGING HYMN)

Now I look down the harbor. All manner of boats, overloaded with fleeing population, pulling out from docks. (SOUND OF BOAT WHISTLES)

Streets are all jammed. Noise in crowds like New Year's Eve in city. Wait a minute. . . . Enemy now in sight above the Palisades. Five great machines. First one is crossing river. I can see it from here, wading the Hudson like a man wading through a brook. . . . A bulletin's handed me. . . . Martian cylinders are falling all over the country. One outside Buffalo, one in Chicago, St. Louis . . . seem to be timed and spaced. . . . Now the first machine reaches the shore. He stands watching, looking over the city. His steel, cowlish head is even with the skyscrapers. He waits for the others. They rise like a line of new towers on the city's west side. . . . Now they're lifting their metal hands. This is the end now. Smoke comes out . . . black smoke, drifting over the city. People in the streets see it now. They're running towards the East River . . . thousands of them, dropping in like rats. Now the smoke's spreading faster. It's reached Times Square. People trying to run away from it, but it's no use. They're falling like flies. Now the smoke's crossing Sixth Avenue . . . Fifth Avenue . . . 100 yards away . . . it's fifty feet. . . .

■

Mr. Welles and Mass Delusion

DOROTHY THOMPSON

All unwittingly, Mr. Orson Welles and the *Mercury Theater on the Air* have made one of the most fascinating and important demonstrations of all time. They have proved that a few effective voices, accompanied by sound effects, can so convince masses of people of a totally unreasonable, completely fantastic proposition as to create nationwide panic.

They have demonstrated more potently than any argument, demonstrated beyond question of a doubt, the appalling dangers and enormous effectiveness of popular and theatrical demagoguery.

They have cast a brilliant and cruel light upon the failure of popular education.

They have shown up the incredible stupidity, lack of nerve and ignorance of thousands.

They have proved how easy it is to start a mass delusion.

They have uncovered the primeval fears lying under the thinnest surface of the so-called civilized man.

They have shown that man, when the victim of his own gullibility, turns to the government to protect him against his own errors of judgment.

The newspapers are correct in playing up this story over every other news event in the world. It is the story of the century.

And far from blaming Mr. Orson Welles, he ought to be given a Congressional medal and a national prize for having made the most amazing and important contribution to the social sciences. For Mr. Orson Welles and his theater have made a

greater contribution to an understanding of Hitlerism, Mussolinism, Stalinism, anti-Semitism and all the other terrorisms of our times than all the words about them that have been written by reasonable men. They have made the *reductio ad absurdum* of mass manias. They have thrown more light on recent events in Europe leading to the Munich pact than everything that has been said on the subject by all the journalists and commentators.

Hitler managed to scare all Europe to its knees a month ago, but he at least had an army and an air force to back up his shrieking words.

But Mr. Welles scared thousands into demoralization with nothing at all.

That historic hour on the air was an act of unconscious genius, performed by the very innocence of intelligence.

Nothing whatever about the dramatization of the "War of the Worlds" was in the least credible, no matter at what point the hearer might have tuned in. The entire verisimilitude was in the names of a few specific places. Monsters were depicted of a type that nobody has ever seen, equipped with "rays" entirely fantastic; they were described as "straddling the Pulaski Skyway" and throughout the broadcast they were referred to as Martians, men from another planet.

A twist of the dial would have established for anybody that the national catastrophe was not being noted on any other station. A second of logic would have dispelled any terror. A notice that the broadcast came from a non-existent agency would have awakened skepticism.

A reference to the radio program would have

Dorothy Thompson was a foreign correspondent, columnist, radio commentator, and author.

established that the "War of the Worlds" was announced in advance.

The time element was obviously lunatic.

Listeners were told that "within two hours three million people have moved out of New York"—an obvious impossibility for the most disciplined army moving exactly as planned, and a double fallacy because only a few minutes before, the news of the arrival of the monster had been announced.

And of course it was not even a planned hoax. Nobody was more surprised at the result than Mr. Welles. The public was told at the beginning, at the end and during the course of the drama that it *was* a drama.

But eyewitnesses presented themselves; the report became second hand, third hand, fourth hand, and became more and more credible, so that nurses and doctors and National Guardsmen rushed to defense.

When the truth became known the reaction was also significant. The deceived were furious and of course demanded that the state protect them, demonstrating that they were incapable of relying on their own judgment.

Again there was a complete failure of logic. For if the deceived had thought about it they would realize that the greatest organizers of mass hysterias and mass delusions today are states using the radio to excite terrors, incite hatreds, inflame masses, win mass support for policies, create idolatries, abolish reason and maintain themselves in power.

The immediate moral is apparent if the whole incident is viewed in reason: no political body must ever, under any circumstances, obtain a monopoly of radio.

The second moral is that our popular and universal education is failing to train reason and logic, even in the educated.

The third is that the popularization of science has led to gullibility and new superstitions, rather than to skepticism and the really scientific attitude of mind.

The fourth is that the power of mass suggestion is the most potent force today and that the political demagogue is more powerful than all the other economic forces.

For, mind you, Mr. Welles was managing an obscure program, competing with one of the most popular entertainments on the air!

The conclusion is that the radio must not be used to create mass prejudices and mass divisions and schisms, either by private individuals or by government or its agencies, or its officials, or its opponents.

If people can be frightened out of their wits by mythical men from Mars, they can be frightened into fanaticism by the fear of Reds, or convinced that America is in the hands of sixty families, or aroused to revenge against any minority, or terrorized into subservience to leadership because of any imaginable menace.

The technique of modern mass politics calling itself democracy is to create a fear—a fear of economic royalists, or of Reds, or of Jews, or of starvation, or of an outside enemy—and exploit that fear into obtaining subservience in return for protection.

I wrote in this column a short time ago that the new warfare was waged by propaganda, the outcome depending on which side could first frighten the other to death.

The British people were frightened into obedience to a policy a few weeks ago by a radio speech and by digging a few trenches in Hyde Park, and afterward led to hysterical jubilation over a catastrophic defeat for their democracy.

But Mr. Welles went all the politicians one better. He made the scare to end scares, the menace to end menaces, the unreason to end unreason, the perfect demonstration that the danger is not from Mars but from the theatrical demagogue. ■

Format Radio

Radio programming today consists almost entirely of formats—country, album-oriented rock, and easy listening, for example. These prerecorded formats cut costs because they require fewer staff members. Some stations also use satellite programming, which lowers costs even more because it requires no local disc jockey.

Perspective 4 describes the latest in format radio—the WAVE in Los Angeles, which has eliminated disc jockeys altogether. Perspective 5 describes a very different type of radio, "Sportstalk" on New York's WABC—personalized radio that depends on the host for its success.

Consider:

1. What makes the WAVE an attractive format for advertisers?

2. What makes a program like "Sportstalk" a popular program?

3. What is the difference in philosophy of a radio station that produces a program like "Sportstalk" and one that produces the WAVE?

4. What are the implications for radio if formats like the WAVE succeed and programs like "Sportstalk" become less common? If programs like "Sportstalk" become more common? Which trend is more likely to happen?

Yuppie Radio: New Age Makes WAVE

ROBERT GOLDBERG

The Mideast has its Palestinian Question. New York has the Bernhard Goetz controversy. Out here, they're arguing about the WAVE.

On Valentine's Day, KMET—94.7 on Los Angeles's radio dial—gave up the ghost. The mighty MET, long famous as a hard-driving pioneer of album-oriented rock (and in its 1970s heyday the top-rated music station in L.A.), was transformed by station management into the WAVE, KTWV, America's first New Age radio station. Where KMET cranked out the pounding beat of Led Zeppelin and the Rolling Stones, KTWV offers light pop, relaxing instrumentals, lilting jazz-classical fusion. The WAVE has no disk jockeys—no one to identify the music at all. (You have to call in to find out the titles and artists.) It does, however, have all sorts of soothing sounds: bells, chimes, water running, birds chirping.

In L.A.—a city where entire lifetimes are

Robert Goldberg is a New York free-lance writer.

spent in cars listening to the radio—this transition has been major news. Los Angeles, after all, is the single largest radio-advertising market in the country, and the move from mega-voltage to mellow at 94.7 became an instant *cause celebre*. On one side are the hard rockers. On the other, the smooth groovers.

At Whiskey A Go-Go and Gazzarri's, two venerable rock institutions on Sunset Strip, the '60s holdovers, long-haired and tie-dyed, smirked when asked about the WAVE. "Robot radio," they called it. "Musical wallpaper."

The rock critics have been no kinder. Commented one article in *L.A. Weekly*: "This audio Frankenstein, sewn together out of market-research reports, Arbitron [ratings] books, and some of the blandest music ever visited upon the face of the planet, features no disc jockeys (no disc jockeys would play this [stuff]) only an officiously soothing prerecorded voice (the voice of the stewardess on the Plane-Ride to Hell)."

And yet, all sorts of people around L.A. are getting downright laid-back with the WAVE. Somebody is listening. Favorable letters have poured in: "FABULOUS," gushed one. "Your station gives off the 'positive-energetic-relaxation' feeling." "Congratulations," stated another (from the president of a software company). "Adventurous? Ha! That is a mild word. You are subjecting the general public to vibrational realms heretofore only found in the darkened crevices of avid Dungeons and Dragons players, sci-fi conventions, astral plane travellers . . ."

In *Pulse* magazine, one columnist wrote that the type of New Age music featured on the WAVE "opens the door to a better tomorrow, reminding each of us that love, empathy and compassion lead to survival, growth, self-fulfillment and the eventual realization of world peace.

Over at KTWV, employees feel they are on the crest of a new movement—that New Age is the music of the future, and that the WAVE will be the first of many New Age stations across the country. They point proudly to a play list that includes Steely Dan and Kitaro, Sade and the Windham Hill group. Their philosophy is clear. Listed on the walls of the station are charts with concise columns of adjectives. Under YES—"sensuous," "uplifting," "relaxing," "soothing"; under NO— "intense," "challenging."

Frank Cody, programming director of KTWV, believes the WAVE is an idea whose time has come: "Everything has a life cycle. Mary Tyler Moore went off the air. The Beatles broke up. Album rock had been trending downward for a long time. The people who grew up on rock—on Cream and Blind Faith and Creedence—they left it behind as they got older. Look, as you grow up, there's less of the frustration of adolescence, when you have all this pent-up sexual energy, all this rage. As things fall into place for you, as you find it's OK to like Mom and Dad, it's hard to look at the same old prancing around and pouting onstage and take it seriously. So that audience, as they grew older, they left rock behind. They discovered they wanted to get nice homes, go to nice restaurants, have good clothes, listen to more sophisticated music."

Did anyone say Yuppie? "Please," says Mr. Cody. "don't use the Y word." But former KMET D.J. Jim Ladd insists: "This New Age radio is just the latest Yuppie trend. They're appealing to the lowest common denominator with the highest disposable income." *Los Angeles Times* pop critic Patrick Goldstein agrees: "The WAVE is not geared to music lovers at all. It's geared to advertisers. It's a very smart new way to show advertisers they're reaching the best demographics—the affluent Yuppie audience. To me, the station is like the 'Invasion of the Body Snatchers'—like someone snuck in during the night and replaced the body with something that looks like a body, but isn't a body at all. The WAVE looks like radio, it sounds like radio, but it doesn't have any soul. It's just one more thing in our lives that's ersatz."

The initial figures, however, have been a very real answer to the hard rockers and the critics. According to the Arbitron rating figures, KTWV has been doing pretty well. In fact, the numbers seem to indicate that this New Age, Yuppie-based station may be one of the hottest radio phenomena to come along in a while. Of course, the final word isn't in, but during its first full month, the station jumped from 30th to seventh place among adults in the 25-to-54-year-old range, the so-called "money sell." And in the crucial "afternoon drive" listening period, the station went from 7,900 listeners (or 32nd place) to 58,000 listeners (or third place).

It's hard to argue with success. But diehard KMET fans like Bill Bothmann still want to try. Mr. Bothmann, a self-described 38-year-old "starving genius inventor" (his latest is a coffee-filter lifter) has been circulating to bring back the MET. "My heart was broken," says Mr. Bothmann. "I listened to KMET for 18 years. I felt sick when I turned on my radio and heard KTWV. To take rock and roll and replace it with that—that disease. It's a biological germ. I see it as a plot against the public."

If Mr. Bothmann is unhappy about losing KMET, he's downright mad about the suddenness of the transition, the way it was handled: "After 18 years of marriage, to divorce me on Valentine's Day. I think they're totally sick. Charles Manson, I can almost respect him more than that station management—at least he admits what he does. What they've done is cold-blooded. They're reptiles, going for broke." So far, Mr. Bothmann has collected 4,000 signatures. The WAVE, however, shows no indication of rolling back.

At a Husker Du concert at the Variety Arts Center, one of the hippest places in downtown L.A., the kids in the audience are howling. "The WAVE?! The WAVE?!" sneers a young woman with 18 earrings in her right ear. "It stinks. It sucks. I hate it more than life itself." She readjusts the chains around her waist, and turns to her friend. "Yeah," the young man with six inches of white hair, all sticking straight up, agrees. "It's a hindrance to the development of the human race." They nod at each other and turn to go. "But hey," he turns back. "In 10 years, I'll probably be listening to it." ■

The Sultan of 'Sportstalk'

FREDERICK C. KLEIN

I'm Arthur George Rust Jr., and this is Sportstalk.
You're on the air.
CALLER: *Mr. Rush?*
AGRJ: *It's Rust, with a T.*
CALLER: *I'm a big fan of yours.*
AGRJ: *Not that big. You don't know my name.*
CALLER: *I was nervous.*

Who wouldn't be a little nervous? We're talking radio station WABC here, 50,000 watts from the Big Apple, with a na-tional audience of millions after the sun goes down, not to mention Canada.

And the guy on the other end of the phone is Art Rust Jr., 58, the World's Greatest Authority on sports. Don't believe it? Just ask him.

Frederick C. Klein is a reporter for *The Wall Street Journal.*

"You've heard about walking encyclopedias? Well, I'm a walking computer," says Mr. Rust with nary a blush in his Manhattan broadcasting studio. "I know so much it scares me sometimes.

"One time we're in Flushing, doing the show outdoors. There's a couple hundred people watching. A fellow stands up with a piece of paper in his hand. He reads off the names of a dozen old-time Puerto Rican ballplayers for me to identify, guys like Hi Bithorn and Looie Olmo.

"I reel 'em off: 'Hiram *Gabriel* Bithorn, Chicago Cubs, 1942 to '46, White Sox, 1947. Luis *Rodriguez* Olmo, Dodgers, 1943 to '49,' and so forth. The guy's mouth drops open. It was just me up there, by myself. No script. No books. No flunkies looking things up. I tell you, brother, I'm a bitch!"

Art Rust Jr. amazes and amuses the multitudes between 6 and 9 p.m. weekdays on WABC. A veteran of radio and television who does a weekly sports column for the New York Daily News on the side, he has done the Sportstalk show for six years now. It's different from the others that clog the airwaves nightly, he avers.

"First, I'm the biggest—nobody else has a fraction of my audience," he says. "Second, I'm black. That gives me a whole new dimension—a different way of looking at things. Third, I deal strictly in sports facts, not trivia. That's because I don't think there's such a thing as sports trivia. One man's trivia is another man's history. What's more important to most people: Joseph Paul DiMaggio's lifetime batting average, or the Congress of Vienna?"

CALLER: *Hi, Art. This is John from the Bronx.*
AGRJ: *How are you, John. Do I hear water running?*
CALLER: *I'm taking a bath.*
AGRJ: *What's on your mind?*
CALLER: *Those guys running the Yankees! PU! They stink! We acquire Britt Burns! Britt Burns!*
AGRJ: *I was in Florida and I broke that story on his injury. I knew he could play in pain, but I didn't expect that.*
CALLER: *And they traded Baylor to the Red Sox! That's why the Red Sox aren't folding.*
AGRJ: *Mike Easler's not chopped liver.*

CALLER: *He's not Baylor. Besides, the Yankees have no catcher, no shortstop and nothing resembling a pitching staff. Where's George! Get him on the show!*
AGRJ: *I'll do that.*

"Anyway," Mr. Rust continues, "people don't call in with fact questions all that often. We deal mainly with issues here. Racism in sports. Drugs. The pernicious influences affecting college athletics. I'm an educator. I'm a sociologist. I'm a catalyst. I get people thinking.

"I go right at 'em on the racial thing. Anybody who thinks racism went out of baseball when Branch Rickey signed Jack Roosevelt Robinson in October of 1945 has another think coming. Don't believe me? See how many black, fringe ballplayers you can name. There ain't many. If you're black and not a star, you're out. George Foster had it right.

"Same goes for the media. People ask me why, with my knowledge, I never did play-by-play for a big-league team. I tell 'em that when I wanted that job, there was no way they were gonna have a black in the booth. Now, of course, they can't afford me. I get some satisfaction from that.

"I aggravate some people because I'm a brilliant black SOB, and I'm on top. I'm arrogant. I don't take a back seat. I live plush. But I can relate, too. You might be surprised who listens to my show. Mario Cuomo does. And Robert Merrill, the opera star. Richard Nixon's an Art Rust Jr. fanatic! He says he's gonna come on my show some day. What do I think of him? Well, he got caught.

"But it's the ordinary people with brains who really dig me. My call-in regulars and I have a love affair going! Four birthdays ago, Billy from Brooklyn phoned up from the lobby with 10 buddies. He had a case of champagne and a huge cake. Whatta party! When my man Mario from Manhattan got married, he invited me. And I went! You'd better believe I broke some color lines that day.

"The bottom line, though, is the show. This is a performance business, like sports, and if you don't perform, you're history. That's why I understand athletes so well. And you know something?

I've never done a bad show. Believe it! I can make roaches running across the floor sound like the Kentucky Derby."

CALLER: *It's Teddy from Brooklyn, Art. Thanks for taking my call.*

AGRJ: *The pleasure is all yours.*

CALLER: *My question is about Clete Boyer and Brooks Robinson. One year Clete had a better fielding average, but Robinson got the Golden Glove award at third base. Why was that?*

AGRJ: *More than the averages go into the award.*

CALLER: *Who'd you like at third?*

AGRJ: *My guy was the pencil-thin Brooklyn Dodger, Mr. Billy Cox. That man could pick 'em. I'll tell you about another gentleman. His initials were Aurelio Rodriguez. Had a shotgun for an arm! Came up with the Angels in '67. They traded him to Detroit in '71. Then he went to . . .*

■

PERSPECTIVE 6

The Sinking Future of Radio News

As radio recedes into background noise, news programming grows less essential. The declining importance of radio news is the subject of this article from the *Columbia Journalism Review*.

Consider:

1. If part of the media's responsibility is to keep the public informed, what are the implications of these news cutbacks?

2. Do you agree with program director Jeff Rowe, who says that "news . . . isn't vital anymore"?

3. What changes can listeners expect as radio news broadcasting eclipses radio journalism even further?

Radio Daze: Tuning Out the News

JOHN MOTAVALLI

After the third pink slip, Patrick Hennessey began to wonder about his career choice. He had learned to be a radio newsman at WPKN-FM, an eclectic and serious-minded college station at the University of Bridgeport, in southern Connecticut, and after graduation in 1980 he landed a job at a small station in the middle of the state, WMMW-AM, in Meriden. Three months later the news staff was reduced from two people to one, and Hennessey was out of a job.

He moved to Milford, Connecticut, for a job at WFIF, but eight months later the AM station eliminated its entire news department. In 1981, Hennessey found work at a seemingly more stable station, New Haven's WPLR-FM, a popular rocker with a strong signal. He worked his way up to afternoon anchor before that station decided in 1983 to reduce its four-person news staff to one. (Later, he says, the station added "a couple of comedians" to do the morning news, in line with the "morning zoo" craze that swept through rock stations a couple of years ago.)

Still undaunted, he relocated again, this time to southeastern Connecticut for a post as news director at WNLC-AM in New London, where he went back to covering the school board and the sewer commission. But the pay was low, and, although no one had ever questioned his abilities as a journalist, he began to think about switching professions. "I decided public relations would be a better career, at least in terms of eating weekly and other fringe benefits," he says.

By this time Hennessey had learned that what had seemed like his own bad luck was really the

John Motavalli is a managing editor for *Adweek*'s special reports on the media, advertising, and marketing.

effect of a national trend. Since the Federal Communications Commission deregulated radio six years ago, radio news has been in a sharp decline.

According to a study by University of Missouri journalism professor Vernon A. Stone, an estimated 2,000 full-time positions in radio news were eliminated last year alone, while 700 part-time slots were created. In major markets, Stone reports, the average full-time news staff dropped from a median of 2.7 in 1985 to 1.4 last year. According to a survey of nearly 2,000 radio stations by the National Association of Broadcasters and the Broadcast Financial Management Association, news departments got the smallest slice of stations' budgets last year, an average of 4.4 percent, compared with 11 percent for advertising and promotion.

Prior to deregulation, radio stations had to use at least 8 percent of their time for non-entertainment programming, a requirement that many big-city stations, especially FM rockers, were loath to fulfill. Station managers contend that listeners don't want their music interrupted. "If you're running a music-oriented station, outside of morning drive, news should be a low priority," says Jeff Rowe, who has worked as a program director for stations in Chicago and Milwaukee. "Ten years ago there were fewer stations in each market. There's stronger competition now for audiences and ad dollars. News, outside of full-service stations, isn't vital anymore."

One faction of news professionals, especially those in management positions who are adamantly opposed to any return of regulation, contend that the news dearth is a problem of the market that would not be solved by new FCC rules. Ernie Schultz, president of the Radio-Television News Directors Association, argues that the cutbacks have been relatively minor in terms of overall radio news employment, and that the stations that have phased out news tend to be those that were only doing it because they had to. According to Jim Farley, vice-president of radio news at NBC Radio Network, the real culprit is the decline of traditionally news-oriented AM radio. "Yes, there has been a diminution of news, and yes, it's been since deregulation," he says. "But too many people miss the point—that deregulation happened as radio stations, particularly AM stations, have had declining audiences and they've had to make cost cuts. News has been one of the first things to be cut."

Radio turnover in radio station ownership has exacerbated the problem. Farley adds, "There are a lot of new people in our industry, ranging from sleazy speculators to hungry entrepreneurs to ethical business people," he says. "We've got to make new station owners realize that the news people are unrealized assets, not liabilities awaiting the budget ax."

Indeed, after Los Angeles-based Westwood One agreed to buy Farley's own NBC Radio Network from General Electric Company, . . . the network's venerable Washington news bureau suffered severe ax wounds. Some bureau employees were laid off, others were transferred out of radio, and a third group was moved to Mutual Broadcasting System studios in Arlington, Virginia, where they will still use an NBC Radio Network News signature while also filing reports for Mutual. (Westwood One, which started out as a distributor of recorded rock concerts, bought the Mutual Broadcasting System at the end of 1985.)

Radio journalists complain that the post-deregulation era has also brought about a decline in the quality of radio news. In order to survive in today's climate, news services that depend on radio have branched out to entertainment and soft "life-style" news, and have found ways of packaging hard news into shorter, faster-paced newscasts. The Associated Press radio news network, for example, has added a two-minute "light" *Newswatch* report and a one-minute *NewsMinute* report, both geared to rock stations, plus *Segue,* a series of one-minute shows on entertainment that started this summer. The trade newsletter *Inside Radio* notes that the coming of life-style news will "eclipse radio journalism even further. . . . Plainly there will be fewer radio journalists and very ill-defined news departments."

The decline in emphasis on news has not escaped the attention of Congress. In introducing a bill . . . that would make "meritorious" public service a requirement for renewal of a broadcast license, Ernest F. Hollings, the South Carolina Democrat who chairs the Senate commerce committee, scored station owners for caring only about the "bottom line on their balance sheets."

Station managers and owners contend that those who want news will seek out news-oriented stations. Tom Cohen, senior counsel to the communications subcommittee of the commerce committee, disagrees: "Most people only listen to a couple of radio stations, and if that's the case and there's no news on the station, then that person's access to news is going to be limited."

The fate of the bill is unclear, and the Justice Department has said it will recommend a veto if it is passed. The issue is not likely to die, however. "The trends are clear," Cohen says. "Each year it's getting a little worse." ■

The Importance of Radio as an Advertising Medium

Like magazines, radio can target an audience according to demographics such as interests, income, and age. The programming you choose defines you as an audience for an advertiser. To Charles D. Peebler, chief executive officer of a major advertising agency, radio is a very important part of the marketing mix. Consider:

1. According to Peebler, what are radio's advantages for advertisers?

2. Why would Peebler's agency advise *The New York Times* to advertise on radio?

3. Which specific audiences does Peebler define that radio can deliver?

Radio's Unique Ability to Target and Deliver Specific Audience Segments

CHARLES D. PEEBLER

I am CEO of the only major advertising agency in America that commits nearly 15 per cent of the advertising funds placed in its trust to radio. For the most part, the rest of the top shops award radio anywhere from 5 to 10 per cent of the media spending pie. In fact, Bozell, Jacobs, Kenyon & Eckhardt, according to published and accurate reports appearing in the trade press just a few months ago, in 1985 was this nation's Number 1 buyer of radio time, not just on a percentage basis, but in actual dollar volume as well.

Why should that be? Have we discovered the ultimate marketing and media mix? I would love to say "yes," but it wouldn't be true. Do we know something that all other agencies don't know? I

hope so, but I don't think it has anything to do with the way we evaluate radio. I believe we assess radio's value in a manner not dissimilar to most other agencies. What then accounts for our obvious faith in the medium? Radio attracts and reaches its publics . . . all of them, young and old, men and women . . . by getting close to them . . . by delivering the programming and the values that each targeted audience segment wants to hear. So it's only natural that our buyers relate to radio's exceptional ability to get close to the customer. I'm a member of a small and vanishing breed of advertising executives who grew up "watching" radio. You heard me right. For those of you too young to remember [and sometimes I wish I were], we didn't merely listen to it on the radio . . . we watched it on the radio. Radio brought us soap operas and westerns, action and

Charles D. Peebler is chief executive officer of Bozell, Jacobs, Kenyon & Eckhardt.

drama, comedy and variety, mystery and history, ballads and boogie.

Which of us watched it on the radio . . . and how many of us watched at the same time . . . depended on the appeal of the program. They didn't call it targeting back then, and markets weren't segments, but the objectives were the same . . . and believe me, they knew how to reach their audience. Radio brought to us entertainment, information and amusement. We brought it to our imagination. It was a pretty good trade-off then . . . and it's a pretty good trade-off now.

Newspaper Clients

In case you were not aware, one of our clients of whom we are most proud is *The New York Times*. In addition, we also represent, with equal pride, the *Minneapolis Star-Tribune* and the *Omaha World Herald*. But we'll turn to *The Times* to help me make my point. It's easy for us, you might say, to demonstrate our belief in radio by putting millions of Chrysler dollars into broadcast. After all, with a budget the size of Chrysler's, they're important players everywhere. But that certainly couldn't and wouldn't be true with *The New York Times*.

Their target market is too educated and the income level too high. In other words, radio is a terrible advertising medium for *The New York Times* . . . right? Wrong! Radio is, in fact, a great buy for *The New York Times*. It helps us reach precisely the audience we must: younger, better educated and high or higher income. We fine tune our demographics with the same care with which the New York Philharmonic's first violinist tunes his Stradivarius . . . and then we orchestrate the campaign.

By the way, I'd be remiss if I didn't point out that we not only try to buy radio creatively, we try to be creative on the radio.

Ringing the Cash Register

If there is one common thread among our heavy radio clients, it is that they are action-oriented. When they advertise, they expect something to happen—now—at the counter and at the cash register. Perhaps that's another reason why we buy radio at double and even triple the rate of the overall U.S. agency community.

Ten Bozell, Jacobs, Kenyon & Eckhardt clients spent over $1 million each in radio last year. Number 1, Chrysler and Plymouth, had cars to sell . . . and they wanted action. American Airlines was close behind. They had seats to fill. And you better believe they wanted sales action, too . . . and like Chrysler, they relied on radio to help them get it.

Our Number 3 radio user, American Stores, lives in a totally different world. But they coexist in the same medium, and for many of the same cash register reasons. Where else can they tailor advertising to reach women 18 to 34? Then tailor it again to reach more women 35 to 49? And finally, custom fit it once again for ages 49 to 54. And just as important, they can actually afford to make different commercials appealing to each separate age group. Whether you're American Stores or Zale's Fine Jewelers, you talk to the millions of women in today's workforce, many of whom can be reached most effectively in their cars as they commute to and from the job.

Or, if you're Greyhound or McDonald's, we know how important it is for you to reach blacks, Hispanics and other minorities . . . or young adults, or seniors. Radio helps us find them and reach them, affordably and frequently. ■

For Further Reading

Books

Laurence Bergreen, *Look Now, Pay Later: The Rise of Network Broadcasting* (New York: New American Library, 1970).

Peter Fornatale and Joshua E. Mills, *Radio in the Television Age* (New York: Overlook Press, 1980).

Irving Settel, *A Pictorial History of Radio* (New York: Citadel Press, 1960).

Christopher H. Sterling and John M. Kittross, *Stay Tuned: A Concise History of American Broadcasting* (Belmont: Wadsworth, 1978).

Periodicals

Broadcasting

Electronic Media

Journal of Broadcasting and Electronic Media

RTNDA Communicator, published by the Radio/Television News Directors Association

Television/Radio Age

The Television Industry

The Importance of Ratings

The nation's major television ratings service is the Nielsen Company, based in New York. Since 1950 they have been providing the numbers that stations use to verify their audiences. In turn, advertisers buy time on stations at prices based on these numbers: a higher Nielsen rating typically means that a TV commercial during higher-rated programs will cost advertisers more. Ultimately, this brings higher profits to stations that televise the ratings leaders. In this article from the *Columbia Journalism Review*, Charles Fountain describes what happens when stations "hype" their ratings.

Consider:

1. How has the profitability of local news affected the influence that ratings have on programming?
2. Describe some of the methods that stations have used to draw higher Nielsen numbers.
3. How is the use of people meters likely to change ratings results?
4. What does Fountain mean when he says that with the ratings numbers, "perception is reality"?

The Great Ratings Flap

Between Rigged Nielsens and Newfangled People Meters, How Can You Tell Who's on Top?

CHARLES FOUNTAIN

Talk to a television news director about ratings and you'll soon be awash in report-card metaphors. It's a telling parallel, for his anxiety and trepidation are much the same as that of the adolescent who holds his report card at arm's length for a moment or two, nervously of-

Charles Fountain teaches journalism at Northeastern University in Boston.

fering up a hasty prayer before stealing a first look. *Oh please, God, I'll stop disobeying my parents if only you'll let me have a C in geometry.*

Oh please, God. I'll never ask for anything again. Just let this book show us with a 12 at six o'clock.

Ratings have been around for as long as broadcasting: NBC attempted some random phone surveys as early as 1928, and the first formal system was in place by 1930. And, from the first, ratings have been a preoccupation, even in news. Bill Leonard, a former CBS News president, recounted in his memoirs... a conversation he had in 1946 with WCBS radio station manager Richard Swift, after Leonard had been hosting a critically celebrated news mélange called *This is New York* for about three months.

"Your numbers don't seem to be adding up," is how Leonard remembers Swift opening the conversation.

" 'You mean the ratings,' I said hesitantly.

" 'That's right.'

" 'Ratings aren't everything,' I tried.

" 'Name something else,' said Swift."

Journalists have traditionally resisted the pressure to pay homage to these intimidating numbers conjured up through an arcane blend of science and black magic. News's function, after all, was public service, not profit. News ratings,

particularly local news ratings, were thus an internecine preoccupation, the province of astigmatic numbers-crunchers; the argot of ratings was a language that few in the newsroom understood and fewer still cared about.

But while, from a reporter's perspective, news may remain a public service, increasingly its by-product is profit. Newscasts today are the most profitable programs most local stations air, and television journalists are consequently less and less able to hold themselves aloof from the numbers. Like their counterparts in entertainment, news managers are watching the numbers as never before, clamoring about their inaccuracy (except when their own station shows up in first place); reacting more quickly to the numbers with programming and personnel moves; and, in some cases, setting out to manipulate and distort those numbers. As a result, while the general public has for years known how the leading

prime-time entertainment series ranked in the Nielsens, news ratings have now become headline news as the struggle for a larger audience share produces competitive strategems worthy of a J. R. Ewing.

A well-publicized example occurred in Los Angeles last May, when KABC-TV broadcast a special series on the Nielsen families during its regular eleven o'clock newscast. The report was a close look at how the Nielsen system works—who the families are and how they are chosen, what information is compiled and how it is compiled, and how the networks and local stations use the information that Nielsen provides. It prompted immediate cries of foul from KABC's Los Angeles competition and touched off a noisy nationwide debate over journalistic ethics. At issue was the timing of the series. It ran during the heart of the May "sweeps" period, and critics charge that KABC was trying to short-circuit the ratings process by producing a series that Nielsen families—those families with diaries or meters in their homes—would quite naturally want to watch, thus artificially inflating KABC's ratings and skewing the May "book" for the entire Los Angeles market.

"What [KABC] committed was, at the very least, unethical, and at the very most, fraudulent," charged KNBC news director Tom Capra.

Trying to get a leg up on the ratings is nothing new. Local television "report cards"—the ratings books—come out four times a year, and for years stations have endeavord to put forth their best efforts during these sweeps months. One news director likened the process to a full-dress inspection in the military: "You dress up and polish everything and try to put your best foot forward."

The practice is called hyping (or hypoing) the ratings; and more often, instead of putting a best foot forward, what stations do during the sweeps is the journalistic equivalent of flashing a little thigh. The newscasts are loaded wtih "special series," heavily advertised and promoted, aimed at maximizing audience and ratings, and sometimes pandering to the baser instincts. A perennial favorite is teen-age prostitution. Other

standbys include homelessness, runaways, and the mentally ill. Most, however, move into the fringes of newsworthiness: in Los Angeles, during the May sweeps a year ago, viewers were offered series on sexual attraction ("Find out what revs up your sex drive and turns on your neighbors"); devil worshipers; female gangs; extramarital affairs; kittens; super foods that feed millions; senior citizen employment tips; senior citizens in soap operas; senior love ("Age has nothing to do with young love or young lust. Meet some seniors who know how to make a good thing last"); back trouble; car thieves; and two different reports on summer tanning ("What's going on this summer? Not much if you like bikinis. Find out how you can get toned, tanned, and turned on this summer. Watch Cynthia Allison's sizzling report, all this week").

And how about the $1 million in prizes that Milwaukee station WITI offered its viewers during the November 1986 ratings sweep?

Hyping the ratings has become so sophisticated that it is now broken down into subcategories. "Everybody hypes," says Pete Megroz, vice-president for television-station sales and marketing for Arbitron. "Our industry all of a sudden is concerned with the difference between normal hype and abnormal hype."

In other words, a series on summer tanning, while it may send Edward R. Murrow into a sepulchral spin, is okay—normal hype. Its purpose is to entice as many viewers as possible. But KABC's series on the Nielsen families—despite carrying news value far in excess of anything on summer tanning—was cheating. "What KABC was trying to do was to influence the sample," says Megroz, "not influence the general population."

The ploy worked—at least at first. The Nielsen families watched. And since, in Los Angeles, one Nielsen family represents between ten and twelve thousand households, KABC was a resounding winner in the May book, with a 10.5 rating, two full points better than KNBC. In the wake of the furor over the series, however, Nielsen threw out the numbers for the eight newscasts in question, and the adjusted figures left KABC tied with KNBC.

In Minneapolis there was a different wrinkle but a similar furor. KARE, Channel 11, commissioned a research project that coincided with the May sweeps. A questionnaire was mailed to homes in the Twin Cities asking viewers to "watch Channel 11 as often as possible for the next seven days," and then to check off their reactions to the various KARE anchors and special series. KARE, traditionally a weak third in the market, saw its ratings jump dramatically, more than three points in the immediate metro area, and two points overall, propelling the station past KSTP into second place, close on the heels of WCCO, the much-honored and much-respected leader in the market.

WCCO took KARE to court, charging that the station "has gained an unlawful and unfair advantage in competing for television viewership and television advertising revenues in the local television market, and plaintiff has suffered, and will continue to suffer, resulting damage." WCCO further argued that KARE, "given their success in achieving rigged ratings . . . [is] likely to repeat [its] wrongful actions, thereby causing plaintiff irreparable harm and injury."

At issue is not only the timing of the mailing, but also its size. Atkinson Research, the company that conducted the survey, refuses to say how many questionnaires were mailed, but WCCO alleges that the mailing was in the "tens of thousands, and potentially hundreds of thousands"—out of all proportion, WCCO charges, to the number of questionnaires that KARE would have needed to secure statistically valid research data. One of the questionnaires even went to WCCO anchorman Don Shelby.

The judge in the case has enjoined the parties involved from discussing it, but plenty of angry words were uttered before he issued his order. WCCO general manager Ron Handberg, in announcing the suit, called the survey "outrageous and appalling. It's the most outlandish attempt to doctor local TV ratings I've ever seen. I do not see how the people at KARE-TV can produce something like this and still sleep at night."

Nothing so determines the standing of a local station as its ratings. In unsuccessfully seeking an injunction that would have prohibited the Nielsen company from throwing out the ratings of the Nielsen families newscasts, KABC claimed that "it has been the traditional leader in Nielsen for TV news in Los Angeles and has spent millions of dollars promoting itself as the top station. The unlawful actions of Nielsen are threatening to rob KABC of its long-standing and hard-earned status as the 'number one news station.'"

From the help-wanted ads in *Broadcasting* magazine ("Sun Belt Number One looking for the anchor that will keep us there") to convention gossip ("They've been a strong Number Two for years, but they just hired a new female co-anchor, added an entertainment reporter, spent $100,000 on a new set, and beefed up their advertising and on-air promotion. They're really making a big pitch for the fall book"), position in the market is as much a part of a station's identity as are its call letters.

Sometimes it seems as if nothing else matters—not the awards that may clutter the newsroom walls, not the loyalty of long-time viewers, nor the praise of critics for journalistic innovation and solidity. To be proud of the product is not enough, says Jeff Rosser, news director at WNEV-TV in Boston, a station that produces a newscast that most critics agree is the journalistic equivalent of those of its rivals, but a station that traditionally finishes a distant third to Boston's WBZ and WCVB. "How far do you think I'd get if I tried to convince my news staff that it's enough [just to be as good as everyone else]?" he says. "They'd look at me like, 'What planet did you just come from?' Winners want to be recognized as winners. They don't want to just go home and have their wives and kids say, 'It's okay, honey, you're a winner to us.' I want to be a winner to the world."

High ratings, of course, mean more than being recognized as a winner. In a top-ten market, a single point's difference between two stations' newscasts can mean a difference of a million dollars a year in revenues—which goes a long way toward explaining the industry's obeisance to the ratings.

It also explains the perennial concern in the business about their reliability. One problem is that different rating systems can produce different results. When household meters came into use, for example, they gave quite a different picture of viewing patterns—particularly when it came to news programs—from the picture provided by diary-keepers. "The truth is that news ratings are always lower in metered surveys than in diaries," says Pete Megroz of Arbitron. "With diaries, people often fill in what they'd like you to believe they're watching. So news does very well. Public television does very well. People would rather have you believe that they were watching the news instead of the thirty-seventh rerun of *Gomer Pyle,* but the truth is a lot of them are watching *Gomer Pyle* and the meters show it."

Moreover, it seems likely that the new people meters, as compared with diaries, will show higher numbers of younger, upscale viewers, viewers who may already have a living room cluttered with electronic gadgetry—stereos, tape decks, VCRs, computers—and will settle comfortably into the new technology. By contrast, the diary system has always been suspected of a built-in bias toward older viewers, the theory being that they may be more likely than younger people to take the trouble to fill out the *TV Guide*-like diaries. Some people in advertising and television are afraid, too, that viewers who are given people meters will tire of punching in and out every time they watch television, and that the ratings picture will be even more muddied than it is now.

For the time being local news programs will be rated by people meters in only one market, Denver, where Arbitron's ScanAmerica service has been in place since April. The new technology will otherwise be limited to the measurement of network audiences, for which a special national sample is used. And, for the networks, people meters will be the only game in town: on September 14, [1987] Nielsen discontinued its old system of rating network shows by household meters and diaries. (Arbitron is not a significant player in the network-rating game.)

The arrival of people meters brought welcome news to CBS. After finishing a consistent third in the network ratings all summer long, Dan Rather was back on top when the first official people-metered report came out. This did not necessarily mean, however, that viewers were suddenly liking Rather better. Throughout the summer, when the old numbers, based on household meters, were showing Rather running third, the already-in-place but not-yet-official people meters showed him first. Nobody seems to know why this was.

That audience-rating is not an exact science is hardly a revelation. In New York, Boston, Washington, and a dozen other sizable markets, the Nielsen and Arbitron numbers often disagree to the point of having different stations rank first, second, and third. Many people in television think one main difficulty is that the samples are simply too small. Nationally, only 2,000 homes speak for the more than 88 million homes with television. During a local sweeps period, one diary routinely represents more than 2,000 homes; in a metered market, a meter can represent more than 10,000 homes. Nielsen and Arbitron insist, however, that increasing the size of the sample would not significantly change the numbers. In any case, broadcasters are not eager to pay for the peace of mind that a larger sample might or might not bring; in markets the size of New York and Los Angeles, a station's outlay for ratings information already runs around $1 million a year.

"Is [the system] one hundred percent accurate?" says Melvin Goldberg, executive director of the Electronic Media Rating Council, a watchdog group funded by broadcasters and ratings organizations that oversees and audits the ratings process. "No, nothing is. But, as a measure, this is what you have. This is, quote, the truth."

In other words, as a political campaign, perception is reality. Short of a television station putting employees in every home in its viewing area or installing cameras to watch the watchers, the verdicts handed down by these samples will continue to be gospel, and stations will consequently continue to seek an edge in the ratings. Policing them as they seek this edge is likely to be a growing matter of interest and debate. Nielsen's action in delisting KABC was the most dramatic ever taken by the industry. The more common "punishment" for trying to tinker with the sample is for the service to "flag" the ratings—to put a notation in the front of the book alerting advertisers to anything that might have skewed the ratings. But the numbers themselves stand, without an asterisk or any disclaimer other than the fine print at the front of the book. Imagine an umpire who catches a pitcher doctoring a ball and simply discards the ball, leaving the pitcher on the mound with his emery board and nail file.

Advertisers don't seem to care; the numbers are what count. But as the gimmicks start to run amuck and the number of flags increases, so, too, do the cries for better controls. The difficulty in setting up such controls, however, is that no one is really in charge.

"Who is supposed to deliver the sanctions?" asks Mel Goldberg of the Electronic Media Rating Council. "How do you measure the sanctions, and where is there a judge or a jury? And how do you know what is and is not bad? Remember, we're not saying this is a crime."

Goldberg's council has drawn up a set of recommended guidelines for limiting ratings distortion, and both Nielsen and Arbitron have put their clients on notice that they are likely to be quicker to pull ratings if incidents such as that at KABC recur. "It bothers me if this kind of practice is going to encourage the U.S. government to stick its nose into the ratings business," says Arbitron's Megroz. "There are a lot of broadcasters today who say, 'We're headed towards deregulation and that's great. My God, let's not do anything that will cause the government to stick its nose back in our business.'"

Given the unlikelihood that the stations themselves will exercise restraint, a solution to the problem is probably years down the road. People meters, if they prove successful, will deliver fifty-two weeks of reports replete with demographics, and that would render the sweeps periods obsolete and eliminate the hyping—unless it was done routinely throughout the year, in which case it wouldn't by hyping but business as usual. But it will be at least two years before New York has people meters, and it will then be a long time before the system is established in other markets. Indeed, it is unlikely that it will ever be completed: Megroz believes that metering will never be economically feasible for any but the top thirty or so markets.

So the sweeps will be here through our lifetime, and so, presumably, will the efforts to dress up the newscasts to accommodate them. It's a matter of competition, and the newspaper critics who decry television's practices may be forgetting their own heritage. It was not so long ago that ill-bred, ill-mannered, and ill-kempt newspapermen—reporters who would betray their mothers for a scoop and sell out their papers for a free meal—routinely engaged in behavior in pursuit of circulation that was far more egregious than the airing of a few sexy news specials.

Still, the Republic survived and nostalgia has even endowed that lusty era with a certain romance. Perhaps we are merely suffering TV's insecure and footloose adolescence, and a generation from now, when the industry, together with its anchors, has begun to take on a little more gray around the temples—when the number two and three stations have given up on news and the monolithic survivor dominates the market with a 55 rating and an 80 share—we'll look back on these spirited times and sigh about what fun it was every three months to be able to count on an in-depth look at the sexual mores of the runaway children of homeless members of organized crime . . . and how it affects *you*. All this week, at six and eleven. ■

PERSPECTIVE 2

The Declining Network Audience

As described in Perspective 1, the use of people meters to measure TV viewing did show a smaller audience for network programs than earlier measuring devices. Another major factor affecting the network audience is the fracturing of viewership as people choose cable and independent stations and use the TV set to show movies. Overall, CBS took the biggest drop, but the following chart shows that viewership at all three networks was down.

How Network Viewership Declined

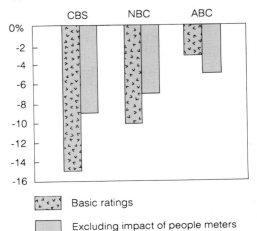

Percentage change in network ratings for all programs
1987–88 vs. 1986–87 season

Basic ratings

Excluding impact of people meters

Note: Data as of April 10, 1988

PERSPECTIVE 3

Tabloid TV

Because ratings are such an important factor in the economics of TV, stations are constantly looking for programming that will deliver the necessary numbers. One choice is tabloid TV, as described in this article from *The Wall Street Journal.*

Consider:

1. What factors have led to the fracturing of the TV audience?

2. How is the current wave of tabloid TV different from the TV sensationalism of the 1950s, 1970s, and 1980s according to the author?

3. Do you think it is accurate to trace this new trend's beginning to "The Oprah Winfrey Show"? Why? Why not?

4. Do you agree with Bonnie Kaplan, executive producer for Geraldo Rivera, that the goal of these shows is "to enlighten"? Why? Why not?

TV Is Going Tabloid as Shows Seek Sleaze and Find Profits, Too
Titillating Channels

DENNIS KNEALE

Uh-oh. "A Current Affair" is scheduled to go on the air in just a few hours. The news magazine show has attracted several million viewers with its nightly fare of real-life murder, mayhem and sex. But this time, as the senior producer scans a videotape, he frets that the show may have gone too far.

As the episode begins, the camera zooms in on a shot of several policemen and a woman in front of the mobile home where her four children have been stabbed to death. She is sobbing. "Oh, no, my babies, my babies." A narrator observed that one child had been stabbed 20 times, and "the tip of the knife [had] broken off in her skull."

But that isn't what bothers Peter Brennan. "Is that blood?" the producer, who is colorblind, asks as the camera slowly pans over the wreckage inside the mobile home. He is studying a suspicious spot on the carpet. "Is it red?" he asks.

"It's more brown," Maury Povich, the show's host, observes. "But blood turns brown." The two men debate whether to cut a big chunk of the footage, but they decide against it. Tonight, as

usual, "A Current Affair" will give its viewers a full measure of gore.

Television has gone tabloid. The seamy underside of life is being bared in a new rash of true-crime series and contrived-confrontation talk shows. They are cheap to make—$25,000 to $50,000 an episode, one-tenth the average cost of an episode for a network series. And the shows rake in big profits.

Except for the most sensationalist shows, advertisers don't seem to raise any objections to the sex or violence, either, as long as the shows deliver the viewers. And they do. Tabloid television is luring an audience that is highly prized by advertisers: women, especially those between the ages of 18 and 49, who typically control a sizable portion of the family budget.

"America's Most Wanted," a show that features profiles of fugitives from the law, counts young women among its most loyal viewers. Some of the blue-chip companies that have advertised on the show: American Telephone & Telegraph Co., Nissan Corp. and Kraft Inc., to name just a few.

For years, television operated on the premise that the biggest audiences are lured with the least objectionable programs. Nowadays, that formula

Dennis Kneale is a staff reporter for *The Wall Street Journal*.

doesn't seem to work as well as it once did. The videoscope is increasingly cluttered. Some 500 game shows, talk shows, and series reruns compete for the fragmented attention of television viewers.

The new shows rise above the crowd by focusing on the sleazy, the sordid, and the downbeat. Re-enactments of actual crimes are popular, and, even more perverse, the shows sometimes ask real-life victims to play themselves in the drama. Among the other topics explored in graphic detail: mothers who murder their babies, love triangles, the children of inter-racial lesbian couples. One show featured an interview with 38-year-old Siamese twins joined at the heart.

Two of the most popular shows, "A Current Affair" and "America's Most Wanted," are the product of Fox Broadcasting Co., which is controlled by Rupert Murdoch, the newspaper-tabloid king from Australia. NBC has jumped into the genre, too. It announced . . . that "Unsolved Mysteries," which also features crime re-enactments and had aired periodically, would become a regular weekly series. . . . "The Morton Downey Jr. Show," a talk show in which controversial guests and the audience are verbally battered by an acerbic host, [began] national syndication [in 1988].

Coming soon: a series that features actual murder trials, a series on missing children, and, yes, even more shows with dramatic re-enactments of real crimes. The producers of one show have broadened the category, probably out of necessity. They plan to offer "Crimes of the Century."

Television has long dabbled in sensationalism. The 1950s had professional wrestling matches. The '70s had weirdo programs ("Real People" once aired a segment on a man who ate dirt). In the 1980s, local news programs offer heavy doses of gore, especially during the ratings sweeps.

But the new wave is more outrageous than ever before. Television producers are discovering that fictional violence isn't enough for viewers anymore. "People are jaded by the preponder-

ance of crime fiction," says Michael L. Linder, the executive producer of "America's Most Wanted."

Today, viewers apparently need an extra jolt to stay tuned. Producers have found a rich lode to mine in the terrible things that happen to ordinary folks. The message to viewers: This could happen to you.

"Some people are going to exploit the trend in a merciful way," says "Unsolved Mysteries" producer John Cosgrove, "and some will exploit it mercilessly."

Consider some recent examples:

—In a crime re-enactment on "America's Most Wanted," a rapist bursts into a woman's home. He forces her to the bed, hits her in the face, stuffs lingerie into her mouth and ties her hands behind her back. Only then, does the camera veer off. All this unfolds in the grainy, slow-motion style of filmmaker Sam Peckinpah.

—In a recent special with Geraldo Rivera as host, "Murder: Live From Death Row," 30 million viewers saw footage of an actual murder of a convenience-store customer. The producers used the videotape from the store's security cameras. Mr. Rivera interviewed several convicted murderers about their crimes, encouraging them to share the grisly details. The highlight of the show: a prison interview with mass murderer Charles Manson.

—On "Morton Downey," the host and a guest re-enacted the strangling of Jennifer Levin by Robert Chambers in Central Park. (Mr. Chambers, who claimed he accidentally killed the young woman during "rough sex," was recently sentenced to prison in the case.) Using a pair of pink panties procured from someone in the audience, Guardian Angel Lisa Sliwa tied Mr. Downey's hands behind his back, then squatted on top of him as he lay on the floor.

"He pulls off the panties and strangles her," says Robert W. Pittman, the president of Quantum Media, Inc., which owns the show. "It was great. . . . Television works best when you get to be a voyeur."

Curiously, for all the gore, tabloid television hasn't sparked much of a reaction among the most vocal critics of sex and violence on television. The National Coalition on Television Violence, a group that records every fictitious violent act on television, says it sees no need to track tabloid television. Indeed, the Coalition's Dr. Thomas E. Radecki praises "America's Most Wanted" for its role in capturing fugitives at large. (The show encourages viewers to call a toll-free number with tips to help police catch suspected criminals; the show's producer says such tips helped lead to the capture of nine fugitives.)

"Oprah," a daytime talk show with Oprah Winfrey as host, may have triggered the trend. Her show first aired several years ago in Chicago, then went national in the fall of 1986. She quickly trounced Phil Donahue, then the reigning top gun of talk, by focusing on the bizarre.

Self-proclaimed porn addicts, witches and bigots have been among her guests—and her show's ratings have soared. Jealous rivals have taken to calling the show "Nuts 'n' Sluts" and "Freak of the Week."

Debra A. DiMaio, the show's executive producer, invokes a defense frequently put forth by tabloid-television producers: We don't make this stuff up, it's real life. Besides, she says, when viewers complain about a show on sex, they do so only after having watched every minute of it.

Even for Ms. DiMaio, things tend to blur after a while. Asked about a recent segment the show did on child murderers, she says: "Are you talking about kids who kill kids, or kids who kill their parents?" "Oprah" aired segments on both.

To keep up, Ms. Winfrey's rivals have had to resort to ever-racier fare. "The pressure to do 'I was impregnated by an alien from outer space' is greater," Phil Donahue says. One of the problems, he says, is that the public has less and less interest in hard news. To do a segment on the Persian Gulf, he says, "we try to sneak it in between the male strippers." This troubles him, but he isn't about to change it. "Nobody wants to be a dead hero," he says, "least of all me."

Advertisers still shy away from shows on the outer fringe of tabloid television, such as "Morton Downey." Joel Segal, an executive vice president of advertising agency McCann Erickson Inc., says he would like to reach the Downey audience but won't risk it. "I worry about what he might do," Mr. Segal says.

Mr. Downey runs wild on his show. He insults guests—"Zip it!"—and has assaulted at least one of them. Mr. Downey was recently cleared of criminal charges after slapping a gay activist and telling him to "keep your bodily fluids to yourself!" (The incident happened while the show was being taped, but the segment hasn't been aired yet.)

"Sex sells, sensationalism sells," Bill Boggs, the show's executive producer, says. Not all of the segments are outrageous, he says—just enough to keep 'em coming back.

The ratings earned by "America's Most Wanted" proves that point. After only six weeks, the show [was] the top-rated on the Fox lineup. It [got] 60% more viewers than what it replaced ("Werewolf") and draws an 11% share of viewers nationally. (In Washington, D.C., it draws a 28% share.) That record is better than several network series that air on twice as many stations as "America's Most Wanted."

"The future of TV is very much real-life," Mr. Brennan of "A Current Affair" says. "It's what Shakespeare wrote about—rage, jealousy, greed."

"A Current Affair" made its debut on Fox's New York station last fall. It is currently syndicated to 69 markets.

Extensive reporting and scoops are rare. The show is filmed on the cheap—$35,000 an episode. A sampling of segments from the past two weeks: graverobbers, a profile of a porn star, and a trade show for mercenaries. That segment had buxom beauties in bikinis firing M-14s.

Mr. Brennan says all the show's segments have a moral message or a national angle. And, he says, there are limits. A few of his rules: no shows on hookers, drug addicts or child molesters. He also says he won't allow corpses to be shown because death is too private.

What about the recent story that did show a

corpse? ("Portrait of Evil," was about a man who killed his parents.) Says Mr. Brennan: "Terrible. I won't defend it. I apologize for it. We've done plenty of things we regret."

Geraldo Rivera's new talk show also explores the extremes of tabloid television. In a show on drugs, Mr. Rivera interviews a grieving mother whose daughter died of a drug overdose.

"The girl's body rotted for three days" at a friend's home before someone called the police. Mr. Rivera tells viewers—twice. Later in the program, Mr. Rivera interviews a man who had been shot by drug dealers. The man pulls open his shirt to bare a long scar and the bullethole. The camera zooms in for a close-up.

During the show, Mr. Rivera says he would cut the hands off anyone who gave his nine-year-old son cocaine. In a follow-up show, he points to two addicts and says if they tried to rob his house, "I'd blow their heads off." Both lines get wild applause from the audience.

But, the object isn't sensationalism, Bonnie Kaplan, the show's executive producer, insists. "The goal is to enlighten." ■

PERSPECTIVE 4

Minorities on Television

In this article, David Ehrenstein discusses the role that the characters portrayed by actors Bill Cosby and Eddie Murphy play in creating the image of blacks on television and in the movies. Ehrenstein challenges the idea that these portrayals improve the image of black people in American society.

Consider:

1. Do you agree with Ehrenstein that for both Murphy and Cosby, "white notions of black life provide the ruling assumptions that their comedy relies on"? Why? Why not?

2. Does the reality portrayed by the Huxtable family on "The Cosby Show" do a disservice to blacks, as Ehrenstein claims? Why? Why not?

3. Ehrenstein says that, "At first glance, Murphy has the impact of a complete original—a smart, attractive black youth who uses his intelligence and quick wit at every opportunity. . . . But it's *only* an image." Do you agree? Disagree? Explain.

The Color of Laughter

DAVID EHRENSTEIN

With 1988 marking the twentieth anniversary of the Kerner Commission Report on the status of black Americans, the media are filled with polls and observations about the evolution of race relations over the past two decades. One "poll," at any rate, seemingly proves those relations have vastly improved: In television, Bill Cosby dominates the ratings, while in the movies, Eddie Murphy is king of the box office.

Although black entertainers have enjoyed widespread popularity over the decades—regardless of the nation's racial climate—the phenomenon of Cosby and Murphy is something quite new. They're not simply popular; they're probably the *most* popular performers, black or white, in America today. "This is the Cosby decade—America loves black people," declares the hero of the film *Soul Man* (1986), a noxious farce about a pampered white yuppie who enters Harvard Law School by dyeing his skin and passing for black to qualify for a minority scholarship. But what does "love" of Cosby constitute in the era of Howard Beach, Al Campanis, and the first president since Andrew Johnson to veto civil-rights legislation?

Indeed, whatever the Nielsen ratings say, race relations have eroded dramatically since the days of the civil-rights movement. "All in the Family" reiterated the clichés of racism through Archie Bunker's crass remarks—always neutralized, of course, by his heart of gold. The show's

mockery of racism in fact merely trivialized it. The trend has accelerated in this decade with such films as *Soul Man,* which uses its ostensibly prointegrationist stance to spout racist jokes; the Eddie Murphy vehicle *Trading Places* (1983) which plays off the incongruity of a black con passing for a respectable citizen, and *Adventures in Babysitting* (1987), which bases its comedic premise on the (white) belief that all urban blacks are criminals. Sometimes the humor is merely condescending, as in the "Blacks Without Soul" sketch in *Amazon Women on the Moon* (1987), which features a black man's inability to "talk black." What's the joke? Or is being black in and of itself some sort of comic relief?

Cosby and Murphy would appear to be immune to such catering to racism. But, in fact, they're centrally implicated in it. In both their cases, white notions of black life provide the ruling assumptions that their comedy relies on. The domestic bliss of the Huxtable household is perceived by whites as the exception to the rule of black family life, reaffirming the notion that racism wouldn't be a problem if only blacks were more like "us." Similarly, Murphy's fast-talking cop/con man (the roles are interchangeable) toys with white expectations of violent black behavior without ever challenging the possible reasons for that violence: He stands up to whites while reassuring them he doesn't take offense at their fearful expectations. Television's top Superdad and Hollywood's slickest hipster operate not as cultural purveyors of black American life, but rather as safety valves, generating laughs that mask the conflict between black aspirations and the maintenance of white power.

David Ehrenstein writes about film for the *Los Angeles Herald-Examiner.* He is the author of *Film: The Front Line 1984* and, with Bill Reed, *Rock on Film.*

In his 1976 book-length essay, "The Devil Finds Work," James Baldwin recalled his earliest moviegoing experiences viewing the likes of Stepin Fetchit, Willie Best, and Mantan Moreland, the three black actors most strongly associated with stereotyped images. "It seemed to me," Baldwin wrote, "that they lied about the world I knew, and debased it, and certainly I did not know anybody like them—as far as I could tell; for it is also possible that their comic, bug-eyed terror contained the truth concerning a terror by which I hoped never to be engulfed." In short, the lie of the stereotype held within it a grain of truth—blacks were largely at the mercy of hostile forces beyond their control. The "bug-eyed" terror of these actors may have been fake, but the fear blacks faced every day in white society was all too real. Yet even if the stereotype contained some truth, its real power was in its use as a social leveler: This is who you are, the stereotype insists, and this is *all* you are.

At first glance, "The Cosby Show" is a successful attempt to break the chokehold of such traditional black stereotypes. The Huxtable family—close-knit, clean-cut, parentally controlled—seems to undercut white racism even as it serves as an ideal for black viewers: "This is who you are" becomes "this is who we *should* be." And it would be ridiculous to expect anything else from Cosby, whose early comedy routines were founded on a frank refusal to deal with racial difference—a refusal that whites found utterly charming. Black and white children were at base no different, his routines suggested, so black and white adults should be, too.

Likewise, the world of "The Cosby Show" is founded on assumptions of complete racial harmony and total integration. But while the notion of a world without racial strife may have been admirable in the integrationist sixties, on eighties television this idyllic conceit becomes little more than a monstrous blocking mechanism. The characters seem incapable of *imagining* (much less experiencing) racial adversity—even in a comic context. Black identity is reduced to a visual style, a fashion statement.

Yet you can't help but wonder what would happen if the Cosby kids were to wander beyond the confines of their plush prison of a home. Theo, for instance, would most likely encounter whites who would see not a nice, well-mannered teenager, but simply a black adolescent male—an object of almost instinctive white fear and hatred. And what would happen when Vanessa tried to hail a taxi, only to be ignored by cabbies fearful of ending up in a black neighborhood? Fit only for the "Cosby Show" universe, these characters would dematerialize in the real world.

Denise, the fashion trend-setter of the Cosby clan, *is* one character who has ventured out of the house—although only into a spin-off show, the tellingly titled "A Different World." Needless to say, it's the *same* world: At college, Denise is as safe as she would be in the Cosby living room. The show's action invariably revolves around such heart-stopping issues as unfinished term papers and borrowed money—at a time when black students at "liberal" schools like the universities of Michigan and Massachusetts are subjected to racial harassment.

But "A Different World" doesn't cover its tracks as well as "Cosby." Reality asserts itself in the obvious sensuality of its star, Lisa Bonet, despite the show's determination to repress her sexuality. Although she's seen longing for a handsome, light-skinned black youth in the opening credits, this beautiful young woman's love life is practically nonexistent, save for a few passing dates. The main male characters seem to have giant signs around their necks that read, "No sexual threat"; intimations of eroticism—male or female—would instantly upset the decorum the show works so hard to maintain. The show's producers need to keep Bonet "untouched" for the same reason that MGM plastered Lena Horne against a pillar in forties musicals rather than give her dramatic roles and raise the troubling specter of a black woman's sexual power. But given "A Different World's" studied superficiality, it's doubtful that Denise would do anything really troublesome like eloping with a white man, or (worse still for the light-skinned character) an obviously black one. Besides, troublesome behavior is the stock-in-trade of that other black superstar, Eddie Murphy.

From the moment of his first appearance on NBC's "Saturday Night Live," Eddie Murphy was totally and uncannily in control. His gleeful send-ups of stereotypes past and present—Buckwheat, Velvet Jones, Raheen Abdul Muhammad—were brought off with an infectious sense of fun. A gifted mimic with enormous reserves of personal charm, he rapidly emerged as the show's star, only to quickly abandon television to conquer movies. Murphy triumphed in *48 HRS* (1982) and *Beverly Hills Cop* (1984), action pictures shrewdly tailored to his comic persona. It seemed as if Murphy could do no wrong. Even *The Golden Child* (1986), a confused fantasy-adventure that suffered a critical drubbing, racked up enormous box office, thanks to legions of loyal Murphy fans.

At first glance, Murphy has the impact of a complete original—a smart, attractive black youth who uses his intelligence and quick wit at every opportunity. And unlike the Cosby kids, he's *constantly* encountering whites who are either oblivious to him, scared of him, or who expect an obsequious underling. Murphy confounds them with the image of a free, powerful black man. But it's *only* an image; his freedom and power exist within very clear confines.

"I'm your worst f--kin' nightmare, man—I'm a nigger with a badge," Murphy announces in the red-neck barroom scene in *48 HRS.* For black audiences, watching Murphy swagger through the bar was a new thrill—a twist on routines first seen in "blaxploitation" thrillers a decade before. To whites, the scene meant something else. Here was Murphy *acting* the part of an "angry black man," a la the black-power activities of a decade earlier—but the payoff, of course, was that he didn't *really* mean it! It was as if all the black anger that has raged through years of political struggle had suddenly revealed itself to be, at heart, nothing more than a routine—a joke. Whites in the audience were off the hook: Eddie

(and, by extension, all blacks) wasn't *really* angry with them. It's only a few short steps from there for reassured whites to conclude that they're not racist simply because they enjoy Eddie Murphy.

As for sexuality, Murphy is, despite his "dirty" language, almost as circumspect as Lisa Bonet. On-screen, Murphy almost never has a love interest (his recent attempt at having one in *Coming to America* only proves how impossible this is). In his concert films, such as *Eddie Murphy RAW* (1987), Murphy talks almost nonstop about sex. . . . Race, meanwhile, is given the kid-glove treatment: Murphy teases whites who get "worked up" after seeing a *Rocky* film. Moreover, he casts himself as the nice guy when he recounts a fracas he got into at a disco a few months before. As Murphy tells it, the disturbance was all a misunderstanding: How could anyone think that Eddie Murphy would want to cause trouble?

"I'm not an angry comic. My life has been real nice," Murphy confessed to an interviewer in 1983. To another writer, he confided, "I'm not a conservative-type black man. I wouldn't be believable as a doctor or a lawyer. I'm an aggressive black man." The statements aren't contradictory, for in the first case, Murphy is talking about his personal life, and in the second, his performing persona. He *plays* the "angry black man"—not because he *is* one, but because he inherited the role from the last important black comedy star, Richard Pryor.

Looking at Murphy in *RAW,* it's impossible not to think of Pryor's brilliant, often brutal routines, which seem to sum up several decades of black experience. Murphy, for example, has adopted with relish Pryor's use of the word "nigger" (always controversial among blacks because it created such pleasure for whites—a dirty thrill sanctioned by a comic's honesty; Pryor, in fact, no longer uses the word). Indeed, Murphy, the middle-class kid from Long Island, has frankly taken up everything about the lower-class, bohemian Pryor—except his comic edge.

Unlike Murphy, Pryor dealt with the truly taboo subject of growing up on society's margins. And therefore—even if personal problems hadn't short-circuited Pryor's career—there were clearly limits to how far he could go. Pryor's television show was too hot for the networks, while the characters in his concert routines—junkies, winos, pimps—were too raw to be adapted into fictional narrative form. Whatever Pryor's success in translating his life to the screen in *Jo Jo Dancer, Your Life Is Calling* (1986), the film was a deadly serious attempt to deal with black American life as he knew it. White America, however, wasn't interested.

It's no surprise, then, to see Pryor today staring out of the poster for his latest film, *Moving,* with his face transfixed by something not unlike the "bug-eyed terror" that so disturbed Baldwin. Nor is it surprising to discover that in the film, a comedy about a black family transferring to a new home, racial friction plays no role whatsoever. The social atmosphere that makes *Moving* a bankable project is the same one in which Murphy's unthreatening brand of black comedy thrives.

As the eighties draw to a close, a new awareness of the unfinished struggle with racism seems to be emerging. The trouble is that, in the decades since the last major battles, no cultural context has arisen from which to view racism. Murphy offers trivialization of the problem while Cosby carefully constructs a world in which racial problems never intrude.

Black American lives aren't automatically encapsulated by perfect families and slick hipsters—particularly when such clichéd characters are the only black faces on view. More is needed. Some of it will be funny. But before the laughter flows, black entertainers will have to get a lot more serious. ■

PERSPECTIVE 5

Cable TV's Growing Future

In the last ten years, cable operators have been encroaching on the audience that once belonged entirely to TV network affiliates and independent stations. More than half the nation's homes are wired for cable. The economic implications for commercial stations, of course, are far-reaching. This article from *Advertising Age* describes the attractiveness for advertisers of the growing cable audience.

Consider:

1. What makes the cable audience, compared to the broadcast television audience, so attractive for advertisers?

2. What are the economic advantages to the advertiser of buying ads on cable instead of on broadcast?

3. What are the advantages to cable operators of people meters, as opposed to the traditional diary ratings system? (For more information on people meters, see Perspective 1, pages 87–93).

4. Explain how the Cable Planning System is used to target audiences. What advantages does the use of this system offer an advertising agency?

As Milestones Fall, Cable Carries Weight

LEN STRAZEWSKI

After years as the shunned stepchild of broadcast television, cable TV is coming into its own as a national advertising medium, say agency media buyers and cable industry analysts and leaders.

Building on increased penetration—recently reaching 50% of U.S. homes—affluent demographics, improved programming and falling broadcast TV ratings, cable networks are beginning to show on national advertiser buying schedules as 2% to 10% of the total media budgets, analysts and media buyers say.

By the end of [1987], cable network advertising revenue is expected to top $1 billion, with more than $878 million generated from national advertisers—up 18% from last year—and $264 million from local spot sales—up 38%—from last year, according to reports from Paul Kagan Associates, a Carmel, Calif.-based industry analyst.

By 1996, Kagan expects ad revenue to quadruple to $4.5 billion with national advertising reaching nearly $3 billion.

"What has changed is the relationship of supply and demand," says Radford Stone, VP-national marketing, New York-based Cabletelevision Advertising Bureau. "This is still an oversupply in cable and that has kept the CPMs [costs per thousands]* down, but there is an increasing demand for more impressions, particularly in high demographic cable households which broadcast television is not delivering."

Len Strazewski is a Chicago-based free-lance writer.

*CPMs = Cost per 1,000 homes delivered to the advertiser. (M is the Roman numeral for 1,000.)

Broadcast TV ratings have been dropping overall, Mr. Stone notes, and falling particularly fast in cable households as new exclusive programming draws viewers. Moreover, recent studies, including a 1986 survey, have shown that many of the cable networks have a key affluent viewership 10% or more above the national average.

ESPN, for example, has an audience heavily weighted to male affluent viewers and MTV appeals most strongly to young affluent viewers 25 to 34 years old. And according to composite data from a 1986 study, cable households in general are more affluent—18% more likely to have incomes more than $50,000—and better educated—14% more likely than the average to have college graduates.

"Broadcast television under-delivers these valuable households," Mr. Stone says. "That has left media planners scrambling to add impressions to meet their strategic goals. That means shifting 2% to 3% of their budgets into cable."

Costs haven't hurt, either. Although cable ratings may be low—a 2 or 3 share for some shows compared with a 15 to 20 share for typical broadcast TV programming—CPMs are as much as four times lower—$3 to $4 compared with $12 for network television.

What media buyers aren't getting in total number of viewers they are making up with total impressions, buying more frequent cable spots in upscale cable homes.

"That's been the tactical response from many buyers," Mr. Stone says.

"And while we are glad to see that happening, we would prefer to see cable showing up more as part of strategic media plans from the beginning. That is also beginning to happen."

Mr. Stone says a recent CAB survey of leading national advertisers indicates that 20% of the largest national advertisers, including heavyweights Nabisco Brands, Coca-Cola Co. and Mars Inc., are committing up to 10% of their media budgets to cable.

Some national advertisers actually are designing spots for cable. PepsiCo, for example, recently premiered a 90-second Pepsi-Cola spot featuring Michael Jackson on MTV before slotting a shorter version for broadcast.

One reason for the upswing, industry insiders and outsiders agree, is recognition by agency media buyers of the value of cable. Agency media planners, longtime skeptics of cable's value as an ad medium, are now becoming outspoken supporters. They point to such breakthrough events as ESPN's National Football League contract, C-SPAN and CNN's live coverage of the Iran-contra hearings, Turner Broadcasting's colorized classic films and innovative original programming such as Showtime's "It's Garry Shandling's Show."

"As programming has improved, so has penetration. And the households cable attracts are, in turn, attractive to advertisers. Subscribers tend to be younger, better educated and affluent," says Beverly O'Malley, director of electronic media for Saatchi & Saatchi DFS Compton, New York.

Erica Gruen, the agency's associate director of electronic media, agrees. "We're seeing cable come into its own, not only financially, but in terms of programming. In fact, because of its attractiveness to subscribers, cable's efficiencies can be better than most broadcast alternatives by as much as 40% to 60%."

An agency study of cable by Ms. O'Malley and Ms. Gruen released this summer points to the Nielsen ratings of early 1987 showing that for the first time, the network prime-time ratings dropped below 50%, down 3% from the previous year, and independent broadcast TV stations fell to less than 8%, also down 3% from the previous year. Meanwhile, cable and cable-carried super-

stations such as WTBS in Atlanta and WGN in Chicago increased their ratings 15% to 7.3% in prime time.

"Ratings on cable may still be small, given the sheer number of networks competing for their share of the viewing pie, but the overall growth pattern can no longer be denied," the study says.

For 1988, the study predicts continued growth of cable sports programming as a big advertising drawing card, the movement of one-hour action adventure shows such as "Riptide" and "Airwolf" to cable in lieu of syndication, more original cable programming and the continued development of special interest networks such as MTV and Nickelodeon, CNN and The Discovery Channel.

MTV's Nickelodeon and its later-hour counterpart Nick at Night has been a particular surprise this year, drawing toy and cereal advertising for its daytime children's programming and package goods spots at night. Russ Naiman, VP-advertising sales for Nickelodeon and Nick at Night, would not disclose total ad revenues, but says Nickelodeon's revenues doubled over the last three years and Nick at Night more than doubled over the last year.

Daytime highlights include "Double Dare," a kid's game show that has generated a 3.5 share and reruns of "The Monkees," an almost 20-year-old musical sitcom that has become a cult hit.

Nighttime highlights include other television classics such as "Car 54, Where Are You?" and "Laugh-In."

Another factor spurring the growth of national advertising on cable is media-planning technology. For years, agency media buyers and cable industry leaders have bemoaned the lack of accurate ratings and a means to compare the value of broadcast ratings and cable ratings.

The introduction of people meters, however, has improved TV viewing measurement, Mr. Stone notes, and has proved cable industry claims that diary-based measuring techniques were under-reporting cable usage. The new Nielsen data from the meters shows broadcast TV with smaller shares during prime time than ever before (73), with daytime scoring 61 and late-night day-parts 54.

Last summer, when broadcast networks ran reruns, cable viewership increased sharply, according to the latest Nielsen figures. On a 24-hour basis ad-supported cable network's ratings rose by 40% during the summer months, resulting in a gain of 866,000 homes per average hour while pay-cable services increased by 18% or 288,000 homes per quarter.

By daypart, ad-supported cable ratings increased 33% in prime time, 42% during daytime and by 21% on weekends. The Nielsen study shows that advertiser-supported cable and pay cable had audience shares of 22 and 20, respectively, for 42 total, larger than the broadcast total of 41.

To guide media planners in using the new data, CAB also introduced the Cable Planning System. A computer-software product based on the popular Lotus 1-2-3 personal computer spreadsheet program, the Cable Planning System is designed to use product-use demographic data with ratings information to target impressions in households with greater product buying propensity.

"Essentially, media planners use it to put the majority of impressions in front of the people who buy the product," explains Carol Lansen, senior account exec at CAB. Now in use at most major agencies, including Young & Rubicam, BBDO, Ogilvy & Mather and others, the system was designed to help media planners budget for cable purchases.

For example, if cable households have a 110 product usage index—10% more likely than the average to buy a product—they account for about 55% of sales, making them a good target for advertising. However, because broadcast TV delivers only about 45% of cable households, the planning system reveals that as a medium, broadcast TV is under-delivering the key households. The system then advises buyers as to how much cable time must be purchased to balance the buy.

"It's a very straightforward system," says Kevin Burns, manager of broadcast and new technologies at O&M, New York. "It gives you a for-mula for figuring out what you should be buying in cable." O&M, he says, has been buying substantially more cable, because of the system and improved programming.

"Using cable has become more of a mainstream consideration," Mr. Burns says. "In some cases, there is no reason to buy any cable at all, but in a lot of situations, particularly when a cable network skews toward a particular audience . . . buying cable households becomes very important. In those situations, the Cable Planning System helps figure out what's needed."

Gene DeWitt, president of DeWitt Media, New York, a media-buying and consulting company, says the system "is the first objective means of calculating how much of a TV budget should go into cable."

Previously, he says, media buyers followed their intuition and bought small amounts of cable time on an experimental basis. Some small advertisers saw cable as a bargain and put 20% to 40% of their budgets in it. The planning system, how-

Cable TV gross revenue estimates

Year	Total cable ad revenues*	% chg
1980	$ 58	—
1981	122	110
1982	227	86
1983	353	56
1984	572	62
1985	751	31
1986	930	24
1987	1,142	23
1988	1,395	22
1989	1,685	21
1990	1,982	18
1991	2,329	18
1992	2,705	16
1993	3,142	16
1994	3,555	13
1995	4,041	14
1996	4,500	11

* In millions of dollars

Source: Cable TV Advertising, Paul Kagan Associates, Carmel, Calif.

ever, quantifies the audience and eliminates the guesswork.

"To me, cable is just television and buying cable requires the same analysis as buying television," Mr. DeWitt says. "You've got to know who the audience is and how many impressions they are receiving. After that, it's a question of money. If I can buy cable impressions at $5 CPM with as good or better qualified audience and am being charged a $12 CPM for broadcast television, I'm going to buy more cable. Cable is the last bargain left in television advertising." ∎

CHAPTER FIVE

For Further Reading

Books

Erik Barnouw, *Tube of Plenty* (New York: Oxford University Press, 1975).

Todd Gitlin, *Inside Prime Time* (New York: Pantheon Books, 1985).

Todd Gitlin, (ed.), *Watching Television* (New York: Pantheon Books, 1986).

Jeff Greenfield, *Television: The First Fifty Years* (New York: Abrams, 1977).

Newton Minow, *Equal Time: The Private Broadcaster and the Public Interest* (New York: Atheneum, 1964).

A. M. Sperber, *Murrow: His Life and Times* (New York: Freundlich, 1986).

Periodicals

Broadcasting

Cable Today

Cablevision

Channels (formerly *Channels of Communication*)

Electronic Media

Emmy, Published by the Academy of Television Arts and Sciences

Journal of Broadcasting and Electronic Media

TV Guide

Television/Radio Age

The Movie Industry

Today's Movie Business

Movie income is up—it was $4.2 billion in 1987—but so are costs, and the movie industry is struggling to adjust to a movie market that is just as fickle as ever. No one—not even professional filmmakers—can predict which movies will be hits. In this overview of the current state of the movie industry from *The New York Times,* reporter Aljean Harmetz details the current realities.

Consider:

1. What is meant by the term "vertical integration"? How is it affecting the movie business?

2. How would you define the term "movie studio" today? How do movie studios today differ from those in the 1930s?

3. How has the advent of videocassettes affected the movie business?

4. Why does Harmetz conclude that "the movies have always been an uneasy blend of art and commerce, but, today, commerce is the clear winner"? What are the reasons for the growing emphasis on profits?

Now Playing: The New Hollywood

ALJEAN HARMETZ

Things change all the time in Hollywood. Raunchy teen-age comedies clogged the theaters like cholesterol in aging arteries for six years, then disappeared overnight, to be replaced in the fall of 1987 by courtroom melodramas and steamy love stories. Three months ago, the stock market crash put upstart companies at risk, those fragile new movie makers dependent on stock sales and one hit movie.

What does the shifting business of the movie industry mean for people who don't own stock in movie companies, who simply want to find a movie to see over the weekend? Quite a lot, actu-

ally. There are more movie theaters than ever before, [in 1987] there were 511 new movies to fill them, an outpouring of movies greater than any year since 1970. That basketful of new movies contains many interesting, quirky or daring independent films that would have had no chance to be made or distributed six years ago. It also contains some dreadful films that are pushed into theaters solely to make them valuable for sale four months later on video cassettes.

Whatever the changes, the major studios will stick around. They always do. Like chameleons, they adapt to each decade—changing ownership, shedding their sound stages, producing television series for the networks and building video-

---

Aljean Harmetz is a reporter for *The New York Times.*

cassette companies. The studios of the 80's are very different from those mythological creatures that controlled popular culture 50 years ago. But they still carry the same names—Metro-Goldwyn-Mayer, United Artists, 20th Century-Fox, Paramount, Warner Bros., Columbia and Universal. And, even though they no longer have 250 actors under contract as M-G-M did in 1935, they still control most of what goes on in the movie industry.

"The strong will survive and become stronger and the weak will disappear," says Martin Davis, chairman of Gulf and Western, the parent company of Paramount Pictures.

What is going on right now is a grab for power, with the small getting big and the big getting huge, immense, gargantuan.

Every big studio is now a conglomerate or has been purchased by a conglomerate. Companies that were created to sell video cassettes are becoming movie studios. So are theater chains. Independent films that would never have reached theaters outside the big cities a few years ago are being played in middle-sized towns. And theaters have been popping up like mushrooms in every shopping mall.

In [Nov. 1987], the National Association of Theater Owners said that there are more movie theaters in the United States now than there have been at any time since the association started keeping track in 1948; 22,721 movie screens, with more opening every month. And more and more of those theaters are owned by the movie studios. In the last two years, the studios have bought 14 theater chains, totaling nearly one-fifth of the theaters in the country.

Ticket sales reached $4.2 billion last year, making the 1987 box office the best in Hollywood's history. Revenues from video cassettes are even higher. Over the holiday season, the Walt Disney Co., which in the 1930's was a producer of cartoons but is a major movie company today, sold 3 million cassettes of the 32-year-old animated film "Lady and the Tramp," bringing the studio $60 million.

Paradise is not trouble-free. Jeffrey Katzenberg, chairman of Walt Disney Studios, points out

that 1987 was a great year for exhibitors but not necessarily for the studios. "The consensus is that there was simply too much product," he says. "If you divide the film rental by the number of pictures that were released, a disproportionate amount of money went to a few successful films."

Over the Thanksgiving weekend, there were more than 30 movies available. But two Disney movies, "Three Men and a Baby" and "Cinderella" and two Paramount movies, "Planes, Trains and Automobiles" and "Fatal Attraction," sold more than 60 percent of all tickets. Christmas weekend the rewards were more evenly spread, but the new Bill Cosby movie "Leonard, Part VI," was still a disaster.

The Era of the Mega-Studio

For 1988, the buzzword in Hollywood is vertical integration. The major studios—and even some of the minor ones—intend to make and distribute movies, show them in their own theaters, manufacture and sell the video cassettes six months later, then syndicate their films to their own television stations, bypassing the networks, and, in the case of Disney, play them on a studio-owned pay-cable channel.

In this era of deregulation, the studios are attempting to control their own destiny, something they have been unable to do since the Federal Government forced them to get rid of their theaters in 1948 and the advent of television dumped moviegoing out of first place as America's popular entertainment.

As a matter of fact, the label "movie studio" is somewhat archaic. Paramount is part of Gulf and Western's "Entertainment Group," along with Madison Square Garden, the New York Knicks basketball team and 894 movie theaters. And 20th Century-Fox, which is controlled by the press baron Rupert Murdoch, has started a fourth television network after buying five television stations for $1.6 billion.

MCA, the parent company of Universal, has a thriving studio tour, a mail order gifts company, a company that runs the concessions at Yosemite National Park, WOR-TV in New York and a 50 percent ownership in Cineplex Oden, one of the largest theater chains in the United States and Canada.

Warner Communications, which shares ownership of the MTV and Nickelodeon cable channels and is the sixth largest operator of cable systems, is buying a 50 percent interest in 454 of Paramount's theaters. Amusement parks bring Disney most of its revenue. In December Columbia was reorganized by its owner, Coca-Cola, leaving Coke with 49 percent of the stock in a new company, Columbia Pictures Entertainment, made up of Columbia, Tri-Star Pictures, Loew's Theaters and all of the television companies Coca-Cola had purchased.

Goodbye Bijou, Hello Multiplex

Almost all the new theaters are multiplexes, single buildings that house eight or 10 small movie screens. Last fall, Cineplex opened the nation's largest movie complex, a theater with 18 screens on the Universal Studios lot. With 6,000 seats, the Universal Cineplex is roughly the size of Radio City Music Hall, but it can play 18 movies instead of one.

Multiplexes and video cassettes have greased the way for a vastly increased number of small, oddball English-language films that were independently produced: "Sammy and Rosie Get Laid," "Slam Dance," "Square Dance," "Dirty Dancing," "Matewan," "Maurice," "The Dead," "The Whales of August," "Dogs in Space," "Wish You Were Here," "The Glass Menagerie" and "Barfly," to name a few recent movies.

To put this trend in an even more startling perspective, more than 40 percent of the Academy Award nominations last year went to movies that were not made or distributed by the eight major studios. And the best actor and best actress awards in 1985 were won by William Hurt for "Kiss of the Spider Woman" and Geraldine Page for "The Trip to Bountiful," movies that were distributed by Island Pictures, one of the small, independent distributors that have sprung up to challenge the major studios.

Together, video cassettes and multiplexes have essentially killed the civilized single-screen art theaters that played mostly foreign films or showed old American movies in repertory. But, together, they have fueled the rise of what Hollywood calls "specialized" movies. (Art film is a dirty—i.e. uncommercial—word today.) These low-budget films—"She's Gotta Have It" cost less than $200,000, "River's Edge" cost a little over a million dollars, the opulent "Room With a View" cost $3 million—often get made only because hungry video-cassette companies need product and are willing to underwrite a film maker with one or two million dollars. However, getting a film made is futile unless people can see it. And the multiplexes have made that possible.

These efficient concrete pillboxes sitting astride shopping malls have replaced the rococo Regents and Bijoux, the old Main Street picture palaces. And they also need product. In a Los Angeles shopping mall, three Cineplex screens were playing Steven Spielberg's "Batteries Not Included" over Christmas, but the theater was also showing "Barfly" and "The Glass Menagerie."

Worries and Costs at a Risky Time

But, as Mr. Katzenberg points out, there is also a product glut that is expected to last another nine months. This competition—which means that unsuccessful movies start losing theaters after a week and thus have no chance to build an audience—is especially worrisome to the young independent film companies.

"There's no discrimination," says Ira Deutchman, president of marketing at Cinecom, the distributor of "Matewan" and "Room With a View." The exhibitors just book everything for two weeks. In order to make a movie worth something for home video, it has to play in the theaters, and the result is that there's more garbage in the marketplace than ever before."

There is also a new get-tough attitude toward the unions. The average cost of making a major studio movie last year was about $16 million, with an additional $8 to $10 million spent on marketing. The bloated budgets have had several effects, including using nonunion employees and studios in Canada and states where filming is less expensive than in California.

Although there is a certain amount of featherbedding, the outlandish costs cannot be dumped into the laps of the unions. They are as much or more a result of $4 million star salaries—for example, Warren Beatty and Dustin Hoffman got a joint $10.5 million for "Ishtar," a box-office disaster. They are also caused by the inability of studios to keep control over producers and directors.

The "average" costs are skewed by such plump turkeys as "Howard the Duck" with a budget of $35 million, "Pirates" at $31 million and "Tai-Pan" at $25 million. But, even when a movie costs $10 million or $12 million, a studio has to aim for the largest possible audience. At those prices, a major studio rarely takes chances as United Artists could a decade ago when it gave Sylvester Stallone $1 million to make "Rocky." To feed their distribution machines, studios will often release low-budget independently made films, like "Can't Buy Me Love," which was a box-office success last summer for Disney.

By the way, "Howard the Duck," "Pirates," and "Tai-Pan" put together sold less than $25 million worth of tickets. Which reinforces a basic lesson about making movies. It's still a risky business. Certain stars—Clint Eastwood, Sylvester Stallone, Eddie Murphy, Arnold Schwarzenegger and Michael J. Fox included—can guarantee an audience for a movie. But only for the right movie. When Clint Eastwood tosses away his Magnum to play a dying singer in "Honkytonk Man" and Sylvester Stallone tries comedy opposite Dolly Parton in "Rhinestone" and Mr. Fox, as a factory worker, copes with a crazy mother and sister in "Light of Day," nobody buys tickets.

Today's Stars: Sequels

There is still a star system. Andrew McCarthy, for example, is a star for teen-age girls, as the success of "Mannequin" proves. But stars don't have the weight they carried when M-G-M meant Metro-Goldwyn-Mayer, and the company's sound stages and Chinese villages sprawled over a hundred acres in Culver City. Now MGM is just one more high-rise building in Beverly Hills, part of Kirk Kerkorian's MGM/UA Communications Co. And none of the five most successful movies of all time had a star. The only stars of "E.T.," "Star Wars," "Return of the Jedi," "The Empire Strikes Back" and "Jaws" were their directors and producers, Steven Spielberg and George Lucas.

The major star in Hollywood today—second only to Mr. Spielberg—is the sequel. "Crocodile Dundee II" is almost finished. "Rambo," "Rocky IV" and "The Karate Kid Part II" earned more money than their ancestors. Audiences are comfortable with the familiar, as the mathematical stew of "Jaws IV," "Star Trek IV" and "Superman IV" proves. The movies have always been an uneasy blend of art and commerce, but, today, commerce is the clear winner. George Lucas made nearly as much money from "Star Wars" toys and games as he did from the movies. And sequels provide the extra time to maximize the profits by turning the movie into a novel, a T-shirt, a lunchbox, and bedsheets.

No one has ever accused the movie industry of taking its heart out of its pocketbook. Luckily, blockbusters are unpredictable enough that a few serious personal films like Robert Benton's "Kramer vs. Kramer" and James L. Brooks's "Terms of Endearment" win Academy Awards and make lots of money. So studio heads occasionally gamble. No matter how confident they look in their Mercedes-Benzes and their Ray-Bans, all studio executives are convinced that success is impermanent. Even at Paramount—which has stayed at the top of the Ferris wheel for two years with "Top Gun," "Crocodile Dundee," "Beverly Hills Cop II," "The Untouchables" and now "Fatal Attraction" and "Planes, Trains and Automobiles"—there is terror.

In the decade since the success of "Star Wars" and "Animal House," the studios have concentrated on a core audience of 12 to 22. Now, as the pool of teen-agers diminishes, studios are having to raise their sights—or at least the age levels at which they aim their movies. And Hollywood's copycat mentality means that executives and producers will try to replicate good movies that sell tickets as well as bad films that sell tickets. It takes 18 months from first idea to final print. The success of a taut courtroom thriller, "Jagged Edge," in the fall of 1985 led to a number of films which were intended to appeal to adults last fall, including "Fatal Attraction."

Mini-Majors: Here Today

If you think of Hollywood as a three-layer cake with the major studios on top and the independents on the bottom, the rather squishy middle layer consists of the mini-majors or boutique companies. Mini-majors don't own studio lots and they tend to come and go pretty quickly. Because they don't have those thick libraries of old movies and television series to shore them against a bad year at the box office, they can run out of cash and customers.

Among the dimly remembered companies from a few years ago are Time-Life Films, Melvin Simon and ABC and CBS's film divisions. Today's mini-majors are Orion, Cannon, Lorimar, De Laurentiis Entertainment Group, Tri-Star and New World Pictures. Because producers and directors knock on the doors of the major studios first and travel to the smaller companies only when the majors turn them down, the mini-majors are likely to be offered less commercial—and sometimes more interesting—projects. It was Orion that distributed and partly financed "Platoon," reaping millions of dollars and four Academy Awards.

Orion appears in good shape, with a successful classics division, Woody Allen, a television series—"Cagney and Lacey"—to syndicate, as well as shrewd management. Tri-Star is backed by Coca-Cola. New World runs on low-budget and teen-age exploitation films. The others are cautionary examples of what can happen when you don't have a hit.

At the Cannes Film Festival two years ago, Menahem Golan, the chairman of Cannon, thumbed through a glossy brochure of his upcoming films and assured a reporter that he simply had to be successful because Cannon movies were financed by selling foreign and video-cassette rights before the camera started to whirl. Dino de Laurentiis, who could charm the devil and cooks the best pasta in Hollywood, used something of the same formula. But budgets at both companies expanded like rubber bands. De Laurentiis Entertainment Group had to write off the $18 million "King Kong Lives" as well as "Tai-Pan." And pre-sales don't cover these multi-million-dollar marketing costs.

Lorimar should survive because of its golden touch in television—its shows include "Dallas," "Falcon Crest" and "Knots Landing." But, with no box-office hits in 25 movies, Lorimar's dreams of becoming a major studio have been put on hold. It still owns the old M-G-M lot, but heavy debt has forced it to jettison television stations and two advertising agencies.

Coming Attractions

What of the future? There are a number of warning signs. The stock market meltdown means trouble for small companies. Selling shares in new companies will become considerably more difficult and a number of small companies whose stock has crashed will go under. And a few top executives are already murmuring that the theater chains may find themselves in massive trouble by the end of 1988 if the movie cycle ebbs as it seems to do every three years.

However, there is little doubt that the studios will continue to survive. Whether the multiplexes will prosper or die with the advent of high-definition television or pay-per-view or some other new revolutionary technical device is unknown. But whatever the technology, that technology will remain in the service of entertainment.

As one movie mogul said a few years ago, "It doesn't matter to me if people want to watch movies on soda crackers. I'll find a way to glue our films to saltines." ∎

PERSPECTIVE 2

Viewpoints on the Representation of Blacks in Films

In 1917, the black-owned Lincoln Motion Picture Company produced two movies, which were rented to black educational and social organizations, to overcome what the filmmakers believed was a negative image of blacks in America. The Lincoln Motion Picture Company soon folded, but criticism of racial stereotypes in the movies nonetheless has persisted as an important cultural issue.
    Consider:

1. Do you think the portrayals of blacks in films are attempts to reinforce the rest of society's stereotypes of black behavior? Why? Why not?

2. Do you agree with Richard Wesley that "mediocrity is much more easily rewarded in Hollywood than innovation"? Why? Why not?

3. What does Charles Fuller mean when he says that "making motion pictures is like getting into a car with a group of people"?

4. What does Reginald Hudlin mean when he says that in Hollywood "you're dealing with people who don't want to make any movie that they haven't seen before"? What is the effect of this attitude on black moviemakers, according to Hudlin?

Color Bars: A Panel Discussion

Over the decades, American movies have offered a cavalcade of stereotypical images—scolding mammies, shuffling chauffeurs, gun-toting avengers, genial sidekicks, sexy whores, and sly pimps. These clichés have one common denominator. They reflect the expectations and attitudes of white moviegoers rather than the realities of black life. In the late eighties, are white audiences, and the film industry, at last ready for films that deal with black life on its own terms?

This roundtable on the current state of black film features **Charles Fuller,** playwright, whose work for film and television includes *A Soldier's Story* (adapted from his Pulitzer Prize-winning play *A Soldier's Play*) and *A Gathering of Old Men*;

Richard Wesley (*Uptown Saturday Night, Native Son*), whose plays have been produced at Joseph Papp's Public Theater and on Broadway; writer-director **John Sayles** (*The Brother From Another Planet, Matewan,* and the upcoming *Eight Men Out*); and **Reginald Hudlin,** independent video- and filmmaker (*Reggie's World of Soul*), who is currently at work on his first feature film, *The Kold Waves*. Writer Thulani Davis moderates.

Thulani Davis: I recently read an article that asked, "Did Spike Lee pave the way for the independent black filmmaker?" And I thought: I have to call the writer on that, because I would say black filmmaker Oscar Micheaux paved the way fifty years ago. Micheaux made films for black audiences in segregated America. He didn't explain black life, since he knew his audience would already understand the language; he wasn't dealing with white people or white America. He *assumed* there were stories that were meaningful to *us*.

In the eighties, ironically, some of those assumptions that were developed in a segregated America have come back to us. Much as in a Micheaux film, the black world of *She's Gotta Have It* is not explained: Either you can roll with it or you can't. Reggie, you do something similar in *Reggie's World of Soul.* So I want to ask you about Reggie's world, as opposed to some world that we have all come to know quite well—like, let's say, Bill Cosby's world.

Reginald Hudlin: My mission is to put on film uncut funk, stuff that's never been seen. I've never heard real black kids say, "Hey, go to school!" or "Just say no!" Kids hear that and say, "Yuuh!" I've recently been out to Hollywood, and they have no idea what's going on. They go from an air-conditioned house into a car, into a parking garage, into an office. No funk, you know? Yet I can just open my window and the dialogue rolls right in. But the only way to make sure that stuff gets on-screen is to be in control of the project.

Davis: Charles, you've worked in Hollywood a long time. How important is control over the final product?

Charles Fuller: If I felt that I was going to spend my life making motion pictures, I would certainly want control. But it has been my experience that the contract they send me doesn't give me control of anything but the periods, commas, and semicolons.

Richard Wesley: My best ideas have never gone on the screen, because I simply wouldn't allow them to exist in a Hollywood matrix. A writer has infinitely more freedom in the theater than in film, unless, of course, he has the good fortune, wherewithal, and initiative to do what John [Sayles], Reggie, and Spike have done. But when I

was younger, I was not patient. I wanted to see my ideas come to fruition instantly, and the best way to do that was to go into the theater.

So over the last fifteen years, my worst ideas and my worst writing are on the screen. And I don't mind making that admission, because I learned very early on that mediocrity is much more easily rewarded in Hollywood than innovation. So I sit back and wait till my agent calls me and says, "So-and-so has an idea for a film. They would like you to write it." If it doesn't clash too much with my own political, social, and ideological positions, I'll do it.

For instance, in 1975, I wrote [the movie] *Let's Do It Again,* then I came home and wrote [the play] *The Mighty Gents. Mighty Gents* was my expression of myself; *Let's Do It Again* bought my car. I've been able to live like that for the last fifteen years.

When I worked with Sydney Poitier, it was understood from day one that he was the boss. The only ideas that would go down on paper were his ideas, and the dialogue would be preapproved by him. There were to be no African-American cultural colloquialisms, because he's not into that; the characters were to exist according to a particular formula. So you could get the work done pretty quickly.

Davis: Does the vast difference in the size of the audiences for theater and film affect you?

Fuller: The numbers in television are very exciting—I like reaching that many people in one shot. But I still prefer the stage to motion pictures; there's a lot more risk. Making motion pictures is like getting into a car with a group of people. You may be driving, but the director's beside you, the producer's behind you, and the actors are there, as well. But a play is like riding a motorcycle. If you fall off, you fall by yourself. And you also have the rain on you; you've got the wind blowing at you. I'd rather take risks on my own.

Davis: John Sayles probably feels like he's on a motorcycle most of the time. John, when you have an idea, how do you proceed?

John Sayles: You learn how screenplays get bent out of shape when you write them for other people. I co-wrote one movie called *The Challenge,* and the director said, "Well, I know they're all Chinese in the script, but let's make them all Japanese because I can get Toshiro Mifune and who knows the difference anyway?"

Davis: You don't even have to change the costumes . . .

Sayles: Right. So after that, I decided I would finance things myself. Now when I come up with a project, I ask myself: Is there any way I can control this whole thing? Or: Is there a way that I can put seed money in and talk other people into it? *Brother From Another Planet* was made with my own money.

Davis: When I saw *Brother,* I thought: A white person must have made this, because the notion that black people might be slaves on other planets seemed too much. But I also thought much of the time you had black humor down, and through the [white] aliens, you showed some black perceptions of white people that you might see in Richard Pryor.

Sayles: One of the reasons I stuck myself into the film as an alien was to make it accessible to white people as well as black, and I needed a guide. A lot of the film is about assimilation, and about how far you can go into another culture.

Every time that you write a character who's not like yourself, it's like refracting light, and the result is either clear or soupy. Hollywood makes soup of most people's experiences, be they black or white; there's not a whole lot of recognizable human behavior in Hollywood movies. So when I make an independent movie, I try to think: Who are the people that I know but whom I never see onscreen? I try to be more like a reporter, even if the film is science fiction. I'm trying to get somebody else's voice up there on the screen, and for a long time, a lot of people have been left out of the conversation.

I know a lot of black actors who are extremely underemployed. One of the revelations when we were casting *Brother From Another Planet* was reading [résumés that said] "Tony Award," and then you say, "Well, what did you do between 1967 and 1970?" and they say, "I didn't work."

Davis: How many black writers are there in Hollywood these days?

Wesley: Of the more than six thousand writers in the Writers Guild [West], just over 120 are black. And most of them have been writing for television: "The Cosby Show," "Amen," "Silver Spoons," "The Golden Girls," "Benson."

Davis: Has it changed much over the last fifteen or twenty years?

Fuller: My first job—I have to smile when I think about it—was offered to me by Anthony Quinn. We met at a hotel on Central Park South, and I was wearing a dashiki, combat boots, and an Afro out to here. Quinn and this Arab guy were telling me how *Across 110th Street* was the greatest film of the century. But they needed somebody to rewrite all of the love scenes between the black characters. At that time, 1972–1973, as far as I know, there were no more than fifteen black people working on the Coast as writers, and of the fifteen, only two were screenwriters, the rest were TV hacks.

Davis: A lot of our discussions often revolve around how black people represent the race, yet as a writer, I find that you rarely think of your characters in terms of: "This black man will be all black people." But do any of you have an agenda for your work?

Fuller: I stopped going to the movies when I was growing up, because I really didn't see any images of black men that supported the reality that I knew in my own life: The images I remember were Mantan Moreland, Willie Best, Stepin Fetchit. But my father and his brothers were a bad group of black men, and I knew a lot of black men who would kick your ass if you got in their face. *Those* were the kind of men I wanted to write about. So I'm always in the business of improving the image of black men in this world. OK? That is why I do it, why I started doing it, and I will die doing it.

Sayles: One reason there were a lot of characters in *Brother From Another Planet* was so you don't have to worry, "There's one black in this movie: Does he have to be a good guy?" It's funny—you see a lot of mainstream movies and TV shows with interracial gangs. But you go around New York and there aren't that many interracial gangs. Hollywood is not worried about being accurate, but about balance and protecting their flanks from any criticism.

Hudlin: I guess it's a little trickier for me because I do comedy, and the first thing that happens when we get political is we lose our sense of humor.

Now, if I'm going to take up ninety minutes of someone's time, I feel I have an obligation to say something. But at the same time, I want my film shown on Forty-second Street. When I think of an audience, I think of the people I grew up with back in East St. Louis: There are still these little blue-haired librarian ladies there who know who Grand Master Flash is, and liked their record "White Lines." The Corn Belt, the flyover audience, is much hipper than most people think.

Davis: Has Spike Lee's success made your projects more feasible?

Hudlin: Due to *She's Gotta Have It,* this is probably the best time in the history of the world to be a black filmmaker. All of a sudden, every studio in town is saying, "Yeah, black filmmakers! Are there any more? Get the fad book, Charlie!" But you have to be aware that it's a trend. And you're dealing with people who don't want to make any movie that they haven't seen before.

If you look at the history of independent film, there are movements. In my generation, there's a trend toward fiction, toward politics with enter-

tainment, as opposed to filmmakers in the seventies, who were fueled by the political fires of the time and made films that were much more straightforward, like a punch to the chest. Some people could see the current trend as a softening, an attempt to be more accessible to an audience.

Davis: Does that make it easier to raise money?

Hudlin: The problem has always been money. The key is not talent. There's always been an abundance of very talented filmmakers and writers and actors. And even people with extraordinary amounts of money in Hollywood often can't get a film made.

And while I've gotten a tremendous amount of support for my independent projects, there are lots of times when it comes down to the fact that no one cares but you. Then it's a matter of your willpower to create a film out of nothing. There's no other motivation. At some point, you use up all your fantasies of success, and there's nothing left but will: "I can't go down."

These days, there are more and more middle-class blacks who have disposable income to invest in ventures like film. A lot of these people wanted to be writers, but their mothers said, "I'm going to pay for you to go to school, so you're going to go to get your MBA." And these people with first-generation money see black independent film as a reasonable, [although] high-risk, investment.

But in terms of traditional sources of money for independent films, it's a bad time. Federal grants, where most independent filmmakers get their money, are controlled by the government—and we know who controls the government. Then you have PBS—again, heavily dependent on the government. If you've noticed, there are more black people on NBC than there on PBS. PBS is a useless entity. We should get rid of it. If I don't watch it, and I'm an independent filmmaker, who's watching it?

Davis: Are you better off when Hollywood is making movies like *The Color Purple* and *Native Son*?

Hudlin: I could care less about whether *The Color Purple* exists or not. I won't pay my six dollars to see it. But it does affect what I do tangentially. For a whole year I was asked, "You're a black filmmaker: What do you think about *The Color Purple?*" And I'd say, "I think you ought to go see a black independent film: That's what's happening."

Davis: Making a film is only half the problem, though. The other half is getting it distributed.

Sayles: There are two ways you can distribute a film. Either you make something that people want—or think they want—or else you drive the print around in your car. That's how Melvin Van Peebles distributed *Sweet Sweetback's Baadasssss Song*. No distributor wanted his movie. I think he went down to a theater on Peachtree Street in Atlanta and said, "Look, I will buy a month of your time." And the film ran for something like a year and a half.

Hudlin: Yeah, *Sweet Sweetback* was important not only because of its cathartic value—the main character kills a white cop and gets away with it—but because, as Van Peebles was quoted as saying, that movie made a million dollars before the first white person saw it. It was a business revolution as well as an aesthetic one.

Wesley: The current push toward black independent films is a swing of the pendulum back to the direction black filmmakers were moving in prior to the fifties. The Depression had catastrophic effects on the black community—black-owned banks, insurance companies, and other financial institutions—so the black community moved away from economic independence to a position of integration. But integration—like so many other things in America—is based on economic viability, and black people in this country have always been economically weak. And so they leave themselves open to the utter contempt of the people they're trying to integrate with.

When black filmmakers protest their position in Hollywood by taking up placards and picketing in front of a theater, saying, "Give us a job, give us a place in Hollywood," they're admitting that the black nation is an impotent essence within the United States. But black people have never been as impotent as some aspects of our leadership have attempted to make us feel over the past sixty years. Oscar Micheaux spent thirty years of his life, from 1918 through 1948, making at least a film a year, and he did it without one-tenth of the financial and educational resources that are available to black people today.

Today there are black-run theaters in major markets. But no black independent filmmakers have ever contacted them about the possibility of exhibiting their films there. It's a gold mine waiting to be tapped.

We now have—possibly for the first time in the history of our people—a generation of young black entrepreneurs. Kids coming out of Harvard, Wharton, and Howard don't want to become clerks for a Fortune 500 company only to realize that middle management is as far as they're going to go. They want to work on their own, and for a lot of them communications is the place to be. So I expect that you'll see more and more filmmakers and young business people coming together to form the kind of distribution and financial networks that are necessary to allow filmmakers to make the kinds of films they want. They're beginning to see the handwriting on the wall. ∎

PERSPECTIVE 3

Who Decides Which Movies Are Made?

Moviemakers constantly search for good stories to tell, but finding a riveting thriller or a sensitive romance means sifting through scripts for all the movies that *don't* get made. In this short article for the *Los Angeles Times,* David T. Friendly provides a quick glimpse at the process.

Consider:

1. What does the movie executive mean by the statement, "In this business, reading is information"?

2. Do you believe, as most of these scriptreaders assert, that every script is completely reviewed? Why? Why not?

3. What is the impression of the role that scriptreaders play in the movie-making process?

Hollywood Weekend: Word-Working Time

DAVID T. FRIENDLY

A t 3 p.m. last Sunday, as millions of Americans tuned in Super Bowl XXI, Karl Schanzer nestled in his favorite chair in the den—but the TV wasn't even turned on. Schanzer, a creative affairs executive for 20th Century Fox, was about two-thirds through his weekend homework. By kickoff he had already read eight scripts, a synopsis and a treatment—roughly 1,000 pages of text—and he still had five scripts left.

At 1 a.m. he finally crawled into bed. At 5 a.m. he got up to finish the last screenplay in time for the studio's Monday morning creative meeting. It was there that he finally learned the Giants had blown out the Broncos.

In Hollywood, weekend reading—not football or baseball—is the local, national and sometimes *only* pastime. This is the mental equivalent of prospecting for gold. Between Friday evening and Monday morning, studio executives must read anywhere from six to 16 scripts along with assorted synopses, treatments and the occasional novel. They plow through scripts in development at the studio, "spec" scripts (submissions on speculation from writers without deals yet), writing samples, "hot" submissions that come in at the last minute and, of course, scripts smuggled from competing studios.

David T. Friendly is a staff writer for the *Los Angeles Times.*

All in search of the mother lode, the undiscovered blockbuster.

Even for seasoned, lightning-fast readers, the quantity can be exhausting and frustrating. "There is always more to read than there is time for," says one junior executive. "If you're watching a game or something, there's always a script saying, 'Read me! Read me!' It's not the guilt that motivates you, it's wanting to have the edge on the competition. In this business, reading is information."

Every Friday afternoon the required reading list for the "weekend read" at each of the major studios gets distributed to the creative team. (Heavy reading dominates weekends because weekdays are devoted to a heavy diet of meetings, business meals and political in-fighting.) On Monday morning, in a meeting usually chaired by the president of production, each script is discussed and each of the executives is polled for reaction. While a short synopsis (known as "coverage") is attached to each of the scripts, most executives questioned in an informal sampling said they rarely skipped anything on the list.

"You always have homework Sunday night and invariably you are panicked Monday morning as you try to finish," says Jane Rosenthal, vice president of production at Walt Disney Pictures where the assigned reading last weekend totaled 13 items. "The reading load is excessive in this business."

Depending on reading speed, executives can easily spend the vast majority of their weekends with their noses buried in mountains of pages. "They really do all of that reading," says David Obst, a screenwriter and former executive at CBS Films. "People are willing to forgo any sort of life whatsoever to avoid the embarrassment of being unprepared. They are literally willing to drown in words."

So what do you do when you simply conked out in the first act of say, "Squadron" (inevitably described as "Platoon in Space"), and the boss wants to know what you thought? "I think it's dangerous to bluff," says one veteran executive. "You

can fool some of the people some of the time, but eventually you're going to get caught."

Others are not always so fastidious. "It depends on the situation," says one creative affairs executive who insisted on anonymity. "If everyone hated the script, it's easy, because then you just jump on the bandwagon. The problem is that if you say you liked it, you have to defend your opinion."

Executives are not always the best actors though. A high-priced comedy writer recalled— with understandable anger—a meeting with the head of a small production company. The company had commissioned a comedy script from him and his writing partner and insisted it be done in six weeks.

"We turn in the script and the meeting is canceled twice. Finally we go in to see the guy, and he starts off with some good notes and intelligent questions. Then he gets very vague. I finally ask him, 'Did you read this script?' And he says, 'Well, not all in one sitting.'"

Clearly, speed is a valuable asset in this game. The sheer volume of material is a good motivator, but most executives queried said that it takes between 1 and 1½ hours to read a typical 120-page script.

There are exceptions. Twenty-six-year-old Ellen Collett, a Yale graduate and now director of development at Gale Ann Hurd's ("Aliens") Pacific Western Productions, says she can read an entire script in 15 minutes. "I can do it between phone calls," she says. "On a good weekend, I can easily get through 20 scripts."

For those with less supernatural abilities, there are some shortcuts. Executives who instantly dislike the subject and the writing will usually quit reading by page 30. Jackie Gerken, executive in charge of creative affairs at DEG, says she limits herself to five scripts a day on Saturday and Sunday but reads all of them all the way through. "Any more than that and the material starts to blur," she says.

But when the weekend list is as high as 14 to 15 scripts, the executives sometimes have little choice. Climbing that paper mountain can create some difficulties in maintaining a social life. "You feel guilty if you are not reading for neglecting your work, and you feel guilty if you are reading for neglecting your personal life," says one exasperated woman executive. "You can't win."

It's not all drudgery though. The fulfillment comes, these folks say, when late at night, just when they're about to fade, they open the cover page of the 12th script of the weekend and suddenly they are entranced with a story or a dazzling writing style. "There's nothing better," says Disney's Rosenthal. "Then you just stare at that stack and say, 'Hmmm, what else is in there?'" ■

PERSPECTIVES 4 & 5

Who Should Hold Control Over Hollywood's Creative Output?

In 1986, MGM began "colorizing" several pre-1950s movies. Ted Turner, who owned MGM at the time, said that colorization would make the movies more appealing to television audiences because TV viewers do not like black-and-white movies. In 1988, Congress held hearings on the issue of artists' rights, and George Lucas and Steven Spielberg were among those who testified. Despite the pleas of Lucas and Spielberg, Turner and several others have continued the colorization process.

Consider:

1. Do you agree with George Lucas that "art in all forms belongs to the people and . . . must be protected by public institutions, not multinational corporations" Why? Why not?

2. Are movies, as Lucas asserts, parallel examples to other works of art that therefore should be protected by government action from alteration, such as changing the sound track, speeding up the pace, or editing out entire segments? Or should the owners of the movies have the right to make any changes they wish? Why?

3. What is the distinction that Spielberg makes between moral rights and economic rights as they apply to movies?

4. How does Spielberg propose to protect artists' moral rights? Do you believe his proposal would work? Why? Why not?

In Defense of Artists' Rights
'The Beginning of the Battle To Preserve Our Humanity'

GEORGE LUCAS

I am not coming to Washington as a writer-director, or as a producer, or as the chairman of a corporation, I am coming to speak as a citizen. A citizen of what I believe to be a great society. A great society that is in need of a moral anchor to help define and protect its intellectual and artistic heritage. Under current law, it is not being protected.

The recent destruction of our film heritage by colorization is only the tip of an iceberg. American law does not protect our painters, sculptors, recording artists, authors or filmmakers. If something is not done now to clearly state the moral rights of artists, current and future technologies will alter, mutilate and destroy for future generations the subtle human truths and highest human feeling that talented individuals within our society have created.

Art in all forms belongs to the people, and it must be protected by public institutions, not multinational corporations that are driven by greed and self-interest. A copyright is held in trust by its owner until it reverts to the public domain. It belongs to the American public; it is part of our common cultural history.

For more then 100 years, and in 76 nations, the arbitrator of a work of art has been the creator or creators of that work. Who better than the person whose hard labor and unique talent created the art should determine what is an appropriate alteration?

Buying a copyright does not make an artist. The copyright owner does not suddenly become talented or creative, does not suddenly have the ability to write a novel, play music, paint pictures or make films. An artist's creative talent is not something that can be transferred. And it is the artist's unique vision made concrete in art that must be respected, that piece of our creative heritage that must be protected.

America needs a declaration of moral rights for artists. Such a declaration has been provided for in the moral rights clause of the Berne Treaty.* It has worked for many years in many different countries. It is simple: A person's creative work "cannot be altered without that person's permission." Any legislation short of this is a patchwork that will confuse, and stir up ongoing debate.

Creative expression and imagination are human qualities; they are part of the very essence of what it is to be human. People who alter or destroy works of art, and our cultural heritage, for profit or as an exercise of power are barbarians, and if the laws of the United States continue to condone this behavior, we will become a barbaric society.

The preservation of our cultural heritage may not seem to be as politically sensitive an issue as "when life begins" or whether it should be terminated, but it is just as relevant and important because it goes to the heart of what sets mankind apart. Creative expression is at the core of our

---

George Lucas's film successes include "Star Wars" and "Return of the Jedi." He is chairman of the board of Lucasfilm.

*Author's Note: The 100-year-old Berne Treaty established international copyright standards for 76 countries.

humanness. Art is a distinctly human endeavor. We must have respect for it if we are to have any respect for the human race.

This is just the beginning of the battle to preserve our humanity. Today, engineers with their computers can add color to black-and-white movies, change the sound track, speed up the pace and add or subtract material to the philosophical taste of the copyright holder. Tomorrow, more advanced technology will be able to replace actors with "fresher faces," or alter dialogue and change the movement of the actor's lips to match. It will soon be possible to create a new "original" negative with whatever changes or alterations the copyright holder of the moment desires.

The copyright holders, so far, have not been completely diligent in preserving the original negatives of films they control. To reconstruct old negatives, many archivists have had to go to Eastern Bloc countries where American films have been better preserved. In the future it will become even easier for old negatives to become lost and be "replaced" by new, altered negatives. This would be a great loss to our society. Our cultural history must not be allowed to be rewritten.

The other arts have not been hit quite as hard as film. But one day, it may also be profitable to alter on a massive scale paintings, literature or a recording artist's performance. A clear statement of our national values must be made now. Are we going to be a society totally controlled by greed and profit? Congress makes the laws, and laws represent an awareness of a higher moral order. Law by and for greed denies our humanness.

The assurance of the artist's moral rights adds stability. The corporations, which hold many of the copyrights, are unstable entities. They are bought and sold, and corporate officers change on a regular basis. There is nothing to stop American films, records, books, and paintings from being sold to a foreign entity or an egocentric gangster who would change our cultural heritage to suit his personal taste.

I accuse the companies and groups who say the U.S. law is sufficient of misleading the Congress and the American people for their own economic self-interest.

I accuse the Motion Picture Association, for example, of seeking to protect their own narrow interest on the issue of film piracy and thereby save themselves $1 billion, without acknowledging the moral rights of the artists who created those films.

I accuse the corporations that oppose the moral rights of the artist of being dishonest and insensitive to America's cultural heritage and of being interested only in their quarterly bottom line, and not in the long-term interest of the nation.

The public's interest should ultimately dominate all other interests. And the proof of that is that even a copyright law permits the creators and their estate only a limited time to enjoy the economic fruits of that work. Ultimately that work returns to the public domain, and the public should receive what it paid for by virtue of the taxes and military service used to preserve the cultural environment in which these things could be created.

That's why the U.S. Senate should weigh carefully the fate to our cultural heritage. Attention should be paid to this question of our human soul, and not simply to the accounting procedures and monetary considerations. Attention must be paid to the interest of those who are yet unborn, who should be able to see this generation as it saw itself, and the past generation as it saw itself, and how it worked with the mediums that were available to it, whether with a black-and-white palette or a color palette.

There are those who say American law is sufficient. That's an outrage! It's not sufficient! If it was sufficient, why would I have to testify before the Senate? Why would John Huston have been so studiously ignored when he protested the colorization of "The Maltese Falcon"? Why are films cut up and butchered without so much as a holler of protest? Where can an artist go to protest?

Vandalizing a work of art and then putting a disclaimer on it saying this was not what the artist originally intended is not sufficient. Excluding some artists from moral rights protection because they were commissioned to do a piece is not sufficient. Is an artist who works for hire any less of an artist? Is the Sistine Chapel ceiling any less a work of art?

I hope the Senate will have the courage to lead America in acknowledging the importance of American art to the human race and extend proper protection to the creators of that art—as it is accorded them in much of the rest of the world communities. ■

In Defense of Artists' Rights
The Creation of Art Is Not a Democratic Process

STEVEN SPIELBERG

The Berne Treaty gives voice to the idea that art and the artist are not commodities to be treated like sausage. The Berne Treaty gives to the artist a specific standing to object to defacement of his/her work and it recognizes moral rights as distinct from economic rights. That distinction is at the heart of the debate.

To sign the treaty, a country must have a moral rights concept in its domestic law sufficiently clear to comply with the requirements of the treaty. The powerful economic interests that oppose moral rights for artists maintain that U.S. law *is* sufficient to qualify for Berne membership and no further recognition need be given to the moral rights of its artists. No film fantasy is as outlandish as that claim.

Under what law is the work of film artists, for instance, protected for today and for future generations? Where is the law that defines their moral rights?

What law gave Frank Capra moral rights to protest the colorization of "It's a Wonderful Life"?

What law gave John Huston legal support to seek redress for his disgust at a similar act of defacement performed on "The Maltese Falcon"?

What law protects those of our colleagues, living and dead, whose honor and reputations are offended by the electronic speeding up or slowing down of their films, or the capricious editing of scenes to fit the films into arbitrary time slots?

What law protects against the offense of honor and reputation of our *foreign* colleagues whose films undergo similar humiliations when they are exhibited in the United States? Sir David Lean has complained that nowhere in the world can "Dr. Zhivago" be seen as he originally made it.

Bertrand Tavernier, president of the French Society of Film Directors, has said that his first introduction to the United States was through

Producer-director Steven Spielberg's films include "Jaws," "E.T.," "Back to the Future," and "Empire of the Sun." He heads his own company, Amblin Entertainment.

American films of the '30s and '40s. He saw "Mr. Smith Goes to Washington" and applauded when Jimmy Stewart, as the idealistic young senator, declared that "Lost causes are the only kind worth fighting for." Tavernier saw and understood that perseverance and morality could persuade the Senate.

The last refuge of those who oppose strong moral rights legislation is the absurd contention that if the original negative is untouched, the "real" picture is somehow still intact. This is an argument made of nonsense. No one sees the original negative. Ever! They are made to be duplicated. It is in that duplication that they have their only life and their only audience.

Not a single original negative ever won an award, not a single original negative ever made someone laugh or cry.

There are those who say the marketplace enjoys this defacement, wants to see black-and-white films in pastel colors and will tolerate any disfigurement. Comments like those reveal a lack of understanding of the creative process. The creation of art is not a democratic process, and in the very tyranny of its defined vision lies its value to the nation. The public has no right to vote on whether a black-and-white film is to be colored anymore than it has the right to vote on how the scenes should be written, whether the next angle should be a close-up or a wide shot, whether music should enter or fade out or what kind it should be, or on any of the thousands of other artistic choices made by the artist in the turbulent process of creation. The public does have a right to accept or reject the result but not to participate in its creation.

If our adversaries think the current copyright law protects us, they are wrong. To comply with the law's warnings about misrepresentations, a film defacer would merely have to attach a disclaimer before the film is projected, stating that it has been colorized, or electronically shortened, that scenes have been edited, that the composition has been changed or other "improvements" have been added.

The current law does not protect *the film,* it does not protect *the artists.* It protects *the con-*

sumer and does not in any way bestow on the United States the credentials that clearly are required by the Berne Treaty.

How did this magical notion arrive that something is there that isn't there? Powerful economic interests have gathered and in a massive and cynical act of self-service, they have invented it. They have performed this reverse intellectual somersault to rationalize their insensitive and untenable position; namely, that what is good for their special interest is good for the U.S.A.

A community of artists also lives, has a voice and contributes to the national health and welfare. We request that the Congress rebalance the competing interests of "show" and "business." We urge that Berne-implementing legislation contain our proposal that without the agreement and permission of the two artistic authors (the principal director and principal screen writer), no material alterations may be made in a film following its first, paid, public exhibition.

In the interest of fair play and honor among the civilized nations of the world, we ask the Senate to stand up and perform an act of political courage; to resist the economic powers that insist you serve them only and not us; to recognize the moral principal involved here as of greater importance to our national self-esteem than another buck on the bottom line; to grant that Berne requires moral rights in American law *that do not now exist.* ∎

CHAPTER SIX

For Further Reading

Books

Tino Balio, *The American Film Industry* (Madison: University of Wisconsin Press, 1976).

Jack E. Ellis, *A History of American Film,* 2nd ed. (Englewood Cliffs: Prentice-Hall, 1985).

Robert Sklar, *Movie-Made America* (New York: Random House, 1975).

Jason E. Squire, (ed.), *The Movie Business Book* (New York: Simon & Schuster, 1983).

G. S. Watkins, (ed.), *The Motion Picture Industry* (Philadelphia: American Academy of Political and Social Science, 1947).

Periodicals

American Film

Film Comment

Hollywood Reporter

Variety

Video Times

The Recording Industry

CHAPTER SEVEN

Electronic Composers

As synthesizers replace traditional instruments, music has gone digital. Reproducing the sounds of an entire orchestra with one keyboard is affordable for even the amateur musician. In this article from *Business Week,* the authors describe the potential of digital sound.

Consider:

1. How have synthesizers changed the economics of the music business?

2. What musical benefits do music systems like the Kurzweil 250 offer for musicians and composers?

3. What are the benefits of MIDI?

4. Do you agree that musicians are being given unprecedented creative tools or will all the music eventually sound the same? Explain.

Music Is Alive with the Sound of High Tech

TERRI THOMPSON, CARLO WOLFF, and DAN COOK

In the 1960s composer Walter Carlos created a sensation with a recording he called *Switched-On Bach.* Using one of the first music synthesizers, devices that electronically mimic a variety of musical instruments, Carlos spent months creating sounds, recording the music bit by bit, and editing together thousands of snippets of tape. The result: a top-selling album of electronically produced classical compositions that sounded as if they were played on a harpsichord—sort of.

From Bach to rock, musical technology has changed since then. Carlos still flouts convention:

Terri Thompson, Carlo Wolff, and Dan Cook are reporters for *Business Week* magazine.

He's had a sex-change operation and now is called Wendy. But electronic music is no longer the stuff of the avant-garde. These days, anyone capable of playing a keyboard instrument can be a one-man band. For only hundreds of dollars, today's electronic instruments will respond with sounds respectably close to those of a concert grand piano, a whole orchestra, a vast choir, or just about anything that the player can dream up.

Sax and Violins. With a technique called digital sampling, the sound of a car door slamming or a dog barking can be turned into music that can be played at any pitch. These sounds are captured and stored as numerical values on floppy disks; to clone sounds, the sampler merely recalculates the numerical values. Flip a switch and you can "sample" patches of existing recordings. If you don't like it as a violin, punch a key and it's a saxophone. If you want to see it as sheet music, print it with a personal computer.

Artists from Stevie Wonder to French composer-conductor Pierre Boulez are embracing the new technology. Instead of practicing in soundproof rooms or copying sheet music a note at a time, musicians wearing headphones are sitting at music workstations that look more like a control panel at NASA than musical instruments. Indeed, the new technology is revolutionizing the way music is played, composed, studied—and enjoyed.

Even New York's Juilliard School, the most respected conservatory in the U.S. and a bastion of classicism, has embraced high tech. It opened its first electronic studio in 1987 thanks to donations of synthesizers and music editing equipment from Yamaha International Corp., a leading producer of new music technology. "It's the wave of the future," says Dean Bruce MacCombie. "Better to get involved with it than to pretend it doesn't exist."

It exists, all right. Sales of electronic keyboards and related equipment jumped more than 40% in 1986, to $1.3 billion, according to the American Music Conference, a nonprofit organization that promotes music participation by amateurs. In 1986, Americans bought 2.6 million electronic keyboards—twice the number sold in 1985 and more than five times the 1984 total. They also bought 350,000 synthesizers in 1986, compared with 220,000 in 1985. That's because the plunging cost of the computer power needed to make electronic systems work means they are affordable to more people. At the same time, escalating labor and material costs have caused prices for acoustic pianos to nearly double over the past five years. Last year just 166,555 new pianos were sold, compared with 282,172 in 1978.

Today an estimated 25 million people in the U.S. play keyboard instruments. And thanks to the new musical technology, predicts Robert Moog, the first to use a keyboard rather than knobs and dials on a synthesizer in the early 1960s, "musical activity on the part of amateurs will increase."

Despite the pioneering developments in the U.S., it took the Japanese to make the market sing. Composer Larry Fast, who has been creating synthesizer music for 20 years, remembers working on a synthesizer that used a mainframe computer and cost $2 million when he was a researcher at AT&T Bell Laboratories in Murray Hill, N.J., in the 1970s. But in 1983, Yamaha swept into the U.S. with its DX7. The portable keyboard did everything the monster at Bell Labs could—and sold for $2,000. Today, for a mere $400, "you can get a Yamaha synthesizer with features that were lacking in the DX7," says Fast. And other foreign manufacturers, including Casio, Akai, Roland, and Korg, now dominate the market along with Yamaha.

Steinway Sound. The U.S. is not completely out of the picture, however. Although Moog's original company folded in 1977, he has joined forces with Raymond C. Kurzweil, a computer scientist and entrepreneur, who has put his small, Waltham (Mass.) company, Kurzweil Music Systems Inc., at the forefront of electronic music. While many developers of electronic instruments concentrated on adding new sounds to composers' vocabularies, Kurzweil set out to reproduce faithfully the sound of traditional instruments and the response of high-quality piano keyboards.

In 1983, Kurzweil introduced its prototype of the Kurzweil 250. Instead of using analog circuits, like those in the first electronic synthesizers, this new generation of musical instrument has gone digital. To create the sound of, say, a key on a Steinway piano, it simply calls from its computer memory the sound of that note and reproduces it through speakers. To all but the most discerning, the sound is very close to the real thing.

But that system—and similar ones from Ensoniq, E-mu Systems, Lowrey Electronics, Oberheim Electronics, Sequential Circuits, and Yamaha—can do far more. They sound just as good mimicking a violin, a flute, or a massive chorus. And they can do all those things at once.

The Electronic Keyboard Crescendo

Retail sales, in millions

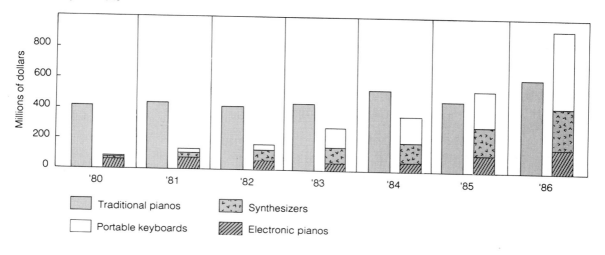

A musician can "layer" sounds on top of one another, so a single keystroke can simultaneously produce the same note sounded by a guitar, piano, or a full string section. Or, with a so-called sequencer function, the musician can play a part on one instrument and store it, then add another part while the first part is being played back, and so on, gradually creating a full orchestra.

But it's not just the individual instruments that are driving the revolution in music. It is an industry standard known as MIDI, short for Musical Instrument Digital Interface. While companies trying to automate factories still can't agree on protocols that will let their dissimilar equipment communicate, in 1983 music makers agreed on MIDI. It allows a musician to hook up synthesizers, electronic drums, and organs to a single keyboard and connect the entire system to a personal computer, regardless of the manufacturer. MIDI is the conduit through which all the signals pass from one instrument to another.

That way, all the information can be stored in digital form in the computer's memory, rather than on recording tape. So the composer can manipulate it in ways that were unheard of a few years ago. Play a tune on the keyboard, and the written notes appear on the computer screen. Change a note on the screen, and the computer plays back the corrected version. Don't like the tempo? Have the computer change it. Or alter the key, or change the violin part to a flute. Nor does the composer have to be adept at the keyboard. A saxophone player, for example, can hook up a so-called "wind-controller" and play music into the system, then tell the composer to play it back through the synthesizer. Or MIDI can turn the sound from the saxophone into an entire orchestra.

Miami Heist? Professional musicians quickly saw the potential in linking instruments to computers. Since the MIDI standard was introduced, sales of computer hardware and software based on MIDI have shot up to about $500 million, and the market is expected to double within the next three years. The latest generation of personal computers from Apple, Atari, Commodore, and IBM accommodates the technology. Many brands of musical software are available for $50 to $500. And the five top manufacturers of synthesizers are building MIDI into all but their lowest-priced instruments.

Such changes are not without controversy. The biggest battle centers around the so-called digital sampling technology. These devices are so adept at stealing others' sounds—even styles and human voices—that composers soon will have at their disposal unlimited electronic "sidemen" stored on computer chips. Put Beverly Sills singing a high C into the memory, for instance, and a digital sampler can play it back as a high D, or any other note. Hit two keys at once, and you hear two Beverly Sills. Play a few notes in sequence, and you have Sills singing a melody she never sang before.

Professional musicians have taken the issue to court. David Earl Johnson, a struggling percussionist, is suing the producers of *Miami Vice,* claiming the theme music of the popular TV show rips off his conga sound. Johnson says that the composer of the score with the pulsating beat had sampled his conga playing at a recording session and later used his sound without compensating him. To protect his latest record album, Frank Zappa has taken the precaution of copyrighting against sampling.

Now that entire orchestras can be replaced by synthesizers, some worry that thousands of musicians may be put out of work. Others fear that music as an artistic endeavor will stagnate as the new crop of musicians becomes ever more dependent on technology.

Most, though, believe new technology is giving musicians unprecedented creative tools. After all, what past composer could invent new instruments at will, make music from any sound, and hear their compositions just seconds after they were written?

"We want to revolutionize music making," says Jeffrey G. Gusman, R&D manager at Yamaha Communications Center Inc. in New York. "We are supplying the artist with the tools he needs." Even Bruce A. Stevens, president of venerable piano maker Steinway & Sons, believes "there is a world of opportunity for the use of computers" in music. Nor does he expect it to put him out of business. He is convinced that after musicians learn how to play an electronic keyboard, they'll want to upgrade to a fine acoustic piano.

No one is happier with the new wind blowing through music than Wendy Carlos. It will lead to "a lot of alternative styles," she says. "This is the first time I've felt I haven't needed to apologize for producing electronic music." ∎

PERSPECTIVE 2

Recording Industry Sales

These charts show that although the recording industry is collecting more money, the sales of most types of recordings have declined. Sales of cassettes and compact discs are up, but LP and singles sales fell substantially.

Records Growing Again . . . But Fewer Bright Spots

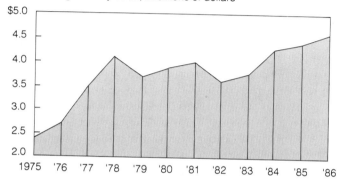

Total recording industry sales, in billions of dollars

Recording industry sales by type

	1986 Sales (in millions)	Change from 1985
Cassettes	$2,489.5	+4%
LPs	983.0	-23
CDs	930.1	+139
Singles	228.1	-19
8-Tracks	10.5	-58

PERSPECTIVE 3

The Role of Music in Our Lives

Music is all around us today—on the radio, in the office, in the market and the shopping mall. In this essay, Bernard Holland asserts that the sheer availability of music has somehow cheapened it, taken away its special pleasures.
    Consider:

1. What does Bernard Holland mean when he says that "the musician who makes time start and stop plays at being God"?

2. Do you agree with Holland that "the wondrous accessibility [of the great works of music] has rendered them invisible"? Why? Why not?

3. Has music's accessibility ruined your enjoyment of it? Why? Why not?

A New and Awful Silence
Serious Music Is Losing Its Measure

BERNARD HOLLAND

The electric clocks in my house keep better time than the ones I wind, yet I scarcely look at them. It is the ticking, I think, that comforts me. I like to lean my ear against these various pendulums and, back and forth, gently rock my life away.

These ticks and tocks give a meter to the passage of the day; they are a metaphor for silence. Silence, after all, is not an absence of noise but a subtle acknowledgment of this metronomic beat, the force that both brings new life and inscribes tomorrow's obituaries. There is luxury and terror in this act of resignation, this silent attention to the ticking of our lives.

Silence's most eloquent contradiction is music—not because music *breaks* silence with its sounds but also it interrupts its motion. All the arts do this: books freeze events between two covers, pictures pin them against a wall. But music goes viscerally to the source of our mortality. It stops time in its tracks and reinvents it. What a supernatural act it is to command a tempo and a rhythm, to set time in motion and bring it to a halt. In a life of temporal endlessness, the musician who makes time start and stop plays at being God. This is music's comfort and its triumph: that somewhere there exists an antidote for decay.

Music scarcely exists anymore, having multiplied itself into silence. This probably makes no sense at all to you, but let my try to explain. To call music an interruption is also to say it is an event, something that can seize our attention only if it is preceded by uneventfulness, and then succeeded by it. When I first heard Bach's B minor Mass some thirty-five years ago, that's how I experienced it—like a monolith rising out of an empty plain, a magisterial presence defined by the emptiness around it.

I fear I shall never have that sensation again. The plain is no longer empty. Developers have taken it over. On my FM radio the B minor Mass is now but a commercial break away from the *Goldberg Variations* and the *St. Matthew Passion*. My days have become chains of such great events.

The technologies of the ear (the radio, the record player, the compact disc) both give and take away. How marvelous that Mozart's twenty-seven piano concertos, Beethoven's nine symphonies, and Bartók's six quartets are only fingertips away. And how horrible. It is a cruel trick that the wondrous accessiblity of these great works has rendered them invisible.

We have, of course, only ourselves to blame. Science and the arts once met in a world of mutual congratulation. Stars moved to the music of the spheres; ancient musicians sang to the Pythagorean scales, serenely conscious of their geometric purity. But science is no longer as sure of its answers. Solutions retreat as we approach them. Thus we calculate our progress in degrees.

This calculation has made of us a society of measures—how tensile the steel, how quick the 100-meter dash, how slow the drip from the ketchup bottle. *How well* has given way to *how much, how many*.

So it should not surprise us that music has become quantitative too. One record on my shelf fills me with wisdom; three more records multi-

---

Bernard Holland is a music critic of the *New York Times*.

ply it. One of my colleagues claims more than 50,000 items in his collection, and I know hardly any in my business with fewer than 10,000. Such a privilege—to have in one's home the capacity to hear Brahms's Fourth Symphony played nineteen different ways!

In the South of my youth, where concerts were as rare as eclipses of the moon and Ernest Tubb ruled the airwaves, each new long-playing record was a discovery; the ecstasy was in that first moment, never to be relived. Listening machines and their paraphernalia advertise to us what they cannot fulfill—a reenactment of epiphanies. Each new Brahms Fourth promises such a rediscovery. Will Toscanini via RCA, or Bruno Walter according to CBS, bring us close enough to touch that first thrill again? Some avenues bring us nearer than others, but none near enough. We measure these nearnesses one against the other, and ask: who shall be first among Brahms Fourths?

Fishing in my pitiful collection of records the other day (my filing system is of the I Ching persuasion), I did find a recording of Brahms's Fourth. I put it back on the shelf, I'm not quite sure where. I am not worried. I know how it goes—the key of E minor, two beats to the measure, upbeat swoops down, upbeat swoops up, very beautiful in its austere way. This is how I relive (and therefore live) this music—in my imagination.

The imagination is our great healer. It is also the world's leading interpreter of the Brahms Fourth Symphony. The nineteen performances that other critics have at their fingertips seem puny beside it. And my imagination does other things—it calms the wow in my turntable, smooths the distortion of my woofer.

The walls of records in my colleagues' homes, arranged, catalogued, cross-catalogued; the giant loudspeakers the size of refrigerators looming in their living rooms—all help explain to me why musical masterpieces no longer move me as they once did. The technological prowess of these new instruments of music is amazing. But they cost dearly: they usurp our capacity to dream. As a young man, I cherished the B minor Mass, the *Quartet for the End of Time,* the *Symphony of Psalms* principally as voices speaking within me. On my shelf today, they are measured like real estate, by the frontage foot.

The ear plots its escape, but fails. Even the streets are not safe, and subway platforms ring with Bach's solo violin sonatas or the Spanish guitar. New England villages worthy of two gas pumps now add summer music festivals to their inventories. One approaches their outskirts apprehensive, car windows rolled shut. In restaurants, Mozart serves as aural garnish for the fish of the day.

We are strangled by the very volume of our resources, dwarfed by them too. I think back to my friend with his claim to 50,000 records. How small he seems beside them, like a computer scientist facing an immensely potent machine that he does not quite know how to address. Modern science instructs us—shames us with the fact—that the universe has become very big and we very small. Beethoven, you will remember, promised us to take fate by the throat; one wonders if its size today might not exceed his grasp.

Music, indeed, seems to have become that popular science-fiction nightmare—the manmade creature that grows beyond expectations, seizes autonomy, and smothers its masters. The quartets, the masses, the songs and sonatas that once rose as isolated protests against the vastness of time have become something very different. They have swollen, then merged and melted into time's fabric. They have become a form of silence themselves. ∎

The Cost of Sound

The recording industry includes not only all the recording artists, but also all the employees of recording studios that produce the sounds you hear. This article describes the interrelationship between recording company profits and the recording studio business.

Consider:

1. What major factors have affected recording studio profits in the last ten years?
2. How does changing technology affect the costs?
3. What is "organic recording"? Do you agree that it may be the trend for future music? Why? Why not?

The Beat Goes On, But It Costs Lots More

WILLIAM K. KNOEDELSEDER JR.

When a singer goes into a recording studio to cut an album, the money for the session is usually paid by a record company in the form of an advance against the artist's royalties on the eventual sale of the record.

The success of the studio business, therefore, is tied directly to the performance of the record industry at large. In recent years, that has meant hard times for studio operators.

For example, according to the Recording Industry Association of America, the major record companies released 4,170 new albums in 1978. The following year, as the record industry began to feel the effects of declining sales, only 3,575 new albums were released.

William K. Knoedelseder Jr. is a writer for the *Los Angeles Times*.

In 1980, the number fell to 3,000. By 1984, with the record industry in a full-blown depression, the number had dropped to 2,170.

In 1985, the number of new releases started inching upward again as the record industry began recovering from its slump.

The problem is, the recovery has been fueled largely by the sale of older records reissued on compact disks—records that don't require additional time at the recording studio. In 1987, with record company profits at an all-time high, the major companies released only 2,406 new albums—still far below their output 10 years ago.

Making matters worse for the studios, belt-tightening by the record companies has reduced the average recording budget for an album from about $125,000 a few years ago to between

$80,000 and $100,000 today, according to studio operators.

And with home studios siphoning off recording time, studio operators estimate that their share of an average album's recording budget has fallen to between 50 and 60 percent.

In 1967, the Beatles' classic album "Sgt. Pepper's Lonely Hearts Club Band" was recorded using what was then state-of-the-art studio technology: a four-track tape-recording machine. That meant that four different elements—vocals, guitars, drums and piano—were recorded separately and then combined on a single half-inch tape.

In the ensuing 21 years, technological advances in sound recording have made four-track recording seem almost as primitive as, well, chiseling in stone.

Today, the state of the art is 48-track recording. For music lovers, the advances have meant better-sounding records; for studio operators, they've meant huge expenses. A 24-track recorder—considered the minimum for professional recording—can cost $25,000 to $90,000. A 32-track digital recorder costs about $140,000.

One studio operator estimates that to keep up with technology and remain competitive, a studio must completely upgrade its equipment "every 2½ or three years—consoles, tape machines, new mikes, the whole schmear."

When Chris Stone opened his famous Record Plant studio in 1968, "fully equipped, including construction, right down to the floor tile, it cost $75,000," he said. "Today, that same room would cost $1.5 million."

After a five-year onslaught of computerized pop music—what one sound engineer described as "two-skinny English kids, a synthesizer and a drum machine"—studio operators say they are witnessing a backlash.

"Right now, the cutting edge is live music; some of the new young bands are looking down on synthesized sound," said one veteran recorder, adding with a chuckle: "They actually think they've discovered something new; they're calling it 'organic recording.'" ■

CHAPTER SEVEN

For Further Reading

Books

R. Serge Denisoff, *Solid Gold* (New Brunswick: Transaction Books, 1975).

Robert Metz, *CBS: Reflections in a Bloodshot Eye* (Chicago: Playboy Press, 1975).

James R. Smart, *A Wonderful Invention: A Brief History of the Phonograph from Tinfoil to the LP* (Washington: Library of Congress, 1977).

Don Weller, *The Motown Story* (New York: Scribner's, 1985).

Periodicals

Billboard

Down Beat

Music Index (a separate index that covers articles on the music industry)

Rolling Stone

The Book Publishing Industry

PERSPECTIVE 1

How Much Do Authors Earn?

In the only comprehensive contemporary study of authors' earnings, Paul William Kingston and Jonathan R. Cole reveal that very few authors are rich. Published in 1986, this study of more than 2,000 authors by the Columbia University Center for the Social Sciences and the Authors' Guild Foundation shows that millionaire authors like Judith Krantz and Stephen King are extremely rare. Instead, most writers pay for their writing time by holding other jobs. (The study was conducted in 1979, and although the dollar amounts today would be somewhat higher, the percentages of writing income would be about the same.)

Consider:

1. What were the three factors that transformed writing in the 1800s into a somewhat profitable profession?

2. What do the authors mean when they say that writing "remains a profession which does not reflect the normal correlation between income and esteem"?

3. According to the survey, which type of writing earned the most imcome for writers?

4. How would you characterize the working life of today's typical writer, based on these results?

The Wages of Writing

PAUL WILLIAM KINGSTON and JONATHAN R. COLE

Robert Benchley once defined a freelance writer as "one who gets paid per word, per piece, or perhaps." . . . In the public mind, the prevailing stereotypes of this [the writer's] condition appear to consist of contradictory images. One version is of the writer living in a cluttered garret working away on manuscripts, living in relative poverty. A contrasting image is of the author as the well-rewarded "talent," an image no doubt fostered by blockbuster contracts for paperback and movie rights. Such is the nature of stereotypes, of course, that one can find some measure of truth in both these images. . . .

The American experience with professional authorship did not really reach a take-off stage until the first quarter of the nineteenth century.

Paul William Kingston is Assistant Professor of Sociology at the University of Virginia. Jonathan R. Cole is Professor of Sociology and Director of the Center for the Social Sciences at Columbia University.

Although gothic adventures produced in England and written principally by women working in anonymous secrecy were imported to America, there was no fortune to be made in that business. Most women authors during that period received a small flat fee—somewhere between five and twenty guineas per book. As William Charvat points out, it was not until Cooper's success in the early 1820s that we could claim to have one single American novelist who was financially successful. In fact, he dates the profession of authorship in the United States to the 1820s when James Fenimore Cooper and Washington Irving discovered that readers were willing to buy their books on a regular basis.

Charvat points to three key factors that transformed the occupation of writing into one which was more profitable. For one, authors began to write on diverse subjects of general interest. This broke down formal barriers between reading groups, and books began to appeal to a wider audience among those who were literate. For another, an increasing number of people were able and willing to pay for books; others could get them through a growing number of circulating libraries. Finally, authors were helped by the astuteness, entrepreneurial spirit, and increasing business experience among publishers, who began to forge a closer linkage between authors and their readers. While these factors improved the economic condition of authors, they were themselves dependent on the ability of authors to produce manuscripts in a timely fashion and on the increased prestige of authorship within the society.

What were the actual incomes of American authors during the middle half of the nineteenth century? As noted, until the 1820s no American novelist was financially successful. Toward midcentury the pattern that we observe today held for most men and women of letters. The vast majority of active authors, many of whom had significant reputations, worked only part time at writing. Most of these writers could not make ends meet on writing-related income. In order for them to pursue their writing interests, they had to hold second jobs. In fact, by midcentury there were probably more part-time, or what we have called the "intermittent full-time," authors than there were writers devoting themselves exclusively to literary activities.

It was not unusual for prestigious writers to secure relatively lucrative positions through political patronage. Hawthorne's job at the Boston Custom-House, arranged by friends, is a case in point. This position protected him from financial bad weather for quite some time. Hawthorne notes, however, in "The Custom-House," which appears as an introduction to the second edition of *The Scarlet Letter,* that few of his colleagues at the custom-house even knew of his work, and if they did, they could not have been less interested:

None of them, I presume, had ever read a page of my inditing, or would have cared a fig the more for me, if they had read them all; nor would have mended the matter, in the least, had those same unprofitable pages been written with a pen like that of Burns or of Chaucer, each of whom was a Custom-House officer in his day, as well as I. It is a good lesson—though it may often be a hard one—for a man who has dreamed of literary fame, and of making for himself a rank among the world's dignitaries by such means, to step aside out of the narrow circle in which his claims are recognized, and to find how utterly devoid of significance, beyond that circle, is all that he achieves, and all he aims at.

Other notable nineteenth-century authors who had a difficult time of it included Thoreau, who lived from hand to mouth and apparently did not mind, and Emerson who wrote in 1838 that he owned a house, $22,000 worth of stocks earning 6%, and an income from lectures varying from $400 to $800 a year. Even though some novelists began to live off their writing by the 1820s, it was not until after the Civil War that a single American poet could live comfortably with income derived from writing.

At the time of his death in 1891, Melville left an estate worth $13,261.31. Melville's will shows that he had about $4,500 in cash, another $8,000 in U.S. registered bonds, and $600 worth of personal books, which numbered roughly 1,000 volumes. After expenses, the net value of the estate then came to approximately $12,000.

The total income that Melville derived from English and American sales of his first five books as well as the English sale of his sixth, *Moby Dick,* was approximately $8,000, amounting to roughly $1,600 a year for five years, but his liabilities exceeded assets for this period. For the period 1860 to 1868, Melville was practically without any income whatsoever from his novels, magazine publications, or lectures. During these years he heavily relied on income generated from his father-in-law's estate, though it was not sufficient to support a household with four children. A second job became essential. In 1866, Melville began working as Inspector of Customs in the District of New York at a salary of $4.00 a day, that is, approximately $1,250 a year. This position was actually quite precarious since the New York Custom House, notorious for its corruption, was almost invariably under scrutiny for its well-known feather-bedding, and jobs were never secure.

What is perhaps most remarkable about the economic situation of literary figures in late eighteenth- and early nineteenth-century Britain and America is how similar it is to the current financial position of authors. Of course, much has changed. The size of the reading public, the proportion of the population that is literate, the number and types of books published, and the sheer number of people who are authors, have grown, if not exponentially, certainly at a very rapid rate. Nonetheless, it appears to be as true today as it was in the 18th century that few authors are capable of subsisting on writing-related income. To be sure, writing has been freed from a system of patronage, and the profession of authorship is one which carries with it substantial prestige. But it remains a profession which does not reflect the normal correlation between income and esteem. While most highly respected occupations also yield substantial incomes, this is not the case with authorship. We can point to the occasional author who makes substantial sums of money from writing, whether it be an Alexander Pope in the eighteenth century or a Normal Mailer today. But for the vast majority, it remains either a low-paying occupation or only one of several occupations which support individual writers and their families.

Income from Writing

Most authors cannot make ends meet from their writing alone.

▲ For the year 1979, the representative (i.e., median) author in the survey earned a total of $4,775 from writing; that is, 50 percent earned less than this amount. (This dollar figure represents total income derived from book royalties, magazine and newspaper articles, motion picture and television work, and so on.)

▲ A quarter of the authors earned less than $1,000 from their writing; 10 percent of the authors had a writing income of more than $45,000; 5 percent, more than $80,000.

▲ For authors without any other regular paid position, the median writing income was $7,500; for part-time authors, $2,600.

▲ The representative author had an hourly writing income of $4.90.

▲ The representative author (as indicated by the median) received 98 cents of every writing dollar from books, including both royalty payments and subsidiary rights; the remaining two cents came from articles and scripts. Royalty payments alone typically accounted for 87 cents of every dollar.

▲ About half of the recently published authors (1977–1980) within each writing genre—with the lone exception of genre fiction writers—earned less than $5,000 in 1979 from writing.

▲ Authors' income from writing is subject to sharp short-time fluctuations; in 1979, 5 per-

Continued

cent of the authors earned about ten times as much from their writing as in the year before, while another 5 percent earned only one-fifth as much as the year before.

▲ A quarter of the authors earned five times as much from writing in their best year as in 1979, and 10 percent earned fully fifteen times as much in their best year as in 1979.

The Writing Occupation. Analyses of the financial return from writing must take into account the great diversity of the economic lives of authors.

▲ Forty-six percent of the authors held a regular paid position besides freelance writing.

▲ Most of the other jobs held by authors were in the professional occupations.

▲ The representative author (as indicated by the median) devoted twenty hours a week to actual writing or work directly related to a book or article. Thirty-four percent of authors without another job spent forty or more hours a week writing; 28 percent of those with another job wrote less than ten hours a week.

▲ The mixed occupational career of many part-time authors was apparently a matter of economic pressure rather than preference. Forty-six percent of the part-time authors expressed a definite willingness to drop their other work if they could match their present total income by writing full time; another 22 percent thought that they would "possibly" like to make such a change.

▲ The large majority of part-time authors found writing more satisfying than their other jobs.

Writing Income and Characteristics of Authors and Their Work.

▲ Prolific authors, of course, earned more than others. Forty-three percent of the authors with no more than two published books to their credit earned less than $2,500 from writing in 1979, in contrast to the 12 percent of authors who had published at least ten books.

▲ Genre fiction* was the most lucrative kind of writing: a fifth of genre fiction authors earned at least $50,000 in 1979, almost three times the rate of adult nonfiction writers.

▲ Winners of honorific awards for their writing earned a little more than authors who had not received such recognition. Among the prizewinners writing income remained unrelated to prestige of the award.

▲ The median income of male authors (60 percent of those in the sample) was $5,000 in 1979; for female authors, $4,000. Thirty-seven percent of the men and 40 percent of the women earned less than $2,500; 11 percent of the men and 6 percent of the women earned more than $50,000 from writing.

▲ Considered together, black, Hispanic, and Asian authors did not have signficantly different writing incomes from white authors.

▲ Where authors lived had little to do with how much they earned from writing: 44 percent of New York-based writers earned less than $5,000 from writing in 1979 compared to 51 percent based in California and 52 percent based in the South. Nor were New Yorkers more apt than authors located in other regions to earn upward of $50,000.

▲ The financial fate of writers was not affected by their social class origins; incomes are much alike among those coming from white-collar and blue-collar families.

▲ College graduates fared no better, on the average, than authors with less formal education. Among the graduates, the prestige of the colleges attended had no discernible effect on subsequent writing-related income.

---

*romance novels, westerns, and mysteries, for example

"Books—wow. I love books."

PERSPECTIVE 2

Anatomy of a Best-Selling Publisher

Authors whose books sell well today usually owe a portion of their success to sophisticated marketing strategies developed by mass market publishers. Crown Publishers is Judith Krantz's literary home, and in this article excerpted from *Manhattan inc.* magazine, Gerri Hirshey describes how Crown helps its books succeed.

    Consider:

1. What does Gerri Hirshey mean by "the glitter at the top [of Crown Books] rests on a mountain of schlock"?

2. How does Crown's marketing system work to assure that its books will be best-sellers?

3. What does Crown's Bruce Harris mean when he says, "What we learned about promotion was that you make noise *before* you publish the book"?

4. What does Crown's approach tell you about mass market publishing in America?

Hype House

GERRI HIRSHEY

Three years ago, on one of his regular perambulations through the roseate atrium of Trump Tower, Donald Trump noticed a small, well-groomed blond woman casing the joint. She looked familiar. He made some inquiries of his staff. Yes, they told him, that was Judith Krantz. And when he introduced himself, she was full of questions: "She told me she was writing a book; she had the name and everything: *I'll Take Manhattan,*" says Trump. "She asked me what the specific color of the marble was, where it came from. She said that the centerpiece of the book was going to be life in Trump Tower, the life of a glamorous, successful young woman."

Crown Publishers, Inc. released the latest novel by its glamorous, successful author, in May of 1986 with a $500,000 promotion budget and a glittering $30,000 party in—where else?—the atrium of Trump Tower. A celebration seemed in order; since they teamed up in 1977, both virtual unknowns in hardcover trade books, Krantz and Crown have enjoyed four megasellers and have signed a new contract (with Bantam Books for paperback publication) for three more.

Indeed, Crown is the Trump of commercial fiction, a savvy *arriviste* capable of erecting bestsellers with great speed and power, claiming bookstore real estate on the strength of its huge sales volume, rushing from manuscript to miniseries with the stroke of a pen.

Together with Krantz and a handful of other best-selling authors, Crown has done nothing less than change the way the publishing industry does business, building elaborate castles in the air—castles like *Scruples, The Two Mrs. Grenvilles,* and *Princess Daisy*—then using mass-marketing techniques to make them down-to-earth best-sellers. Deploying a mighty sales force and a state-of-the-art distribution system, Crown can nail down prime real estate—what Donald Trump calls a "Tiffany location"—in bookstore windows, eye-catching racks, and booksellers' catalogs. With revenue from its huge remainder and promotional book divisions, Crown can finance front-list gambles.

Over and over in her fiction, Krantz tells her own story, and that of Crown Books: Unknown Gets Make-over, Then Makes It Big. Before they were transformed, Krantz was a magazine writer best known for "The Myth of the Multiple Orgasm" in *Cosmopolitan*; Crown was largely a remainder book operation with a couple of fluky

Gerri Hirshey is the author of *Nowhere to Run: The Story of Soul Music* and is also a staff writer for *The Washington Post Magazine*.

best-sellers like *The Joy of Sex* and *How to Avoid Probate*. Until it published *Scruples*, Crown was a nearly invisible giant; its front-list make-over was a bold act of wealth and will. But in its fifth and most visible decade, Crown has taken a front position in the hardcover trade wars, showing the rest of the publishing industry new ways to sell, promote, and distribute. Since 1978, Crown has had sixteen fiction and five nonfiction best-sellers.

For part of this past summer, Crown had four books on the *New York Times* list; *I'll Take Manhattan,* Jean M. Auel's *The Mammoth Hunters,* William Caunitz's *Suspects,* and Tama Janowitz's *Slaves of New York.* In nonfiction, Robert Lenzner's *The Great Getty* left its competition, *Getty,* eating dust. Last year's hot beach novel was Dominick Dunne's *The Two Mrs. Grenvilles. Smart Women/Foolish Choices* ignited the raging ain't-men-beasts genre, and before the tears dry, Crown will follow up this spring with *Women Men Love/Women Men Leave.*

Crown also excels at packaging glossy lifestyle books under its Clarkson N. Potter imprint. Recent hits include Terence Conran's *House, Bed and Bath,* and *Kitchen* books, Martha Stewart's *Weddings,* Lee Bailey's *Good Parties,* and Suzanne Slesin's *The International Book of Lofts. How to Buy and Maintain a Fur Coat* and *How to Write Erotica for Fun and Profit* are also selling well.

Despite its late entry into high-stakes hardcover trade, Crown now claims to merchandise with the big guys—Simon & Schuster, Random House, and Bantam. Exact figures are hard to come by, since it is a privately held, family-owned and -operated corporation. A 1985 estimate in *BP Report,* an industry newsletter, put revenues at $75 million. Howard Kaminsky, executive vice president of Random House, describes Crown as "miraculous. . . . I think they're terrific publishers; year in, year out, they *make* books."

In fact, the glitter at the top rests on a mountain of schlock. Besides cookbooks and diet books and reprints of mysteries and westerns,

there are also self-help books on varicose veins and tomes on Celtic manuscripts. Likewise, Crown's audio divisions cater to a wide range of tastes, from Brahms to the Turtles. As company president Alan Mirkin says, "A publishing company can't live on best-sellers. We're just seeking to have a number of them. It gives everybody a shot of extra vigor and vim. On the other hand, the rent is often paid by the books that no one's heard of."

Crown is also nonpareil at selling other publishers' failures and overstocks through its most successful division, Outlet Books. Remainders range from Poe & Shakespeare to *Why Do Shoes Squeak & 565 Other Popular Questions, Hitler's Teutonic Knights,* and *The Dirtiest Little Limerick Book Ever.* So resourceful is Crown, there is virtually no book it can't get rid of. Its giant warehouse in Avenel, New Jersey, can be the beginning and the end of the line for books. Those that died even as remainders are sold to book-safe companies, which hollow them out as jewelry caches.

"It reminds me of Swift's premium meats," says Krantz's agent Morton Janklow. "Their famous campaign was 'We use every part of the pig except the oink.' And that's what Crown does."

Crown stands for hard work and hype. "Sales driven," says its editorial director. Says Mort Janklow, "They're terrific marketers with no literary pretensions." No literary presence, is the countercharge. "They're respected for their marketing," says one publishing vice president. "But they ain't respected for their editorial acumen." Indeed, the review pages have always been a much tougher sell for Crown than soft TV features or the life-style pages.

Consider, again, the career of Judith Krantz. In 1977, Janklow took on a manuscript written by the wife of a friend, producer Steve Krantz. He took it to fledgling Crown editor Larry Freundlich. Janklow had a proposition: together they would *make* a book.

Janklow: "I said, 'Look, Crown has this huge marketing machine, Outlet Books, all this, but nobody knows you're alive. You haven't done serious fiction, real fiction. I have a book that I can put into that pipeline."

The marketing plan for *Scruples* changed publishing history, developing techniques that virtually insured best-sellerdom long before the first paying customer took a copy home.

Freundlich, who had been hired "to make Crown a front-list publisher," says he knew the book would founder if he couldn't sell it to the rank and file. "I believe that Crown has arguably the best trade sales force in the business, except for Random House," he says. "But the Crown sales force has been used to making its money by selling items other than hot front-list fiction.

"I thought a substantive fact had to be delivered to them so they wouldn't just see it as editorial chauvinism. So I suggested we get an early reprint offer."

Freundlich invited a Warner paperback executive to his home in Bridgehampton and gave him a manuscript by an unpublished, unknown author. He told him Crown was *committed,* was going to take its huge sales force and *drive* the books into the store, producing 106,000 copies in first printing—even topping the norm for Harold Robbins. Warner could make a preemptive reprint bid *right then.*

Freundlich got $500,000 from Warner. A sale to Doubleday's book club added $10,000, but Freundlich felt he hadn't reached what he calls "critical mass." To garner the final particles that would detonate his sales force and sustain its momentum, Freundlich booked a flight to London, where he intended to put *Scruples* on the block.

"Conducting an auction among English publishers was not very genteel in those days," he says, clearly pleased with himself. "There were eleven publishers in the auction," he says, "and by the end of the day we had £57,750—over $100,000. That certainly did stir things."

But *Scruples* still needed an active mix of packaging and word.

"The promotional part of it," confesses director of publishing Bruce Harris, "I got from my wife, who'd been in the promotion department at Avon. I'd seen what the paperback people were doing for books like *Sweet Savage Love,* making a big noise about books and authors that people had never heard of." Paperback people were given to promoting such genre fiction with high-gloss prepublication press kits and art heavy on overripe cleavage, flaming mansions, and dark-eyed beauties lidded with the look of lust. Crown produced such a press kit for *Scruples,* but the lady wore a veil. She was a classy dame, it suggested, and the material inside detailed a hot portfolio of assets. The lady was everywhere, on posters, brochures, and expensive bound galleys with a hitherto unheard-of four-color cover.

"What we learned about promotion was that you make noise *before* you publish the book," says Harris. "You just don't wait until afterwards. Now everybody does it. But at the time, it was very unique."

"Finally," says Krantz, "*Scruples* was number one, and I think it was the first time that a first novel by a first novelist became number one. Oh, I don't know about *Catch-22* or *The Naked and the Dead.* There were a few landmark novels that may have made number one. But no other first novelist has ever had four number one best-sellers in a row."

When Freundlich first took *Scruples* to Crown founder and chairman Nat Wartels, he insisted, as he does today, that "at least one hundred pages is literature." Ten years, three more novels, and countless copy editors later, its author writes sentences like the following: " 'Of course you do,' Maxi murmured maternally, pulling his head to her marvelous breasts like sun-warmed fruit of the gods."

Maxi is the heroine of the latest Krantz project, *I'll Take Manhattan.* A joint hardcover/paper deal with Crown and Bantam was signed in 1984. The hardcover was released in May of 1986; production for the miniseries began just one month later. . . . The *Manhattan* miniseries includes a reprise of the real party Crown threw for the book's publication. That affair was so lavish, so va-va-voom visual, that producer Steve Krantz duplicated it right down to the champagne flutes. Watching Crown's party footage (shot for promotions) against rushes from the miniseries, it's nearly impossible to distinguish TV fiction from Crown fete. Things got curiouser still when another Crown author, James Brady, working as a celebrity interviewer for CBS-TV, found himself in Trump's hall of mirrors interviewing Judith Krantz during the filming of the miniseries. Brady's crew was filming another crew filming a story starring, among others, Donald Trump.

Donald Trump appears in both the Crown and the miniseries footage, playing himself. So does Crown's director of publicity, Nancy Kahan. In the miniseries footage, Kahan wears a pink evening suit—the same one she wore to the Crown party. She dances and she smiles. Though Crown, Bantam, and Krantz decline to release exact figures on the new contract, one might reasonably estimate Krantz's deal at between $10 million and $15 million, before royalties, subsidiary rights, and dramatic sales. With the last of the three books due to be delivered in 1993, Crown and Krantz are assured of nearly a decade more of best-seller bliss.

"It's a wonderful life," says Nancy Kahan. "Sometimes I have to pinch myself." ∎

PERSPECTIVE 3

The Fate of Serious Fiction

In many countries, fiction historically has provided a major means of political expression. Great fiction writers have often provoked social change. In this short excerpt from his book *The Art of the Novel,* Czech author Milan Kundera argues that today's fiction no longer provides this political outlet.
Consider:

1. Why does Kundera feel that the novel may disappear? Do you agree? Why? Why not?

2. Why does Kundera say that today's worldwide political atmosphere is not conducive to fiction-writing?

3. If, as Kundera asserts, the world has been reduced to a series of stereotypes, how does this affect the novel?

The Art of Serious Fiction

MILAN KUNDERA

If the novel should really disappear, it will do so not because it has exhausted its powers but because it exists in a world grown alien to it. . . . Like all of culture, the novel is more and more in the hands of the mass media; as agents of the unification of the planet's history, the media amplify and channel the reduction process; they distribute throughout the world the same simplifications and stereotypes easily acceptable by the greatest number, by everyone. . . .

And it doesn't much matter that different political interests appear in the various organs of the media. Behind these surface differences reigns a common spirit. You have only to glance at American or European political weeklies, of the left or the right: they all have the same view of life, reflected in the same ordering of the table of contents, under the same headings, in the same journalistic phrasing, the same vocabulary, and the same style, in the same artistic tastes, and in the same ranking of things they deem important or insignificant. This common spirit of the mass media, camouflaged by political diversity, is the spirit of our time. And this spirit seems to me contrary to the spirit of the novel. ■

Milan Kundera is a Czechoslovakian novelist.

PERSPECTIVE 4

Writers in the Public Eye

The public's perception of a writer's life often differs quite a bit from reality. When someone writes horror stories, like Stephen King does, people sometimes believe he is what he writes. In this essay from *The New York Times Book Review*, King describes some of the inconveniences of being a celebrity.

Consider:

1. How do most of the letter-writers Stephen King describes view his life?

2. What does King's essay tell you about the life of a celebrity author?

3. From what King says, what is his primary motivation to write?

'Ever Et Raw Meat?' and Other Weird Questions

STEPHEN KING

It seems to me that, in the minds of readers, writers actually exist to serve two purposes, and the more important may not be the writing of books and stories. The primary function of writers, it seems, is to answer readers' questions. These fall into three categories. The third is the one that fascinates me most, but I'll identify the other two first.

The One-of-a-Kind Questions: Each day's mail brings a few of these. Often they reflect the writer's field of interest—history, horror, romance, the American West, outer space, big business. The only thing they have in common is their uniqueness. Novelists are frequently asked where they get their ideas (see category No. 2), but writers must wonder where this relentless curiosity, these really strange questions, come from.

There was, for instance, the young woman who wrote to me from a penal institution in Minnesota. She informed me she was a kleptomaniac. She further informed me that I was her favorite writer, and she had stolen every one of my books she could get her hands on. "But after I stole *Different Seasons* from the library and read it, I felt moved to send it back," she wrote. "Do you think this means you wrote this one the best?" After due consideration, I decided that reform on the part of the reader has nothing to do with artistic merit. I came close to writing back to find out if

she had stolen *Misery* yet but decided I ought to just keep my mouth shut.

From Bill V. in North Carolina: "I see you have a beard. Are you morbid of razors?"

From Carol K. in Hawaii: "Will you soon write of pimples or some other facial blemish?"

From Don G., no address (and a blurry postmark): "Why do you keep up this disgusting mother worship when anyone with any sense knows a MAN has no use to his mother once he is weened?"

From Raymond R. in Mississippi: "Ever et raw meat?" (It's the laconic ones like this that really get me.)

I have been asked if I beat my children and/or my wife. I have been asked to parties in places I have never been and hope never to go. I was once asked to give away the bride at a wedding, and one young woman sent me an ounce of pot, with the attached question: "This is where I get my inspiration—where do you get yours?" Actually, mine usually comes in envelopes—the kind through which you can view your name and address printed by a computer—that arrive at the end of every month.

My favorite question of this type, from Anchorage, asked simply: "How could you write such a why?" Unsigned. If E. E. Cummings were still alive, I'd try to find out if he'd moved to the Big North.

The Old Standards: These are the questions writers dream of answering when they are collecting rejection slips, and the ones they tire of quickest once they start to publish. In other

Stephen King has published 17 novels, including 5 novels authored under the pseudonym "Richard Bachman." His latest book is *Gunslinger.*

words, they are the questions that come up without fail in every dull interview the writer has ever given or will ever give. I'll enumerate a few of them:

Where do you get your ideas? (I get mine in Utica.)

How do you get an agent? (Sell your soul to the Devil.)

Do you have to know somebody to get published? (Yes; in fact, it helps to grovel, toady and be willing to perform twisted acts of sexual depravity at a moment's notice, and in public if necessary.)

How do you start a novel? (I usually start by writing the number 1 in the upper right-hand corner of a clean sheet of paper.)

How do you write best sellers? (Same way you get an agent.)

How do you sell your book to the movies? (Tell them they don't want it.)

What time of day do you write? (It doesn't matter; if I don't keep busy enough, the time inevitably comes.)

Do you ever run out of ideas? (Does a bear defecate in the woods?)

Who is your favorite writer? (Anyone who writes stories I would have written had I thought of them first.)

There are others, but they're pretty boring, so let us march on.

The Real Weirdies: Here I am, bopping down the street, on my morning walk, when some guy pulls over in his pickup truck or just happens to walk by and says, "Hi, Steve! Writing any good books lately?" I have an answer for this; I've developed it over the years out of pure necessity. I say, "I'm taking some time off." I say that even if I'm working like mad, thundering down the homestretch on a book. The reason *why* I say this is because no other answer seems to fit. Believe me, I know. In the course of the trial and error that has finally resulted in "I'm taking some time off," I have discarded about 500 other answers.

Having an answer for "You writing any good books lately?" is a good thing, but I'd be lying if I said it solves the problem of *what the question means*. It is this inability on my part to make

sense of this odd query, which reminds me of that Zen riddle—"Why is a mouse when it runs?"— that leaves me feeling mentally shaken and impotent. You see, it isn't just *one* question; it is a *bundle* of questions, cunningly wrapped up in one package. It's like that old favorite, "Are you still beating your wife?"

If I answer in the affirmative, it means I may have written—how many books? two? four?—(all of them good) in the last—how long? Well, how long is "lately"? It could mean I wrote maybe three good books just last week, or maybe two *on this very walk up to Bangor International Airport and back!* On the other hand, if I say no, what does *that* mean? I wrote three or four *bad* books in the last "lately" (surely "lately" can be no longer than a month, six weeks at the outside)?

Or here I am, signing books at the Betts' Bookstore or B. Dalton's in the local consumer factory (nicknamed "the mall"). This is something I do twice a year, and it serves much the same purpose as those little bundles of twigs religious people in the Middle Ages used to braid into whips and flagellate themselves with. During the course of this exercise in madness and self-abnegation, at least a dozen people will approach the little coffee table where I sit behind a barrier of books and ask brightly, "Don't you wish you had a rubber stamp?"

I have an answer to this one, too, an answer that has been developed over the years in a trial-and-error method similar to "I'm taking some time off." The answer to the rubber-stamp question is: "No, I don't mind."

Never mind if I really do or don't (this time it's my own motivations I want to skip over, you'll notice); the question is, Why does such an illogical query occur to so many people? My signature is actually stamped on the covers of several of my books, but people seem just as eager to get these signed, as those that aren't so stamped. Would these questioners stand in line for the privilege of watching me slam a rubber stamp down on the title page of *The Shining* or *Pet Sematary*? I don't think they would.

If you still don't sense something peculiar in these questions, this one might help convince you. I'm sitting in the cafe around the corner from my house, grabbing a little lunch by myself and reading a book (reading at the table is one of the few bad habits acquired in my youth that I have nobly resisted giving up) until a customer or maybe even a waitress sidles up and asks, "How come you're not reading one of your own books?"

This hasn't happened just once, or even occasionally; it happens *a lot*. The computer-generated answer to this question usually gains a chuckle, although it is nothing but the pure, logical and apparent truth. "I know how they all come out," I say. End of exchange. Back to lunch, with only a pause to wonder why people assume you want to read what you wrote, rewrote, read again following the obligatory editorial conference and yet again during the process of correcting the mistakes that a good copy editor always prods, screaming, from their hiding places (I once heard a crime writer suggest that God could have used a copy editor, and while I find the notion slightly blasphemous, I tend to agree).

And then people sometimes ask in that chatty, let's-strike-up-a-conversation way people have, "How long does it take you to write a book?" Perfectly reasonable question—at least until you try to answer it and discover there *is* no answer. This time the computer-generated answer is a total falsehood, but at least it serves the purpose of advancing the conversation to some more discussable topic. "Usually about nine months," I say, "the same length of time it takes to make a baby." This satisfies everyone but me. I know that nine months is just an average, and probably a fictional one at that. It ignores *The Running Man* (published under the name Richard Bachman), which was written in four days during a snowy February vacation when I was teaching high school. It also ignores *It* and my latest, *The Tommyknockers*. *It* is over 1,000 pages long and took four years to write. *The Tommyknockers* is 400 pages shorter but took five years to write.

Do I mind these questions? Yes . . . and no. Anyone minds questions that have no real answers and thus expose the fellow being questioned to be not a real doctor but a sort of witch doctor. But no one—at least no one with a modicum of simple human kindness—resents questions from people who honestly want answers. And now and then someone will ask a really interesting question, like, Do you write in the nude? The answer—not generated by computer—is: I don't think I ever have, but if it works, I'm willing to try it. ∎

CHAPTER EIGHT

For Further Reading

Books

Lewis A. Coser, Charles Kadushin, and Walter W. Powell, *Books: The Culture & Commerce of Publishing* (New York: Basic Books, 1982).

Kenneth C. Davis, *Two-Bit Culture: The Paperbacking of America* (Boston: Houghton Mifflin, 1984).

John P. Dessauer, *Book Publishing: What It Is, What It Does* (New York: R. R. Bowker, 1974).

James D. Hart, *The Popular Book* (Berkeley: University of California Press, 1950).

Periodicals

AB Bookman's Weekly (collector books)

Book Research Quarterly

Publishers Weekly

Support Industries

PART III

Advertising

How Much Does It Cost to Make a Commercial?

Slick production, carefully chosen music, and well-crafted pictures have turned commercials into TV's most expensive programming. In this article, Alex Ben Block explains what makes TV commercials so expensive. Consider:

1. What are the major elements necessary for a TV commercial and what do they cost?

2. What justification do advertising agencies give for the high costs? Do you agree? Why? Why not?

3. Ultimately, who ends up paying for the cost of the commercials?

Where the Money Goes

ALEX BEN BLOCK

During the 15 years Norman Seeff was a much-sought-after still photographer, best known for record album covers featuring performers like the Rolling Stones and Ray Charles, he was lucky if his annual income approached $100,000. Four years ago he began directing TV commercials. This year his income will be around $750,000. Yet Seeff's compensation is only in the midrange for top commercial directors. While he earns at least $7,500 for each shooting day, better-known directors charge $15,000. Joe Sedalmaier of Chicago, the brains behind Wendy's "Where's the beef?" campaign, among others, commands $20,000 a day.

Well-crafted commercials these days cost an average of $125,000 for 30 seconds of sales

pitch. The most expensive can run up to a million dollars per half-minute. A two-hour feature film, by contrast, averages about $90,000 a half-minute.

Advertising agencies "produce" TV commercials, but they rarely make them. That's done by the highly fragmented TV commercial production industry, composed of thousands of small operations ranging from production companies to small contractors who design and build sets. It is a business of specialists. Certain directors, for example, do only comedy or drama, others only food shots. Norman Seeff is known for his ability to improvise dialog that manages to slip in key advertising points.

Seeff, 47, works exclusively with producer Richard Marlis, 35, who operates one of about 2,000 small commercial production companies. Their clients range from MasterCard to Pizza

---

Alex Ben Block is a reporter for *Forbes* Magazine.

Hut. Marlis' eight-year-old firm, operating out of an old four-bedroom stucco house near the Sunset Strip in Hollywood, will gross $6 million this year, with a profit margin on its commercial productions of 20%, or $1.2 million (a net of about $200,000 after other overhead and taxes).

Marlis keeps careful track of production costs on a Macintosh computer, programmed with a standard industry form that has space for 276 different expense items. An art director, for example, makes $550 a day, a hairstylist $400, and a director of photography $2,000. Total personnel and equipment costs of an average Marlis-Seeff production: $60,000 to $70,000 per shooting day. Few commercials take less than two days.

Production costs are only part of the total bill. When a commercial is shot on location, budgets frequently go through the roof. A study by the Television Bureau of Advertising told this horror story: "A total of 25 people [flew in] for the shoot [in Hawaii] . . . at a room rental rate of more than $150 per person per night. Not to mention the costs of meals at the most expensive restaurants. And the client was with them. . . . This was not an isolated case."

When all is done, the advertising agency adds on about 18% of the budget as its fee.

There is a certain momentum to all this: Once a client has started spending big money, it's hard to stop. There is, for example, the so-called famous faces phenomenon. A commercial's cost obviously starts ballooning when a client wants a readily recognizable person to pitch the product. Jack King of Ingels Inc., a Los Angeles-based broker that matches celebrities with advertisers, says even minor stars on a network TV series can command $250,000 for each commercial.

Pepsi's new Michael Jackson campaign . . . cost between $2 million and $4 million, not counting Jackson's fee. Jackson himself is earning $15 million ($10 million cash and $5 million in concert tour support). "When you wake up in the morning and you've got Michael Jackson for one more day, you want the best possible people and often they cost more," says award-winning director Joe Pytka.

Egos are getting as inflated as the money, and efficiency is increasingly sacrificed for "art." Larry Postaer, creative director of Rubin Postaer & Associates in Los Angeles, made a recent $250,000 Honda commercial in south Florida, where he says he could roll the cameras only one hour a day. Why? He felt the light was right only for a half hour in the morning and another half hour at twilight. "From experience you learn that cars look flat and unattractive in direct light, so you have to catch the shot when the angle is just right," argues Postaer. The rest of the day, at a cost of about $9,000 an hour, the large crew and rented equipment sat idle.

Outrageous? "If a commercial results in the sale of, say, 50,000 cars at $12,000 each, that's $600 million," declaims Postaer. "So it's not unreasonable to spend a quarter of a million dollars for a commercial."

Because of mounting costs, fewer commercials are made today, and those that are tend to air for longer periods. One major agency, Leo Burnett Co. of Chicago, which made 1,200 commercials a year two decades ago, last year produced only 410. Yet, in a variation of Parkinson's Law, the costs keep rising. "With fewer commercials, the impact of each is magnified," says Al Stauderman, president of Connecticut-based Bird Bonette Stauderman, which consults with advertisers on production costs. "That way the agencies can justify spending even more money." ■

PERSPECTIVE 2

New Technology Breeds New Marketing Research Techniques

Traditional TV ratings systems are being replaced by more sophisticated technology, which can check not only whether viewers watched a commercial but
also whether they bought the product. This article describes the new audience
research system.

Consider:

1. Define single-source ad research. How does it differ from traditional au-
    dience research?
2. What are the economic consequences to advertising agencies if single-
    source ad research succeeds?
3. What is the ultimate goal of single-source ad research?
4. What are the disadvantages of measuring consumer practices using single-
    source ad research?

Single-Source Ad Research Heralds Detailed Look at Household Habits

JOANNE LIPMAN

Information Resources Inc. knows what Paxton
Blackwell of Williamsport, Pa., eats for breakfast. It monitors the television shows he
watches. It tracks the coupons he uses, where he
shops, the brands he buys. It even knows which
newspapers he reads.

Mr. Blackwell doesn't mind the Big Brother-
style surveillance—not the meters on the family
TV sets or the surveys he answers on reading hab-

Joanne Lipman is a staff reporter for *The Wall Street Journal*.

its and brand preferences. "I'm crazy about surveys anyway," he says. "I always wanted to be a
Nielsen family."

In fact, Mr. Blackwell's stint as an Orwellian
guinea pig makes the A. C. Nielsen Co. television
ratings system look about as sophisticated as an
abacus in a computer store. He is part of a fledgling science called single-source research, which
could revolutionize the advertising business. It
goes far beyond mere TV ratings to track exactly
what ads people see and how that affects what
they buy. If perfected, single-source systems will

do something no research has done before: show how—indeed, if—advertising works.

Excess Advertising?

Of course, ad agencies may not want to know. Not only could the research prove that some ad campaigns are flops, but it may show that some companies advertise too much. That's a frightening thought for ad agencies, which work on commission.

"I would expect many advertising budgets are beyond the saturation point," says Edward Dittus, a marketing director for SAMI/Burke Inc., a research firm developing a single-source system. A recent Information Resources analysis found, for example, that only seven of 20 brands' sales were affected at all by the level of TV advertising.

But single-source efforts are riddled with problems. One example: figuring out how to analyze all the information derived from following a person's TV, reading and shopping habits. "We're going to get truckloads of data," says Bob Warrens, a senior vice president with ad agency J. Walter Thompson Co. and a member of an Advertising Research Foundation panel studying how to analyze the data. "The computer-analysis systems that can make this stuff very useful to us simply don't exist. There's nothing sophisticated enough."

Another hitch is cost. Right now, single-source research costs advertisers hundreds of thousands of dollars a year *per brand*. Moreover, it tracks purchases only at grocery stores and drugstores.

Yet for all its problems, advertising executives say it will become widespread within five years, and the race to be first and best in supplying single-source data is fierce. Chicago-based Information Resources, Dun & Bradstreet Corp.'s Nielsen unit, and Control Data Corp.'s Arbitron Ratings Co. and SAMI/Burke units all are developing single-source systems, and others may follow. None of the systems is complete; each has substantial drawbacks. But each firm insists its system is best and will prevail.

'Wave of the Future'

"It's the wave of the future, and we want to be the first one out there with the best product," says Andrew Tarshis, president of NPD/Nielsen Inc., a joint venture of Nielsen and NPD Group, a Port Washington, N.Y., market-research firm.

The basics of single-source research are straightforward, although the companies' methods and technology differ. After recruiting a test panel of households—which receive small payments or inducements like coupons—the research firm meters each home's TV sets and quizzes family members periodically on what they read. Their grocery purchases also are tracked, with electronic scanners that read the universal product code on packages. For background, most systems also track retail data, like product sales.

By sifting that information, researchers can find out if, for example, people exposed to 50 Twinkie ads will buy more Twinkies than people exposed to 25 Twinkie ads—and if so, how many more. They also can pinpoint television shows that attract very specific audience segments—a show with an above-average proportion of viewers who buy Twinkies, say, or one with a below-average proportion of Twinkie buyers but promising demographics.

A Campbell Soup Co. single-source experiment with its V-8 juice shows how the system works. Using an index of 100 for the average household's V-8 consumption, Campbell found that demographically similar TV audiences can consume vastly different amounts of V-8. In early 1987, for example, "General Hospital" had a below-average 80 index, while "Guiding Light" had an above-average 120 index. The results were surprising, because "General Hospital" actually had a slightly higher percentage of women 25 to 54 years old—the demographic group most predisposed to buy V-8—and so would ordinarily have been expected to be a better advertising forum to reach V-8 drinkers.

The Information Resources data that Campbell used isn't representative of all U.S. homes, and so isn't yet meaningful enough to act on. But when reliable information becomes available, Campbell will be able to rearrange its ad schedule to raise the average index. Thus, the advertising would reach more of the right people, says George Mahrlig, director of media services, "and hopefully it would translate into sales." As the data and analysis improve, he adds, "we should be able to analyze and find out how many commercials it takes to change a household's buying pattern."

Some industry executives are skeptical, however, that advertisers ever will use single-source data to buy TV ad time on a show-by-show basis. Currently, agencies buy packages of ad time that include a number of shows. "It becomes prohibitively expensive" to buy specific programs, says Thompson's Mr. Warrens. He says single-source data should be used more broadly—for example, to test whether a candy bar usually pitched to mothers in prime time will sell even better to teen-agers on weekday afternoons.

Single-source data has come in for criticism for other reasons, too. In a new Thompson study, Mr. Warrens concludes that it may encourage short-term promotions, like coupons, that have readily measurable effects. Other industry executives say that the impact of advertising is cumulative, and that monthly or quarterly single-source data would lead advertisers to emphasize the short term.

The various single-source firms, meanwhile, are arguing over whose system is best. At this point, many industry officials say, Information Resources is the most advanced, with 12,000 households wired in 10 markets across the country. Participants have identification cards that they present to cashiers at participating stores; details of their transactions are stored electronically by household.

But the firm's participants don't constitute a representative national sample, in part because its system requires cable-TV hookups.

Involving the Subject

Nielsen, on the other hand, which is testing its single-source services in 1,500 homes and promises to be in 15,000 by [1989], is criticized for its product scanner. Unlike Information Resources participants, Nielsen families must scan their products with hand-held electronic "wands" at homes, keying in information about coupons and sometimes even prices.

"Our research indicates that no more than about 5% of the population is willing to scan their products at home," says Gian Fulgoni, president of Information Resources. Campbell's Mr. Mahrlig adds, "The more passive the better. Anything you get people that involved in is going to create some kind of effect on them, and you don't know what it is." Nielsen counters that its system is better because it allows tracking of purchases from a wider range of stores.

The rivalry between Information Resources and Nielsen is all the more intense because Nielsen last fall tried to acquire Information Resources. The Federal Trade Commission blocked the sale.

Arbitron and SAMI/Burke, meanwhile, have 600 Denver-area homes wired. But their system doesn't track product prices. In any case, they won't decide [right away] what to do with their program, says Arbitron's president, A. J. "Rick" Aurichio.

Still, Mr. Aurichio says researchers have just begun to tap the potential of single-source systems and ultimately could go far beyond supermarket and drugstore purchases. With the people meter, he says, "we have the ideology to ask further questions right on the TV screen. We could even find out whether you've used fast-food or bought a new car."

Learning About Grape-Nuts in Denver

Can General Goods Corp. persuade Denver to buy more Grape-Nuts cereal?

Arbitron Ratings Co. used its single-source research project to try to find out. The Control Data Corp. unit tracked 200 Denver households, monitoring everything from the TV shows they watched to their grocery purchases. Its goal: to see if General Foods, without raising ad spending, could reach more Grape-Nuts buyers with its ads and thereby boost sales and market share.

The analysis was an experiment in which General Foods wasn't involved. But the data, collected in the first half of 1986, is real—and it shows how single-source analysis may someday transform the way companies advertise.

Broad Penetration

Arbitron began its analysis by examining the grocery purchases of all 200 homes. It found that 18% had bought Grape-Nuts in the six-months period. That was a strong showing, placing the cereal fourth, behind General Mills Co.'s Cheerios, purchased by 24% of all homes, and Kellogg Co.'s Raisin Bran (20%) and Corn Flakes (19%).

But Grape-Nuts showed less strength when Arbitron looked at how much of the cereal the 200 households bought. While the average home bought about 250 ounces of cereal in the six months, only about 40 ounces of that total was Grape-Nuts—well below average.

The analysis strongly indicated that a new Grape-Nuts marketing strategy was in order: General foods must try to reach the large number of current users and persuade them to buy *more* Grape-Nuts. And it must try to reach those current users more often.

"As simple as that (strategy) may be, it's almost revolutionary," says Jim Spaeth, a vice president of SAMI/Burke Inc., one of Arbitron's sister companies working with it on the single-source project. "I've never seen ad strategy driven by the data like that."

To reach current users, Arbitron first had to pinpoint them. It knew that women 25 to 54 years old were the major grocery buyers in homes. So, it looked at Grape-Nuts prime-time TV schedule to see which shows had big audiences of women in that age group whose households bought Grape-Nuts.

The results were discouraging. Five of nine shows in the schedule had far higher ratings for women in households that *don't* buy Grape-Nuts than for women whose households do. The result: "Wasted impressions," Mr. Spaeth says, because if the strategy was right, the ads were hitting the wrong people.

The differences in ratings make a big difference in cost. For example, the show "Stingray" was watched by a high proportion of households that don't buy Grape-Nuts, so the cost of reaching 1% of the target group—women 25 to 54 in households that bought Grape-Nuts—came in at a hefty $25,000 for the show. The "ABC Wednesday Night Movie," which reached much more of the target group, cost just $2,500 per 1%.

Changing the Schedule

Using that data on specific shows, Arbitron made a new ad schedule, adding shows with high ratings for the target audience, like "20/20" and "MacGyver." The new schedule reached the target group 62% more often.

Moreover, the cost for each 1% of the target group reached by the new schedule dropped, to $4,888 from $8,010, and the cost of the total TV schedule was almost unchanged. Based on figures compiled by Broadcast Advertiser Reports, an Arbitron unit that tracks TV commercial spending, the actual schedule cost $857,100. The revised schedule would cost $845,700.

"It brings a new level of clarity to the use of television," Mr. Spaeth says. "TV used to be cheap. It isn't so cheap anymore. It's high time we became more precise and efficient about how we use it."   JOANNE LIPMAN

Using Emotional Pitches to Sell Products

Advertisers appeal to an audience by using information and emotion. In this article from *Adweek,* Kim Folts describes the results of a study that looked at the effectiveness of using emotional appeals to sell products.

Consider:

1. According to Stuart Agres, by what means does an advertisement best form a double bond with consumers?

2. What methods were used to test the subjects' emotional responses?

3. Which type of advertisement fared best and why?

4. Which kinds of emotional ads were most effective and why?

Psychological Appeal in TV Ads Found Effective

KIM FOLTZ

The opening shot is a whirl of action: A man in the throes of a medical emergency is being rushed to a hospital emergency room. Filmed walking on the street after he is well he talks about how he was lucky that his heart attack wasn't fatal and how, from the start of his medical crisis to his recovery, he was comforted by the fact that he didn't have to worry about how his family was going to be taken care of. The scene ends with a shot of him hugging his pregnant wife.

It's not an uncommon kind of commercial pitch these days, but it may have uncommon appeal. Television commercial micro-dramas, like this one for Prudential Insurance, that draw viewers emotionally into the commercials and attempt to set up a psychological connection be-

Kim Foltz is a reporter for *Adweek* magazine.

tween the consumer and the product have been growing in popularity, but many advertising experts worried that these "soft" sells weren't the best sellers. That opinion may soon change: New research suggests that commercials that incorporate a psychological appeal may, in fact, be very effective. "Our philosophy is that it really does take two kinds of benefit promises to persuade a

Emotional Pitches Do Sell Well

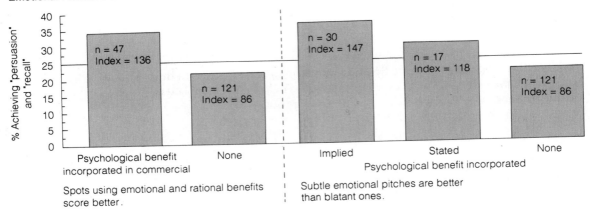

Spots using emotional and rational benefits score better.

Subtle emotional pitches are better than blatant ones.

consumer to buy a product," says Stuart Agres, executive vp/director of strategic planning for Lowe Marshalk. "A commercial should address product benefits such as 'Our detergent gets clothes whiter and softer,' as well as psychological benefits such as 'Our detergent will boost your esteem in the eyes of your mother-in-law.'"

Agres is convinced that commercials that meet both the rational and psychological criterion form a double bond with consumers, increasing initial acceptance of a product and creating brand loyalty.

To find out exactly what role, if any, psychological benefits played in TV commercials, Agres decided to conduct some tests. No easy task this. "In consumer research on commercials the tendency is to ask very rational questions about the commercials and people naturally respond about the highly rational aspects of the ads," he explains. American consumers aren't well trained to talk about emotions and aren't good at articulating the psychological aspects of ads."

Nonetheless, Agres pressed ahead. The agency developed a method of testing the communication of emotions in commercials which used cards with drawings that represented different emotional states. Using this device, research subjects could be shown commercials and then asked to pick the cards that best represented their feelings about the ad and its product. Using specially filmed spots for three imaginary clients,

a bank, a shampoo and a computer, Agres found that spots that used a rational/emotional pitch scored the best with consumers.

Pushing the test a step further, he added a price-discount wild card. Again, he found that consumers remained more loyal to brands that also offered a psychological benefit in their ads. Here's how it worked. A test group was shown white-card concepts for two shampoos, one that offered rational benefits (Alegro) and another that offered both psychological and rational benefits (Avanti). The price of Avanti remained constant. Alegro's price was repeatedly discounted. "Avanti's emotional/rational benefits had created such a strong bond with our test group that many would not switch until the discount reached $1," says Agres.

Pleased with the results, Agres still wanted further validation of his theory. He decided on a double-blind test by respected researchers outside the agency. He got New York-based ASI Market Research, which specializes in analyzing commercials for their consumer-recall and persuasion qualities, to put together a reel of 168 commercials from a wide variety of categories for both new and existing products. Each had been scored on how well it performed in terms of consumer recall and persuasion.

The spots were then sent to professor Russell Belk, a marketing research expert at the University of Utah. Belk analyzed the ads and separated them into two groups: those that contained only rational benefits and commercials that incorporated psychological and rational benefits. He found that 121 of the commercials had rational benefits only and that 47 utilized both psychological and rational benefits. Belk had no idea of how the spots had scored on ASI's tests.

The analysis of the results was more than encouraging. The tests showed that emotional advertising is capable of performing well: commercials with combined rational/psychological benefits scored better than those with only rational benefits when it came to consumer recall and persuasion (see chart).

But not all "emotional" ads performed the same. The test showed that emotional ads that implied a psychological benefit scored better than those that out-and-out stated the emotional payoff to the consumer. "What this shows is that emotional ads have to be done right if they're going to be effective," explains Agres. "A subtle approach works better because it has a chance to get past the consumers' natural barrier of skepticism."

While Agres' research makes big strides in understanding the impact of emotions in ads, the investigation is far from over. "This is just the beginning," he says. "We're just starting to open up the question of what's going on with emotions and advertising."

Agres is likely to get a lot of help finding the answer. . . . [H]e's presenting his research at an American Psychological Association conference in New York. "I'm sure this will be very interesting to them," he says. "Once you get academics investigating a topic, everyone else follows." ■

PERSPECTIVE 4

Anatomy of a Commercial (Chicken-Style)

Creating commercials can be expensive (see Perspective 1, page 153), and it can also be a challenge—especially when the product is chicken and the advertising agency decides to feature live birds in the ads. Debbie Seaman explains one agency's idea of a creative commercial and how it worked.

Consider:

1. What was the goal of this commercial approach?

2. What difficulties did the agency face in trying to turn chickens into movie stars?

3. In your opinion, was this creative idea worth the trouble? Why? Why not?

Smart Move: Caps, Gowns, Chicks

DEBBIE SEAMAN

If the creative team at Della Femina, Travisano & Partners/New York had known what it was in for when it decided to do a spot starring live chickens, it just might have chickened out.

As copywriter Joe Della Femina (brother of chairman Jerry) put it, "The only thing dumber than chickens are a writer and art director who do a commercial with chickens.

"That *chair* is intelligent compared to a chicken," he added, gesturing across the agency's conference room, where he sat with art director Raul Pina, vp/account supervisor Joanne Tilove and Linda Tesa, vp/director of radio and TV production.

They were discussing a hilarious new 30-second spot for Gold Kist Young 'n Tender Brand Chicken. To illustrate that "these chickens are at the top of their class," DFT&P put a barnyard of the birds in caps and gowns—certainly a different way to "dress" a chicken. As the birds strut their stuff to the strains of "Pomp and Circumstance," the sincere-sounding voice of Percy Rodriguez explains how these chickens are smarter than ordinary chickens. This could be ironic, considering what the agency had to say off the air about chicken IQs. However, the copy goes on to qualify "smarter" by explaining that these chickens probably eat better than people do.

Throughout the spot, we are treated to touches such as a member of the "class" falling asleep and being nudged awake by a mate. Then there's the chicken marching by with a diploma under its arm, er, wing. Near the end, to the line "They're in a class by themselves," there's a shot of caps tossed in the air, accompanied by a chorus of chicken cheers. These sounds, Della Femina noted, were made by "a bunch of clucks at the agency."

Commercials for Young 'n Tender have been recipe-oriented for the past three years, and the client wanted a campaign to promote brand awareness. After several ideas didn't pan out, the agency went back to the drawing board. Della Femina recalled being so "punchy" that he thought, "Let's just think about it as if we had no restrictions upon us at all."

Ruminating about chickens good enough to be Young 'n Tender, Della Femina thought of graduation—"going from being something else to something better"—and then inevitably of the traditional commencement march, "Pomp and Circumstance." He and Pina never considered using animation (like another new spot for the brand) because "the humor of the idea was in the costumes and gowns being on something live."

People at Gold Kist warned the creative team that chickens were virtually untrainable, but it was undaunted—even when one director after another turned down the job. DFT&P has the Meow Mix account, so it has had a lot of experience with directors who *can* work with animals. "But those directors were reluctant to touch it," pointed out producer Tesa.

Fortunately, the agency happened to have a reel from Fallon McElligott in Minneapolis, and on it were commercials for Gold'n Plump chickens using, yes, live chickens—and lots of them. DFT&P tracked down the director, Jim Hinton of Wilson-Griak Productions in Minneapolis, and offered him the Gold Kist job. Not surprisingly, Hinton wasn't wild about the idea but finally accepted.

Debbie Seaman is a reporter for *Adweek* magazine.

One thing Hinton knew that the agency *didn't,* for example, was that the minute a hat goes on a chicken's head, it's head falls forward. So for each chicken, there had to be one crew member to do such things as stroke the bird's neck to keep its head up—and hope it would stay up when the cameras started to roll.

It was Hinton's idea to include the sleeping chicken—after all, it was probably the easiest shot to get. For the first shot of the "class" grouped together, crew members had to hold the chickens above their heads—and wear slickers and garbage bags for their own protection. ("You say people get dumped on . . . ," quipped Della Femina.) Among other problems the crew faced were chickens walking backward when they were supposed to go forward. The DFT&P folks credit Hinton with "the patience of a saint."

They couldn't always say the same for themselves. "At the beginning of the day, we were feeling sorry for the chickens," Pina remembered. "At the end of the day we felt like kicking the cages. *Barbecue* was on my mind at the end of the day!" But the caterers for the shoot had been warned not to serve, well, you know what. By the final day of the shoot, the chickens had taken over the set, and a lot of people decided to eat out.

When the shoot was over, Hinton reportedly said that, while he'd enjoyed working with the agency, he'd never do a live-chicken commercial again. "I feel we owe him one," Pina said—and he wasn't referring to another live-chicken spot. ■

PERSPECTIVE 5

Minorities in the Marketplace

Market segments, such as minorities, are always intriguing to advertisers, who want to learn how to target each type of audience. This article from *Advertising Age* shows that advertisers are learning about the Hispanic market very slowly. Consider:

1. How well have major corporations targeted the Hispanic market?
2. What are the benefits that marketing to Hispanics can offer an advertiser?
3. What are the arguments that advertisers give against expanding advertising that targets Hispanics?

Marketing to Hispanics

ED FITCH

Percentages can be misleading.

A quick look at one set indicates that corporations are increasing budgets, rolling out the red carpet to the U.S. hispanic market. According to *Hispanic Business,* Santa Barbara, Calif., companies spent $490.7 million targeting U.S. hispanics in 1987, a 23.3% increase from 1986.

But further examination shows that if corporate America is laying down a red carpet, it is amazingly thin.

Corporations spent $4.2 million *less* targeting U.S. hispanics in 1987 than Pillsbury Co.'s total ad budget in 1986, a year in which it was ranked as the No. 16 advertiser.

Philip Morris Cos.' 1986 ad budget was almost $1.4 billion. Philip Morris also happened to be the No. 1 hispanic market advertiser in 1987. Its '87 hispanic budget was $13.3 million—less than 1% of its 1986 ad spending.

Hispanic market proponents rather wistfully argue that companies should spend 7.5% of their budgets on the segment to reflect hispanics' percentage of the U.S. population. Some compa-nies—notably Adolph Coors Co,. the No. 3 hispanic advertiser—divert about 7.5% for hispanic marketing. But they are an exception.

Because the numbers show it is unrealistic to expect most companies to equate ad expenditures with hispanic population, those having a vested interest work to convince non-advertisers to enter the market.

"We can't go to the well all the time," says John Pero, New York-based VP, director of national sales, Univision, the leading Spanish-language TV network. "Although the perennial advertisers are spending more, a lot of companies are sitting back and not doing anything."

Spanish-language media and hispanic agencies encounter a familiar litany of reasons companies prefer to stay out: Research is inadequate or suspect; general-market ads reach hispanics; the market will assimilate; it's not worth the cost; hispanics don't buy our products; we don't have the marketing or distribution expertise—the list goes on. "It's like knocking your head against the wall," Mr. Pero says.

"Hispanic Marketing Issues: A National Survey," just-released research conducted by Miami-based Tinsley Advertising's Conceptos International division and the University of Miami, opens up some windows in that wall, tracking the opinions of brand managers and marketing and advertising executives at major corporations.

"For one thing, only 1% of the respondents feel strongly that the so-called hispanic market would disappear," says Joe Albonetti, VP-executive director of Conceptos International and the study's author. In fact, 63.2% strongly agree that the market will grow and become more important. And 70% feel that Spanish-language adver-

Hispanic Market Ad Expenditures

	($000,000)	% chg.
1987	$490.7	23.3
1986	398.0	19.3
1985	333.5	17.2
1984	284.5	26.8
1983	224.5	35.2

Ed Fitch is a reporter for *Advertising Age.*

tising is essential, even in reaching younger, more assimilated hispanics.

A sizable 70% also admit that their company doesn't give hispánic marketing the attention or budget it deserves, while only 8% say it is over-emphasized. "And the longer companies are involved in hispanic marketing, the more they feel they aren't doing enough," says Mr. Albonetti.

Budgets are limited, says Bonnie Garcia, national manager-hispanic market development at Detroit-based Stroh Brewery Co. "I would love to do something to reach the Puerto Ricans and Cubans, but we have to concentrate on the bulk of the market first. The company has its priorities and that is to establish the general market first."

Hispanic marketing often is pushed onto the back burner. "It's a peripheral issue for everybody who isn't directly associated with the market," says Victor Ornelas, manager-promotions and marketing communications, Seven-Up Co., Dallas.

Ms. Garcia says that awareness of the segment is very high among Stroh brand groups and that targeting hispanics is seen as a long-term, but crucial, marketing strategy. "We're unlike A-B [Anheuser-Busch], Coors or Miller, because we're the new kid on the block, just expanding into different markets."

The Conceptos' study shows that companies' decisions to target hispanics are proactive and not reactive, however. Although those that market to hispanics are more aware of their competitors' hispanic market activity than those who are not involved, the decision to enter the market is not a defensive posture.

Most companies decide to target the hispanic market because they sell products in heavily hispanic areas and find the segment's growth attractive, particularly in light of a maturing general market.

"Companies are more concerned with finding a way of building their brands than looking over their shoulders," says Mr. Albonetti. "It's not being used primarily to outmaneuver competitors or as a way to gain share of market from them," a view that is held equally by category leaders and lower-tier competitors.

Top 15 Advertisers in the Hispanic Market

		1987 budget ($000,000)	from 1986
1.	Philip Morris Cos.	$13.3	77.3%
2.	Proctor & Gamble	12.0	50.0%
3.	Adolph Coors Co.	9.8	145.0%
4.	Anheuser-Busch Cos.	8.0	23.1%
5.	McDonald's Corp.	7.0	11.1%
6.	Johnson & Johnson	6.0	71.4
7.	Colgate-Palmolive Co.	5.0	66.7%
8.	Ford Motor Co.	3.0	—
	Goya Foods Inc.	3.0	—
	Sears Roebuck & Co.	3.0	—
	Nabisco Brands Inc.	3.0	20.0%
	AT&T	3.0	20.0%
	Dart & Kraft Inc.	3.0	20.0%
	American Home Products	3.0	76.5%
	Lever Brothers	3.0	N.A.

At Kraft Inc. the strategy is completely offensive. "We view the segment as a growth opportunity for selected core brands that have high consumption among hispanics," says Jim Macdonald, ethnic marketing manager at the Glenview, Ill.-based marketer.

The survey's response to another possible reason, "Our competition is marketing to hispanics and they could gain an edge if we do not," also downplays competitiveness as a factor. Only 58% of the respondents say this is important or very important, placing nine other considerations as more crucial. This casts doubt on the snowball theory, which holds that once one company in a category enters the market, its competitors will follow.

"This is one of the most important findings," says Mr. Albonetti, "and it may be disconcerting to people who are trying to create a bandwagon feeling." Fortunately, he says, most of the companies that have entered the market have met their goals.

Not every marketer is satisfied with the effort. About 12% of the survey respondents started and then dropped hispanic marketing programs. "No one can be complacent about that," Mr. Albonetti says.

The first marketer in a product category to jump into the segment is the most successful because of hispanics' documented brand loyalty, says Fil Fernandez, marketing program manager-hispanic marketing, Polaroid Corp., Cambridge, Mass.

The fourth most mentioned reason why companies market to hispanics is that they feel their product has a particular appeal to hispanics. But because product goods essentially are alike, "the appeal of a specific product is generated by advertising," Mr. Albonetti says. "If you're the first in you can make tremendous share gains because competition is less and hispanics are brand loyal and enjoy the attention."

Being able to prove that hispanics will find their products appealing is the most important reason for reconsidering a hispanic marketing program, according to non-participating companies. If research indicates strong product usage among hispanics, 80% say it would be a very important consideration. Data displaying good potential of the market as a whole is cited as being very important by 70%.

"Research has gotten the market to where it is, but because it has been promotional in many instances, it has fueled suspicion of the numbers," says Mr. Albonetti. Those with a vested interest in the market have to provide cleaner, more actionable data, he says.

Recently, Univision and Telemundo Group commissioned studies by Audits of Great Britain and Market Opinion Research, both widely respected by general marketers. And the Spanish Radio Advisory Council asked corporations and general-market agencies to select a methodology they would trust.

Although Spanish-language media research may not equal that found in the general market. Larry Goldstein, project manager, Advansers, St. Louis, admonishes corporations that use research as an excuse for not participating.

"There may not be data available in all markets, but the available data is reasonable," he says. "Companies can proceed with what's there."

One of the more interesting ironies is that 60% of those companies not marketing to hispanics base this decision on reasons other than research. Although they say they want more believable data, only 19% researched the market, finding "hispanic media inefficient within the context of overall brand marketing."

Mr. Ornelas agrees that those trying to convince companies to enter the market have to provide better information. "But corporations have to do a better job of providing their own research."

Most companies that aren't marketing to hispanics say the cost isn't worth the budget. Despite Mr. Garcia's contention that corporations will find hispanic marketing programs and media "surprisingly efficient," the No. 1 reason cited by non-marketers is that they cannot affort to divert resources from current marketing programs. The No. 2 reason is that potential sales do not offset the costs.

"The reason they stay away is because they say they can't divert funds and lack resources," says Mr. Albonetti, "not because they don't think the market holds potential.

"But they're not blind. They're attuned to the fact that it's a hot segment. Even the skeptics filled out a 12-page survey, which shows a certain degree of interest." ■

CHAPTER NINE

For Further Reading

Books

Stephen Fox, *The Mirror Makers: A History of American Advertising and Its Creators* (New York: Morrow, 1984).

A. Jerome Jewler, *Creative Strategy in Advertising*, 3rd ed. (Belmont: Wadsworth, 1989).

Roland Marchand, *Advertising the American Dream* (Berkeley: University of California Press, 1985).

Michael Schudson, *Advertising: The Uneasy Persuasion* (New York: Basic Books, 1984).

John Wright, (ed.), *The Commercial Connection* (New York: Doubleday, 1979).

Periodicals

Advertising Age

Adweek

Journal of Advertising

Journal of Advertising Research

Public Relations

Understanding Public Relations

In this excerpt from Doug Newsom and Alan Scott's introductory public relations text, *This Is PR,* the authors describe the different types of work public relations people do.

Consider:

1. Do you believe that the public still views people in public relations as "flacks" and "hucksters"? Why? Why not?
2. Describe briefly each of the functions of public relations.
3. How does public affairs work differ from other types of public relations?
4. How does promotion differ from publicity?

PR—What Is It?

DOUG NEWSOM and ALAN SCOTT

Television viewers of the evening series soap *Dallas* were given a jaundiced view of public relations when the CBS show introduced "a slithery character" called Leslie Stewart, a PR woman who promised to help J. R. Ewing improve his image. J. R., recovering from a gunshot wound, was trying to regain control of the family oil business. The PR character showed him a new logo for Ewing Oil at their first meeting and promised to make him someone everyone would want to work for, "the richest, most desirable man in town."

PR practitioners protested. CBS's management described Stewart as "almost a female J. R., and not intended to be a caricature of the ethical PR person." The weekly national newsletter *pr re-*

Doug Newsom teaches journalism at Texas Christian University. Alan Scott teaches journalism at the University of Texas at Austin.

porter said the PR character's conduct would deserve censure under the ethics code of the Public Relations Society of America because she promised specific results in areas over which she had no control.

The complaints of PR practitioners were based on their concern that erroneous ideas about what public relations is and can do would be reinforced. CBS knows better. One of the best examples of a genuine example of public relations techniques occurred at CBS.

On Sunday afternoon June 2, 1957, CBS's *Face the Nation* had as its guest Nikita Khrushchev, then First Secretary of the U.S.S.R.'s Communist Party. A real coup? Not in the Red-hunting days of the 1950s—especially when Khrushchev chose this occasion to say, "I can prophesy that your grandchildren in America will live under socialism."

Monday morning newspaper headlines enlightened those who missed the telecast, and by Monday afternoon it was clear that CBS had rocked the ship of state. Secretary of State John Foster Dulles was outraged, and President Eisenhower was also reported to be upset. Broadcast stations and networks generally have been more sensitive than individual newspapers to public clamor, especially from the government. Thus on Tuesday morning CBS executives began a marathon meeting that went well into Wednesday.

CBS News saw the program as a plus; corporate executives did not, fearing restrictive legislation in Congress or loss of licenses for the network's five affiliated stations. According to Sig Mickelson, then president of CBS News, it took the arrival of an outside public relations counsel to resolve the dilemma:

He encouraged the adoption of an affirmative position rather than a negative one. He urged CBS to take the offensive: show pride in Face the Nation *rather than embarrassment; brag to the country about having made a major contribution to better world understanding rather than apologize for having given the Russian leader an opportunity to speak directly to the American people.*

Even more significantly the CBS response— reflected in full-page ads in the New York and Washington newspapers on the next morning— became the springboard for a campaign on behalf of broadcasters' freedom of the press that was to last for several months. The campaign demanded First Amendment protection for broadcasting.

The *counseling* of public relations not only restored CBS's faith in itself and aroused public opinion to speak in its support but also, for the first time, raised the critical issue of constitutional freedom for broadcast news, which was already guaranteed for printed news. This was no false front, no image making. The threat was real, and it was serious.

In many minds, of course, PR has long been associated with image making and the false front. Public relations practitioners have been looked upon as "flacks," "hucksters," P. T. Barnum-style con artists interested only in taking your money and getting you inside the tent.

Such an impression of public relations practice might have been the key to the downfall of the only U.S. president to resign from office.

After reviewing the 1,120 pages of *R. N., The Memoirs of Richard Nixon, Time* magazine described "a few admissions about what he thought was just a public relations problem."

Nixon's ignorance of PR is apparent in his diagnosis of his own legal and political situation after the break-in at Democratic National Committee headquarters in the Watergate office complex. When the break-in was shown to involve officials of his 1972 reelection committee and former White House aides, he tried to shield the event from public scrutiny. The cover-up did not restore public confidence, though, and Nixon thought it had been just a PR ploy that had failed. He said after the cover-up he sensed "a cloud of suspicion still hung over the White House. Yet I felt sure that it was just a public relations problem that only needed a public relations solution." Nixon was equating "cover-up" with public relations. Before the Watergate episode was over, other players in the drama also equated PR with "stonewalling it," that is, not talking to the news media, and with "PR scenarios," where role playing to predict possible public effects was used until the most attractive set piece could be found in which to place the staged action. It was never pointed out that PR involved encountering a problem openly and honestly and solving it.

Yet, as media scholars David Clark and William Blankenburg point out, "Ideally, public relations is not just a matter of saying good things, but of doing good as well. Though much of PR is just a slather of frosting on stale cake, the best is a disclosure of an active social conscience."...

PR and Related Activities

Public relations may include all of the following activities, but it is never just any one of them: press agentry, promotion, public affairs, publicity and advertising. PR activities also coexist with marketing and merchandising, terms that are not synonymous. Since many people confuse public relations with one or more of these activities, let us distinguish among them.

Public Relations PR is responsibility and responsiveness in policy and information to the best interests of the institution and its publics. The public relations practitioner is the intermediary between the interest represented and all of the involved publics. Public relations involves research into all audiences—receiving information from them, advising management of attitudes and responses, helping set policy that will demonstrate a responsible attention to these attitudes and responses and constantly evaluating the effectiveness of all PR programs. This inclusive role embraces all activities having to do with ascertaining and influencing the opinion of a group of people.

Press Agentry Because PR had its origins in press agentry, many people think that is all there is to public relations. Press agentry involves planning activities or staging events that will *attract attention* to a person, institution, idea or product. Sometimes these are just stunts, but pure hokum is seldom palatable these days. There is nothing wrong with simply attracting crowds and giving people something to see or talk about, provided there is no deception involved. Today's press agents are polished pros who steer clear of fraud and puffery, unless it is strictly in fun and is recognized as such.

Although a press agent's principal aim is to attract attention, rather than to educate or achieve understanding, some press agents manage to do both. An example of good press agentry was a series of free outdoor concerts with a program of light classical music offered by the Dallas Symphony Orchestra one summer to stimulate interest in its season ticket sales drive. The events attracted a warm response from music lovers, and probably helped people see the symphony as a "fun-giving" rather than as a formal institution. "Press agentry" can be one element in an overall public relations effort.

Promotion There is a hazy line between the old press agentry and today's promotion. Although promotion incorporates special events that could be called press agentry, it goes beyond that into *opinion making,* for promotion attempts to garner support and endorsement for a person, product, institution or idea. Promotional campaigns depend for their effectiveness on the most efficient use of various PR tools; and *more* is not always better. Examples of promotion are the various fund-raising drives conducted by churches, charities, health groups and conservation interests. Among the successful promoters in the country are the American Red Cross, the American Cancer Society and United Fund organizations. Promotion, fund raising and all that goes with such drum beating are a variety of PR activities, incorporated into an overall public relations program. What makes promotion activities worthwhile is the merit of the cause. The legitimacy of the cause is also important from a purely pragmatic viewpoint: It won't receive media coverage if it isn't legitimate.

Public Affairs Many public relations people are using the term *public affairs* to describe their work. This is misleading, however, because public affairs is a highly specialized kind of public relations that means *community relations* and *governmental relations,* or dealing with officials within the community and working with legislative groups and with various pressure groups such as consumers. It is a highly significant part of a public relations program, but it is not the whole program. Eighteen months before the Dallas/Fort Worth Airport was to open, two PR firms were hired—one to handle public affairs, the other to handle media relations. There were good reasons for having two firms. Public affairs was complex, not only because the airport was paid for by cities in two different counties, but also because the airport was located astride two counties and within the municipal boundaries of four suburban cities. The media relations were complex as well, since they involved arranging the special events, advertising and publicity connected with the opening; producing informational materials about the airport; and conducting media relations that were international in scope.

In the military, *public affairs* is the term commonly used to designate a broader responsibility than *public information,* which is merely publicity—handing out information. Because of a rather shortsighted law that precludes government use of people identified as public relations personnel, military public affairs officers often have broad public relations functions, that is, responsibility for all facets of both internal and external public relations.

Publicity   Because publicity is usually involved in helping to call attention to the special events or the activities surrounding a promotion, there is confusion over this term. Essentially, publicity means *placing information in a news medium,* either a mass medium such as television or newspapers or a specialized medium such as corporate magazines or industry newsletters. Publicists are writers. Use of the term *public relations* by institutions to describe publicity jobs is unfortunate. Publicists perform a vital function—disseminating information—but they generally do not help set policy. (Only PR counselors, usually at the executive level, are in a position to effect substantive management changes.)

A college student's first awareness of public relations activity is often through some personal experience with publicity. A note comes from home, "Congratulations on making the dean's list. Love, Aunt Susie." A clipping is attached. How did that get into the hometown newspaper? Mother? No. The university's news bureau sent a story with that student's name and others from the same town.

Publicity isn't always good news. For campus PR people, the political strife of the sixties and early seventies was an ulcer-provoking period. At Drake University in Des Moines, Iowa, radicals planted a bomb that exploded in the science building. The university's public relations office gave information to the local and campus news media immediately. The next day, the office sent out a four-page mailing piece that included a letter from the president telling what had happened, describing the extent of the damages, estimating when repairs would be made and emphasizing that the incident was not caused by university students. The mailing piece also carried reproductions of the newspaper stories and photographs. It was sent to alumni, parents, students, faculty, staff and others on the university's mailing list. Such prompt action helped clarify a situation that could have resulted in actions even more detrimental to the university such as the removal of students by concerned parents or the withdrawal of funds and support by alumni and donors.

Advertising   Advertising is concerned with *buying time or space* for ads and helping to *design and write copy* for ads. Advertising is usually separate from PR and should complement the total PR program. If a public relations person has no expertise in advertising, an agency should be hired to work under his or her supervision. Advertising is needed for special events and successful promotion. Although it is a major part of marketing, it is a distinct activity with its own needs for research and testing. Advertising as paid-for time or space is a tool of PR, often used to complement publicity, promotions and press agentry (for example, the appearance in supermarkets of the Jolly Green Giant).

Marketing   As in advertising, research and testing play a vital role in marketing, but the kind of testing advertising uses may be only a part of market research. Marketing specialists want to know if there is a *need or desire* for a product or service and, if so, *among which audiences* and in *what form* is it most likely to be received. Marketing is directed toward consumers, although it must interact with other publics such as the sales force, dealers, retailers and the advertising department. Market research is invaluable to the PR practitioner because it provides information about consumers—and relationships with consumers are an important PR consideration.

All marketing activities have public relations implications and occasionally a direct impact. For example, a marketing campaign launched to promote a new type of double-edged razor blade turned into a public relations problem when samples of the product (enclosed in an envelope with promotional literature) were inserted into newspapers, provoking complaints about, for instance, a dog cutting its mouth and children getting to the blades before their parents. Most often, however, marketing is an asset to public relations.

Merchandising Merchandising, often confused with marketing, is concerned with the *packaging* of a product, an idea or perhaps even a president. Its research asks what subtle emotions play a part in acceptance of the product, what shape of package is easiest to handle, what color is likely to attract more attention, what kind of display will make people react. The answers are important information for salespeople and dealers and should supplement the marketing and advertising research in a campaign. Merchandising experts are strong in the area of graphics, color, tactile responses and emotional reactions to physical imagery. Their work is vital, often part of the public relations milieu. However, it is not in itself public relations. . . .

PR Issues: Managers/Futurists

By the mid-1970s as many as one in five Fortune 500 companies had a "futurist" on the payroll, owing to the acceleration of crises. Their role is to serve management as an early warning system. The 1970s was an era of uncertainty. Most Americans worried about economic problems, shortages of natural resources, especially energy, and a lack of confidence in American institutions. These concerns have continued in the 1980s, giving impetus to planning based on predictions of internal company development and external social, political and economic conditions. Detecting emerging issues and watching social and economic trends has become an important PR function, casting PR people more in their role as social scientists. Information and intelligent analysis can help restore confidence in our economy and government. The challenge to PR practitioners is to provide leadership in developing creative, pragmatic communications programs, giving the public full information that is candid, factual and understandable. Further, PR workers must draw more extensively on their innovative skills to maintain good relations with their audiences. Audiences are the public of public relations. ■

PERSPECTIVE 2

Edward L. Bernays Talks About the Business

Edward L. Bernays, often called the Father of Public Relations, wrote the first book on the subject, *Crystallizing Public Opinion,* in 1923. He was interested in mass psychology—in how to influence large groups of people. In this article, Bernays traces the evolution of the public relations profession.

Consider:

1. What are the characteristics of each of the stages of public relations that Bernays describes?

2. Is each of the stages Bernays describes exclusive of the others? For instance, do elements of Period 3 still exist today?

3. What would be the roles of a public relations professional who operated in each of these periods?

4. How do you view the public relations profession today?

Father of PR Analyzes Its History

EDWARD L. BERNAYS

As I see it, public relations in the US has had five periods.

▲ *Period 1.* Public relations for independence (late 1700s to 1800)
▲ *Period 2.* Public relations in the period of expansion (1801–1865)
▲ *Period 3.* Public be damned period (1866–1900)
▲ *Period 4.* Public be informed period (1901–1919)
▲ *Period 5.* Public relations of mutual understanding (1920 to present).

In the first period, public relations for independence, public opinion of the colonists, people power, became unified for independence. The methods the group leaders and opinion molders, among them Samuel Adams, John Dickinson, Thomas Paine, Patrick Henry, Thomas Jefferson, used would today be called public relations strategies and tactics. Oratory, newspaper exposure and correspondence rallied public opinion and the people to the cause of freedom and independence. The Boston Tea Party would today be called a media event.

Edward L. Bernays authored the first book on public relations, *Crystallizing Public Opinion,* in 1923. Bernays is still active in public relations today.

In the second period, 1800 to 1865, public relations of expansion, the United States developed and expanded in a manner unprecedented in history—industrially, financially, technologically.

In 1832, the telegraph revolutionized communications. Four-page newspapers proliferated. Reform movements agitated the society, free secular education, votes for women, world peace, establishment of labor unions and prohibition. The ideologies of Alexander Hamilton often conflicted with the ideologies of Thomas Jefferson and Andrew Jackson. The greatest issue in public opinion was the question of slavery.

In the third period, the public be damned period 1865 to 1900, the post civil war period, the inventions of electric power and the internal combustion engine accelerated industrial development and output. Laissez faire prevailed. Robber barons were in the saddle. Public utilities and other monopolies proliferated. The statement made by William Vanderbilt, the railroad magnate, in 1879 characterized the period, when he said "The public be damned" in response to a question by a newspaperman. Vanderbilt's statement fell like a bombshell on the social and economic scene. It accelerated anger of the people, already antagonistic to the despotic power of the railroad magnates and the monopolistic utilities and other "malefactors of wealth."

It should not be forgotten that this period also saw the rise of the press agent.

In the next period, the public be informed period 1901–1919, counter reaction to the practices of businessmen and unscrupulous politicians came from activist groups of varied kinds. Speaking in numerous large magazines of national circulation, *McClure's, Everybody's* and others for this nationwide reform movement were investigative reporters, known as muckrakers. Ida Tarbell, Lincoln Steffens, Stewart Edward White were among them. From 1901 to 1916 they exposed excesses of business and politicians through their concentrated attack. President Theodore Roosevelt, responding to the public mood, in a public relations gesture proclaimed the Square Deal and brandished the Big Stick.

In 1912, the year I graduated from Cornell University, Woodrow Wilson was elected to the presidency of the United States. Recognizing the growth of people power he proclaimed the New Freedom. It gave the people a greater recognition of their power. It also brought to business a greater recognition of people power.

Of the next period, 1920 to today, the period of mutual understanding. Eric Goldman, professor of American history at Princeton University in his book, "Two Way Street, the Emergence of public relations," writes as follows: "Public relations counsel marks the third stage in the evolution of public relations thought in the United States. The public was not to be fooled in the immemorial way of the press agent."

In those early days from 1919 on, a virtual conspiracy of silence prevailed in the media about public relations.

Between 1930 and 1940 public relations prospered. The stock market crash and the devastating depression that followed put business in the doghouse. Business recognized this and tried to reestablish itself through new public relations strategies.

In the 1950s bigness of corporations, corporate mergers and conglomerates worried the public.

In the 60s and 70s distrust in our leaders and institutions affected our people. Watergate and the Vietnam war weakened their trust in their leaders, not only at the level of the national government but with all our institutions. Watergate had a particularly bad impact on public relations' new nomenclature and titles developed. A variety of new titles was concocted. Public affairs manager, public issues director, community affairs manager were among the favorite terms used by public relations people. They were apparently unaware that these new titles were also in the public domain. Anyone could use them. And they might also become victims of anti-social individuals using the title. ■

PERSPECTIVE 3

Public Relations and Politics

Today, public relations is an integral part of the political process. In this excerpt from their book *PR: How the PR Industry Writes the News,* Jeff and Marie Blyskal discuss how public relations people shape what we learn about politicians and government agencies.

Consider:

1. What do the Blyskals mean when they say that events become "part of the third-party endorsement of the product being sold"?

2. Why do government agencies need public relations, according to the Blyskals?

3. Do you agree that the public relations activities described here are necessary? Appropriate? Why? Why not?

How Political Public Relations Shapes the News

JEFF and MARIE BLYSKAL

Political PR (often overlapping and blurring the term "politics") is at least as old as the Republic itself and probably older, according to PR historians. For example, Edward L. Bernays points to the Boston Tea Party as the equivalent of today's media event that was "staged to dramatize American resistance to British authority." Scott Cutlip and Allen Center, authors of the textbook *Effective Public Relations,* say President Andrew Jackson's political opponents created myths about "Davy Crockett in an effort to woo the frontier vote away from Old Hickory. Crockett's press agent was Matthew St. Clair Clarke."*

For the public, the problem with political PR is that it is often intertwined with real events or with events that appear to have a significance of their own. Here is a realm of PR in which ideas, programs, policies, laws, and the politicians themselves are the products to be sold. And because of the credibility of threatened congres-

sional or legislative action; of U.S. warships in Central America; of leaks, speeches, and trial balloons; and even of Greenpeacers being detained in the Soviet Union, these very "events" become part of the third-party endorsement of the product being sold.

PR helps "package" a political product for sale, often in subtle ways. When former New York governor Hugh Carey went to Washington in 1976 to get federal loan guarantees for a near-bankrupt New York City, he brought union and business leaders with him to show that the state and city were united in getting themselves out of trouble. "That was terrific PR," says [New York political consultant David] Garth. "He wasn't just a governor with a city in trouble that wanted a handout; he went down as a group of the brightest leaders working on a problem but needing some help."

Likewise, a governor or other politician's tour of a flood area or disaster site serves a PR function. If the politician does not participate in this news cliché, it could generate negative publicity that implies the politician doesn't care. But more importantly, the extra publicity sets the stage for state or federal assistance for the affected area. Explains Garth: "Politicians don't

---

Jeff and Marie Blyskal are award-winning journalists who have written for several national publications.

*Another American legend, say Cutlip and Center, was Daniel Boone—"the creation of a landowner promoting settlement in Kentucky."

have to lobby each other in private conversation. If they need assistance, they ask for it. But you might be asked to create a public climate of need to get support for congressional funding. A disaster no one knows about will have a difficult time getting aid." Even floods and tornadoes need their own PR representatives.

Examples of political PR disguised as real news abound.

1. During the 1984 presidential campaign, President Reagan's own chief PR man, Michael Deaver, "admitted" in a press interview that Reagan sometimes naps during cabinet meetings. The press loved it, since it raised the "age issue" against Reagan. But the "age issue" never did develop into a big campaign problem, despite Deaver's remarks. Why not? Because Deaver's comment was apparently designed to defuse the issue by having the White House raise it before the Mondale campaign could. Having thus gotten Reagan's age into the open, the White House was then able to dismiss it, in part with Secretary of Defense Caspar Weinberger's comment that he too would like to doze during long, boring cabinet meetings.

2. In January 1985, the *New York Times* ran a series of articles that accused the city's chief medical examiner, Dr. Elliot Gross, of producing a series of misleading or inaccurate autopsy reports on people who died while in police custody. Almost immediately after the series ran, the *New York Post* ran a front-page story trumpeting WHAT THE TIMES DIDN'T PRINT about Gross. The *Post* charged that the *Times* story was weak, unfair, and contradictory and that the story's primary sources were enemies of Gross. The *Post* also hinted that the *Times* story was a PR campaign against the chief medical examiner by Michael Baden, Gross's predecessor who was ousted by New York mayor Koch in 1979. "Baden openly boasted he had so much clout with the *Times* he could get any story he wanted published," said the *Post,* quoting the widow of another former— and "legendary"—New York medical examiner, Dr. Milton Halpern.

What the *Post* didn't print, however, was the fact that Gross's PR man, Howard Rubenstein, who had given the newspaper the story, was also the *Post*'s PR man. According to the *Daily News, Post* executive editor Roger Wood would not comment on Gross's connections with the *Post*. [In April 1985, a mayoral investigatory body found that Gross had not been guilty of any wrongdoing.]

3. In the early eighties, stories about the business potential of outer space began appearing in the press. *Fortune* and *BusinessWeek* were two to cover the "news." Those stories were initiated by NASA, says David Garrett, the agency's public affairs officer, to help generate commercial customers for the space shuttle. Similarly, NASA placed stories in *Ebony* and *Jet* in 1983 "to get the black community interested in science and technology," says Garrett.

NASA, like the Pentagon, is always looking for the PR angle to justify its budget. Flybys of the space shuttle over Boston, New York, and Washington and the shuttle's visit to the Paris Air Show in spring 1983 are only the most overt publicity stunts to build public excitement and support. NASA also sends a "space mobile," films, and exhibits to schools around the country for educational—and PR—purposes aimed at the voters of tomorrow. NASA newsletters, detailing recent discoveries and successes, are sent to science teachers in 35,000 U.S. schools. The agency's protocol division handles influential guests (like opinion leaders in Congress, the Office of Management and Budget, and aerospace companies) at space launches and now at shuttle landings. "We invite people who can get support for the agency," admits Garrett. Most recently the influential people brought in to be influenced by the PR included Wall Street brokers and others from the financial community who will help invest in the commercialization of space.

4. One of the most spectacular political PR news stories, however, was one that a major news organization hyped for its own ratings. In early 1984, CBS News's *60 Minutes* and the short-lived *American Parade* aired interviews with former president Richard Nixon. CBS played to the last row: "You have never seen him less guarded, more direct, or more outspoken," said a CBS News advertisement. "I have never known a president to speak for the record as unguardedly as Nixon has," said *60 Minutes* executive producer Don Hewitt.

The disturbing thing about this whole affair—aside from the fact that CBS News bought U.S. broadcast rights to the interview for $500,000—is that it was a clear political PR production. Nixon's interviewer was Frank Gannon, a friend of the former president who had done PR with Ron Ziegler for a time in the Nixon White House. The press made almost nothing of this matter. Gannon claimed the Nixon interview was the first of many celebrity interviews to come from Gannon's production company, Historic Video Productions. . . .

Gannon says the interview was his own idea, but that one of Nixon's motives was undoubtedly to boost his own image and put Watergate to rest once and for all. The effectiveness of the PR is frighteningly evident in the press that followed the event. AFTER DECADE, NIXON IS GAINING FAVOR,

headlined the *New York Times* in August 1984, the ten-year anniversary of his resignation; "Richard Nixon is back," said a *USA Today* story around the same time; "[The CBS broadcast] will probably enhance Nixon's re-emergence," said *Newsweek*.

Only *Parade* magazine put the whole affair into proper perspective. It quoted the August 1974 wonderings of George Frampton, one of the lawyers on Leon Jaworski's Watergate special prosecuting force. Said Frampton then: "I wonder if ten years from now history will endorse the notion that Mr. Nixon has 'suffered enough.' . . . The prospect of Mr. Nixon publishing his memoirs . . . should remind us that, unlike his aides who are convicted of crime, Mr. Nixon will have the 'last say' about his own role in Watergate if he is not prosecuted."

Parade went on to quote a March 14, 1984, *Washington Post* account of a Nixon appearance: "The cream of America's business and industrial establishment welcomed Richard Nixon back into the fold. A sellout crowd of 1,600 at the Economic Club of New York . . . gave him three standing ovations. . . . Nobody mentioned Watergate." ∎

PERSPECTIVE 4

Public Relations Techniques

The Internal Revenue Service certainly can use some press relations advice. In this speech, delivered to Internal Revenue Service employees in Cleveland, Ohio, Frederick Buchstein outlines the principles of effective public relations.

Consider:

1. Explain the differences between advertising, public relations, and press relations, according to Buchstein.

2. Describe the process by which stories are evaluated and published and/or broadcast, according to Buchstein.

3. Outline the steps that Buchstein suggests to help establish good press relations.

4. What is the least painful approach to handling negative information, according to Buchstein? Do you agree? Disagree? Explain.

Public Relations: How to Make the Best Use of Contacts with Editors and Reporters

FREDERICK D. BUCHSTEIN

Perhaps we should take a moment first to define the difference between advertising, public relations and press relations. For purposes of today's remarks, let's consider advertising as a communication technique which utilizes space or time that is purchased to tell a company's story. Public relations is the technique which utilizes the editorial columns in the print media and/or the noncommercial time of radio and television to tell the corporate story. Press relations is the branch of public relations which treats the media as an audience unto itself and a conduit to other audiences.

This anecdote from *Reader's Digest* illustrates the difference between advertising and other corporate communications.

If you work for a circus and put "The Circus is Coming to Town on Monday" posters all over town, that's advertising. If you put the posters on an elephant and parade him through the town, that's sales promotion. If you lead the elephant through the mayor's flower garden, that's publicity. If you can get the mayor to smile about it, that's public relations.

And if you can get the press to publish the story on page one, that's press relations.

Press relations is a fine art which cannot be practiced without first understanding the relationship between journalists and organizations

Frederick D. Buchstein is Director of Research for Dix & Eaton, Inc., a public relations agency.

such as the Internal Revenue Service and the way the media works.

How to Live with the Media

Let's first talk about how you and journalists get along.

Like it or not, the Internal Revenue Service and journalists have to do business with each other. The IRS needs the news media to reach tax avoiders and evaders, and taxpayers. Journalists have to talk to the IRS to get the news that affects their readers and viewers. It's a shotgun marriage to be sure.

But since divorce isn't possible, you have to learn how to live with the media and survive. And that's what you're here today to do. You're going to learn to view and to use the media as potential allies in getting your message across to your publics.

Before revealing the secrets of press relations, I'm going to tell you something about the media itself.

It portrays you as bad guys. When was the last time you saw a TV program portraying an IRS agent as a good guy?

To even begin to change these attitudes, you have to understand how the media works.

Remember that newspapers and TV and radio stations are profit-making businesses.

The size of what is known as the "news hole" in a newspaper—that portion of the paper devoted to news and editorial comment—is dictated each day by the amount of advertising sold for that day. The news hole can be as small as 30 percent of the total paper. Many publishers strive for a 40 percent to 50 percent news hole.

Each day the editor gets a set of dummies or layout sheets which have the ads' sizes marked. He must take the remaining space and allocate it to the various standing elements that make up the paper such as the comics, stock tables, the horoscope, editorials, columns and so on. What's left is further divided into news categories—local, state and national—with an attempt to keep the categories balanced. The best stories go on page one.

With rare exceptions—such as a presidential assassination attempt—the editor, working with a layout or makeup man, has no flexibility in changing the size of the news hole. The TV or radio news director fills air time instead of space. He fills about 22 minutes of air time in a 30 minute TV newscast.

Every day, everywhere, there's news: there's a murder in the city. On a highway, a tank truck has overturned. In the suburbs, there's a leak in a water main. None of these can be anticipated, nor can their coverage be scheduled in advance.

In addition to local news, there are international, national and state happenings that demand coverage. All these events must compete for the few inches available in each day's newspaper, or for a few seconds of air time.

So the reporter/editor duet has the problem of getting the most interesting and important news pared down to the minimum length it takes to tell the story.

The majority of national and international news comes from the Associated Press, United Press International, or other wire services such as Dow Jones. And since a newspaper can have as many as seven editions a day, the paper must be continuously revised, updated and redesigned to keep pace with breaking news. The *Plain Dealer,* for example, has state, Greater Cleveland and final sports editions.

Broadcast media have nearly impossible deadlines: the late-breaking lead story on a network news program can change a dozen times in the half-hour before air time. Radio stations try to find a new headline or angle on a breaking story every hour on the hour, 24 hours a day. They're also striving for scoops.

What this means is that a reporter may spend two hours interviewing a business executive or an IRS manager, an assignment his editor emphasized could make page one or be the play story. When the reporter gets back to the newsroom, however, late-breaking news may have bumped his story to the back of the paper—or out of the paper altogether.

Reporters do not edit their own articles. They do not have control over the editing process, do not decide where the story will be played in the paper, and do not write headlines. All of this often happens after the reporter has turned in his copy and gone home for the day or out on a new assignment.

To lessen the possibility of error, the reporter usually writes in the "inverted pyramid" style. The six most important elements—who, what, when, where, why and how—are put in the first couple of paragraphs. The rest of the facts follow in descending order of importance, so the story can be cut from the bottom to fit the space allocated for it. *The Wall Street Journal* has pioneered the use of the delayed lead. The reporter sets the scene with a vignette or anecdote and then gets to the point of the story. All reporters look for punchy, colorful quotes for their stories.

Between the time an article leaves the reporter's typewriter or VDT and reaches the public, the story is constantly edited by people who did not witness the event and who have no firsthand knowledge of the story.

The reporter turns his story over to an editor, who checks the facts, sees if the reporter has the best lead possible, edits for length, and decides where the article will appear in the paper.

The editor may hold the story for the next day, rewrite it, combine it with another story, or kill it. The reporter may not know what happened to his story until after it is published.

Today, most copy editing—and even story writing—is done on computer terminals called VDTs which are used to set type. Accuracy is im-

Job	What he does	What can go wrong
Newsmaker	Makes news.	Refuses to talk to the reporter in search of facts. Purposively misleads reporter or gives only part of the story. Doesn't know how to explain what happened so any dummy can understand it.
Reporter	Gathers facts. Writes the story. Forwards it to the editor.	Fails to understand what the story means. Fails to get the facts right. Fails to put the story into context for the reader. Writes a dull story that no one reads. Is too dumb, lazy, busy, or facing too tight a deadline to overcome the above. Is anti-business. Ignores the facts so he can tell a good yarn.
Business editor	Manages reporters to make sure the news is covered and features written. Fights with the sports, city, and other news editors for page one space. Must live with managing editor's policy decisions, whims and fancies. Tries to balance coverage of what readers want and need to know against space availability.	All of the above. Ignores reporter's advice and overplays or underplays a story. Like his reporters, he can fail to realize when he has a good story or is being bamboozled. Like his reporters, he bows to policies and whims of the publisher's.
Copy editor	Edits the story for language, logic, accuracy. Writes the headline.	He's in a hurry or misunderstands the story and screws up the headline or rewrite. Readers can't yell at him because they don't know who he is.
Makeup editor	Oversees printers who physically produce the paper.	Trims the meat out of the story to make it fit in allotted space.
Paper boy	Delivers the paper.	Tosses the paper into a puddle or bush. Never delivers it when you want it. Wants a tip for delivering bad news to your doorstep.
Reader	Selectively reads the news.	Avoids business news when it's on the business page. Only reads the headlines. Is more interested in the sports page and funnies.
Newsmaker	Reads the story about himself.	I didn't say that. That stupid reporter got his facts wrong. Why didn't I say more? Why wasn't my story on page one? Why didn't I get more space? I'll never talk to a reporter again. Where's my p.r. man. I want my name in the paper again.

proved—the time between typewriter and news-stand is shortened.

From the editor, the story advances to the copy desk where detailed editing occurs. Unnecessary words and phrases are eliminated, spelling and punctuation are corrected and facts are double-checked. Leads are punched up.

The editor tells the headline writer how many lines, how many words and even how many letters he can use, to capture the major thrust of an article. Headline writing is one of the most difficult jobs in the newsroom, and a three-word headline can't always be one hundred percent accurate.

Here are just a few headlines which were actually published which don't say what the writer obviously meant to say:

What was the copy editor for the Wilmington, Delaware, *News Journal,* thinking when he wrote, "Fire officials grilled over kerosene heaters."

And how many editors at the *Minneapolis Tribune* let this headline get into the paper, "6 found slain in Miami; missing toddler sought."

I'm sure that the chap who wrote this headline just plain got tired of significant news, "British left waffles on Falklands."

Almost all of this reporting and editing—whether in print or electronic journalism—is done at a hectic pace against extremely tight deadlines—a major contributor to errors.

The film or videotape editor has the unenviable task of cutting several hundred feet of film down to a ten-second clip. Some broadcast news stories are covered in a single sentence.

This is where the danger of out-of-context quotes becomes very real. Television and radio demand short, colorful quotes, even though a longer, more reasonable, but less attention-grabbing statement may be more accurate. Broadcast journalists will seek out those people who can articulate complex ideas in one or two short sentences. They also want stories that are easy to illustrate.

The tremendous speed at which news is gathered, written, edited, and published or broadcast, can produce results that disappoint

both you and the reporter. The public may never know the reasons why, but sometimes the real issues never make it to the newspaper or TV screen.

Stories lose touch with reality for other reasons, too.

How to Develop a Press Relations Program

With a little luck and a great deal of skill, you can get your message published or aired without it being butchered by the system.

The trick is that you must master the art of press relations. The time to start a press relations program is before the crisis develops. Practitioners of pre-emptive press relations survive and thrive. Practitioners of reactive press relations take unnecessary risks.

What you should expect and hope for is that the stories that are generated by you or about you are fair, accurate, unbiased, and, hopefully, favorable.

This goal will not be reached or even approximated unless you take the time to develop ongoing relationships with the reporters and editors who cover the IRS.

What this means is that you must get to know personally the reporters and the kinds of stories they do. Get-to-know-each-other lunches are a good way of doing this. Hand-delivering press releases is another. This gives you the opportunity to let the reporter ask you questions. Occasionally, suggest stories that are not pure puffery. Let him know about developing trends. For example, what is new about the way the IRS is handling its collections. Talk about collection successes.

Try and be fair in releasing breaking news stories. Nothing raises a reporter's hackles quicker than the knowledge that he is getting the news second. If you must break a story at such a time that favors one publication over another, offer to give the "hurt" party a personal interview or additional information. The reporter in this position is looking for a second-day lead—a new angle on a developing or breaking story.

Don't let your friendly reporter get the idea

that you're a publicity hound. Only reporters are allowed to have big egos.

Also, don't think for one moment that just because you know a few reporters that you won't ever get burned by the news media. It just ain't so. Friendship doesn't sweep bad news such as layoffs, plant closings, scandals, or red ink under the mat. And if you make a PR blunder, you are going to pay for it. Remember the brouhaha that erupted when General Motors announced a rash of layoffs and asked for contract concessions and then went ahead and announced a new incentive bonus system for top managers. Timing is critical.

Whenever you deal with a reporter, make sure that he has an updated fact sheet on the collection Division. You'd be surprised at how many errors are repeated year after year because the reporter's files are out of date. Such handouts make the reporter's job easier and reduce the chances that stories about you will be inaccurate. Give him copies of news stories about you that are accurate—this is particularly important when you are involved in a controversy or breaking news story.

Most business news stories are gathered by phone, through personal interviews, at press conferences and through press releases. What we're going to do now is learn how to use these important public relations tools.

Let's start with the press release. Perhaps only one out of every 500 is ever published. The other 499 are thrown in the trash can because they are missing vital information, are irrelevant, poorly written, unintelligible, illiterate or addressed to writers who are dead or who have been fired. The National Right to Work Committee used to send me five copies of the same release. Some were addressed to Frederick D. Buchstein, Fred Buchstein, and etc. Some releases are thrown out because they have absolutely no news value. If the release doesn't have direct—and quickly recognizable—meaning to the newspaper's readers, it won't be used.

The handout also needs a punchy opening paragraph—or a lead, as it is called—to make an editor want to read it and then to publish it.

A press conference offers information for stories that explode on the front pages of the newspapers or it can blow up in your face.

The number one reason for calling a press conference is to present information that is of such complex and significant nature that the newsmen will have to ask additional questions for clarification and understanding.

The media expect that any story that doesn't require extensive questions and answers will be delivered to them as a news release.

The best assurance any organization can have that it will get good media turnout for its press conference is to earn a reputation for calling one only when something of real importance has occurred or is contemplated. When an organization has that kind of reputation, no editor or reporter would consider not attending. Nothing can be more detrimental to an organization than to call an unwarranted press conference. Reporters are going to be very skeptical about wasting their time when you call another meeting.

If you are convinced that a press conference is in order, arrange it so that newsmen can get the story and all the information quickly and accurately. Hold the press conference at a convenient place and at a convenient time for the media. Have visual aids available—photographs, drawings, models, films, etc. Have written information available—news releases, fact sheet, speech, or statistical information. Arrange the room so that there is adequate equipment—microphones, chairs, typewriters, television platforms, electrical outlets, telephones, adequate lighting, etc. Keep the number of speakers (and the length of their talks) to a minimum. Most times, one or two well-informed people can present all of the information and answer all of the questions.

Keep it short. Reporters have other stories to cover and you'll be helping them if you provide them with the information, answer their questions, and let them go. Even the reporters who want a special interview will appreciate being able to do it after their colleagues have gone.

Before you call a press conference, analyze the situation clearly and be very certain in your own mind that this is the best way to present the information to the press. After all, there may be many times when you would just as soon not have to answer their questions, where they may want to ask you about unrelated activities, or times when they can embarrass you by asking questions about topics you do not care to discuss.

Reporters often interview managers by telephone. It's a quick and easy way to get information for a story.

The phone interview presents a number of problems for the person being interviewed. You can't read the reporter's face for reactions to what you are saying. Personal chemistry between you and the reporter is virtually nonexistent.

Since phone interviews tend to be shorter than in-person ones, don't beat around the bush. Say what you have to say and shut up. If after you hang up, you remember something you should have told the reporter, call him up and tell him.

How to Handle Controversy

Don't forget that if you are giving your opinion on a subject that may be controversial—a collection or IRS ruling—any reporter will give others a chance to make their points, too. They correctly assume the public is entitled to both sides of any story.

Even in situations where the story is totally one-sided—a manager or IRS profile, for example—any reporter worth his salt is going to look for elements to balance the story. He knows the story is going to be much more believable—and interesting—if he writes about dirty socks as well as the new haircut.

There are a number of tricks which will allow you to go through an in-person interview and survive. If properly done, the manager can help dispel a negative reputation or perception.

Try and have the reporter come to your office. You are more relaxed in familiar surroundings. And the reporter gets to see you in your environment. This helps to humanize you.

Prepare carefully. In any interview, print or film, you must be prepared. Playing it by ear can be dangerous. The best preparation is to anticipate the most likely questions, attempt to research the facts, and then structure effective answers. A PR man with a news media background can help you anticipate the most likely questions.

Don't try to memorize your lines—keep your answers conversational. The written materials you use to prepare for an interview can often be provided to a reporter as background information. Always give a reporter a printed fact sheet on your organization. Don't assume he has up-to-date information on you.

If it's a face-to-face interview, remember that you are in a discussion with another person who will respond to human courtesies. Be polite—be friendly—offer the reporter a cup of coffee. Set up an informal situation. If you can, find a couple of easy chairs instead of remaining sphinx-like behind your desk. This says to the reporter that you are going to converse as equals.

You should not take the reporter to task for an editorial you disagreed with, or an article you thought contained an error. You wouldn't be impressed if the reporter told you how much he disliked the IRS.

Use simple, straightforward words, and don't be too formal. The aim of communication is to convey an honest, ungarbled message—concisely.

Don't ask for the privilege of saying something off the record. Most reporters don't even want to hear off-the-record remarks. It's like giving them a lobster dinner and then asking them not to eat it. The temptation is just too great. And don't ask a reporter for editing rights or expect to get an advance copy for approval. Most news media have specific policies preventing this. He might, however, agree to reading back to you the technical parts for accuracy.

Answer direct questions as briefly and as directly as possible, elaborating only when necessary. Some executives feel an easy way to answer a reporter's questions is a simple yes or no; the less said the better. Few reporters will let a news source off the hook that easily. They'll ask you to explain, and if you don't, you'll look like you're hiding something. Explanation doesn't mean being evasive or wordy, but simply that you shouldn't be so brief you will hide your message.

A simple yes or no answer is usually disastrous. And if it's a loaded question—don't respond with a loaded answer.

When there are legal or proprietary reasons that keep you from answering a question, say so. If you must use this kind of answer, explain what the legal or proprietary reasons are. And never just say "no comment." It's been used as a hiding place so many times—by so many—that it automatically raises a red flag in the mind of the reporter.

If you truly don't know the answer to a question, don't be afraid to say, "I don't know, but I'll find out." But then make sure you do follow up, or find someone who knows more about the issue than you do to follow up for you.

Arguing with reporters is the one surefire way to make certain the story will be negative. You can rarely win battles or arguments with reporters and televised interviews will reflect even indirect hostility. Some reporters try to create an adversary relationship in the hope that you will drop your guard—have you ever watched Mike Wallace? If you know the attempt is deliberate, you should be able to handle it.

You should also look out for the reporter who does just the opposite: he makes you so comfortable that you're soon chatting away like old friends. Don't forget that you're still being interviewed—and will be quoted.

Finally—and most importantly—tell the truth—even when it hurts. Nobody likes to admit that business is bad, that employees are being laid off, that another chemical is on the EPA suspect list, or that the company has made a mistake.

Yet, telling the truth is almost always the least painful route. If the news is bad enough and big enough, it's going to get out anyhow—and we're much better off telling it in our own words.

Planning for Your Audience

Okay, now that you know everything there is to know about press relations, you can rush out and get yourself on page one of *The Wall Street Journal* and an interview on the Today Show. Presto, you're a media star. And all it takes is a little pal-ling around with reporters and a few free lunches. Right? Wrong.

Successful and positive public relations takes planning. There are questions to be answered such as what it is you want your press relations to do for you. Do you want to become a spokesman for the entire industry? Do you just want to see your name in the paper? Do you want to increase the visibility of your institution? Do you want more depositors? Do you want to publicize a new type of account? Do you want to change your image from that of an old-fashioned S&L to that of a financial planner? Do you want the public to have a better understanding of the IRS?

Then, you have to identify your audiences and decide how to best reach them. Which group is giving you the most concern? Tax evaders? Tax avoiders?

Then you have to decide how you are going to reach these audiences. Are you going to rely strictly on stories the news media are willing to run? Are you going to get involved in public relations advertising, direct mail and special events? Or are you going to publish a newsletter?

How will you know after all the time and money is invested in an ongoing press relations program whether it was worth all the trouble and expense? In other words, before you launch your press relations program you have to set some goals for it and figure out how to decide whether you succeeded in reaching them.

You might even want to get fancy and conduct a communications audit or survey to find out what your problems are. A follow-up survey would tell you whether your press and public relations campaign has helped alleviate them.

This ends the lecture portion of this media survival course.

I'd like to take a few minutes now to recommend some actions you can take to improve the news media's understanding of what you do and why it is important to readers, listeners and viewers.

Hold a media update session with the business reporters in your area. Invite them to your offices to explain what it is you do, how you do it and why you do it. Over coffee and donuts, talk about your jobs. Show them your offices. Answer their questions. Learn about them. Don't worry if you don't get a story out of this session. It is designed to position you as experts and to increase understanding. Fair and objective stories that do result are icing on the cake.

Once a year—or more often, as appropriate—issue a press release on how much money you have collected in your region, as well as how much has been collected nationally.

Take advantage of opportunities to address groups like Kiwanis, Rotary and the Lions.

Take advantage of opportunities to make public service announcements on the television and radio. Talk about issues of importance. PSAs are free for the asking.

If you know that you have a story that when it breaks will spur page one headlines, prepare for it. Appoint a spokesperson. Make sure that person can present the facts in the most accurate and positive manner possible. Anticipate the questions and your answers. Be responsive to the reporters. ■

PERSPECTIVE 5

Ronald Reagan's Public Relations Legacy

In this article from *Advertising Age,* Steven W. Colford discusses several of the public relations strategies originated by the White House staff during Ronald Reagan's presidency. Colford says that many of these public relations approaches will become staples of U.S. politics.

Consider:

1. For what purposes did the Reagan administration use focus groups? Was it a useful strategy? Discuss.

2. Colford says that one of the hallmarks of the Reagan presidency will be "an unprecedented use of the tools of Madison Avenue to sell the president and his policies to U.S. citizens." Besides the use of focus groups, describe three examples of the use of Madison Avenue techniques.

3. List the strategies that the Reagan administration used to deal with the news media. Did they work? Explain.

4. Explain the comment of political scientist Larry Sabato that "leadership is about manipulation to some degree, but it's . . . bad if the president can't see beyond his own symbols, and I wondered sometimes if he [Reagan] could."

Hail to the Image
Reagan Legacy: Marketing Tactics Change Politics

STEVEN W. COLFORD

Three months before President Reagan's trip to Moscow, a small group of people sat in a room in Philadelphia and listened to some of the things the president would say in his public speeches at the summit.

Actually, they did more than listen. They helped determine exactly *what* the president would say. Did they think he should emphasize human rights? Did they like this phrasing better than that? What should he say about the Strategic Defense Initiative, known as Star Wars?

The group constituted yet another staple of marketing and advertising enlisted in the cause of the Reagan presidency: the focus group. It was as if Procter & Gamble Co. were pretesting a new Cheer campaign.

Whatever else may be said of the Reagan administration, one of its hallmarks will be an unprecedented use of the tools of Madison Avenue to sell the president and his policies to U.S. citizens.

Although there's wide disagreement over the appropriateness of using such techniques in politics, there's virtual unanimity that no president—and perhaps no corporation—ever used them as effectively as the Reagan administration did, at least during its first term.

Despite evidence that President Reagan's image-builders faltered during the Iran-contra affair and that the president has been unmasked by

Steven W. Colford is a reporter for *Advertising Age*.

the kiss-and-tell books of former insiders, it's likely that parts of his marketing program will become increasingly important tools in U.S. politics.

"No presidency has been more image conscious or image driven than that of Ronald Reagan," wrote former *New York Times* reporter Hedrick Smith in "The Power Game." "Quite obviously, image-making or political public relations was not invented by Reagan," he continued, but "it reached new peaks of sophistication in the Reagan era."

February's focus-group session, for example, was hardly exceptional for the Reagan administration, according to Larry Speakes, the former White House spokesman, and others familiar with the Reagan presidency.

Focus groups, invariably under the direction of Richard Wirthlin, the president's longtime pollster, were used before previous summit meetings as well as before important speeches, Mr. Speakes said in an interview.

"Before State of the Union speeches, for example, Wirthlin would sit a group of people down in Washington and would register what was hot and what was cold and how they reacted to certain sections of the speech."

The president may not have been aware of the focus groups and what they produced, Mr. Speakes said. "I don't know how much of it was actually presented to the president. It was used more to help the staff prepare a speech or message and understand what parts were most effective. We would look at [poll] results to determine what was sellable [and] how."

Focus-group testing of speeches was but a small part of the White House image-building plan. The strategy also included:

▲ Sharply restricting the president's discussion of issues—his ad themes, in Madison Avenue parlance—to those few he could turn to his advantage.

▲ Careful scheduling and staging of "photo opportunities" for maximum positive publicity.

▲ Limiting the availability of the president to the media, particularly print media.

▲ Timely speechmaking before friendly regional audiences—regional marketing, in effect—to bolster public sentiment for the president and against Congress.

▲ Delivering weekly radio messages, often maligned as wasting time on small audiences but, in fact, a major instrument in "positioning" the president for positive coverage on slow-news weekends.

▲ Exploiting to the hilt the best "spokesman" a campaign could hope for—in this case the president himself.

The staging of the Reagan presidency probably began even before the election was over. Phil Dusenberry, vice chairman of BBDO Worldwide, New York, said he thinks a lot of the marketing groundwork was laid after Mr. Reagan lost the Republican presidential nomination to Gerald Ford in 1976.

"He didn't let any grass grow under him," said Mr. Dusenberry, who worked on the Tuesday Team, Mr. Reagan's ad hoc agency for the 1984 campaign. "He had a syndicated newspaper column, he had his radio program that he used to build support from the grass-roots level and he was always out on speaking tours, talking to all groups.

"There's nothing like using hometown newspapers and [broadcast] stations to get your message out and make it stick, repeating it, theming it again and again and again."

"Theming it" was in fact a key to the Reagan presidency. After the 1980 election, his closest advisers—Michael Deaver, Ed Meese, James Baker—decided that sticking to a short, tight agenda would help control what was reported, especially by the electronic media.

"What we did in the first year was concentrate on the president's economic message and mission," Mr. Speakes said, "and we made sure that everything he did was connected to and reinforced that idea.

"If someone came into the Oval Office during that time, regardless of who or for what—even if it was just for a photo opportunity—we'd manage to tie it to the economy and curtailing taxes. We simply would not change our methods or our policies, even if other issues came up that could have sidetracked us."

"Ronald Reagan kept saying the same things, repeating the same basic themes, over and over and over," said Ed Ney, former chairman of Young & Rubicam. "That is brilliant strategy, whether you're selling a product or, as president, selling what you believe in. . . . Find the benefits of what you're selling, deliver your message, make it interesting and do it consistently.

"And the president was well positioned by his advisers, and the American public bought what [it] wanted to buy," he continued, adding that the Reagan administration's use of such marketing practices as polling, research and "sales" and media planning was unsurpassed in political history.

"We may have seen the greatest salesman ever," Mr. Ney said.

"Reagan—and his people—defined their agenda, at least in the first term, and refused to be distracted from it," agreed Hodding Carter, former Department of State spokesman for Jimmy Carter's administration. "And that's very important to selling anything—that you don't try to sell too much.

"And it was made attractive by the extraordinary capacity Reagan had to translate his positions into human terms, and to make them appear warm and acceptable even when a lot of people were opposed to the specifics."

The Reagan administration also embraced regionalism in a way that would make regional marketing enthusiasts such as Campbell Soup Co. proud.

"Whether it was education or taxes, it didn't matter," Mr. Speakes said. "If the president was traveling to promote a policy, we'd be sure to travel to the region where there were congressmen or senators important to the issue.

"We'd have the local media there from the region that was important to the legislator, and then he could be out front [in staged photo opportunities] with the president and be seen with the president by that legislator's constituents. If it was trade or textile legislation, we'd be sure to go on a southern swing to South Carolina, where we could be seen with [Sen.] Strom Thurmond."

That regionalizing often helped the Reagan White House leapfrog Congress and take its case directly to the people.

Using the Media

Nowhere was the Reagan White House more diligent than in its use of the media, particularly television. "He had an entire team that had thought through how they would deal with the media," said Mr. Carter, now a political commentator for ABC-TV and head of Main Street Communications, Washington.

"TV was his be-all and end-all," said Larry Sabato, a political scientist at the University of Virginia. "And there I don't know that he so much controlled them as frustrated them with his limited exposures and infrequent news conferences. . . . The genius of Reagan's people was simply giving them such limited access and so few pictures that they knew what would be on the evening news."

"That business of evasiveness from the media was elevated to art form," said Mr. Smith, the former *Times* reporter, in an interview.

It took many forms, Mr. Smith said. There was, for example, the seemingly insignificant de-

cision to move the daily White House briefings from noon to early morning.

That was done, Mr. Smith said, to make sure the president didn't have to react to statements from the State and Defense departments, both of which had morning briefings for the media. Instead, he could make a preemptive strike with his own remarks.

"By making the first comments on major overnight news and foreign developments," Mr. Smith wrote in his book, Mr. Speakes "could shape the Washington slant on the news before Congress or other agencies could react."

"When the press office obfuscates and tries to keep the press hidden, it limits the amount of news coming out," said Tom Shales, *Washington Post* TV critic. "But it also serves to make the press more aggressive, and then when the public tunes in the news and sees that, it asks, 'Why is [ABC-TV White House correspondent] Sam Donaldson so rude?' That doesn't hurt the president at all; it just makes him look better and the press worse."

The president's weekly radio messages were an important part of the marketing plan. The folksy addresses were discontinued early in his presidency. But at the recommendation of Joseph Holmes, an employee in the White House TV office, President Reagan resumed them in April 1982.

"We were never able to get an accurate audience count, but then we never worried about that part of it," Mr. Speakes said. "It was the ripple effect that was important. We knew what the president said in that message on Saturday would be picked up. . . . So the size of the radio audience didn't matter. . . . It was another tool in the communications package that we had put together."

No detail was too small for the Reagan image-builders. Mr. Deaver, for example, didn't like the tan drapes of the Oval Office—they washed out the president's color when he was televised there. So, soon after the president's first term began, Mr. Deaver replaced the drapes with $20,000 worth of backlighting.

And when Mr. Reagan prepared to accept the

Republican nomination for a second term in 1984, a special design team hired by Mr. Deaver redid the convention podium in warm, earthy colors and eliminated all sharp angles from the area surrounding the president.

The idea was to show the president as a sea of calm in the middle of a hall of loud, sweaty and excited GOP delegates, Mr. Smith said.

Embracing Reagan-Like Traits

Some admen working in politics already are trying to transfer Reagan-like traits to their candidate clients.

"Ronald Reagan, whether in a speech or whatever, communicated one-on-one, even if he was talking to millions," said Thomas Edmonds, a political consultant and president of Edmonds & Associates, Alexandria, Va.

"And that's what I'm trying to do more and more with my clients in terms of trying to capture the real person," he added. "I've already, with some clients, sat down and done commercials with a camera over the shoulder and the candidate very relaxed, until we can capture that same essence."

Adapting the Reagan techniques to other campaigns probably can work on a limited scale, experts say. But attempting a wholesale replication of the Reagan marketing program is foolhardy, they also say, because its most essential element is the one least reproducible: Ronald Reagan, master spokesman and trained actor who never forgot his training.

"There were even differences in what he did in front of a TV camera vs. what he did on a stage," Mr. Speakes recalled. "For example, when he was on stage, he knew he could do a grand gesture. But when he was [before the] TV camera, it was much smaller because he knew a big gesture would be too big."

"We may never see another president who is quite as consistent in manipulation and following scripts as Reagan," said the University of Virginia's Mr. Sabato. "And that can be both good and bad."

"Leadership Is About Manipulation"

"I think in the public sense what he did can be good because leadership is about manipulation to some degree, but it's also bad if the president can't see beyond his own symbols, and I wondered sometimes if he could."

But conservative Roger Stone, President Reagan's Northeast political director in 1976, 1980 and 1984, said he thinks too much has been made of the president's "communications mastery."

"There's no question he had good people around him deciding which were his best camera angles, but the basic product had to be there to sell," Mr. Stone said. "And Ronald Reagan is exactly what he appears to be." . . .

On the other hand, the Reagan image . . . [was] tarnished during the second term, and that could affect the next president.

"I think, especially with some of the books that have come out about Reagan, there's likely to be a backlash by the public," Mr. Smith said. "Maybe the new slickness for a candidate will be a well-calculated non-slickness."

"If you're not another Babe Ruth in communications who can hit them out of the park like Reagan, then it would be my advice not to try," said Alex Castellanos, a partner in Murphy & Castellanos, an Alexandria, Va., media consulting company that worked on Robert Dole's presidential bid.

"I think that because of the backlash to the Reagan era, people already are looking for less image," Mr. Castellanos said. "An ultrareal kind of candidate, a sort of anti-Reagan." ■

CHAPTER TEN

For Further Reading

Books

Edward L. Bernays, *The Engineering of Consent* (Norman: University of Oklahoma Press, 1955).

Scott M. Cutlip, Allen H. Center, and Glen M. Broom, *Effective Public Relations,* 6th ed. (Englewood Cliffs: Prentice-Hall, Inc., 1985).

Marin Linsky, *Impact: How the Press Affects Federal Policymaking* (New York: Norton, 1986).

Freaser P. Seitel, *The Practice of Public Relations,* 2nd ed. (Columbus: Charles E. Merrill, 1984).

Periodicals

Public Relations Journal

Public Relations Quarterly

Public Relations Review

Issues and
Effects

PART IV

Ownership and News Gathering

PERSPECTIVE 1

Media Ownership

Media ownership today is of four major types: (1) concentrated ownership—companies that have holdings within one industry, such as newspaper chains or broadcast network affiliates; (2) cross-media ownership—companies that own more than one type of medium (newspapers and radio stations, for example); (3) conglomerates—companies that own media properties but also own businesses that are unrelated to the media industries; and (4) vertical integration—companies that attempt to control several aspects of one media industry, such as movie production and movie distribution. The following article is a profile of the Hearst Corporation, which has been a major media power since the turn of the century.

Consider:

1. Which of the four types of media ownership does the Hearst Corporation represent?

2. What role does the Hearst family play in controlling the company?

3. How does the Hearst approach to launching a new magazine differ from that of its competitors?

4. What advantages does a privately-owned media company such as Hearst have over a publicly-owned company?

Citizens Rich

WILLIAM P. BARRETT

In a television spot promoting the *San Francisco Examiner,* the ghost of William Randolph Hearst talks with his 38-year-old grandson, Will Hearst III, who now heads the Hearst Corp.'s flagship paper. "Are you sure you know what you're doing, Will?" the ghost asks. "I don't know," replies Will. "Did you?"

It's a bit of byplay that the once severely troubled Hearst publishing organization can

William P. Barrett is a reporter for *Forbes* magazine.

now afford. In [1987], the centennial year of the enterprise founded by the legendary Hearst—the man whose life inspired the film *Citizen Kane*—revenues are expected to top $2 billion, perhaps for the first time. *Forbes* estimates that the cash flow after existing debt service nears a rich $280 million. After taking into account the effects of the Oct. 19 Black Monday crash, *Forbes* estimates the Hearst empire's net worth in the neighborhood of $3.5 billion. Besides newspapers, magazines and TV stations, the wealth includes vast real estate holdings on both coasts. As a family media fortune, the Hearsts stand a close second to their private-media archrival, the Newhouse organization, which *Forbes* estimates to be worth about $3.75 billion.

Estimates are necessary because Hearst—like Newhouse—is a secretive outfit that doesn't reveal its finances. "I hope you say somewhere I didn't verify your numbers," says Frank A. Bennack Jr., Hearst Corp.'s Texas-born president and chief executive, when interviewed by *Forbes.* Even within the company, financial information is shared only on a strict need-to-know basis. Many of Bennack's top managers have never seen a budget or financial statement besides the one for their own divisions.

But as the TV advertisements show, Hearst, one of the country's best-known private companies, has been putting on more of a public face in the past few years. For the first time in decades, it has been borrowing big money and acquiring properties. Since Bennack took the helm in 1979, Hearst has shelled out more than $1.5 billion to acquire or develop new businesses. These include well-established magazines like *Redbook* and *Esquire,* and feature syndicates like North America and Cowles. In TV, Hearst has bought KMBC-TV in Kansas City, Mo. and WCVB-TV in Boston, while joining partners in starting national cable networks like Arts & Entertainment and Lifetime. It has added book publishers like William Morrow & Co. and Arbor House. Even in newspapers, which for a long time have taken a back seat to magazines in the Hearst scheme of things, the company... purchased the 407,000 daily-circulation *Houston Chronicle.*

"We're not halfway through our acquisitions program," Bennack says proudly of his company, whose management is so lean it doesn't even have an acquisitions department. Moreover, the overall quality of Hearst properties has risen sharply, and the papers in no way resemble the sensational, often inaccurate Hearst press of yesteryear. The *San Francisco Examiner* and the *San Antonio Light,* for example, are now two of the country's better papers of their size (daily circulations around 145,000).

Hearst, which in its 1930s heyday accounted for 14% of the country's daily circulation and nearly double that on Sunday, is no longer primarily a newspaper company. Its 15 daily papers, about half in smaller markets, plus three weeklies, contribute 31% of the company's revenues (one number Bennack does give out) but only a puny 9% or so (our guess) of the net cash flow.

The magazine division, on the other hand, fueled by such ad-laden powerhouses as *Good Housekeeping, Cosmopolitan* and the successful startup *Country Living,* brings in 42% of the revenue, according to Bennack, and maybe 45%, we estimate, of the net cash flow.

The booming broadcast division (six TV and seven radio stations) is perhaps nearly three times more profitable than newspapers on far less than half the revenues. Even the syndication division, headed by King Features Syndicate, which dominates its field peddling Beetle Bailey, Blondie, Popeye and other comic features to newspapers, throws off more than half as much cash on the papers on less than one-seventh the gross.

Hearst, however, is by no means becoming a conglomerate. "The more diverse we are, the better off we're going to be," says Bennack, who works out of the same six-story, storefront-lined building on Manhattan's Eighth Avenue that W. R. himself commissioned a half-century ago. But he means diverse within communications. Aside from real estate, Hearst has now shed all its non-media-related holdings, in 1979 selling the last of the once-vast mining stock holdings on which the family fortune was originally based. In the last two years Hearst has unloaded its 17.5% interest in Southwest Forest Industries Inc. of Phoenix, a dress pattern company and a Maine paper mill, as well as a string of weekly newspapers around the Los Angeles area.

Frank Bennack presides over a company with a lot of lucrative niches in the magazine field. For one thing, it is the country's biggest publisher of monthly magazines in an era when weeklies seem to have the glamour. It has the country's largest collection of nonnetwork-owned ABC television affiliates, giving Hearst considerable clout over network programming. A subsidiary in Des Moines, Communication Data Services Inc., employs 1,400 people and processes about 50 million subscription renewals a year. Among Hearst's other publications is a tony British magazine, *Harpers & Queen,* that has run more than 400 pages an issue. Some of its trade publications, such as *Floor Covering Weekly,* lead their fields.

Because of the way it is structured, Hearst has plenty of money available for more acquisitions. Virtually all of the stock—including 100% of the voting stock—is held by a family trust that is dominated not by the Hearst family but by executives of the Hearst Corp. Dividends, while hardly insignificant, are held to a relatively small proportion of the available cash flow: *Forbes* figures that William Randolph Hearst's 40 or so living descendants, grouped in five branches, one for each of his five sons and spread among four generations, will get around $40 million this year. (The descendants include the two surviving sons, Randolph A. Hearst, 72, the company's board chairman, and William Randolph Hearst Jr., 79, who carries the largely symbolic title of editor-in-chief of Hearst newspapers.)

The rest of the money—after taxes maybe $175 million—is available for acquisitions and capital spending. The founder arranged things this way. Quite clearly, he didn't want his heirs milking the company into oblivion. Until the mid-1970s, family members confirm, the total payout to the heirs was just $150,000 a year, and as recently as 1983 it was estimated at about $15 million.

In his 125-page will, old W. R., who died in 1951 at the age of 88, deliberately kept corporate control away from his five sons, all then in their 30s or 40s. Stock worth two-thirds of the company was left to charitable foundations established by W. R., and the other one-third—which held the voting rights—was put in a trust for the benefit of the sons and other heirs. The boards of all three trusts consisted of the five sons—plus eight non-family company executives, who could outvote them. It was an ingenious arrangement: Besides avoiding estate taxes, it kept the business in the family, but insulated it from possible fights or potential incompetence within the family.

"A brilliant will," says Bennack, who prefers to dwell on the result rather than the cause and definitely means no offense to the five sons, who collectively earned no college degrees and have so far gone through 16 marriages. "He structured it to avoid a breakup of the company." Indeed, however they felt when the will was read more than a third of a century ago, the older descendants have come to accept the will. "We weren't happy about it [the 8-to-5 split] at first," says Randy Hearst, who with brother Bill is one of the family trustees. "But it's worked out well. It was a good thing."

Rumors that certain younger Hearsts are unhappy with the payout and favor a public stock offering periodically sweep middle-management ranks. Says one intimate, "I think some of the family members took notice last year when Sallie Bingham [a dissident daughter of the Louisville Binghams] helped force a sale of the family's newspapers and came away with around $40 million."

Bennack, who is a trustee, replies that his 12 fellow trustees, including the 5 from the family, fully support his policies. "There is a balance that must be made between current and future beneficiaries," he says. "We are of the opinion that acquisition and growth is the preferred strategy for the building of wealth over the long term."

As things stand, the family trust will expire with the death of the last of Hearst's eight grandchildren alive at his demise, probably around the year 2035. Then the Hearst Corp. stock will be distributed to the remaining heirs. But for the next half-century or so, the company can remain intact—and private, although a sale or public stock offering is permissible under terms of the trust.

Thus, with the possible exception of some junior family members, no one is unhappy with the current situation—or with Bennack. "We like his style and the way he operates," says Randy Hearst. "He's very good with the family. We're all on the same wavelength."

Bennack will be remembered as a builder. His regime stands in sharp contrast to that of the late Richard E. Berlin, who ran the empire until his retiremenet at the age of 79. If Bennack is a builder, Berlin was a preserver. Berlin held the reins from 1940 until 1973. He took over a sagging company whose assets were heavily encumbered. There was also the constant threat that Hearst executives would lose control over Hearst Consolidated Publications Inc., the one publicly traded portion of the empire. Holders of its preferred stock had the right to take over that board if four consecutive quarterly dividends were missed.

To keep the company intact and to free up the assets, Berlin cut expenses and preserved the empire. He spent most of the 1950s and early 1960s shutting down or merging money-losing Hearst newspapers in New York, Chicago, Detroit, Boston, San Francisco, Milwaukee and Pittsburgh while selling off Hearst Corp. land. He eventually also bought out the shareholders of Hearst Consolidated, totally privatizing the business and eliminating the need for public financial accountings.

But, having come up in hard times, Berlin showed no taste for expansion or much change as he aged. (One noted exception: With extreme reluctance, in 1965, he agreed to the hiring of Helen Gurley Brown as editor of faltering *Cosmopolitan*; she quickly turned it into one of the company's biggest moneymakers.) Like many another shrewd executive before him and since, Berlin made a big mistake: He stayed on too long. Times changed, and he didn't recognize it. It was no longer a time for retrenchment, but for expansion and risk-taking. In 1953 Berlin showed how far behind the times he had fallen: According to one book on the Hearsts, he turned down a chance to buy *TV Guide,* now one of the world's most profitable magazines, for $75,000, reportedly dismissing television as a fad. As Gannett, Newhouse and what is now Knight-Ridder voraciously grabbed up media properties, Hearst struggled to keep its head above water.

Randy Hearst recalls there was a love-hate relationship between Berlin and the family—one perhaps intensified by those puny $150,000 yearly dividends. While that payout was augmented for many family members by high-paying jobs with the corporation, their power was limited.

Besides the passing of Dick Berlin's preservationist regime, the catalyst for change and the enrichment of the Hearst family was the Tax Reform Act of 1969. Among other things, the law required charitable foundations to divest themselves of large interests in profitmaking businesses. That meant the two charitable foundations W. R. set up to hold two-thirds of the company—governed by the same 13 trustees as the family trust—had to sell out.

Hearst heirs prevailed upon the nonfamily trustees—against some resistance from Berlin, who was in ailing health and about to retire— to go along. In a kind of leveraged buyout, the corporation itself in 1974 bought that majority interest not owned by the family trust for about $135 million, in effect bringing the company under 100% family ownership. As it turned out, the Hearsts had themselves quite a bargain. By March 1978 the Hearst Corp. had paid back the money it borrowed to finance the buyback and had reduced long-term debt to an almost invisible $1.4 million, as against stockholders' equity of $135 million—according to a Hearst Corp. balance sheet still on file at the Federal Communications Commission in Washington, D.C.

Along came Bennack, who had risen through the ranks of the company-owned *San Antonio Light* and become Hearst's chief executive in January 1979. Now began Hearst's aggressive expansion. Nearly three years into Bennack's tenure, according to an October 1981 balance sheet filed at the FCC, the long-term borrowing had increased to $128 million. Meanwhile, stockholders' equity had more than doubled, to $283 million. Bennack's team was off and running. (*Forbes* estimates the long-term debt now at about $600 million, still rather small for an expanding company of this size.)

"We realized there were enormously underutilized assets and we had to diversify," says Bennack. In bidding for increasingly expensive media properties, Hearst had an advantage over some of its publicly owned competitors: It had no outside shareholders to satisfy with short-term performance. This meant that it didn't matter much if an acquisition temporarily diluted earnings if, long range, it enhanced the company's assets. "We are able to be unconcerned with what quarter or even what year an acquisition occurs," Bennack says.

Few companies these days would dare launch a new magazine without tons of research. Marketing studies can last more than a year, for example, and usually end with the mailing of at least one glossy brochure describing the proposed publication, possible stories, departments and even headlines, to potential subscribers. All of which costs a considerable amount of money and wastes time. In the end it may prove only, in Bennack's words, "that the readers liked the brochure." Boiled down, these are cover-your-behind tactics indulged in by insecure executives who are afraid to take risks.

The Hearst way is to latch on to a promising idea, ignore direct mail, put an issue or two on newsstands—via a Hearst distribution subsidiary—and see if it flies. "We don't do a great deal of research," says Gilbert C. Maurer, Hearst executive vice president and president of the magazine division. "Is it good or not? We want to get to that as fast as we can." The results are apparent quickly. That's how *Country Living,* launched in 1978, became a big hit. That's also how Hearst was able to fold *Cosmopolitan Living* in 1982 after just a few issues. "It didn't cost us very much," says Maurer, "to learn that the young *Cosmopolitan* girl isn't interested in her apartment."

There have been other magazine problems.

Hearst closed *Science Digest*—"It didn't work," says Bennack—and *Harper's Bazaar* is feeling the heat from Newhouse's *Vogue*. But the overall picture is quite good.

The long-term approach is evident in other ways. In one of its potentially most lucrative moves of all, Hearst is trying to exploit its vast real estate holdings around San Simeon, Calif., where the Hearst castle, given to the state in 1957, is a popular tourist attraction. The company owns a 77,000-acre cattle ranch that includes a breathtaking 14-mile-long stretch along the Pacific Ocean. In spite of opposition from environmentalists, Hearst has unveiled a 15-year plan to build a series of developments, including 650 hotel rooms, tourist stores and a golf course.

Much of Bennack's efforts, too, have been devoted to making up for the short-run, no-capital-spending, hold-the-fort philosophy that ruled the company during the Berlin years. By the time Bennack took over, a lot of damage had been done, especially to the newspapers.

He has since shut the Baltimore *News-American,* sold the Boston *Herald-American* and turned the *Seattle Post-Intelligencer* into a moneymaker by entering into a government-sanctioned monopoly pact, called a joint operating agreement, with the *Seattle Times* that permitted pooling of mechanical and business departments and an increase in advertising rates.

Then there's Los Angeles, where Hearst in 1961 voluntarily abandoned the morning field to the Chandler family's *Los Angeles Times* in exchange for an afternoon monopoly. Buggy whips, anyone? The company wanted out of a competitive situation, but in so doing moved into an untenable position in a town where the afternoon paper is a dying breed. The resulting *Herald Examiner* now loses an estimated $15 million a year and is kept alive, many feel, primarily out of deference to Bill Hearst Jr., who sees it as a memorial for his father. Some Hearst officials say the *Herald Examiner* has just a few years to live, unless a planned overhaul proves unexpectedly successful.

Hearst Corp.: The Empire at 100

Below, a look at the properties and financials of the intensely private Hearst Corp., a century old and stronger than ever. Revenues [in 1987] will top $2 billion. All numbers are pretax estimates, and asset values of the media properties have been reduced in light of the October 19 Black Monday stock market crash.

Property	1987 revenues	1987 cash flow* ($millions)	Asset value
Magazines	$873	$126	$1,125
Includes Good Housekeeping, Cosmopolitan, Country Living, Town & Country, Redbook, Connoisseur, Harper's Bazaar, Esquire, Popular Mechanics, Sports Afield, Colonial Homes, House Beautiful, Motor Boating & Sailing; 56 foreign editions; special issues; 7 magazines in U.K.; 2 U.S. distribution companies, 2 U.S. fulfillment companies			
Newspapers	650	55	910
Includes Houston Chronicle, San Francisco Examiner, Los Angeles Herald Examiner, Albany (N.Y.) Times-Union and Knickerbocker News, San Antonio Light, Seattle Post-Intelligencer; 11 other papers in Texas, Florida, Michigan and Illinois			
Broadcasting	262	99	1,005
Includes WCVB-TV Boston, WBAL-TV Baltimore, KMBC-TV Kansas City (Mo.), WISN-TV Milwaukee, WTAE-TV Pittsburgh, WDTN-TV Dayton; 7 radio stations in Baltimore, Pittsburgh, Milwaukee and San Juan, P.R.			
Books/Business publishing	140	25	200
Includes William Morrow & Co., Arbor House, Avon Books, 24 trade/professional publications and titles including American Druggist, Diversion, Motor, and Floor Covering Weekly			
Syndication/Production	90	15	100
Includes King Features, North America Syndicate, Cowles Syndicate, television production			
Cable television	50	15	150
Includes 6 cable systems in northern California, electronic data bank, and one-third interest in Arts & Entertainment Network and Lifetime Network			

Property	1987 revenues	1987 cash flow* ($millions)	Asset value
Real estate and other	35	3	550
Includes 77,000-acre cattle ranch with airstrip, San Simeon, Calif.; 65,000-acre Jack cattle ranch, Cholame, Calif.; 70,000-acre Wyntoon timber ranch, McCloud, Calif.; 135,000 acres of timberland in Maine and Canada; Manhattan office buildings and condos, Bronx warehouses, San Francisco office building and parking garage; California printing company			
Total	**$2,100**	**$338**	**$4,040**
Less: Estimated long-term debt service and debt		−60	−600
Total net cash flow (before dividends) and net worth		**$278**	**$3,440**

*Net income plus depreciation and amortization. Assumes full-year ownership of all properties acquired in 1987.

Up the coast in San Francisco, there's the *Examiner,* oldest of the Hearst properties and the self-styled "Monarch of the Dailies." The paper had become wildly profitable in 1965 after the company formed a joint operating agreement with the rival *Chronicle,* owned by the de Young family. But those were the Berlin years, and Hearst rolled over and played dead, while the de Youngs kept hustling. Within a few years the morning *Chronicle* had amassed an overwhelming 3-to-1 circulation lead, a dominance that could kill the *Examiner* when the agreement terminates, possibly as soon as 2005. To its credit, Hearst recently has poured big money into the product—witness the eyecatching TV ads involving Hearst I and Hearst III. Although the paper seems to be appealing to a wealthier audience, circulation gains so far have been minimal.

In Bennack's native San Antonio, the *Light,* caught in a bitter war with Rupert Murdoch's slightly larger *Express-News,* is falling into the red. And Hearst's expensive ($415 million) new acquisition, the financially dominant *Houston Chronicle,* will face increased competition from the rival *Houston Post* if the delayed deal for its purchase by turnaround artist William Dean Singleton goes through.

But, unlike Dick Berlin, whose main job was to keep the wolf from the door, Frank Bennack can deal with the newspaper problems from a position of strength: The magazines are minting money, the TV dollars are rolling in and the company's borrowing power and cash flow are both sufficient to finance whatever spending is necessary. A near basket case 35 years ago, Hearst Corp. is today one of the best-managed media companies in the world. ■

Media Salaries

Washingtonian magazine published this list of media salaries, which is especially interesting because all of the major media are represented in Washington, D.C.

Consider:

1. What is the difference in salary between a reporter for a major newspaper and a reporter for a major TV station?

2. How do the salaries of the network anchors compare to the salaries of network correspondents?

3. How do salaries at public broadcasting stations compare to those at commercial stations?

4. How do the salaries of corporate media executives compare to the people who work for them?

Who Makes What?

ROBERT PACK

It's a classic case of local boy makes good: Weatherman and all-around good ol' boy Willard Scott has parlayed being a personality into megabucks. The 54-year-old Alexandria native is far and away the highest-paid Washington-based newsie, according to broadcast-industry sources, who place his total annual take at nearly $2 million—an estimated $1 million from making personal appearances and giving speeches; a $500,000 salary for telling which way the wind blows on NBC's *Today* show; and an estimated $400,000 for endorsing products. Scott is said to negotiate his own deals, so he avoids having to pay agent's fees, at least for his contract with NBC

Robert Pack is a Washington, D.C.-based free-lance writer.

and his endorsements. And such is his value to NBC that the network allows him to do his weather reports from Washington two days a week and to do them from other locations at will, in order for him to meet his busy schedule of appearances.

Scott is one of the few local newspeople whose total yearly income rivals that of the three network anchors. Dan Rather's latest contract nets him an estimated $3.6 million a year from CBS, twice as much as each of his competitors, NBC's Tom Brokaw and ABC's Peter Jennings. Although Washington is among the half-dozen largest markets in the US, anchors on local television stations still lag behind some of the network people who operate out of Washington.

Second to Scott locally is ABC's Ted Koppel, whose take from the network is pegged at $1.5 million by broadcast sources. In addition, he makes an estimated $200,000 a year for giving speeches, bringing his annual income to a total of $1,700,000. Heavy-duty talker Larry King is third, earning about $1,515,000—$800,000 from Mutual Broadcasting System, $475,000 from Cable News Network, and the remaining $200,000 for writing a book and a column in *USA Today*. Fourth is David Brinkley at $1,200,000—two-thirds of which he receives from NBC and the remainder from writing and lecturing.

Other Washington-based network types: Lesley Stahl of CBS, Sam Donaldson of ABC, and Chris Wallace of NBC, $600,000 each; Robert MacNeil and Jim Lehrer of PBS, $400,000 each; Bill Plante of CBS, $350,000; Phil Jones of CBS, $300,000; Judy Woodruff of PBS and NBC's Andrea Mitchell, $250,000 each; and Bernard Shaw of CNN, $225,000.

Two former local favorites have gone on to the home of the networks and are taking a hefty bite out of the Big Apple. Sportscaster Warner Wolf is said to earn $750,000 a year at WCBS, and Maury Povich receives about half that from Fox Broadcasting for hosting the *Current Affair* show.

At the local stations, the highest-paid is WUSA's Gordon Peterson, who nets $500,000 for his anchor duties and another $100,000 as Martin Agronsky's replacement on the Saturday-night talk show now known as *Inside Washington*. Behind Peterson are Frank Herzog at $430,000—$250,000 as WJLA's lead sports anchor and $10,000 a game for doing the radio play-by-play on fifteen Redskin games during the 1987 regular season and another three culminating in the Super Bowl; WJLA's Renee Poussaint, $400,000; WUSA sportscaster Glenn Brenner, $375,000, plus a $1 million annuity if he leaves; and WRC sportscaster and *Sports Machine* host George Michael, $350,000. Michael's wife, Pat Lachman, a Channel 4 writer, makes about $75,000, bringing the Michael family to $425,000.

Other Washington broadcasters:

Jim Vance, WRC-TV anchor: $300,000. One broadcasting source says Vance's salary has consistently been overstated and that WRC has used his cocaine problems as an excuse to play hardball in contract negotiations.

Donnie Simpson, disc jockey, WKYS Radio: $250,000.

Bob Ryan, WRC-TV and WMAL Radio meteorologist: $230,000.

Susan King, WJLA-TV anchor: $225,000.

Maureen Bunyan, WUSA-TV anchor: $200,000.

Dave Marash, WRC-TV anchor: $200,000.

Mike Buchanan, WUSA-TV features reporter: $200,000. One broadcasting observer says Buchanan is burned out, living off his reputation, and vastly overpaid.

J. C. Hayward, WUSA-TV anchor: $175,000.

Bruce Johnson, WUSA-TV reporter and anchor: $150,000.

Joel Spivak, WRC-TV anchor: $150,000 ("if he's still there by the time your story runs," says a broadcasting source).

Susan Kidd, WRC-TV anchor: $150,000.

Bill Trumbull, WMAL Radio: $135,000.

Joe Krebs, WRC-TV reporter: $125,000.

Pat Collins, WRC-TV reporter: $110,000.

Chris Core, WMAL Radio: $100,000.

Mark Feldstein, WUSA-TV investigative reporter: $80,000.

And in the how-the-mighty-have-fallen department, former NBC anchorman Roger Mudd, who was making well over $1 million a year before he and the network parted company early last year, is now said to be earning much less, perhaps as little as $75,000, at PBS.

The average reporter at the *Washington Post* earns $55,711 a year, according to the Newspaper Guild. Salaries for the paper's 204 reporters range from a low of $20,606 to a high of $91,459, and a journeyman reporter—one with at least four years' experience—is guaranteed a minimum of $38,064. The guild says that twenty other daily newspapers have higher minimums for journeymen than the *Post* does.

White male reporters earn the highest salaries at the *Post;* black females the lowest. White male reporters average $59,307 a year; black males, $54,984; white females, $52,445; and black females, $46,796. Overall, white reporters average $56,714 and blacks average $51,878.

The *Post's* 30 columnists, critics, editorial writers, and cartoonists earn an average of $66,886, while photographers average $51,165.

National-desk reporters earn more than other newsroom employees; in general, the best and the brightest reporters are the ones selected for the highly competitive national staff. Moreover, national staffers tend to have more experience than other *Post* writers. Here are 1987 salaries of selected *Post* employees:

Dale Russakoff, national reporter: $73,425.

Howard Kurtz, New York bureau chief: $64,461.

Albert B. Crenshaw, Business editor: $59,592.

Ward Sinclair, national reporter: $56,625.

Edward Walsh, national reporter: $56,249

Raymond Lustig, photographer: $56,243

Alison Muscatine, Maryland editor: $56,000.

George Lardner Jr., national reporter: $55,588.

Thomas Kenworthy, Capitol Hill reporter: $55,516.

Dita Smith, assistant foreign editor: $52,148.

Peter Perl, assistant Maryland editor: $51,672.

Richard Homan, assistant foreign editor: $50,761.

Lewis Diuguid, assistant foreign editor: $49,000.

Saundra Saperstein, Metro reporter: $46,197.

Suzanne Tobin, Sports make-up editor: $46,134.

Al Kamen, national reporter: $46,635.

Curt Hazlett, Business copy editor: $45,500.

Vanessa Barnes-Hillian, photographer: $43,680.

Patrice Gaines Carter, Metro reporter: $37,122.

John Anderson, Metro reporter: $33,506.

David Saltman, former Style editorial aide: $17,368.

The top corporate executives at the *Post* receive generous compensation plans, but they are paid substantially less than their counterparts at their main rival, the *New York Times.* The three biggest earners at the news-media giants:

The New York Times Company

Walter E. Mattson, president: $2,250,909.

Benjamin Handelman, senior vice president: $1,429,348.

Arthur Ochs Sulzberger, chairman and CEO: $1,240,416.

The Washington Post Company

Katharine Graham, chairman of the board: $1,175,975.

Richard D. Simmons, president: $1,033,313.

Joel Chaseman, chairman and CEO, Post-Newsweek Stations: $686,074.

The difference in compensation between the two companies is largely attributable to stock options: Mattson realized nearly $1.5 million and Hendelman almost $1 million by exercising their right to buy stocks at substantially below market price during the past year, while none of the *Post* executives exercised stock options.

Other media salary figures:

Ben Cason, Kim Willenson, and Barry Sussman, former top editors at United Press International: $126,000 a year.

William Safire, columnist, the *New York Times:* $100,000 salary (in addition to $360,000 in book royalties).

Christine Dolan, former political director, Cable News Network: $75,000. ∎

Competition Forces Networks to Rethink Their Strategies

Since their formation in the first half of the twentieth century, the Big Three television networks—ABC, CBS, and NBC—have dominated the audience and the ratings. In this Perspective, media observer Merrill Brown explains the implications for the networks of today's new audience viewing patterns.

Consider:

1. What does Merrill Brown mean, referring to the television networks, when he asks, "Can elephants learn to waltz?"

2. What factors have caused changes in the networks' share of the audience, according to Brown? Why?

3. What competitive disadvantages do the networks face, according to Brown?

4. What advice does Brown offer the networks about how they can best respond to the new competition?

Can Elephants Learn to Waltz?

MERRILL BROWN

At one time, discussions about the TV business would begin and end with the Big Three networks. Now such discussions merely *begin* with the networks. That is because the networks are crumbling—and the action is moving to competitors. The networks had the most difficult, worst marketed and programmed fall season ever [in 1987], and even the structure of the fall season launch they historically relied on has collapsed. Both the CBS and ABC networks are in tumult at the moment, uncertain of their franchises, uncertain of their short and long term strategies and in the case of CBS, uncertain of their future ownership or even existence.

For years, it has been clear that the networks were on a downward slide. In 1976, the networks routinely reached about 91 percent of the prime-time viewing audience, a figure dwindling below 50 percent already in key periods in heavily cabled markets. Predictably, the networks' ad rates have started to flatten out and even decline in some areas.

What's happened? With the FCC restrictions on station ownership swept away, Wall Street analysts and investors in the early 1980s began to see that media properties could be quite valuable indeed—not just for their earnings but also for

Merrill Brown is the editor of *Channels* magazine, which covers the TV and radio industries.

their enormous annual cash flows. The enormous cash flows represented gushers of untapped borrowing power that could be be used to finance new acquisitions—a "hidden" asset that traditional media owners had generally failed to exploit.

As aggressive newcomers have rushed into the media business over the past six or seven years, they have changed the investment profile of the industry and upset some of its most revered traditions. We are now familiar with some of the brash tycoons who have crashed the once-genteel business of broadcasting: Saul Steinberg, Rupert Murdoch, Larry Tisch, Carl Lindner, the Bass Brothers, George Gillett, and Kohlberg Kravis Roberts, among others. Each in his own way has brought new management practices to the business.

By 1984–1985, the influx of new media investment and management began to shake the foundations of the broadcasting industry. Media companies that happened to be sitting on large cash-flows began to exploit those funds. Production companies like Paramount, MCA, and Lorimar-Telepictures, and others, also began to grow as they filled an unquenchable demand for new programming. Other media entrepreneurs such as Price Communications, Malrite Communications and Heritage Communications also jumped into the expansion game to take advantage of the new investment climate.

All this activity ushered in some serious changes in the economics of television. In 1986 alone, about $5.2 billion was raised in debt financing for broadcasters, according to Paul Kagan—nearly nine times the amount raised for the industry just four years earlier. Ownership of TV stations has gotten more concentrated as well. Thirty years ago, only half of all VHF stations in the 100 largest television markets were group owned; in 1986, nearly 90 percent were group owned.

The pace of station turnover . . . the introduction of new managements and accounting techniques. . . . the experimentation with new programming—this kind of ferment has not been confined to the periphery of the TV industry. It has penetrated to its very core—namely, the Big Three networks. Over the years, as the networks lost viewers to cable, independent TV, and VCRs; as production costs kept growing; as advertisers and their agencies grew bolder in their media buys—each of the networks grew vulnerable and ultimately changed hands.

So far, I've only focussed on the financial and regulatory background of this story. But the real engine for change has been the explosion of new distribution channels—and the wealth of programming innovation that those channels have made possible.

Not so long ago, any American who wanted to watch TV on Sunday evening could only choose between "Walt Disney," "The Ed Sullivan Show," and "The F.B.I." Pretty tame stuff. Now a viewer can watch bicycle racing on ESPN, rock videos on MTV, congressional hearings on C-SPAN, and young people's programming on Nickelodeon. A viewer can watch movies and first-run syndicated shows on independent TV stations. He can buy zirconia diamonds from Home Shopping Channel, check for hurricanes on The Weather Channel, and ask Dr. Ruth how to have the perfect orgasm!

Who exactly are these competitors? I'm talking about at least 28 basic cable networks, five cable super-stations, and the 11 pay-cable networks. I'm talking about the burgeoning program syndication market, both off-network and first-run syndication and barter syndication, an entirely new system for distributing programming. I'm talking about 50 million VCRs, now in over half the nation's homes. And finally, I'm talking about independent TV stations, which have more than doubled in size over the past six years to 250 stations.

With this profusion of new competitors, it hardly needs to be said that we're never going back to the Sunday evening lineup of "Disney," "Sullivan," and "F.B.I." The market has changed forever, becoming irretrievably fragmented. While the fragmentation has made the TV business far less predictable and stable, it may also be making it far more vigorous, competitive and innovative. In a sense, the free enterprise system is triumphing over the network oligopoly. I believe that we're far better off as a result.

Of course, the networks still dominate segments of the volatile TV marketplace, if only because of their unique capabilities and size. But the days when they called the tune are over. In the years ahead, they must increasingly dance to the tune called by the non-network alternatives. Looking at the future, the $64,000 question is: Can elephants learn to waltz? Can the stodgy network broadcast system become as nimble, creative, and cost-efficient as the new TV competitors? And even if they can streamline themselves, how much of their empire will they be able to retain?

The networks' first challenge is to rein in their overbuilt cost-structure—a relic of the 1960s and 1970s TV market—so that they can compete in the lean and mean TV market of the 1980s and 1990s. When Sunday evening was only a three-way race, a bloated cost-structure posed no problem; advertisers had no alternative. But now the marketplace for audiences is wide-open. Now there are new programming vehicles which can deliver more targeted, upscale audiences to advertisers for less money.

For the short-term, at least, the networks have little choice but to lay off staff, slash budgets, and work tirelessly to keep their affiliate stations and advertisers happy—while simultaneously trying to woo new audiences with innovative programming and to expand their worldwide operations. But over the long-term, the networks must do nothing less than redefine the terms by which they will compete. Make no mistake: networks will survive . . . but they won't be the same creatures they once were.

It is impossible to predict what the TV market of the 1990s will look like; the situation is just too volatile. However, let me identify key forces that are restructuring the TV marketplace.

Perhaps the networks' single biggest competitive disadvantage is the FCC's financial interest and syndication rules, which prohibit the networks from owning an equity interest in, or syndicating, most of the programs that they air. As a result, they cannot participate in the enormous revenue stream that independent production companies reap from syndication. As some of you may remember, the networks waged a titanic struggle in Washington from 1982 through 1984 to eliminate the financial-syndication rules. But in the end, Jack Valenti and his Hollywood allies—including the President of the United States—prevailed. Whatever the merits of their arguments, the networks were not and probably never will be as potent a political force as Hollywood.

The financial-syndication rules will come up for renewal in 1990, at which time there will probably be another titanic struggle. But once again, it is highly unlikely that the networks—even in their weakened financial state—will be able to repeal the rules.

A much-underrated source of concern to the networks, I believe, is the growing tension in network-affiliate relations. As competition in local TV markets has stepped up, affiliate stations have grown more disgruntled with the networks. Pressed hard by local competition, affiliates feel they are being shortchanged in their network compensation. Affiliates also resent being locked into clunky programs and limited in available ad time within network schedules that often don't work in their local markets. One bellwether of disaffection among affiliates is their growing habit of preempting the network schedule in prime-time—a habit that grows more attractive as affiliates discover the lucrative payoffs to be had from barter syndication.

To bolster their own sagging fortunes, the networks are insisting on claiming an extra two or three minutes of precious ad time for themselves—depriving affiliates of valuable revenues. But such heavy-handed tactics erode goodwill and intensify the affiliates' resentment toward the networks. While no insurrection is imminent, the deterioration of this relationship is causing additional, serious strains on the network system.

In this context, it is important to mention the changing role of news coverage as a source of network-affiliate tension. One reason that affiliates are feeling so constrained is that technology is liberating them from simply serving as passive carriers of network feeds. Using satellites and minicams, local stations are increasingly able to cover national and international news on their own. Dozens of local stations are using ad hoc services like Stanley Hubbard's CONUS of Minneapolis, which unites TV stations by way of satellite hookups, and enables a Miami station, for example, to obtain pictures from Seattle on demand.

Even as affiliates find themselves less dependent on the network evening news programs, the networks are encountering even more news competition at the national level, potentially a positive development in that it spells the end to the television news oligopoly. The Big 3 now must compete with news programs carried by Independent News Network, the two 24-hour-a-day Cable News Networks, the Financial News Network, and ad hoc syndicated programs. Looking more broadly, network news must also compete with the national newspapers of the 1980s—*The Wall Street Journal, The New York Times,* and *USA Today,* which are available on street corners from Boise, Idaho to Poughkeepsie, New York.

So in terms of the news, the value of what affiliates are getting from the networks is declining dramatically. Technology and economics have remade the face of television news, and in the process, they have weakened another tie that once bound affiliates to networks. Again, you have to wonder: Can the network elephant dance around *this* obstacle?

The list of network headaches grows longer: independent television has reached a unique historical juncture. Collectively, indies are now large enough to mount a serious frontal challenge to the three networks by launching a *fourth* over-the-air network. In the past, powerhouses like Paramount, Metromedia, and LBS Communications failed in their attempts to cobble together network-like arrangements with indies. But then, none of these shadow networks could afford to sustain huge losses over several years, prevent station defections, and also offer top-notch original programming.

All that changed [in 1987] when Rupert Murdoch launched his Fox Broadcasting Network. With the participation of 108 indies which boast access to 84 percent of the nation's TV house-

holds, the Fox network already airs two nights of original, prime-time programming each week—and [expanded] that prime-time schedule [in 1988]. What may distinguish Rupert Murdoch's gamble on a fourth network from previous ones is the rich rewards of "failure," if it comes to that. Even if the Fox network doesn't fly, it is almost certain to raise the value of the seven TV stations that Murdoch owns, and the Fox programming could presumably be sold at sharply higher prices.

The real opportunity of the fourth network concept is the possibility of vertical integration. It's one reason that Lorimar tried to buy the Storer TV Group. It's why MCA bought WOR, the New York superstation. It's why Disney bought KHJ in Los Angeles. By creating original programming, owning an interest in its syndication, and having guaranteed outlets for that programming, the Fox network may be able to vertically integrate several revenue streams and claim an enormous prize. Of course, the Big Three networks cannot even contemplate this arrangement because of the FCC's financial-syndication rules—yet another competitive disadvantage faced by the networks.

Even as independents try to muscle their way into the network business, cable has already crashed the gates. In fact, now that 700,000 miles of cable wire have been laid—providing cable access to 50 percent of all homes, or double the penetration of only five years ago—cable TV is becoming the dominant distribution vehicle for national programming.

Cable has built a remarkable infrastructure, and now stands ready to unleash itself on the television marketplace. Unlike some non-network competitors, cable has some serious, serious money backing it. For example, Time, Inc. owns the second-largest MSO*; the #1 pay television network, HBO; and until recently one-third of a national basic cable network, the USA network—whose other backers are MCA and Gulf & Western. Viacom, a major cable operator, owns MTV,

---

*multi-service operator (cable system)

Nickelodeon and the Movie Channel. Cap Cities/ABC is behind three major cable networks, such as the booming ESPN, which now offers NFL football. And TCI is arguably the most powerful television company in America today.

For years cable was faced with the chicken-and-egg problem—how can you attract advertisers when you aren't in enough homes? And how can you get into enough homes if you don't have the revenues from advertisers? Now that this conundrum is on the verge of resolution, the cable industry, backed with some enormous financial firepower, is poised for a big takeoff.

It's not surprising that investors are *begging* to buy cable systems. Ten years ago cable systems sold for multiples of $300 per subscriber. Last year systems sold for around $1,000 per subscriber. Now cable systems are selling for multiples of $2,500 per subscriber or more. Some analysts call cable the hottest business in the nation!

But cable, of course, has its own problems. Success breeds resentment. And that is precipitating a political response. Broadcasters and the motion picture studios are unhappy that cable is becoming more concentrated, more vertically integrated, and fully deregulated to boot. So along with independent stations, public TV stations, and the home satellite dish community, the studios and broadcasters are pressing for some new ground rules for competition.

For starters, cable's detractors want to institute permanent must-carry rules. They want to reinstitute the FCC's syndicated exclusivity rules. They want to repeal the compulsory cable license. They want phone companies to be allowed to deliver television signals. They want ceilings on cable-company size and a separation between signal distribution and program ownership.

It's unlikely that the broadcast and motion picture industries will ever achieve this ambitious agenda, but they are bracing for a good fight in Washington. At stake is nothing less than broadcasting's future. An historic shift of power is occurring: over-the-air television stations are losing control of their distribution destiny! If leadership in the business passes to cable, the balance of power in the TV marketplace will have shifted.

It's mind-boggling to speculate, for example, about the new economic arrangements that will emerge if the new must-carry rules sunset in 1990, as anticipated. A comprehensive new set of financing schemes, negotiating strategies, and cable-broadcast relationships is going to emerge. Stations will offer money, barter time, or strike other creative deals to ensure that cable will carry their signals.

And in the process, cable just might become the dominant vehicle for national programming. Unless the networks can get their houses in order, broadcast stations may run for shelter by concentrating on local programming, local news and local advertising.

There's a final development affecting network fortunes, and that is the new audience-measuring technologies—the "people-meters." These sophisticated systems are hooked up in 4,000 representative homes this year and are already providing for more accurate and refined audience ratings than the current diary system. And smart money is betting that the people meters will continue to yield disturbing data about how few people actually watch commercials.

The deep, dark secret on Madison Avenue is that most people who use their VCRs to "time-shift" do not watch the commercials. J. Walter Thompson USA estimates that there are some 30 million VCR owners who zip past commercials using their fast-forward button. If the people meters confirm this fact, advertisers would be in a good position to negotiate lower ad rates from the networks.

So what are some of the major trends I see ahead? The emerging vertical integration of program suppliers betokens a significant power shift. Just as the networks dominated the national programming market in the 1950s, 1960s, and the early 1970s, so the major program suppliers will assume that role in the remainder of the 1980s and the 1990s. The market power of these new super-studios will not be as monolithic as the networks; it will be more diffused. However, with so many program distribution vehicles now available, the name of the game is not so much owning distribution outlets as owning the material that goes out over those outlets. It is the programming, after all, which makes or breaks any media enterprise.

Structurally, the 1980s have seen the development of a more diverse, responsive, competitive marketplace than has ever existed before. This is due in large part to the breakdown of network oligopoly but also to the revolutionary impact of new media technologies, which have enabled dozens of new competitors to innovate with program formats, scheduling, and finances. When a viewer can have access to 36 cable chan-

nels or more, who should think that any three players are going to dominate the tube? I'll take the optimistic view of it all and predict that the television of the 1990s will see the airing of more product, more narrowly casted product, and more innovative product.

I should add that all this turbulence has opened up new opportunities for those willing to take risks. This is terrific. Never before have so many entrepreneurs been working so hard, and spending so much, to fathom what the American viewing public wants. It's likely to be an exciting financial development. And it's what is making the television business so vital today. ■

PERSPECTIVE 4

Media Mergers

In this article from *Publishers Weekly,* Irwin Karp suggests that the publishing business is consolidating into fewer, larger groups too quickly, with little opposition to counteract this trend toward conglomeration.

Consider:

1. What would be the result if only about ten major publishers in the United States survived the merger trend?

2. What "powerful reasons" can be made in favor of government controls of publishing? Against?

3. What does Karp mean when he says that conglomerates in textbook publishing put too much emphasis on "product"?

4. What does Karp propose should be done about the number of mergers in the publishing business? Do you agree? Disagree? Why?

Let's Look Much Harder at Mergers

IRWIN KARP

Although the current merger wave is fulfilling an authoritative prediction of "very great concentration, a handful of large publishing companies [that] will make up the U.S. publishing business," little protest is heard from authors' organizations or surviving independent publishers, now at a competitive disadvantage the antitrust laws never intended.

Perhaps they are disheartened by congressional apathy and an antitrust policy that tacitly approves widespread conglomeration in many industries. But Congress might yet act on book publishing mergers because, unlike those in other industries, they threaten fundamental values protected by the First Amendment and the Constitution's Copyright Clause.

In its 1945 *Associated Press* decision, the Supreme Court emphasized that the First Amendment "provides powerful reasons" for applying the antitrust laws to publishers to protect "the widest possible dissemination of information from diverse and antagonistic sources." Recent macro-acquisitions, supplementing the extensive 1970s takeovers, have drastically curtailed diversity of "sources" in trade publishing's constitutionally protected "marketplace of ideas." Where many independent large and medium-sized houses once provided bona fide diversity, truly effective "sources" are being reduced to that "handful of large publishing sources." And although [it is said that] there "always will be room for small, innovative firms that spring up," these companies are no substitute for the many major firms that could distribute nationally and under-

write their authors' prolonged writing projects, and which have now fallen into the hands of the dominant publishing giants.

Conglomeration's constraint on diversity of sources and information in trade publishing's First Amendment marketplace is evidenced all too plainly in the elimination of some acquired firms, recently announced reductions in the number of titles others will be allowed to issue, and an obsessive emphasis on commercial blockbusters that is bound to preempt many other works that would contribute more modestly to the "bottom line." Little wonder that some agents decry, albeit privately, the increasing peril to the middle-range trade book.

In textbook publishing's First Amendment marketplace of ideas, diversity of sources and information probably is at greater risk. A few giant publishers have merged themselves into an even more dominant position that increases their need to provide "product" that offends the fewest possible purchasers. Their takeovers have made textbook publishing more vulnerable to the pressure groups that are seeking, with considerable success, to diminish "information from diverse and antagonistic sources."

The collision of conglomeration with copyright also requires special legislative treatment. Mergers are giving a few giant firms control over larger and larger pools of governmentally created monopolies, i.e. copyrights, magnifying their competitive advantage and power to dominate bookstores and distributors.

The merger wave also frustrates the constitutional purpose of copyright, on which publishing depends. As Supreme Court opinions explain, the Constitution authorized the granting of copy-

Irwin Karp is an attorney and the former counsel of the Authors League.

rights to "authors"—publishers are not even mentioned—to "secure a fair return for [their] creative labor" and thus "supply the economic incentive" to stimulate them to write useful works for "the public good." But mergers have increased the power of the dominant giant firms to compel authors, who negotiate individually, to accept oppressive contract provisions that often deprive them of "a fair return" and benefits of their copyrights.

Ironically, while a permissive antitrust policy permits giant publishers to enhance their superior bargaining position through mergers, the antitrust laws prevent authors from overcoming this disadvantage by bargaining through their organizations for reasonable minimum terms. Congress should level the playing field by adding to the Copyright Act provisions allowing authors' organizations to negotiate with publishers for equitable terms in contracts that convey rights in copyrighted works; there are precedents for such an exemption in the 1976 Copyright Act.

Congress also should legislate to regulate and, where necessary, undo mergers of corporations that exploit copyrights in literary works, and to limit the number of copyrights that can be controlled by any publishing complex.

If Congress fails to act, the current cycle of book publishing conglomeration will erode fundamental First Amendment and Constitutional copyright purposes and, salting these wounds, allow greater foreign ownership of the firms that constitute significant American marketplaces of ideas. Perhaps the Murdoch takeover of Harper & Row will be the "last straw" that impels Congress to act or hold hearings on publishing conglomeration, copyright and the First Amendment. ■

NEWS GATHERING

PERSPECTIVE 5

Politics and the Press

In this Perspective, Governor Mario Cuomo of New York describes how the press and public officials need each other and how they both can learn to do a better job.

Consider:

1. What is the price that Cuomo says the founders of the United States were willing to pay for press freedom? Why?

2. Cuomo observes that journalism is a profession that requires no license. Do you believe journalists should be licensed? Why? Why not?

3. Do you agree with Cuomo that the "tension between those who make the news and those who cover and comment on it" is an important and permanent part of the political process? Why? Why not?

4. According to Cuomo, what is the biggest mistake that reporters can make when they cover politics? Do you agree? Why? Why not?

How Politicians and the Press Interrelate

MARIO M. CUOMO

Let me describe briefly the essence of the relationship between your profession [the press] and mine, and then make a comment about how so much of the communication in my profession is artificial, simplistic and misleading.

And I hope by the time I'm through I won't have to regard this effort as another contribution to that imperfection.

I am in government: you are in the private sector. Part of your job is to describe what we do and what we don't do and comment upon both.

From the beginning this nation conceived of your function as indispensable to the maintenance of a free society. This republican democracy required the fullest opportunity for expression of opinions and revelation of facts. It was an assumption we inherited.

In 18th century Britain, the great struggle to limit the oppressive prerogatives of the government often centered on the issue of the press and the right of the king and parliament to censor or punish or suppress opinions or theories they didn't like.

It was a struggle that those who founded our government were intimately familiar with. And they succeeded in drawing up a document that created free and representative institutions. The First Amendment they 'wrote' as a simple and absolute statement of the relationship between government and the press.

Most of all, remembering their past, they were trying to secure their future by using the freedom of expression as a protection against government's instinct for oppression.

There's nothing complex or convoluted about the language they chose. "Congress shall make no law . . . abridging the freedom of speech or of the press. . . ."

Simple, straightforward, clear.

The amendment was not designed to set up standards of excellence to judge the press by. It doesn't seek to impose conditions on those who decide to publish or write. It simply acknowledges freedom of the press—along with freedom of religion and assembly and speech—as a fundamental right.

The framers of the Constitution could hardly have been clearer about what they intended their words to mean.

"A popular government," James Madison wrote, "without popular information or the means of acquiring it, is but a prologue to farce or tragedy, or perhaps both."

They intended the press to have enormous strength and they didn't intend it naively. Madison and company weren't journalistic innocents: they knew what they were letting themselves in for, that we'd pay a price for this freedom. The journalism of their day made no pretense to political objectivity.

It was overtly partisan and pointed—even vicious—guilty of bad taste and negligence and gross distortions.

But Federalists and Republicans alike were generally agreed that it was a price worth paying. They felt it was better to let the people be ex-

Mario M. Cuomo is governor of New York.

posed to every shade of opinion; to hear every side of the argument, even if occasionally it was done clumsily, or worse. They believed this would be better than to allow government to provide a neat, orderly—but controlled—channel of information.

They saw the freedom of the so-called Fourth Estate as another check and balance in the elaborate web of institutional controls they'd woven around those entrusted with the exercise of power: A way for people to decide for themselves what was in the public good. What party or president or congressperson best served their interests. Better the people than the government. That was the original judgment.

It was a good one then. And it's a good one now.

The principle still works for us. Beautifully. It does what it was supposed to do. It continues to reassure everyone's reasonable freedom by guaranteeing the right of free speech and press.

And does it without insisting on perfection—or even excellence—by the speaker or the instrument.

We know that the press in this country is sometimes disorderly and raucous, occasionally cynical and prying and skeptical.

It remains a profession with no admission standards. Unlike lawyers or doctors or barbers or cabdrivers you don't need a license. Unlike teachers or therapists, you don't have to graduate from college or professional school. Unlike the FBI or the state police, no one checks your background when you join.

Like politics, the press is theoretically open to everyone, although it's customary, if not required, that the members of the press be able to read and write.

But through it all, we have insisted that the press remain free of government's heavy hand. And with the freedom the press has grown strong, even vibrant, and almost always vigilant.

Over and over the press has worked to check the abuse of power, to expose corruption, to fight for fairness, to help keep the electorate informed, involved and educated.

Not perfectly.

Not without mistakes. Even serious ones.

Certainly not without causing some bitterness, even on the part of people as sedate and even-tempered as governors.

In my state, for example, they still tell a story about Governor Horatio Seymour's reaction to the 1863 draft riots when mobs ruled the streets and pillaged stores and looted private homes.

Governor Seymour wrote, and I quote:

"These events were an unmitigated disaster for us all. Commerce was halted, the law defied, and the innocent victimized. Unfortunately the one entirely admirable intent of the mob—to hang Mr. Greeley, the editor of the *Tribune,* from the nearest lamppost—went regrettably unfulfilled."

This kind of tension between those who make the news and those who cover and comment on it isn't just a passing byproduct of our political process. It's an important and permanent part of it.

And yet what would concern me far more than the frequent complaints by public officials would be a constant chorus of praise from elected officials for the stories they read about themselves in the paper.

If they grew happier and happier with the coverage, if they were content with each editorial and comfortable with every story, then I'd really be worried.

Today I'm not worried.

Of course, just as there's great room for improvement in government, surely it is possible to improve the coverage the press gives to politics and public affairs and to improve it without government control or censorship. There's a constant need to strive for greater objectivity, for fairness, for intelligent commentary. But that striving must be voluntary: it cannot be forced.

Attempts to improve the press by regulation, by law, by government are nearly always destined to be counterproductive.

In the end, the best hope for a truly responsible press is the free press itself:

Being self-critical, aware of its limitations, always trying harder to get the story straight, to report conflicting opinions, to ferret out the facts, to question and probe and examine, to help educate—not merely entertain—to grapple with difficult, intricate issues, to focus public attention on problems that aren't easy to grasp or exciting to read about but which are crucial to our future.

That's never been easy but, frankly, I think it's especially hard now.

In this age of electronic imagery—when political campaigns are dominated by 28-second technicolor movies—complexity is increasingly difficult to deal with.

Those of us in politics are tempted to reduce our programs and principles to the simplest level, to a label or slogan that conjures up what it is we stand for, one image that covers all the issues.

For the press, the temptation is to cover us that way.

The temptations are great. Labels make life easier for us all . . . although less honest. With labels we can do a kind of mental shorthand that saves us the discomfiture of thought, allowing us to pigeonhole by stereotype, to settle for caricatures instead of candidates.

How easy it is to describe candidates as "soft on crime," others "hard" on it.

Some "realistic," others "bleeding hearts."

Some "pro-defense," others "anti-defense."

After a while, if we're really good at this process of reduction, we can make the complexities disappear almost completely until—like the Cheshire cat in *Alice in Wonderland*—nothing remains but the image of a grin, a one-word summary of an entire philosophy that a candidate wears like a smile. ■

PERSPECTIVE 6

Prying into Politics

In 1987, the *Miami Herald* reported that Democratic presidential candidate Gary Hart, who is married, had been seen at his Washington townhouse with Donna Rice, a part-time model and actress. Reporters, captivated by the story, eventually confronted Hart with the issue at a press conference. In this Perspective, *Washington Post* reporter Paul Taylor describes his view of what happened when the press met Gary Hart.

Consider:

1. How do you feel about Taylor's question to Hart? Was it justified? Why? Why not?

2. Did the press exceed the bounds of civility in this case, as some critics charged? Why? Why not?

3. Do you agree with Taylor that what he did was "ask Gary Hart the question he asked for"? Why? Why not?

4. How would you define the press' reporting responsibilities in covering candidates for public office?

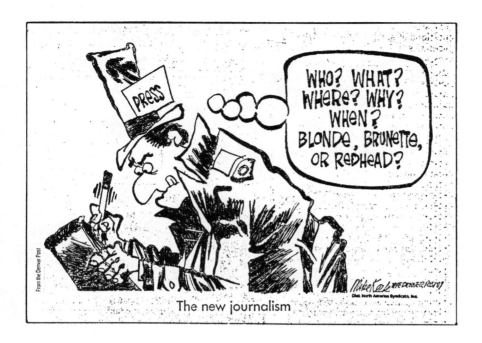

From the Denver Post

WHO? WHAT? WHERE? WHY? WHEN? BLONDE, BRUNETTE, OR REDHEAD?

PRESS

The new journalism

The Question Hart Asked For

PAUL TAYLOR

This originally appeared as a letter to the editor in the New York Times.

I'm the *Washington Post* reporter who put the question to Gary Hart that offended so many *New York Times* columnists. I suspect it offended other folks, too. It's not hard to see why. The question—"Have you ever committed adultery"—seemed to turn me, and by extension my profession, into some kind of morals police. That's not a comfortable role for anyone.

Anthony Lewis wrote (column, May 12) that I was responsible for the "low point" of news cov-

erage of a story in which "reporters and editors salivated in their zeal to learn all and tell all." William Safire said that I was "demeaning" my profession and that "titillaters" in the press like me need to be stopped (column, May 11). A. M. Rosenthal, quoted in another newspaper, said he found the question "nauseating."

Let's review the bidding here: Gary Hart chose to run for president and present himself as a happily married man. During the early weeks of his campaign, he also chose to spend some free time in Bimini and Washington with a woman

Paul Taylor is a reporter for the *Washington Post.*

who was not his wife. He did so despite having assured his top campaign staff that, though it was an open secret he's conducted himself this way in the past, he understood that the fishbowl environs of a front-runner's presidential campaign was no place to engage in such behavior. When the *Miami Herald* broke the story of his relationship with Donna Rice, he criticized the paper's reporting techniques and press ethics generally, said he'd done nothing "immoral" and said he'd always held himself "to a high standard of public and private conduct."

What did Hart mean by his denial of immoral behavior? What exactly was his "high standard"? Was he telling the truth? Did his past behavior bear on his credibility this time? It seemed to me appropriate, under the circumstances, to ask whether he considered adultery immoral (he said he did) and then to ask whether he had ever committed adultery. Hart chose not to answer the second question—which, of course, was his right.

But what about journalists' rights, and our responsibilities? *The New York Times* columnists raise questions about proportionality, civility and privacy. But by carrying their arguments to absurdity, they don't grapple with the issue at hand. Rosenthal advises us that he thinks questions about masturbation are also off limits. Safire worries that newshounds are now going to start asking questions about impotence. What in heaven's name are these guys talking about? Don't they think the political reporters know better?

It is not the job of journalists to win plaudits for civility (though it's certainly nicer when we do). Nor is our job to pry into the most private matters—except when public figures, in conducting and discussing their private affairs publicly, force our hand. Sometimes this job demands that we raise questions we'd rather not ask. *The New York Times* columnists suggest I broke some kind of gentleman's code in this instance. I say, poppycock. What I did was ask Gary Hart the question he asked for. ■

PERSPECTIVE 7

Does Media Attention Distort the Issues?

Some critics charge that by overemphasizing an issue, such as AIDS, the press is manufacturing news. The result of intensely targeting one topic for press coverage is called *agenda-setting*—the ability of the press to influence the choice of issues under discussion at any one time. Focusing so much attention on one topic gives that topic disproportionate public attention, the critics say, at the expense of other important issues. In this article, journalist Ron Dorfman argues that AIDS deserves the attention it is getting.

Consider:

1. Has the issue of AIDS been the subject of a "media-fed national panic," as *New Republic* editor Charles Krauthammer charges? Why? Why not?

2. Do you agree with Dorfman that the AIDS story is "not about a disease, but about our society"? Why? Why not?

3. Marlene Cimons of the *Los Angeles Times* says "the media as a whole downplayed the AIDS story until they realized it wasn't 'just a gay man's disease.' " Do you agree with Cimons? Why? Why not?

4. Dorfman says that in one week he clipped 27 articles about AIDS. Are there other medical stories you feel deserve as much attention? Why? Why not?

AIDS Coverage: A Mirror of Society

RON DORFMAN

In an October 5 *New Republic* piece captioned "Time to cool it," Senior Editor Charles Krauthammer argues that the American people have entirely too much information about AIDS.

Writing after community hostility and a suspicious fire drove the Ray family from Arcadia, Florida, he says: "Obsessive coverage does not create cures. It creates panic."

Krauthammer is an M.D. and is indignant that many people refuse to accept scientific assurances on how difficult it is to transmit HIV, the virus associated with AIDS.

Since a child in Arcadia "is as likely to die by earthquake as he is by sitting in [his] homeroom with young Ray, and far more likely to die in an auto accident," and since the people there "have been told a thousand times who get AIDS and how they get it," their "selective irrationality in the face of improbability is not the product of ignorance but of a media-fed national panic."

To the extent that this is a complaint against news reports and commentary exaggerating the likelihood that AIDS will infect people in the "general" population—which is to say, people who are not homosexuals, not hemophiliacs, and not heroin addicts—it is true enough. But it is a truth unfortunately detached from journalistic and political reality.

"It is not more AIDS information that drug abusers need but treatment for their addiction,"

Krauthammer writes. "It is not more condom ads scientists need, but money to pursue their studies."

But research money and addiction-treatment programs are political products, not scientific discoveries.

Dr. James Curran, director of AIDS programs at the national Centers for Disease Control, observed at a recent Washington meeting on media coverage of AIDS that with this story "scientists and journalists become part of the political process." And the politics of AIDS has more to do with demography than with virology and epidemiology.

As long as the disease was perceived as a threat only to gays and drug addicts, the government was content to let it run its course, proposing no appropriations until 1984 and in fact reducing spending on drug treatment programs.

Under the circumstances, both the research community and advocacy groups had an interest in emphasizing the small but real threat of heterosexual transmission and the ease of prevention by use of condoms, soap, and water. Journalists no doubt reflected that emphasis, and it's a bit unfair to suggest that they should have independently calibrated the scale of risk.

It's not unfair, however, to observe the very real journalistic bias toward aspects of the story that affect the heterosexual majority.

Steve Findlay, responding to a survey in *ScienceWriters,* the newsletter of the National As-

Ron Dorfman, a former editor of *The Quill,* is a Chicago-based freelance writer and media critic.

sociation of Science Writers, said of his editors at *USA Today:* "They are big on covering AIDS, but clearly in the last year the editors are much more interested in heterosexuals and they don't want to hear about gays and drug users. It's a desire to shift the story in ways that may not be warranted."

Marlene Cimons of the *Los Angeles Times,* writing in *Mother Jones* magazine, makes this comparison: "Much as *The New York Times* largely ignores the hundreds of black people murdered every year in the South Bronx and Harlem, but runs prominently on page one the story of a white drama student stabbed to death on a Manhattan rooftop, the media as a whole downplayed the AIDS story until they realized it wasn't 'just a gay man's disease.'"

Both science and journalism strive to report facts, but facts are not policy, and the problem for both, as Curran noted at the CDC-sponsored meeting in Washington, is "how to tell important or inevitable stories without causing panic."

He cited as examples the reports of three health workers who became infected in freak accidents and a case of transmission of the virus through transfusion of blood that had passed screening.

"Even though we knew they would cause problems," Curran said, "we had to report these cases," and so did journalists. Not to have reported them would have led to their ultimate discovery—by political opponents of what Krauthammer thinks is "rationality"—and to the discrediting of the entire public-health education project that both science and journalism have signed on to.

By the same token, media reports of public response to the available knowledge at any given stage of the epidemic have undoubtedly fueled further hysteria. But it is pigheaded to imagine that some journalistic compact or conspiracy could have kept those events under wraps, or prevented them from occurring in the first place.

In Atlanta last February, Laurie Garrett, science correspondent for National Public Radio, noted in a speech to a scientific conference on pediatric and heterosexual AIDS that the critical year was 1983, after the first reports of AIDS in children and in blood-transfusion recipients:

"In San Francisco, for example, gay-owned businesses were boycotted, the police donned masks and gloves before entering gay neighborhoods, firefighters refused to give artificial resuscitation to homosexuals, and people boycotted restaurants. I don't think these and other public responses . . . were created by the media or that the media went out of [their] way to exacerbate them. We simply reported these occurrences."

Also in 1983, Garrett said, funding became a major issue and "I think many of you [scientists] in this room know that you deliberately leaked horror stories about predictions for the AIDS epidemic, cases of unpaid clinical treatment, research problems that were unfunded, and so on. And the media covered those stories."

Whatever was the case in the past, AIDS has ceased to be a story that is primarily about science. The science journalists assembled for the meeting in Washington recognized that fact and wondered what good might come of their discussion.

As Ron Kotulak of the *Chicago Tribune* put it, "It's not our story any more. . . . This disease has become politicized."

B. D. Colen of *Newsday* said "the reaction story has become the tail wagging the dog."

Garrett of NPR said she feels "more and more like a cultural anthropologist, going into Vienna in A.D. 1150 and seeing how the community responds to the Plague."

The one strong recommendation that came out of the meeting, mentioned both by the CDC's Curran and several of the journalists, was the need for vetting of these non-science stories by science editors.

"There's got to be a way for you to peer-review stuff at your own papers," Curran said. "It's bad to see somebody writing stupid stuff at a paper where I know there are two or three experts."

Jim Bunn, who covers AIDS full-time for KPIX-TV in San Francisco, said that for a few years his editors "were sure to ask me to review AIDS stories" done by other reporters. Now, he said, he has to actively check to see who's doing what, "because there are other people who are at a point on the learning curve where they think they know what they're talking about."

Garrett said she knew of a reporter in California who was reprimanded for attempting to correct inaccuracies that had appeared in the paper.

But even where there is a concern for accuracy, and especially at the major media, the autonomy of divisional editors (national, metro, features, editorial, Sunday, etcetera) often precludes the left hand from knowing what the right hand is doing.

And, in the minds of many editors, there was such a thing as too much accuracy; as Cimons of the L.A. *Times* said, the media's greatest contribution to the inappropriate sense of public panic may have been the several years in which the euphemistic "exchanging bodily fluids" survived the knowledge that semen and blood, transferred in traumatic ways such as anal intercourse or hypodermic injection, are the only fluids we really need to be concerned about.

The AIDS story, like "the economy" or "civil rights," has simply disappeared as a discrete editorial entity.

I have a file of clippings on AIDS that I've been accumulating for about a year and a half and which is now about 15 inches deep. With a few exceptions—"Rock Hudson," "obits," and "condom ads," topics I wrote about early in that period—the file is undifferentiated and by now nearly useless.

The volume and variety of coverage have escalated and AIDS has ceased to be a story that goes by that name; it would have to be an editor pretty deep in the sticks who would today instruct a reporter, "Do a story on AIDS."

Instead, there are a multiplicity of AIDS-related stories. The week during which I wrote this column is probably typical. I clipped 27 stories. Not one of them had anything to do with science or medicine. Rather, the stories were about politics, religion, business and economics, lifestyle, the arts, education, and the law. Nearly half of them appeared on a single day, October 1.

▲ The Pasteur Institute in Paris prepares to observe its centennial. It was at Pasteur that Dr. Luc Montagnier first identified human immunodeficiency virus (HIV), the apparent cause of AIDS. Construction is to start in 1988 on a new AIDS and virology laboratory financed by the $50 million realized from the sale at auction of the late Duchess of Windsor's jewels.

▲ A suburban Dallas pediatrician is forced to close his practice after the local newspaper banners his HIV-positive status, gleaned from a lawsuit.

▲ The *Journal of the American Medical Association* reports a Harvard study resulting in a negative cost-benefit analysis of premarital AIDS testing; with 3.8 million persons marrying each year, the tests can be expected to produce only 1,200 true HIV-positives, along with 380 false positives and 100 false negatives, at a cost of about $100 million. Three-quarters of all children born with AIDS are born to unmarried women.

▲ The President's Commission on AIDS is urged by members of Congress to recommend that the president get involved in public education.

▲ Although a lawyer who alleged that he was fired from Baker & McKenzie because he had AIDS has died, his complaint charging the firm with violation of New York's anti-discrimination law will be pursued.

▲ Elizabeth D. Eden dies of AIDS-related pneumonia at the age of 41. She was the former Ernest Aron. In 1972, Mr. Aron's lover, John Wojtowicz, took a number of hostages in an attempt to rob a bank in order to finance Mr. Aron's sex-change operation. The financing eventually was obtained from Mr. Wojtowicz's share of the profits from the film *Dog Day Afternoon*. (*The New York Times* reports, tantalizingly: "Before her sex change, Ms. Eden married Mr. Wojtowicz in 1971.")

▲ District of Columbia officials are counting on

House-Senate conferees to remove from the 1988 D.C. budget an amendment sponsored by North Carolina Senator Jesse Helms that forbids the District to spend any money until it repeals its local ordinance prohibiting insurance companies from considering HIV status in determining insurability.

▲ A Chicago woman saved a man's life by administering CPR when he collapsed on the street. He turned out to be an intravenous drug abuser and to have bleeding gums. Authorities, citing confidentiality requirements, refuse to give the woman information as to the man's HIV antibody status.

▲ Governor George Deukmejian of California says his state's new drug-testing law will not circumvent the Food and Drug Administration's authority generally, but will merely permit speedier clinical trials of AIDS drugs.

▲ The Illinois division of the American Civil Liberties Union criticizes, for irresponsible abdication of leadership, school boards that refuse to enroll children with AIDS knowing that the courts will order them to do so and that their timidity will encourage community panic.

▲ Longmeadow, Massachusetts, mourns the death of 18-year-old Todd White, who had suffered from AIDS since December 1985 and who had been an inspiration to his classmates and teachers at the local high school. Though blinded by complications of the syndrome, White was graduated in June and planned to start college.

▲ Federal officials kick off "AIDS Awareness and Prevention Month" by unveiling print and broadcast public-service announcements and educational materials produced by Ogilvie & Mather under a $4.6-million contract with the Centers for Disease Control. At least some of the television networks will run some of the spots, but none will run any dealing with the use of condoms, leaving decisions on those spots to local stations.

What we have here, clearly, is a story, not about a disease, but about our society.

In urging the media to do less reporting about the "terrors of AIDS," in an effort to reduce the level of hysteria, *The New Republic*'s Charles Krauthammer is, in effect, urging that we blink the collective eye that we keep on that society.

But our nightmares tell us as much about ourselves as do other dreams, and confronting them may in itself be therapeutic. ■

PERSPECTIVE 8

News Gathering and Religion

Among the biggest news stories of the 1980s were the charges of mismanagement and misconduct in various TV religious ministries, especially the ministry of Jim and Tammy Bakker. The *Charlotte Observer,* rooted in the South's Bible country, covered the story long before it captured the attention of the rest of the media. In this article, *Charlotte Observer* editor Richard Oppel discusses why his newspaper considers religion an important issue.

Consider:

1. Why, according to Oppel, is religion an important news issue?

2. What do you believe is an appropriate role for a newspaper such as the *Charlotte Observer* to play in religious coverage? Why?

3. Do you agree with editorial page editor Ed Williams when he says, "Nuts and fools and hustlers can't exempt themselves from our editorial comment by claiming they're acting in God's name"? Why? Why not?

4. Oppel has said, "I don't think the *Charlotte Observer* brought down Jim Bakker. I think Jim Bakker brought down Jim Bakker." Do you agree? Why? Why not?

We Don't Need a Scandal to Make Religion an Important News Beat

RICHARD A. OPPEL

With more than 600 articles [in 1987] alone on PTL, Jim and Tammy Bakker's sullied religious legacy is more than your average church story for the *Charlotte Observer*. But the *Observer* has covered religion intensely at least as far back as the 1930s, when it devoted pages to printing every word of the sermons of a visiting preacher by the name of Billy Sunday.

That's what our readers want. They care about religion, so religion sells newspapers.

The tastes of the Piedmont Carolinas embrace a fascinating mix of interest in race, religion and rock 'n' roll; stock car racing; basketball; textiles and sophisticated electronics; and of far-flung regional banking empires whose revenues dwarf the economies of small nations.

Rich Oppel is editor of the *Charlotte* (N.C.) *Observer.*

When it comes to religion, the *Observer* gives witness to the strange:

▲ Flake Braswell—yes, that's his real name—leader of nearby Union County's True Light Church, sold his upholstering shop and hunkered down to await the end of the world in late 1970. Some of his followers sold their houses and moved into the Ramada Inn on U.S. 74. When Flake rolled out of bed on the first day of 1971 to find the world still there, he bought back his business and explained quietly, "It was a mistake."

▲ Snake-handling preacher Charles Prince of Canton, N.C., was laid to rest in 1985 after being bitten by a rattlesnake and seeking relief in a mason jar full of strychnine. It did not help. They buried Charlie after reading Mark 16:17-18: "And these signs will accompany those who believe: in my name they will cast out demons; they will speak in new tongues, they will pick up serpents, and if they drink any deadly things, it will not hurt them; they will lay their hands on the sick and they will recover."

▲ In June 1987 reporter Dan Huntley visited South Carolina's Oyotunju Village, America's only community devoted entirely to the Yoruba religion, a Nigerian-based, pre-Christian religion. Believers spread herbs from large wooden bowls and carried flaming incense sticks and sanctified the ground around him.

This is Billy Graham's hometown, and the airport parkway is named for him. Randy Taylor, the first national moderator of the Presbyterian Church of the United States—united Northern and Southern factions—was a Charlotte minister. The intellectual thought of this city of 350,000 is driven by the leaders of a dozen large churches.

The Charlotte Area Clergy Association lists more than 570 congregations, and executive director Nancy Mead puts the number at more than 600 if you count "storefront churches without telephones."

The church always has played a major role in the South. After the Civil War, it was one of the few social institutions left standing.

Political movements historically began in the church, and still do. In the 1950s and 1960s, the civil rights movement emerged from black urban churches. In the 1980s, the political right—ignited by issues of abortion, school prayer and textbooks—gains its strength in suburban white churches.

So, religion news for the *Observer* is the stuff of Page One, day-by-day. Religion news consumes a prime news beat and then some. It is not the fusty, dreary dredge tossed to a somber-looking fellow in the back of the newsroom, called "Reverend" by younger colleagues. It is not some abstract body of thought relegated to a weekly "Religion & Ethics" section. We don't have one, although that may make sense elsewhere.

Religion here is news.

For the first 10 ½ months of 1987, we published 1,661 stories involving religion. You may think, as some of our readers no doubt think, that every one of those had to do with PTL. Actually, about 620 were about PTL.

But among the 1,661 stories were other significant stories and significant issues. And there were small stories and issues no bigger than whether slaw or hush puppies were being served at a church meeting.

Reporter Kathleen McClain was in St. Louis when 25,000 delegates of the Southern Baptist Convention in June fought over inerrancy—the issue of whether the Bible is literally true.

We reported in July on the reaction of local churches to the statement by Southern Baptist Convention former president Bailey Smith that "God doesn't hear the prayers of a Jew." The Clergy Association said it rejoiced in Charlotte's ecumenism and regretted any statements encouraging anti-Semitism.

This year we also reexamined the fate of Jewish faculty at Davidson College 10 years after a controversy over whether any non-Christians could gain tenure at the Presbyterian-related liberal arts college. Happily, the few Jews on the faculty say the problem is in the past.

But small stories can be big news to churchgoers, too. One of the biggest annual stories in these parts is the clergy appointments announced at the annual meeting of the 275,000-member United Methodist Church's Western North Carolina Conference at Lake Junaluska.

So reporter Jim Wrinn was there to file columns and columns of a list: "First Street (Albemarle), A. Owen Peeler; Antioch-Bethel, Bruce W. Smith; Bond's Grove-Marvin, Nicholas L. Rochester Jr.; Lilesville, J. Wallace Morton Jr.; Locust-Oakboro, Bruce L. Gwyn. . . ." Our readers expect to see that list.

AP covered for us the fast-growing, 2.1 million-member Assembly of God (AoG) denomination's annual convention in Oklahoma City, where delegates discussed the "crisis situation" of brother Jim Bakker's fall, which demanded "soul-searching."

As always, there were smaller regional meetings. McClain covered the Episcopalians' North Carolina Diocesan meeting on AIDS at Greensboro, while reporter Lolo Pendergast reported on 3,500 Jehovah's Witnesses meeting in Rock Hill, S.C., to talk about world war, famine, terrorism, the spread of AIDS and the approaching end of the world.

We celebrate the milestones, as we did in October when St. Martin's Episcopal Church marked the 100th anniversary of its redbrick sanctuary on East 7th Street, recording old-timers' remembrances from the 1920s, when the church was used as the meeting place for the Sir Galahad Club for Boys.

We note the slips, as we did when we reported the Rev. Richard Leaptrot, a Presbyterian minister in Pinehurst, was arrested on charges of indecent exposure in the Plaza Pussycat Bookstore in Charlotte July 22.

Charlotte is the home for many prominent clergy, including Billy Graham, born on a farm where Park Road Shopping Center now stands. As he moves toward retirement, the 67-year-old Graham frequently returns to his hometown. He was here Nov. 4 to give the eulogy for his longtime associate, Grady Wilson, at First Baptist.

In Charlotte the pastors of a half-dozen major downtown and suburban churches can and will use their pulpits on Sunday to direct social and political action throughout the city, whether it is solving the problem of the homeless or pressuring a local bank to pull out of South Africa.

When one of those pastors, Covenant Presbyterian Church's Doug Oldenburg, moved on to become seminary president, he thanked his congregation for "the freedom of the pulpit" that allowed him to preach a brand of radical economics. His sermons on redistribution of wealth raised hair on the back of bankers' necks many a Sunday.

When Southern and Northern factions of the Presbyterian Church sought leadership to help unify the church several years ago, the Rev. Randy Taylor of Myers Park Presbyterian led the effort and then served as the first national moderator of the unified church.

The pulpits of 70 predominantly black churches are also politically conscious, as any candidate for local office knows. Pre-marked sample ballots commonly are handed out in those churches on the Sundays before election Tuesdays.

Virtually every *Observer* staffer gets swept up into religion news at some point, whether it is business columnist M. S. Van Hecke recording plans for Calvary Church's new $28 million, 10-story complex or sportswriters checking their watches during "prayer pools" (who can come closer to guessing the length of the preacher's invocation?) in the pressbox before high school games.

But several are more intensely involved.

Kathleen McClain, 35, a Rhodes College graduate who worked at the *Cincinnati Enquirer,* is our religion reporter. She is no prima donna. While some of her colleagues nationally may cover simply the "big story," Kathleen works Sundays—attending churches when new pastors are introduced, or a missionary reports back from his or her years in Africa.

And, yes, she writes "Religion Notes," a column that gets in all the fish frys, new associate pastors, Palm Sundays and so on.

Frye Gaillard, 40, our Southern editor, was religion reporter for the *Observer* in the 1970s, providing some of the ground-breaking work on PTL. He wrote often of religion when he was an editorial writer in the early 1980s. Today, he is a frequent speaker before church and clergy groups.

In his book "Race, Rock & Religion" (Easts Woods Press, 1982, $12.95), Gaillard wrote that he "became interested in Christianity per se—the startlingly simple notion that the life and death of Jesus still matter today; perhaps more than anything else."

Ed Williams, 45, a Mississippi graduate and Nieman Fellow, is editor of the editorial page, heading an eight-person staff that regularly comments on religion.

"I was reared as a rural fundamentalism

Southern Baptist, and probably will spend the rest of my life trying to deal with that experience. One thing I know, however, is that religion and religious institutions are important forces in the lives of our readers, and therefore worthy of editorial comment. We write with respect for religion, but we don't hesitate to comment on what people do in the name of religion," he says.

"When the Southern Baptist fundamentalists seem ready to put the clamps on freedom of thought at the Southeastern seminary in Wake Forest, we say it's their right to do so, but we don't think North Carolina—or Southern Baptists—will be well served if the seminary becomes a northern branch of Bob Jones University. When the Bakkers wrap themselves in glitter and greed and call it Christianity, we call it what it is. Nuts and fools and hustlers can't exempt themselves from our editorial comment by claiming they're acting in God's name.

"We comment on people who live up to the teachings of their religion: a carpenter working for Habitat for Humanity, a synagogue running a refuge for homeless women and children, a minister speaking against the Klan or for street people. These are not just public-spirited citizens, they are men and women carrying out the will of God as they understand it. We don't hesitate to speak of the power of God as evidenced in the actions of His people, any more than we'd be hesitant to speak of the power of patriotism or love.

"Revelations 3:16 says, 'Because thou art lukewarm, and neither cold nor hot, I will spew thee out of my mouth.' We take that as an admonition to say what we mean, plainly and firmly," says Williams.

If commentary on religion by Williams and his colleagues isn't present on a Sunday, readers can count on the column of Marse Grant, the retired editor of the Biblical Recorder, who usually is railing away at TV evangelists, inerrant Baptists or political reprobates.

Also, the letters to the editor are filled with people wanting to comment on religion. As long as the writer isn't looping together Biblical verse after verse, we let him or her have at it on religious issues.

So rich is religion in Carolinas life that it hardly could by bypassed as a source of humor. For example, Rabbi Marc Wilson wrote a Viewpoint piece for us decrying the "desecration" of good, rock-ribbed Jewish food by his non-Jewish Charlotte neighbors:

"Smoked salmon is eaten on toast points with creamery butter and chopped egg whites by people named Miffy and Trent. Lox is down-and-dirty two-fisted food, consumed by people named Marvin and Irv (or an occasional Marc), washed down by a Dr. Brown's Cel-Ray or semi-viscous black coffee." Wilson worried, "Brothers and sisters, what will be next? Men of the Word caroming down water slides in three-piece business suits? Church secretaries affirming their faith by posing in the buff?"

At the University of South Carolina stadium in Columbia, Gamecock fans really get to rocking and the whole upper deck swings. This prompted a quote from the immortal coach Joe Morrison: "If it ain't swaying' we ain't playin'." So when Pope John Paul came there, Outfront columnist Doug Robarchek declared, "If it ain't swayin', we ain't prayin'."

We were, by the way, perhaps the only newspaper in the Western Hemisphere that did not print a special section on the Pope's visit. Our judgment might have been different if John Paul were the head fundamentalist Baptist. That would sell.

Each of our seven "Little Observers" includes at least a page of religion news once a month. It is microcosmic journalism:

▲ In our Union Observer, the Rev. Jim McCoy wrote a sermon: "May I raise the corner of the veil of a minister's heart and share with you our most deadly temptation?"

▲ Hickory reporter Bill Chapman told of plans by First Baptist Church in Morganton to sell the stained-glass windows removed from an old sanctuary torn down in the 1960s.

▲ Gastonia reporter Ann Doss Helms reported the decision by West Avenue Presbyterian Church to stay in a neighborhood of a textile mill, a pawn shop, a convenience store and a radiator shop to build a $500,000 addition.

"We believe that Christ calls the church not only into affluent, populated areas, but also into the midst of cities and less than attractive settings," said the pastor.

▲ Photographer Jeff Wilhelm catalogued a 135-year-old church ritual—the Balls Creek Camp Meeting in Catawba County. He wrote: "On the dusty streets between rows of tents (actually wooden buildings), childhood friendships are born. The strongest grow into love. Those that endure blossom into marriage. More children are born, and the circle remains unbroken. Each evening, when the air cools, hundreds of teens 'walk the circle' around the camp, to see and be seen, while the older folks fill the arbor for the evening worship service."

▲ Gene Stowe reported that Union County Gideons—barred from distributing Bibles in the schools—passed out New Testaments on Jan. 28 in the county courthouse square in Monroe.

Worship in our region ranges from a self-proclaimed preacher equipped with nothing more than a Bible and a borrowed concrete-block garage on a red-clay road, to the Rev. Ross Rhoads' Calvary Church, with its computerized attendance reports that record traffic and weather conditions on past Sundays, and its 7,200-seat sanctuary, only exceeded by the city's 13,000-seat coliseum. Rhoads predicts his membership will reach 17,800 by 1995.

The largest denominations in the Charlotte area are the Baptists, who represent about 17 percent of Mecklenburg County's churchgoing population; Presbyterians, 11 percent; AME Zion, 10 percent; Methodists, 9 percent; Catholics, four percent; Episcopalian and Lutherans, two percent each. Practicing Jews number about 1,000 of our population of 450,000.

About 60 percent of Americans are active members of churches or synagogues, according to the "Yearbook of American and Canadian Churches 1987," compiled by the National Council of Churches. The figures, covering 218 religious bodies, showed the total U.S. membership in 1985 was 142,926,363. In Mecklenburg County, about 77 percent of the people are active members.

And maybe the rest are home reading about religion in the Sunday *Observer.* ■

For Further Reading

Books

Ben H. Bagdikian, *The Media Monopoly* (Boston: Beacon Press, 1983).

Benjamin M. Compaine, *Who Owns the Media?* (White Plains: Knowledge Industries, 1979).

A. J. Liebling, *The Press* (New York: Ballantine, 1961).

Walter Lippmann, *Free Press* (New York: Free Press, 1965).

James Reston, *The Artillery of the Press* (New York: Harper & Row, 1966).

Times Mirror, *The People & The Press* (Los Angeles: Times Mirror, 1986).

David H. Weaver and G. Cleveland Wilhoit, *The American Journalist: A Portrait of U.S. News People and Their Work* (Bloomington: Indiana University Press, 1986).

Periodicals

Advertising Age

Channels

Columbia Journalism Review

Editor & Publisher

Folio: The Magazine of Magazine Management

Newspaper Research Journal

Publishers Weekly

Washington Journalism Review

Media Effects

Whose Fault Is It?

Media scholars today generally agree that the media have different effects on different types of people with differing results (called *selective perception*). That is, the media affect what we do, but it's difficult to predict who, when, and how we will be affected.

In Perspective 1, Robert MacNeil challenges the usefulness of television. He says that one of the biggest dangers of television is that it distracts us from other activities and that it trivializes events. In Perspective 2, Jeff Greenfield says that we overestimate the effects the media have on our lives. Consider:

1. What does MacNeil mean when (quoting a Quebec newspaper) he says that television's approach is *"mitraillant de bribes*—machine-gunning with scraps"?

2. Do you agree with MacNeil that "this society is being force-fed with trivial fare with only dimly perceived effects on our habits of minds, our language, our tolerance for effort, and our appetite for complexity"? Why? Why not?

3. Which effects does Greenfield concede to television? Which effects does Greenfield say are debatable? Do you agree? Why? Why not?

4. Do you agree with Greenfield that "television . . . has shown precious little power over the most fundamental values of Americans"? Why? Why not?

5. Which of these arguments is most persuasive? Why?

Is Television Shortening Our Attention Span?

ROBERT MacNEIL

I don't know much about the business of education, but I do know something about my own business, television, and I have a prejudice that I believe is relevant to the concerns of educators.

It is difficult to escape the influence of television. If you fit the statistical averages, by the age of twenty you have been exposed to something like twenty thousand hours of television. You can

Robert MacNeil is executive director and coanchor of public television's "The MacNeil/Lehrer NewsHour."

add ten thousand hours for each decade you have lived after the age of twenty. The only activities Americans spend more time doing than watching television are working and sleeping.

Calculate for a moment what could have been done with even a part of those hours. Five thousand hours, I am told, are what a typical college undergraduate spends working on a bachelor's degree.

In ten thousand hours you could have learned enough to become one of the world's leading astronomers. You could have learned several languages thoroughly, not just to the level required to pass a college course, but fluently. If it appealed to you, you could have read Homer in the original Greek or Dostoyevsky in Russian. If that didn't appeal to you, you could have invested that amount of time and now be at the forefront of anything—nuclear physics, aerospace engineering—or you could have decided to walk right around the world and write a book about it.

The trouble with being born in the television age is that it discourages concentration. It encourages serial, kaleidoscopic exposure; its variety becomes a narcotic, not a stimulus; you consume not what *you* choose and when, but when *they* choose and *what*.

In our grandparents' eyes, such a prodigious waste of our God-given time would have been sinful because that time was not used constructively—for self-improvement, for building moral character, for shaping our own destinies. Our grandparents would have regarded it as sloth, as escapism, as perpetually sucking on visual candies. Yet, our grandparents would probably have found television just as difficult to resist as we do.

Almost anything interesting and rewarding in life requires some constructive, consistently applied effort. The dullest, the least gifted of us, can achieve things that seem miraculous to those who never concentrate on anything. But television encourages us to *apply* no effort. It sells us instant gratification. It diverts us *only* to divert us, to make the time pass without pain. It is the *soma* of Aldous Huxley's *Brave New World*.

Television forces us to follow its lead. It forces us to live as though we were on a perpetual guided tour: thirty minutes at the museum, thirty at the cathedral, thirty for a drink, then back on the bus to the next attraction; only on television, typically, the spans allotted are on the order of minutes or seconds, and the chosen delights are more often car crashes and people killing each other. In short, a lot of television usurps one of the most precious of all human gifts, the ability to focus your attention yourself, something that only human beings can do.

Television has adopted a particular device to do this, to capture your attention and hold it, because holding attention is the prime motive of most television programming. The economics of commercial television require programmers to assemble the largest possible audience for every moment (because that enhances its role as a profitable advertising vehicle). Those programmers live in constant fear of losing anyone's attention—the dull or the bright, the lazy or the energetic. The safest technique to guarantee that mass attention is to keep everything brief, not to strain the attention of anyone but instead to provide constant stimulation through variety, novelty, action, and movement. You are required, in much popular television fare, to pay attention to *no* concept, no situation, no scene, no character, and no problem for more than a few seconds at a time. In brief, television operates on the short attention span.

It is the easiest way out. But it has come to be regarded as a given, as inherent in the medium itself, as an imperative—as though General Sarnoff, or one of the other august pioneers of video, had bequeathed to us, from wherever he now rests, tablets of stone, commanding that nothing in television shall ever require more than a few moments' concentration.

I see that ethos now pervading this nation and its culture. I think the short attention span has become a model in all areas of communication, where the communicators want to be modish, up to date. I think it has become fashionable to think that, like fast food, fast ideas are the way to get to a fast, impatient public reared on television. And I think education is not exempt.

In the case of news, this practice was described a few years ago by a Quebec newspaper as *"Mitraillant de bribes,"* machine-gunning with scraps. The description is very apt.

I believe, although my view is not widely shared, that this format is inefficient communication in terms of its ability to encourage absorption, retention, and understanding of complexity. I believe it is inefficient because it punishes the attentive and the interested by impaling them on the supposed standard of the *in*attentive and the *un*interested.

I question how much of television's nightly news effort is really absorbable and understandable. I think the technique fights coherence. I think it tends to make things ultimately boring and dismissable (unless they are accompanied by horrifying pictures), because almost anything is boring and dismissable if you know almost nothing about it.

If I may pause for a commercial, the "Mac-Neil/Lehrer Report" was founded on the conviction that the attention span of thirty seconds or a minute, which formed the basis of most television journalism, was an artificial formula imposed on the nation by the industry. To claim that it was the only way large numbers of people could be held by news about the real world was false and also insulting to large numbers of intelligent Americans.

We are now seven years along in an experiment to prove the contrary. And we are having some impact. [In] September [1986] we expanded the program from thirty minutes to an hour, the "MacNeil/Lehrer NewsHour."

I believe that catering to the short attention span is not only inefficient communication, but it is also decivilizing. Part of the process of civilizing a young person, surely, lies in trying to lengthen his attention span, one of the basic tools of human intelligence.

A child may or may not have original sin, but he is born with original inattention. He is *naturally* inattentive, like a puppy, except to his basic biological needs.

Rearing a child consists in part in gradually trying to get his attention for longer periods, to cause him finally to direct it himself and to keep it directed until he finishes something. The older or more mature a child is, the longer he can be made to pay attention.

But what so much of television does is precisely the opposite. It panders to a child's natural tendency to be scatterbrained and inattentive, to watch this for two minutes and play with that for two minutes. It is giving up the struggle. It starts from the assumption that he will be bored. It is like conceding that a child likes sugar, therefore you should give him only cereals with lots of sugar in them, or he may not eat and will hate you and grow up to write mean novels—assuming he *can* write—about what wretched parents you were.

I do not think education is immune to the virus. And the responsibility of education is enormous. Educators should consider the casual assumptions television tends to cultivate that bite-sized is best, that complexity must be avoided, that nuances are dispensable, that qualifications impede the simple message, that visual stimulation is a substitute for thought, and that verbal precision is an anachronism.

There is a crisis of literacy in this country and a tendency to excuse it by throwing up our hands and saying, "Well you can't fight the impact of the visual culture. Perhaps we can only join it." But we do not have to resign ourselves to the brilliant aphorism of Marshall McLuhan that the medium is the message. It *is,* but it is not a sufficient message. It may be old-fashioned, but I was taught to believe the Kantian idea that thought is words arranged in grammatically precise ways.

The message of the television medium fights that notion in several ways. One is obvious and perhaps trivial: it ingrains popular verbal habits, like the grammatical shortcuts of Madison Avenue. More seriously, it steals time from and becomes a substitute for deriving pleasure, experience, or knowledge through words. More subtly, even for sophisticated people, it encourages a surrender to the visual depiction of experience, necessarily abbreviated by time constraints, necessarily simplified, and often trivialized.

If American society is to maintain some pretence of being a mass literate culture, then far from reversing the appalling statistics of functional illiteracy, I think the struggle is to prevent them from growing worse. As you know, it is estimated that twenty-five million Americans cannot read or write at all. An additional thirty-five million are functionally illiterate and cannot read or write well enough to answer a want ad or understand the instructions on a medicine bottle. That adds up to sixty million people—nearly one-third of the population. And, since close to one million young Americans drop out of school each year, it is probable that the country is producing at least that many *new* illiterates, or semiliterates, every year.

They land in a society where rudimentary survival increasingly depends on some ability to function in a world of forms and schedules and credit agreements and instructions. They enter a society that already faces the growing problem of finding something productive for most of its citizens to do. It is already a society with a cruelly large number of people who are in some sense redundant, whose share of the American dream is pitifully small.

Literacy may not be a human right, but the highly literate Founding Fathers might not have found it unreasonable or unattainable. We are not only *not* attaining literacy as a nation, statistically speaking, but also falling farther and farther short of attaining it. And, while I would not be so simplistic as to suggest that television is the cause, I believe it contributes and is an influence: for the dull it is a substitute; for the bright it is a diversion.

The educators of this country, especially in the public schools, have had enough burdens thrust on them by society. But I frankly see no other force than educators in the society that can act as a counterweight to the intellectual mush of television. Of course, the home environment is primary, and millions of parents try very conscientiously. But television is now an essential part of every home. The Fifth Column is there, often in many rooms. It is virtually a utility. The school is the only part of a young person's regular environ-

ment where television isn't—or where television wasn't, until recently.

To the extent that schools and universities feel the only way they can reach young people's minds is by importing the values of television, I feel they risk exacerbating the problem. I don't mean there should not be television sets in schools or that television may not be, in a limited sense, a useful tool. Obviously, not all television programs are worthless, and teachers may be able to encourage more critical, more selective viewing—I believe it is called "television literacy"—and may be able to use television to whet the appetite for other disciplines. And there are fine programs designed specifically for instruction. That's not what I'm talking about.

I am talking about the tendency I notice to surrender to the ethos that television subtly purveys: the idea that things are gotten easily, with little effort; that information can be absorbed passively; that by watching pictures children are absorbing as much information as they might through print. That is what I mean by pandering to the easy virtues of television, of letting young people believe that ideas are conveyed by tasty bits; that intellectual effort need not be applied; that you can get it (as they say) quickly and painlessly.

A few years ago I said to my small son, then age nine, "Would you like me to read *Treasure Island*?" He said, "Naw, I know it. I saw it on television." I felt very defeated, since that book happens to be one I love. Later, on a boat, I got him in a captive environment with others who wanted to hear it. I read it and he liked it. But I think of his first response as the equivalent in my generation of saying, "Naw, I read it in Classic Comics." Are we content to let a generation grow up without knowing *Treasure Island* in its complete form? If not, there is only one way and that is by gentle forcing. That is what education used to be all about, and some of the forcing was not too gentle.

Why is that important? On one level, to get the sound of English prose, its rhythms and its rich vocabulary stirring pleasurably in their brains. Because it will echo there all their lives. The other is to stimulate their imagination. I know Walt Disney was a genius. But I personally deplore the way he has made so many classics so visually literal, substituting his (often cloyingly sweet) imagination for that of the child. And television is Walt Disney and his lesser imitators wholesale.

In politics, in sports, in entertainment, in news, if television doesn't like something the way it is, it is assumed that the wide public won't, so American institutions rush to change themselves so that television will like them. Television viability becomes *the* viability. My own code phrase for that pervasive influence on the culture is the short attention span.

Everything about this nation becomes more complicated, not less. The structure of the society, its forms of family organization, its economy, its place in the world have become more complex. Yet its dominating communications instrument, its principal form of national linkage, is an instrument that sells simplicity and tidiness—neat resolutions of human problems that usually have *no* neat resolutions. It is all symbolized in my mind by the hugely successful art form that television has made central to the culture, the thirty-second commercial: the tiny drama of the earnest housewife who finds happiness in choosing the right toothpaste. That . . . has also become the dominant form of political communication, transforming the choice of elected leaders into a slick exchange of packaged insults and half-truths, with the battle weighed heavily in favor of the candidate with the most money and the cleverest ad agency.

Whenever in human history has so much humanity collectively surrendered so much of its leisure to one toy, one mass diversion? Whenever before have all classes and kinds of men, virtually an entire nation, surrendered themselves wholesale, making their minds, their psyches, their bodies prisoners of a medium for selling?

Some years ago Judge Charles Black wrote: " . . . forced feeding on trivial fare is not itself a trivial matter. . . . " Well, I think this society is being force-fed with trivial fare with only dimly perceived effects on our habits of minds, our language, our tolerance for effort, and our appetite for complexity. If I am wrong, it will have done no harm to look at it skeptically and critically, to consider how we should be resisting it. And I hope you will share my skepticism. ∎

Don't Blame TV

JEFF GREENFIELD

One of the enduring pieces of folk wisdom was uttered by the 19th-century humorist Artemus Ward, who warned the readers: "It ain't what you don't know that hurts you; it's what you know that just ain't so."

Jeff Greenfield is a correspondent for ABC's *Nightline* and a syndicated columnist.

There's good advice in that warning to some of television's most vociferous critics, who are certain that every significant change in American social and political life can be traced, more or less directly, to the pervasive influence of TV.

It has been blamed for the decline of scores on scholastic achievement tests, for the rise in crime, for the decline in voter turnout, for the growth of premarital and extramarital sex, for the supposed collapse of family life and the increase in the divorce rate.

This is an understandable attitude. For one thing, television is the most visible, ubiquitous device to have entered our lives in the last 40 years. It is a medium in almost every American home, it is on in the average household some seven hours a day, and it is accessible by every kind of citizen from the most desperate of the poor to the wealthiest and most powerful among us.

If so pervasive a medium has come into our society in the last four decades and if our society has changed in drastic ways in that same time, why not assume that TV is the reason why American life looks so different?

Well, as any philosopher can tell you, one good reason for skepticism is that you can't make assumptions about causes. They even have an impressive Latin phrase for that fallacy: *post hoc, ergo propter hoc.* For instance, if I do a rain dance at 5 P.M. and it rains at 6 P.M., did my dance bring down the rains? Probably not. But it's that kind of thinking, in my view, that characterizes much of the argument about how television influences our values.

It's perfectly clear, of course, that TV *does* influence some kinds of behavior. For example, back in 1954, *Disneyland* launched a series of episodes on the life of Davy Crockett, the legendary Tennessee frontiersman. A song based on that series swept the hit parade, and by that summer every kid in America was wearing a coonskin cap.

The same phenomenon has happened whenever a character on a prime-time television show suddenly strikes a chord in the country. Countless women tried to capture the Farrah Fawcett look a decade ago when *Charlie's Angels* first took flight. Schoolyards from Maine to California picked up—instantly, it seemed—on such catch phrases as "Up your nose with a rubber hose!" (*Welcome Back, Kotter*). "Kiss my grits!" (*Alice*) and "Nanu-nanu!" (*Mork & Mindy*). Today, every singles bar in the land is packed with young men in expensive white sports jackets and T-shirts, trying to

emulate the macho looks of *Miami Vice*'s Don Johnson.

These fads clearly show television's ability to influence matters that do not matter very much. Yet, when we turn to genuinely important things, television's impact becomes a lot less clear.

Take, for example, the decline in academic excellence, measured by the steady decline in Scholastic Aptitude Test scores from 1964 to 1982. It seemed perfectly logical to assume that a younger generation spending hours in front of the TV set every day with Fred Flintstone and Batman must have been suffering from brain atrophy. Yet, as writer David Owen noted in a recent book on educational testing, other equally impassioned explanations for the drop in scores included nuclear fallout, junk food, cigarette smoking by pregnant women, cold weather, declining church attendance, the draft, the assassination of President Kennedy and fluoridated water.

More significant, SAT scores stopped declining in 1982: they have been rising since then. Is TV use declining in the typical American home? On the contrary, it is increasing. If we really believed that our societal values are determined by news media, we might conclude that the birth of MTV in 1981 somehow caused the test scores to rise.

Or consider the frequently heard charge that the increase in TV violence is somehow responsible for the surge in crime. In fact, the crime rate nationally has been dropping for three straight years. It would be ludicrous to "credit" television for this: explanations are more likely to be found in the shift of population away from a "youth bulge" (where more crimes are committed) and improved tracking of career criminals in big cities.

But why, then, ignore the demographic factors that saw in America an enormous jump in teen-agers and young adults in the 1960s and 1970s? Why *assume* that television, with its inevitable "crime-does-not-pay" morality, somehow turned our young into hoodlums?

The same kind of problem bedevils those

who argue that TV has triggered a wave of sexually permissible behavior. In the first place, television was the most sexually conservative of all media through the first quarter-century of its existence. While Playboy began making a clean breast of things in the mid-1950s, when book censorship was all but abolished in the "Lady Chatterly's Lover" decision of 1958, when movies began showing it all in the 1960s, television remained an oasis—or desert—of twin beds, flannel nightgowns and squeaky-clean dialogue and characters.

In fact, as late as 1970, CBS refused to let Mary Tyler Moore's Mary Richards character be a divorcée. The audience, they argued, would never accept it. Instead, she was presented as the survivor of a broken relationship.

Why, then, do we see so many broken families and divorces on television today? Because the networks are trying to denigrate the value of the nuclear family? Hardly. As *The Cosby Show* and its imitators show, network TV is only too happy to offer a benign view of loving husbands, wives, and children.

The explanation, instead, lies in what was happening to the very fabric of American life. In 1950, at the dawn of television, the divorce rate was 2.6 per 1000 Americans. By 1983, it had jumped to five per thousand; nearly half of all marriages were ending in divorce. The reasons range from the increasing mobility of the population to the undermining of settled patterns of work, family and neighborhood.

What's important to notice, however, is that it was not television that made divorce more acceptable in American society: it was changes in American society that made divorce more acceptable on television. (Which is why, in her new sitcom, Mary Tyler Moore can finally play a divorced woman.) In the mid 1980s, divorce has simply lost the power to shock.

The same argument, I think, undermines most of the fear that television has caused our young to become sexually precocious. From my increasingly dimming memory of youthful lust, I have my doubts about whether young lovers really need the impetus of *Dallas* or *The Young and the Restless* to start thinking about sex. The more serious answer, however, is that the spread of readily available birth control was a lot more persuasive a force in encouraging premarital sex than the words and images on TV.

We can measure this relative impotence of television in a different way. All through the 1950s and early 1960s, the images of women on TV were what feminists would call "negative"; they were portrayed as half-woman, half-child, incapable of holding a job or balancing a checkbook or even running a social evening. (How many times did Lucy burn the roast?) Yet the generation of women who grew up on television was the first to reject forcefully the wife-and-homemaker limitations that such images ought to have encouraged. These were the women who marched into law schools, medical schools and the halls of Congress.

The same was true of the images of black Americans, as TV borrowed the movie stereotypes of shiftless handymen and relentlessly cheerful maids. We didn't begin to see TV blacks as the equal of whites until Bill Cosby showed up in *I Spy* in 1966. Did the generation weaned on such fare turn out to be indifferent to the cause of black freedom in America? Hardly. This was the generation that organized and supported the civil-rights sit-ins and freedom rides in the South. Somehow, the reality of second-class citizenship was far more powerful than the imagery of dozens of television shows.

I have no argument with the idea that television contains many messages that need close attention: I hold no brief for shows that pander to the appetite for violence or smarmy sexuality or stereotyping. My point is that these evils ought to be fought on grounds of taste and common decency. We ought not to try and prove more than the facts will bear. Television, powerful as it is, has shown precious little power over the most fundamental values of Americans. Given most of what's on TV, that's probably a good thing. But it also suggests that the cries of alarm may be misplaced. ■

Lewis H. Lapham on the Media

In his book *Money and Class in America, Harper's* editor Lewis Lapham offered several observations about the American media.

Consider:

1. Do you agree with Lapham that the advertising industry "plays with ingenious skill on the themes of perpetual discontent"? Which of today's advertising slogans can be cited as using discontent to sell products?

2. What did *The New York Times* editor mean when he said, "A good author is a rich author, and a rich author is a good author"? What does this say about book publishing? Do you agree? Why? Why not?

3. What does Lapham mean when he says that "the television screen presents a world of Platonic forms and metaphors"?

4. Do you agree that "the popular worship of images thought to be divine has become . . . habitual"? Why? Why not?

5. Do you agree that "Dan Rather's voice is the voice of a committee"? Why? Why not?

Money and Class in America

LEWIS H. LAPHAM

On Advertising

The advertising business plays with ingenious skill on the themes of perpetual discontent that haunt the citizens of an egalitarian society. When everything is more or

Lewis H. Lapham is editor of *Harper's* magazine and the author of *Money and Class in America,* from which these comments are excerpted.

less the same, and when everybody can compete on the same footing for the same inventories of reward, then the slightest variation of result produces a sickness of heart. The collections of goods and services testify not only to social status but also to an individual's worth as a human being. Small and shabby collections belong to small and shabby souls. The more equal people become, the more relentless their desire for ine-quality. "The Americans," Tocqueville remarked in the 1840s, "clutch everything but hold nothing fast, and lose grip as they hurry after some new delight." . . .

On Book Publishing

A prominent editor of *The New York Times* involved with the supervision of the paper's cultural pretensions supposedly once stated the commanding principle with a concision superior to that of my Hotchkiss English master. Explaining the protocols of wealth to a newly arrived subeditor, the editor is purported to have said: "A good author is a rich author, and a rich author is a good author." The maxim is possibly apocryphal, but its point is proved in the bias of the paper's cultural reporting.

Twenty-five years ago a writer who wished to present himself as a serious or important artist was obliged to strike the pose of an outcast. The cultural convention of the period insisted on the image of the writer (or the painter, sculptor or playwright) as a man against the system. Condemned because of his truth-telling to stand outside the palace walls, the writer was presumed to have forsworn the corruptions of Mammon in order to receive the certificate of genius. The critics looked more kindly upon a writer's work if they could imagine him subsisting poetically in an attic, warming himself at the meager fires of a moral and aesthetic principle, directing a fierce guerrilla campaign against the overstuffed complacency of the bourgeoisie.

No more. The romance of the artist as an impoverished seer no longer commands belief. Under the new cultural dispensation, poverty is merely poverty, and behavior once attributed to the vagary of genius has come to be seen as being both boorish and subversive. The phrase "a poor artist" stands revealed as a contradiction in terms. If the artist were any good (i.e., "a real artist" and not a charlatan) he would meet that editor's criterion of being rich. If he isn't rich he has

failed the examination of the market and deserves no sympathy. The bias explains why the literary press so seldom prints unpleasant reviews of well-publicized books. An angry review constitutes an attack not only upon a writer or a work of art but also upon money itself, which, of course, is blasphemy.

On Television

Innumerable teachers and school administrators have remarked on the loss of historical memory among the current generation of American students. A poll conducted during the Bicentennial year showed that 20 percent of those asked couldn't remember what had taken place in 1776; among an audience of college students at the University of Michigan in 1981, nobody in the classroom knew what was meant by the word "Nazi." The effect is much amplified by television, which sustains the illusion that nothing takes time. The television screen presents a world of Platonic forms and metaphors, a world in which history is meaningless and memory irrelevant, where instant fame (reflected in the fleeting smile of a talk-show host) leads to instant eclipse, where politicians come and go in a matter of minutes and a woman's life can be transformed between commercials.

The juxtaposition of images aspires to the simplicity of moral fable. The news footage is reliably grim—riots in the slums of Uganda or Mexico City, murder victims being loaded into police ambulances in Brooklyn. The scenes of poverty and human wretchedness alternate with the advertisements for vacations in sunny Florida, for $20,000 automobiles and unlimited credit, for skin cream and perfume and cleansing lotions all guaranteed to restore the bloom of eternal youth.

The disorientation in time allows people to imagine themselves resident in a magical present. Because the viewing audience seldom can remember what it saw yesterday, the politician, like the actor or the advertising salesman, has no choice but to tell the crowd what it thinks it wants to hear at precisely that moment, counting on the national amnesia to preserve him from the embarrassment of having to redeem his promises with acts.

On Celebrities

With any luck and the right sort of promotion, an individual can become a commodity as precious as an ounce of rhinocerous horn or a designer label pasted on T-shirts, perfume and boxes of chocolate. Celebrities of all magnitudes bestow the gifts of immortality, awakening with their "personal touch" such inanimate objects as throw pillows, automobiles, blue jeans and chairs. Athletes show up on television breathing the gift of life into whatever products can be carried into a locker room. Actors pronounce ritual incantations over the otherwise lifeless forms of cameras, tires and brokerage firms. The popular worship of images thought to be divine has become so habitual that people find it easy to imagine celebrities enthroned in a broadcasting studio on Mount Olympus, conversing with one another in an eternal talk show. By granting the primacy of names over things, the media sustain the illusion of a universe inhabited by gods and heroes as well as satyrs, nymphs and fauns. Barbara Walters struck the appropriate note when, in the midst of interviewing the newly elected President Carter in the autumn of 1976, she said, in the hushed whisper of a suppliant at a woodland shrine, "Be kind to us, Mr. President. Be good to us."

On American Journalists

The fear of change is as traditional among the vicars of the American media as it is among the captains of American industry. Nothing so terrifies most reporters and editors as the arrival of a new idea. Hoping to extend indefinitely the perpetual present in which images pass for reality, the media deal in the semblance, not the substance, of change. Wars might come and go, but the seven o'clock news lives forever. When, in the winter of 1986–87, Premier Mikhail Gorbachev advocated radical changes in Soviet society and foreign policy, the American media insisted that he was lying, that his much-advertised *glasnost* was nothing more than a charade. The Washington columnists held as tightly to their inventories of stereotyped truth as a child to its nurse. To entertain, even briefly, the thought of genuine change was a possibility too painful to bear. . . .

Big-time American journalism is group journalism, and the people who succeed at it learn to speak or write in the institutional voice of *The New Yorker, Newsweek,* or *The CBS Evening News.* Dan Rather's voice is the voice of a committee. More than illness or death, the American journalist fears standing alone against the whim of his owners or the prejudices of his audience. Deprive [*New York Times* Columnist] William Safire of the insignia of *The New York Times,* and he would have a hard time selling his truths to a weekly broadside in suburban Duluth. ■

PERSPECTIVE 4

Stereotyping

Walter Lippmann defined stereotyping in 1922 as the "pictures in our heads" created by repetition. The pictures become our reality. In this article about female stereotyping, Karlene Ferrante gives a historical perspective to advertisers' view of women as passive consumers.

Consider:

1. Do you agree with Ferrante that "although the advertising industry is certainly not the origin of patriarchy, it does reinforce the patriarchal order by stereotyping and objectifying the female body to create insecurities intended to result in sales"? Why? Why not?

2. Do you agree that Christine Frederick's *Selling of Mrs. Consumer* used stereotyping disguised as science? Explain.

3. How does the Mirror Assumption differ from the Gender Assumption? Which one is the most useful, according to Ferrante, in analyzing female stereotyping in advertising? Why?

Making Sense of Sex Stereotypes in Advertising

KARLENE FERRANTE

Out of the political movements of the 1960s came an unprecedented, scholarly effort to document media sexism and racism in the 1970s. These content analyses, summarized in Courtney and Whipple's *Sex Stereotyping in Advertising* (1983), documented the pervasive existence of demographic distortion and stereotypes in advertising. A number of studies compared results over time. It was assumed by many that as women and Blacks achieved equal rights, media portrayals would become less distorted. Implicit in these studies are questions about the relationship between advertising and society: Are defenders of advertising correct in saying that advertising only *reflects* what is going on in society? Does advertising create sex role stereotypes, or does it just use existing stereotypes?

These questions are crucial to a feminist research strategy aimed at social change. And they

cannot be answered through content analyses alone. We need to pay more attention to how advertising is created. My purpose here is to begin to address these questions by taking a look at two companion assumptions commonly made about advertising: the Mirror Assumption (Advertising reflects society) and the Gender Assumption (Advertising speaks in a male voice to female consumers). These assumptions framed not only the origins of modern advertising, but also much of the 1970s discourse on sexism in advertising. Taken together, they lead to the problematic conclusion that the perspective of a dominant group reflects (or should reflect) the perspectives of society at large.

The Mirror Assumption

Advertising reflects society. In his 1985 book *Advertising the American Dream,* Roland Marchand used this as a hypothesis for his historical survey of print advertising during the Great Depression. He concluded that advertising does *not* act as a

Karlene Ferrante is a doctoral student and Jesse H. Jones Fellow at the Jesse H. Jones College of Communication at the University of Texas at Austin.

mirror of American social realities. According to Marchand, some social realities were hardly represented at all. For the most part, content analyses from the 1970s support Marchand's contention that advertising does *not* mirror society. Nevertheless, many people still seem to accept the Mirror Assumption. (Note, for example, that Stephen Fox called his 1984 history of advertising *The Mirror Makers*.)

But what does it mean when the "mirror" reflects and exaggerates some parts of the picture while minimizing or even eliminating others? Advertising pictures reality in a simplified and idealized manner. Characters are not fully developed, and they do not represent specific persons, but rather social types or demographic categories. The result is *stereotypes,* conventional and oversimplified images of types of people.

Stereotypes are powerful in reinforcing societal attitudes about groups of people because stereotyping involves the receiver in creating the message. Jane Root gives an example in *Pictures of Women: Sexuality* (1984). According to Root, ads that juxtapose naturally unrelated images such as cigarettes and a mountain stream push the viewer into assuming there is a connection, and then, into making that connection. Such an ad cannot "reflect" such a connection, since that connection does not really exist in nature. The ad is set up to engage the viewer into creating the association desired—to make meanings, and the meanings made are *personal* meanings.

This internalization process involves not only the processing of information, but a constant re-construction of the self. Admen have made extensive use of the social psychology of Floyd Henry Allport, whose work suggested that the self-concept is socially constructed through interaction with others. The way you are with others, the way others expect you to be, and the way others tell you that you are, all contribute to the social construction of the self.

Advertising continues to create and use self-consciousness to create insecurities that may be calmed only through buying. This self-consciousness is particularly evident among women, and it is engendered by a bombardment with pictures of stereotypically beautiful women, with special emphasis on individual body parts. Although the advertising industry is certainly not the origin of patriarchy, it does reinforce the patriarchal order by stereotyping and objectifying the female body to create insecurities intended to result in sales. The advertising industry is a patriarchal institution which has capitalized on and reinforced women's position in the patriarchal order.

Stereotypes have played an important role not only in defining advertising images of women, but in determining how early admen would conceptualize our entire system of consumerism. A key figure in the early history of advertising was Christine Frederick, an advocate of scientific home economy. In *Selling Mrs. Consumer* (1929), Mrs. Frederick argued that admen should appeal to the instincts of women. Women's instincts were supposedly better developed than those of men, so women would be *naturally* more responsive than men to the appeals they could engineer. At one point she listed 18 female instincts in rank order, including "love of homemaking" and "delight in color, smell, neatness, looks, and feel." Not only did Frederick believe these attributes to be natural, but she seems also to have applied them equally to all women. Such quasi-scientific objectification of women is nothing other than *stereotyping disguised as science.*

Betty Friedan found stereotyping disguised as science in her research of advertising archives for *The Feminine Mystique* (1963). According to Friedan, after World War II, advertising "sold" consumerism to the public *through the manipulation of women's roles.* She reported that marketing research had divided women into three categories: "The True Housewife Type," "The Career Woman," and "The Balanced Homemaker," and tried to persuade women to become balanced homemakers, since they were the most likely to spend the most money over the longest period of time. Friedan's criticism challenged the mirror assumption. It is, indeed, a contradiction in terms to claim to simply mirror society while actively promoting stereotypes intended to mold society.

The 1960s feminist revival led other women

to challenge, first, the stereotypes and, then, the Mirror Assumption itself. On the other hand, I believe that the Gender Assumption will prove useful in feminist analysis of advertising.

The Gender Assumption

This assumption, that advertising speaks in a male voice to female consumers, reflects a basic patriarchal organizing principle of the sexual division of labor. The ideal male stereotype is active, and the ideal female stereotype passive. In abstract communication terms, men speak and women listen. Men act, and women appear. This principle operates not only within individual advertisements (in the form of stereotypes) but also in the *social relations* between admen and consumers.

Historically most advertising executives have been men. The 1931 *Who's Who in Advertising* noted almost apologetically that it had included sketches of 126 women in a volume that gave profiles of 5,000 advertising men. Women have not been excluded from advertising jobs, but traditionally decision-makers have been men, and the traditional perspective of advertising has been a male perspective, which conceptualized the consumer as woman.

Not only does advertising historically represent an elite, male perspective on how to address and persuade the female masses, it also quite literally speaks in a *male voice* in the electronic media. Studies have found that between 80 and 90 percent of voiceovers are male. The male voice of advertising is also reinforced through the classic image of the male authority figure.

It is easy to see the pattern of male voice/female listener. It is a bit more difficult to recognize that such a hierarchical structure is *in itself* an artificially constructed social order. American women did not constitute *themselves* as consumers in need of expert advice. Such hierarchical structures are generally designed and rationalized by groups who situate themselves near the *top* of the structure. Early admen, for example, conceptualized consumers as unintelligent, lethargic, emotional, vulgar, culturally backward,

and, (not coincidentally), female. In *Advertising the American Dream,* Roland Marchand uses phrases from a variety of top advertising men to summarize the elitist attitude toward women as readers.

In a tone of scientific assurance, advertising leaders of the 1920s and 1930s (stated) that women possessed a "well-authenticated greater emotionality" and a "natural inferiority complex." Since women were "certainly emotional," advertisements must be emotional. Since women were characterized by "inarticulate longings," advertisements should portray idealized visions rather than prosaic realities. Copy should be intimate and succinct since "women will read anything which is broken into short paragraphs and personalized."

Such stereotypes were both observed and shaped by early admen. In spite of attempts to appear scientific and objective, there is a circular logic in stating that something is so, and then making it come true. For example, Carl Naether, in his 1928 book *Advertising to Women,* claims that women love to shop, and then provides strategies to make women want to shop. There are many such examples in the history of advertising. A circular logic is employed when such "natural" or "universal" phenomena must be artificially and painstakingly produced. Perhaps these phenomena are not *actually* universal. Perhaps they just seem "obvious" to an elite/provincial group with access to the media. When they really are not true, that group does all it can to make them true.

Challenging the Epistemology of Advertising

This insistence that an elite/provincial (not coincidentally male) perspective is universally valid is advertising's version of objectivism. Epistemologically, it is the same principle that insists that grammatically the generic "he" and "man" also include woman. It is the same principle that allowed slave-owners to create the stereotype of the happy-go-lucky slave, whose carefree existence was made possible by his master's willingness to care for him.

Whenever an elite group succeeds in equating its world view with an objective *reality,* the world views of others are invalidated. This is what happens every time the Mirror Assumption is invoked in relation to advertising. Feminist researchers have done well to stop waiting for advertising to accurately reflect a variety of world views. Thus, letting go of the Mirror Assumption frees us to more fully study the implications of the Gender Assumption. And that, I believe, is the direction we want to go. ■

PERSPECTIVE 5

Television Portrayals of Lesbian Characters

Until recently, lesbian characters are noticeable by their absence from prime-time television programs, according to Marguerite J. Moritz. In this article, Moritz reviews the portrayal of lesbian characters on television.

Consider:

1. Do you agree with Moritz that in the mass media, "lesbians have been virtually invisible"? Explain.

2. Do you agree with Moritz that "the consequent linking of AIDS to homosexuality in general has created a negative social climate for lesbians perhaps just as much as for gay men"? Why? Why not?

3. What arguments does Moritz give for the possibility that the networks may be more receptive to stories that contain lesbian characters?

4. Why does Moritz argue that "gay themes can be money in the bank"? Do you agree? Disagree? Explain.

Coming Out Stories: The Creation of Lesbian Images on Prime Time TV

MARGUERITE J. MORITZ

American television has never had a fondness for minorities. From its inception, its fictional world has been overwhelmingly white, male, middle-class, heterosexual, and professional. Doctors, lawyers, and detectives appear in numbers that defy national statistics on their actual presence in society and in portrayals that depict them as idealized, romanticized, and frequently infallible character types. Since television reflects what is valued by the institutions that produce it, TV's world shows life not as it really is so much as life as the people who shape the industry would like it to appear.

While overrepresentations and idealized representations of social groups signify their high social status, underrepresentations and negative portrayals, of course, carry the opposite message. In addition to constituting a systematic devaluation, this lack of positive representation deprives group members themselves of heroes and role models with which they could strongly identify. It also withholds from the entire audience a valuable source of social knowledge.

In the last three television seasons [Fall 1985 through Spring 1988] lesbian characters and story lines began their fictional coming out, the result at least in part of a changing institutional context in which what was once taboo is now potentially viable and sellable. These changes should not be overstated: They are neither sudden nor sweeping but rather subtle and designed to contain a

Marguerite J. Moritz is an Assistant Professor at the School of Journalism and Mass Communication, University of Colorado, Boulder. Before joining the faculty, she was a television news producer at NBC's WMAQ-TV in Chicago.

minimum amount of risk. Thus these emerging lesbian characters and story lines, like all other characters and story lines, are designed to be acceptable to the larger audience. These texts are created for mass consumption to reflect mainstream cultural values and to satisfy economic imperatives.

Lesbian characters, virtually invisible in the past, are now being created for prime-time television in significant numbers. *Golden Girls, Kate and Allie, LA Law, Hill Street Blues, Moonlighting, Hunter* and *Hotel*—some of the most popular shows on TV—all have had recent episodes (since 1985) with lesbian parts. *My Two Loves,* an *ABC Monday Night Movie,* explored in uncommonly explicit visual detail two women involved in a love affair. In addition, ABC introduced a series in the spring of 1988 which presented the first recurring lesbian character in prime-time history. *Heartbeat,* an hour-long drama about a women's medical group, featured actress Gail Strickland as Marilyn McGrath. Her role as an older woman, a nurse-practitioner, a mother, and a lesbian no doubt gave her considerable demographic appeal. After its initial six-episode spring run, ABC renewed the show and put it on its fall 1988 schedule.

The Barriers

Why has there been such a limited number of lesbian characters on television and why are male gays portrayed two or three times as frequently as their female counterparts? The answer comes in several parts. First, there is the historical tendency in all mass media to relegate women generally to what feminist scholar E. Ann Kaplan describes as "absence, silence, and marginality" and to omit "the female experience from dominant art forms." If women as a group have been framed less prominently than men, lesbians have been virtually invisible. Not only has lesbianism challenged social and religious notions of morality, on a cultural level it stands as an ultimate threat to patriarchy. If the notion of "genuine collectivity" among any women has been regarded as unacceptable by a system in which men dominate, how much more intolerable must the idea be of women who are bonded not only politically, economically or emotionally, but also sexually?

Of course a significant part of the answer to the question of lesbian invisibility on television is also found in the industry itself. Not only is the industry as a whole male dominated, but top program executives and screenwriters are by and large male. After years of dealing with television executives, Alliance of Gay and Lesbian Artists (AGLA) member David Thursdale reached the following conclusion: "Prime-time is dominated by heterosexual males so television's view of the world is their view of the world."

Homophobia inside the television industry may of course be more than matched by similar feelings outside the industry. Representatives of gay activist organizations in Los Angeles say homosexuality is not a popular issue now because of AIDS.

Gay activists are unanimous in saying that AIDS has resulted in far more television coverage of homosexual men than would have been the case had the disease never existed. This increased visibility, not only in television but in all mass media, has resulted in increased public awareness of gays as a group and of gay rights.

Yet the AIDS coverage has its negative side, particularly for gay women. Portrayals of homosexual men now are almost routinely linked to an AIDS story line. The tendency is to equate stories about AIDS with stories on gay life generally. The networks can now argue that they are meeting their responsibility to the entire gay community when in fact their coverage is heavily weighted toward gay men and largely focused on AIDS.

The negative implications for lesbian portrayals on television are fairly obvious. First, intense focus on AIDS has effectively captured center stage and taken the spotlight away from other issues which might relate more directly to lesbian lifestyles. In addition, the consequent linking of AIDS to homosexuality in general has created a negative social climate for lesbians perhaps just as much as for gay men, even though lesbians constitute a very low risk group for the disease.

Perhaps the greatest barrier to more frequent portrayals of lesbian characters is lack of good script material. AIDS has provided a dramatic, highly visible theme on which to develop material about gay men, but lesbian issues have not made a similar emergence. Made-for-TV movies routinely take on socially relevant topics, but because lesbian issues are also rare in nonfiction mass media, their stories tend to remain undiscovered.

One technique for building dramatic appeal into the lesbian characters that made rare TV appearances before the 1985 season was the spider woman approach. Writing in *Esquire,* Richard M. Levine described how the process worked in the early 70s to create texts which relied on negative stereotypes for impact:

One of the worst of these shows, an episode of Police Woman *called "Flowers of Evil," about three lesbians who murdered patients in their old age home ('I know what a love like yours can do to someone,' Angie Dickinson told the trio when she busted them), prompted one of the first organized gay 'zaps' at the networks. A group of lesbians, one a mother with her children, held a sit-in at the offices of the NBC top brass, during which the little tykes expressed their sentiments by parading through the executive washroom. (Coincidentally or not, after that, gay groups generally found NBC more receptive than the other networks to their image-improving suggestions.)*

Nonetheless, a 1986 episode of *Hunter* in which two lesbians play man-hating murderers offered a similarly negative portrayal and engendered another gay protest at NBC. "The networks realized why (we protested) and afterwards came to us and asked us to submit scripts," an AGLA member says. Another gay activist questions the network contention that they simply don't have good lesbian material. "I've seen good scripts submitted where the executives say, 'Change the two dykes into a man and a woman and we'll do the story.' . . . The networks say they don't think people will accept these shows. They say they get far more negative mail on them. But I think they themselves just are not comfortable with the whole topic."

Even shows that pair two straight women can make network executives nervous. CBS twice considered and even announced the cancellation of *Cagney and Lacey* for poor ratings. In an effort to save the program, the network tried the show in different time slots and began market research on how the main characters were being received by the audience. The results, according to network executives, showed that viewers felt actresses Tyne Daley and Meg Foster, (originally cast in the role of Cagney) had a relationship that was "far too intense," lacking in softness and humor. Trade press reports at the time were more blunt, saying that Foster was rejected for her "lack of femininity." Newton Deiter of the Gay Media Task Force says that claim was never substantiated and that the real objection to the Meg Foster character came from network executives themselves who saw the pair as "too strong and too dykey." Cagney was re-cast in the person of Sharon Gless.

Forces for Change

Given barriers to change that pervade the television production system, is it realistic to expect any significant departure from the dearth of lesbian characters on prime time? Gay activists themselves are divided on that issue, although all agree that continued, organized pressure tactics are essential. Beyond that, however, there are other developments that are already working toward change: liberalized censorship policies, successes with homosexual themes in other mass media, the commercial viability for the networks in exploring emerging social issues and the need to generate new material or at least to give a new twist to old themes.

The television networks do not have explicit policies dealing specifically or exclusively with homosexual portrayals. What exists instead are guidelines that are applied generally to homosexuals as well as to other minority groups, and, of course, precedent. Diana Borri, manager of standards and practices for NBC in Chicago, describes the way it works:

The rule is that public taste considerations should be your guide. In the 50s, they couldn't use the word "pregnant" when Lucy was expecting a baby (on I Love Lucy*). Today, I've heard "ass," "bastard," "tits," "bitch"—all words that were never allowed in the past.* Saturday Night Live *broke a lot of barriers.* St. Elsewhere *and* LA Law *get away with a lot.*

Along with a more liberal attitude toward language, a more liberal attitude toward story line also has evolved. Homosexuality was implicitly banned during the first quarter century of television programming. That changed 15 years ago with a made-for-TV movie, *That Certain Summer,* starring Hal Holbrook as a gay father coming out to his son. Since then, several other shows have had homosexual themes, peaking in the late 70s. By 1980, a conservative mood had returned, buttressed by the Moral Majority, Anita Bryant, and shortly thereafter, the discovery of AIDS.

By the second half of the 1980s, attitudes appeared to be shifting once again, this time toward a more liberal approach to language and story themes. In an interview after the 1987 Emmy awards presentations, the producers of *LA Law* were asked how they successfully push the limits of what is acceptable with the censors. They responded by saying that there are very few limits left. The censors, they said, "are no fun anymore. They let us do things and rarely challenge us."

The clearest example of this with respect to lesbian portrayals was seen in the April 1986 *ABC Monday Night Movie, My Two Loves*. Network censors permitted the two women (played by Mariette Hartley and Lynn Redgrave) to have and to display sexual feelings for each other in a way that had not been done before and has not been done since. The two main characters were portrayed by popular actresses who provided significant ratings appeal. The story itself was a complete departure from the typical coming out story. This was about adult choices, not adolescent confusion. The main character was shown to be economically stable and personally capable, an older woman facing an exquisitely difficult decision in her life. The very fact that an attractive woman was shown considering another woman over a man made this a prime-time benchmark.

The same season, the NBC hit show *Golden Girls* devoted an entire episode to a lesbian theme. Warren Ashley was the Standards Department rep on the show and says that from the censor's standpoint it was totally acceptable.

The show was cleared by every NBC affiliate. An estimated 30-million to 40-million viewers watched it and it received an AGLA Media Award. Audience feedback to Ashley's network office was mixed, "... with at least as many positive as negative calls, if not more. I got six letters that were serious enough that they required a response. The basic complaint they all had was that we had presented a lesbian who was not a degenerate."

Yet the kind of sympathetic portrayal done in *Golden Girls* and in a *Kate and Allie* episode a year earlier does deliver an implicit message of approval to the viewer that apparently still worries the networks. The question for censors now is: Are portrayals too positive? "Portraying homosexuality as a better way of living ... would be a problem, just as much as demeaning them would be," Ashley says. Presenting an overly positive portrayal of a heterosexual or advancing that lifestyle as superior undoubtedly never surfaces as a legitimate concern. The fact that a network censor would worry about being too positive in portraying lesbians reflects a double standard that may take years to change.

Network executives are today more than ever in search of material that can attract and keep an audience. The swift and deep penetration of cable television and of home VCR systems both have helped shrink network viewership, as has mainstream Hollywood cinema. With alternative forms of entertainment becoming increasingly appealing, the television industry finds itself no longer in a situation of unchallenged dominance but instead in a relatively marginalized position. Under these circumstances industry executives are keenly aware of other programming successes.

Cable television and cinema both are demonstrating that gay themes can be money in the bank, and that alone may make network executives more open to television portrayals. Indeed, the president of NBC Entertainment, Brandon Tartikoff, cited "lack of predictability" and "contemporariness" as two "essential" ingredients for success in new programs. "The audience now has 35 years of television-watching behind them. TV shows no longer go away. They're just on earlier or later, but they're still on. That audience has seen those story lines over and over again. We have to avoid the predictable; we have to find new wrinkles to the old tales."

The networks have already demonstrated their willingness to cash in on new, topical, and sometimes controversial themes, including homosexual ones. The viewing public is apparently quite willing to be both entertained by and informed about controversial issues, although clearly it can be argued that presentations are oriented toward the implications of these issues for white, middle-class America. *An Early Frost,* says gay writer Vito Russo, "gives the impression that AIDS is not happening to the gay son, but rather to the American nuclear family." In dramatic presentations particularly, scripts often rely on ambiguous endings (such as *My Two Loves*) in an effort to avoid alienating anyone. Constructed in this way, television shows can tap into dramatic subjects and capitalize on their currency, getting ratings without risking audience retribution. ■

Celebrities Versus Heroes and Heroines

The mass media quickly create celebrities and just as quickly abandon them. The media have become our celebrity barometer, says columnist Bob Greene. Consider:

1. According to Greene, what criteria do high school students use in choosing heroes and heroines?

2. Do you agree with Greene that in the United States, "celebrity counts for everything"? Why? Why not?

3. What is the difference between achievement and celebrity, according to Greene?

4. Do you agree that the overwhelming cultural message is that "if you aren't in the movies or on TV or on the professional athletic field . . . your life is pretty worthless"? Why? Why not?

All It Takes to Be a Hero Today Is Fame

BOB GREENE

Many heroic people live in this country of ours. There are inner-city doctors who treat the poor while giving up more lucrative practices in affluent areas. There are police officers who risk their lives daily to keep their towns and cities safe.

There are teachers whose goal in life is to enrich the futures of new generations.

Heroes, all of them.

I bring that up because the 1987 World Almanac Heroes of Young America poll has just been released. The 10 heroes of high school students are:

No. 1: Bill Cosby. No. 2: Sylvester Stallone. No. 3: Eddie Murphy. No. 4: Ronald Reagan. No. 5: Chuck Norris. No. 6: Clint Eastwood. No. 7: Molly Ringwald. No. 8: Rob Lowe. No. 9: Arnold Schwarzenegger. No. 10: Don Johnson.

With one exception, they are all actors. Ronald Reagan is president of the United States, but he is a former actor, and he is televised constantly. The others can all be seen at movie theaters or on home TV screens.

It's probably useless to be upset at the young Americans who were polled. They were just telling the truth. And it is probably too much to expect the young Americans to single out the quiet, unsung heroes among us. In fact, they

---

Bob Greene is a syndicated columnist.

undoubtedly didn't give those quiet heroes a thought.

Actually, the young Americans who were polled were simply reflecting the new truth of life in this country: Celebrity counts for everything. If you are famous, you are a hero. If you are not famous, you are nothing.

The problem here is that this whole syndrome raises unrealistic expectations for young people. How do we instill in them the desire to go out and do their best and let their good work be its own reward? Every message they receive tells them that if you aren't in the movies or on TV or on the professional athletic field—if you aren't making commercials endorsing products—then your life is pretty worthless.

I once had a conversation with Meryl Streep—a celebrity who didn't end up on this year's list of heroes. We were talking about achievement.

"I have a friend who has a son," Streep said, "and the son wants to be a rock and roll star. He doesn't want to play well. He doesn't want to compose music. He just wants to be a famous rock star. I think there's a lot of that out there. People who have no interest in doing anything well—they just want to be famous."

Streep was right: The attitude is widespread, and there is no indication it will get anything but worse. An author may work for years on a book, but the only thing that will matter is the four minutes the author may receive on the "Today" show as part of his or her promotion tour.

So if you're a parent, good luck in teaching your children the best use they can make of their lives is to find something they're good at and they love, and then to go out and work at it until they have come close to perfecting it.

You may make a living that way, but you'll never be looked up to as a hero.

Keep that list in mind: There are medical researchers in this country, and firefighters and cancer-ward nurses.

But the most heroic woman in America is Molly Ringwald. ■

PERSPECTIVE 7

Politics and the Media

ABC's Sam Donaldson reported on events at the White House for more than ten years. In this 1987 profile, Donaldson gives an insider's view of the relationship between the press and politics.

Consider:

1. How does Donaldson feel about the White House's role in setting the news agenda?

2. Does Donaldson feel that the Washington press corps is manipulated?

3. Do you think Donaldson's view of the public's perception of the press is accurate? Why? Why not?

4. How did Donaldson perceive his role as a White House reporter? Do you agree? Disagree?

5. What are the ethical choices that Washington reporters face, according to Donaldson?

A Conversation with Sam Donaldson About the Media and Politics

SHIRLEY BIAGI

"Bray It Again Sam," reads the headline in Time *magazine about a recent White House press conference.* Time *says Donaldson asked an impertinent question. Donaldson is accustomed to the criticism.*

"I have some sort of reputation of asking flamboyant or aggressive questions," he says, "but I have never, ever attempted to do that. I have sometimes asked aggressive questions and needled guests, but it's because I want information, not because I want a show.

"Now, I'm no dummy. If I can get that information and it's interesting and it's interestingly presented, I think that's fine. I think, to get an audience, you have to not be dull.

"Presidents, like most politicans I know, call on people who are interesting. We like interesting people, whether we're going to have them over to dinner tonight or whether we're at a news conference and we're going to call on someone to question us. We don't like dull people, anymore than we like being dull."

Dullness is not one of Sam Donaldson's characteristics. He also does not lack energy. During the week, he follows the president. On Sunday mornings, he is a guest on "This Week with David Brinkley." Sunday evenings he anchors ABC's "World News Tonight."

Donaldson moves everywhere in a hurry. His conversation about himself has an even, practiced rhythm that indicates he is often asked about his work. When he is perplexed (rarely) or intense (often), his eyebrows knit in an upside down W. Sometimes in his voice are hints of his native Texas.

His father died of a heart attack before Donaldson was born, and he was raised by his mother in El Paso, Texas. She sent him to New Mexico Military Institute when he was 14. Then he attended Texas Western College and the University of Southern California. His first job was at KRLD-TV in Dallas, where he spent two years. He moved to WTOP in Washington in 1961.

Donaldson, 52, has been at ABC News since October 1967 and at the White House since 1977. He has covered every national political convention since 1964. The Washington Post has called him "Big Mouth of the Small Screen." His ABC colleague Ted Koppel has called him "perhaps the best White House correspondent ever."

Shirley Biagi is chair of the department of journalism at
California State University, Sacramento.

Being Used in Washington

There's sort of a middle place in journalism where you concentrate on the process, and in the process, if you're the White House correspondent, you go hear the press secretary give you the most rosy scenario of any situation possible, and he wants you to go and tell the American people that. Well, in a sense, you're being used. In another sense that, plus your own judgment, is the news of the day.

To say that people use us in Washington to get out a particular message is to state the obvious reason why we're in Washington as reporters. We are there to find out what's going on and tell everyone about it. So I don't feel used. Now, if the question had been whether I've been lied to, that is a different question. That's where you get even and you cut people off.

How the Public Views the Press

I think most people see the jobs of reporters, whether in Washington or someplace else, as it really is. They understand the press has a function they appreciate—I don't mean in terms of throwing garlands, but I mean that they believe it is important to their lives.

Naturally, newspaper readers or television watchers are not going to endorse every reporter's work or every story and they shouldn't, but I don't buy the idea that the vast majority of the American people has either great hatred or lack of confidence in the American press.

I think that generally most people in this country understand what we're about, they approve of our work in the sense that we ought to be doing it. They don't always approve of every individual, and that's exactly right.

How the Public Views What I Do

People are not sophisticated about my job any more than I am sophisticated about theirs. I think there are a lot of people in the country, for instance, who are intelligent human beings, who somehow think I'm on the White House staff.

I get letters from people saying, "I've written to Ronald Reagan and asked him to fire you from his staff." Well, you say that must be about 3 percent. No, I think some far larger percentage don't understand, really. They understand that I'm at the White House and I report from the White House. They think I'm on his staff. And, of course, there's some percentage who think I'm on Gorbachev's staff.

But if you leave out the fringes, the majority of the people don't understand the techniques that I employ in my business, and that I have to employ. They see the finished product....

My Tough Reputation

There's this myth that I ask the tough questions. Well, to one extent of course, that's flattering. To one extent, that is more than complimentary. It stands me in good stead. But to the other extent, it's a myth, just like any view that I am always rude and crude around the president, in my view, is another myth. It is not true.

But you get typed and cast, for better or worse. One of the problems of this business is that you get typed and people are loath to use you in another way. They think you do what you do, not that you can do something else. You have to try to convince them that it's not true.

In broadcasting, you specialize in what you report and what broadcasts you're on and how they use you. If they use you in a way that management and the public finds pleasing, then they want to keep you there and they don't want you to move on.

But those are the questions that should be asked, I maintain, because people watching want you to ask, and I don't mean just for the theater. I have never asked a question with the thought that, "If I ask this, it will produce good theater, if I ask this it will keep me in the limelight." . . .

To put them on record with [an] answer is worth something, when you go back and something comes up.

One of the ways guests prepare for the Brinkley show is—they're ready for me to start to interrupt, and they immediately say, "Well, please don't interrupt me. May I finish?" even though they know they have been going on, just diarrhea of the mouth, with no point. They know there's a certain element of the audience out there that sees me as rude and crude and hostile and that comment will immediately evoke a sympathetic response, even though they should be interrupted.

Don't Imitate Anyone Else

There was a generation of correspondents at ABC that tried to sound just like David Brinkley. Well, there can only be one David Brinkley, I don't think they did it on purpose. I think it was just when you're around someone who makes such a strong impression, as Brinkley does with that voice and *patois* and the way he talks—well, [*imitating Brinkley*] it's. easy. to. just. fall. in. to. it.

But it was all to their detriment because no matter how closely they imitated him and how smooth they were, who wants a fake David Brinkley? So to say that someone's perception is that Donaldson's gotten where he's gotten by yelling at presidents and by being outrageous—it would be ridiculous for someone to try to pattern themselves after the way they perceive to be the way I've done it. Incidentally, that's not, in my view, the way I've done it.

Learn to Challenge Conventional Wisdom

What I've learned is that the conventional wisdom is usually wrong. So whenever anybody in town says it's going to be this way or that, you seek out the few people who say, "Nonsense. It's going to be some other way." And you present their point of view.

Don't worry about a president having the ability to present his point of view to the country. Be fair to the president, give him a chance. They [the White House] can snap their fingers and command a 9 o'clock address to the nation. They're on the front pages of the papers any day they want. When they pound the table, they're going to be on "World News Tonight," maybe as the lead story.

It's not their viewpoint you have to worry may not get out to the country. It's the viewpoint of the little guy in the wilderness saying, "The MX. It's a turkey missile. It's not worth a penny." You get that guy, you get him on, too. He'll never command as much time as the president. But don't worry that you're counterbalancing as part of Gorbachev's team. Worry about the conventional wisdom going unchallenged.

Now, if the conventional wisdom turns out to be right, and it sometimes does, of course it will prevail. You will not have torpedoed it by putting on the few dissenting voices or other views. But if the conventional wisdom—"We'll take care of this little country of North Vietnam in three months"—turns out to be wrong, you will have done a service to the American people by not allowing it to go unchallenged.

Think if we could have reversed that war just two years earlier, maybe only saved 12,000 American boys. Well, every little bit helps. But 58,000 Americans died in Vietnam in a policy that was wrong. You can take the view it was wrong that we didn't go out to win or you can take the view it was wrong because we had no business there in the first place. But the policy was wrong. It was wrong because it didn't work. The situational ethics of results are such that if the policy doesn't work, we ought to try to know it in advance. We ought to try to figure it out.

Now, I'm capable of being misunderstood when I talk this way. I'm not advocating that you run out and disregard the facts and the quotes and the context and that you purposely withhold information or load your report to suit your own bias. I'm not advocating that. This is not advocacy journalism, which I do not support. The advocacy journalist starts out with a premise and then goes out to support it.

When I say challenge the conventional wisdom, I don't mean start out with a premise that it's wrong, but challenge it. It'll survive the challenge if it's right, and it may change from day to day, and you'll change with it as a reporter. But I think that's the most important aspect of why you try to find out what's really going on, what's really happening.

For my generation of reporters, the two cataclysmic events, Vietnam and Watergate, were such that some of us came to the view that I've just expressed. In the '50s, most reporters and publications were simply garbage in, garbage out. [Senator] Joe McCarthy said he could give a list of 205 communists to the State Department. It was reported uncritically, banner headlines. Not many voices said, "Nonsense. Show us the names and if you can't produce the names, we'll run you out of town because you're nothing but a charlatan."

Today, I hope I can say that Joe McCarthy couldn't exist. A senator could not stand up in Wheeling, West Virginia, and make those kinds of charges and have anyone pay attention to him. Part of that is the sophistication of the American people, but I think part of it is in the way journalists view it.

Ethical Dilemmas

When I first came to town, journalists wanted to be social friends of the people they covered, particularly the presidents. I think most of us believe today that we don't want to be social friends of the people we cover, and particularly of the president. That's not our job. If we want to make friends, there are other people in the world.

I'll tell you what happens to older reporters in this town. They begin to think they're part of the establishment. They begin to think they're part of the ruling class. We ought not to be part of the establishment. If we reporters are the ones who are trying to seek out what's really going on here and we're part of the establishment, then who is going to police us? Who is going to police the establishment? Who is going to stand outside and not really care if they get invited to a state dinner or not?

We are part of the power structure of Washington by virtue of the fact that we carry messages around town, publicly on the air or in print, and that we then carry to the country and to the world a view of what's happening in this town. We are players, no doubt about it.

We are players in the sense of being part of the decision-making process, but I ought not to have a vote or a view taken into consideration when people in government, charged with responsibility, make up their minds about something.

I wouldn't go to the Cabinet room because no one has invited me and I'm not a member of the Cabinet. I'm happy to give the president my views if he wants to watch the Brinkley show or listen to my reports on ABC News. But I ought not to be part of the direct process.

The main caution is, don't believe that your success, your place in society as a reporter, depends on closeness, either socially or from the standpoint of power, with the people you cover. Be an outsider from the establishment.

You will be successful and you will get all the rewards you can stand in the business and all the awards and the important jobs without once going to dinner in Georgetown, without once going to a state dinner, without once being patted on the back by a president who says you're just a terrific fellow. You don't have to have that. And in fact, in my view, it's a detriment because there are enough smart people around who will begin to question your objectivity.

If you're going to befriend someone, befriend someone who's taking it in the neck from the establishment, whether they're people who need assistance or someone who's been fired wrongly from the federal government. The powerful ones don't need your help. They get along very well without it. ∎

CHAPTER TWELVE

For Further Reading

Books

Herbert E. Alexander, *Financing the 1984 Election* (Lexington: D. C. Heath, 1987).

James David Barber, *The Pulse of Politics: Electing Presidents in the Media Age* (New York: Norton, 1986).

Tania Modleski, *Loving with a Vengeance: Mass-Produced Fantasies for Women* (New York: Methuen, 1982).

Joshua Meyrowitz, *No Sense of Place* (New York: Oxford University Press, 1985).

Thomas E. Patterson and Robert D. McClure, *The Unseeing Eye: The Myth of Television Power in National Elections* (New York: Putnam, 1976).

Neil Postman, *Amusing Ourselves to Death* (New York: Viking Penguin, 1985).

David M. Potter, *People of Plenty* (Chicago: University of Chicago Press, 1954).

Periodicals

Communication Abstracts

Communication Research

Journal of Advertising Research

Journal of Communication

Journalism Quarterly

Public Relations Review

Legal and Regulatory Issues

Suing the Press

Several recent cases cited by Rodney A. Smolla in this article show how willing the public is to question the press' sense of responsibility. Once thought of as the protector of the public's interest, the press has increasingly become the target of legal challenges.

Consider:

1. According to Smolla, what motivates the majority of people who bring suits against the press?

2. How does bringing lawsuits against the media serve to make the media "accountable," according to Smolla?

3. Could a suit such as William Westmoreland's serve to enhance the strength of the First Amendment, as Westmoreland argued? Why? Why not?

4. Do you agree that our society today is more in need of a " 'safety valve' of anti-media litigation" than it was a few generations ago? Why? Why not?

The Thinning American Skin

RODNEY A. SMOLLA

It is disgusting, and it is a pack of lies. I—it hurts. It hurts, because words, once they are printed, they've got a life of their own. Words, once spoken, have a life of their own. How was I going to explain to my kids, my family, the people I care about?

Carol Burnett, *testifying in* Burnett v. National Enquirer

*But he that filches from me my good name
Robs me of that which not enriches him
And makes me poor indeed.*

Shakespeare, Othello *(III, iii, 160–162)*

Carol Burnett took the witness stand. With her voice slightly trembling and with tears in her eyes, she explained to the jury why she sued the *National Enquirer.* Her testimony was reported live by the Cable News Network, and the highlights were repeated on the three major network evening news broadcasts:

Q. (Burnett's Attorney): When was the first time you had any knowledge of that article or the contents of that article?

Rodney A. Smolla is Associate Professor of Law in the School of Law at the University of Arkansas.

A. (Carol Burnett): I believe that it was the day that it came out. . . .

Q. What was your reaction?

A. Well, I was absolutely—I was stunned. . . . I felt very, very angry. I started to cry. I started to shake.

William Westmoreland, retired commander of American forces in Vietnam, approached the microphones at the Navy Club in Washington, D.C., to announce that he was commencing a $120 million libel suit against CBS News. A documentary broadcast by CBS and narrated by Mike Wallace entitled *The Untold Story: A Vietnam Deception* had accused Westmoreland of complicity in a conspiracy to doctor intelligence estimates on the strength of enemy forces in Vietnam. As in Carol Burnett's case, the General's remarks were controlled but emotional, seeping with retributive bitterness:

I am an old soldier who loves his country and have had enough of war. It was my fate to serve for over four years as senior American commander in the most unpopular war this country ever fought. I have been reviled, burned in effigy, spat upon. Neither I nor my wife nor my family want me to go to battle once again.

But all my life I have valued "duty, honor, country" above all else. Even as my friends and family urged me to ignore CBS and leave the field, I reflected on those Americans who had died in service in Vietnam. Even as I considered the enormous wealth and power that make CBS so formidable an adversary, I thought too of the troops I had commanded and sent to battle, and those who never returned.

It is, therefore, with the greatest reluctance, and consciousness of the long and bitter legal battle I am about to engage in, that I have advised my attorneys, the Capital Legal Foundation, to bring suit in South Carolina, my home state, against CBS for libel. At this moment, correspondent counsel in South Carolina is filing our complaint against CBS requesting damages for libel. There is no way left for me to clear my

name, my honor, and the honor of the military . . .

The only question is whether CBS had an obligation to be accurate in its facts before it attempted to destroy a man's character, the work of his lifetime. I trust the American judicial system and an American jury will fairly evaluate what I and those in positions of responsibility said and did, and I am pleased to put my reputation and honor in their custody.

William Tavoulareas, the fiesty, iconoclast president of the Mobil Oil Corporation, did not appreciate a story by the *Washington Post* stating that he had "set up" his son Peter in business. The story strongly implied that Tavoulareas had acted in violation of ethical business standards, and perhaps even federal securities law. Tavoulareas tried for a frustrating year to get the *Post* to retract its story, but ultimately felt forced to take the *Post* into court for libel. Tavoulareas stated:

I tried to get them to admit their mistakes. But they're so damned arrogant. I kept telling them I'd sue. But they said I wouldn't because they'd drag me through the mud in discovery. Well, I know my reputation and my integrity, and I knew they'd get nothing on me. I said, "you don't know me. I'm gonna sue."

A comedienne, a general, a corporate executive, each a classic American self-made success story, each wounded by the media, and each striking back, through courtroom attacks that became a cause célèbre, taking on meanings much larger than the lawsuits themselves. They are among the most visible symbols of an astonishing cultural movement. America is in the midst of an explosion of litigation aimed against the media. Americans who feel their reputations have been impugned or their privacy invaded by the broadcast or print media have increasingly resorted to litigation for vindication. Much of this litigation in recent years has been launched by well known cultural figures, many seeking staggering sums

---

*Tavoulareas ultimately lost the suit.

of money. Burnett, Tavoulareas, Westmoreland, Woody Allen, Clint Eastwood, Mohammed Ali, Paul Laxalt, Ralph Nader, Norman Mailer, Wayne Newton, Elizabeth Taylor, Jerry Falwell, E. Howard Hunt, Shirley Jones, Lillian Hellman, Johnny Carson: the list of famous Americans who have taken to suing publishers, broadcasters, reporters, writers, and advertisers in recent years reads as if it were randomly generated from *Who's Who.* The media have been in the uneasy position of continuously reporting about itself as victim, as the lawsuit for libel or invasion or privacy has become one of America's newest growth industries.

Every week a new suit against the media seems to appear, many of the suits brought by politicians, entertainers, sports stars, writers, corporate executives, and other prominent social figures who have themselves previously profited from media attention. And plaintiffs today have no shyness about asking for staggering sums in their complaints. William Westmoreland's complaints against CBS sought $120 million, but there are countless other impressive demands. Former Israeli Defense Minister Ariel Sharon claimed $50 million in his libel suit against *Time* magazine, at one point claiming that *Time* had committed a "blood libel" in a story which implied that testimony before the Israeli investigatory commission into the Phalangist massacres at the Sabra and Shatilla concentration camps in Lebanon in 1982 had put at least part of the responsibility for the massacres on Sharon. Carol Burnett asked for $10 million in her suit against the *National Enquirer.* Beverly Hills physician Robert Fader filed suit for $20 million against *Washington Post* editor Bob Woodward for statements made in Woodward's book on John Belushi. *Wired—The Short Life and Fast Times of John Belushi,* in which Woodward wrote that Dr. Fader prescribed drugs to Belushi and other patients for no valid medical reasons and without regard to his patients' welfare. Norman Mailer sought $7 million in his suit against the *New York Post,* claiming that the newspaper defamed him in reports about the trial of prisoner/writer Jack Henry Abbott. Senator Paul Laxalt sought $250

million against the *Sacramento Bee* for stories linking him to a grand jury investigation of casino operations in Nevada. Former Philadelphia Mayor William J. Green sought $5.1 million from a CBS television station for reporting that he was under federal criminal investigation. Lillian Hellman sought $2.25 million against fellow writer Mary McCarthy after McCarthy said on the Dick Cavett Show that Hellman was "terribly overrated, a bad writer and a dishonest writer," and that "every word she writes is a lie, including 'and' and 'the'." . . .

People like Carol Burnett, whose comic roles have always played on middle class lifestyles, or William Tavoulareas, a self-made man, or William Westmoreland, a proud and courageous soldier, are the heroes of this middle America. Although as individuals each pursued their suits against the media out of sincere and highly personal motivations, as *cultural symbols* their lawsuits (like it or not) take on a larger significance; they are part of a movement toward the restoration of balance and decorum in national life, a decorum that will only be achieved if the media is made accountable. One simply has a hard time believing that simple narcissism could possibly be the prime motivation of Carol Burnett's suit against the *National Enquirer,* William Tavoulareas' suit against the *Washington Post,* or William Westmoreland's suit against CBS. Carol Burnett is an excellent actress, but her trial testimony was no act; the *Enquirer* article had deeply hurt her, and her emotion came through spontaneously and genuinely on the witness stand. William Tavoulareas' response was more a feisty, defiant anger, but it was obviously no less genuine; his efforts to vindicate his reputation became a crusade. And finally, Westmoreland's decision to resort to litigation is worth examining for what it reveals about the interaction between very old-fashioned American values—in Westmoreland's mind and heart, they are captured by the West Point motto, "Duty, Honor, Country"—and the values of the Ronald Reagan 1980's.

At Westmoreland's press conference announcing his decision to commence libel litigation, he spoke at length of his motivation in suing CBS. The most interesting element in Westmoreland's statement was his attempt to reduce the issues in the suit, and his own purpose in pursuing these issues, to the narrowest possible grounds. Was the motivation greed? Surely no one seriously thought it was, and Westmoreland removed any shadow of doubt by declaring, "If I am successful in this case, as I believe I will be, I will not retain any monetary award for my personal use but instead will donate it to charity." . . .

One of the remarkable things about the General's explanation of his motivation was his astute effort to preempt accusations that he was insensitive to First Amendment values, and even more significant, that he was attempting to use the courtroom to retry the central issues of the American experience in Vietnam. "I have dwelled at length upon the tremendous bulwark of liberty and freedom that is the First Amendment to the Constitution of the United States," Westmoreland stated, concluding that his pursuit of redress from CBS would enhance, rather than to detract from the strength of the First Amendment, for he "now feared that public reaction to CBS as the truth came out might lead to weakening of that bulwark through legisled codes of conduct or other attempts to restrain the media." The General was almost doing the media a favor, forcing down medicine that would purge it of its own worst faults.

But wouldn't the litigation contemplated by Westmoreland require the legal system to perform tasks it was never designed to do? Weren't the disputed issues of history raised by *The Uncounted Enemy* beyond the institutional competence of lawyers, judges, and juries? Again, General Westmoreland's instincts were perfect in anticipating and attempting to displace these questions, substituting for them the view that his case would involve the mere workaday stuff of routine litigation: simple scrutiny of the behavior of the defendant—an examination of the conduct and methodology of CBS. Thus, Westmoreland quite presciently declared that "the question before the American people in *Westmoreland* v. *CBS* is not whether the war in Vietnam was right or

wrong but whether in our land a television network can rob an honorable man of his reputation. The question is not whether I was a good general or a bad general. The question is not whether we won or lost the war in Vietnam."

General Westmoreland was totally correct in placing the methodology of CBS in a position of prominence in the litigation; CBS's conduct, it turned out, would be at the legal and factual epicenter of the suit, and much of what would be exposed would not make CBS proud. Despite Westmoreland's sincere protests to the contrary, however, the issues in *Westmoreland* v. *CBS* would also inevitably become the precise issues he disclaimed. Libel suits by their very nature place the "truth" at issue, and the clash of competing truths arising from *The Uncounted Enemy* documentary went to the very heart of American perceptions about Vietnam. Perhaps there was an unwitting concession of this inevitability in Westmoreland's curious use of the phrase "the question before the *American people,*" a phrase that seems to acknowledge the suit's true expansiveness. Indeed, the latitudinal sweep of the lawsuit would be apparent from CBS's own retrenchment in the face of the litigation: CBS would make every effort to make it appear that the fate of independent American journalism was at stake.

What comes through most strongly from Westmoreland's remarks, however, is the obvious sincerity of the General's proclamation that the CBS documentary did in fact deeply wound him, and his abiding faith that the legal system could heal the wound. Without attacking for one second the authenticity of General Westmoreland's feelings, and without meaning to intimate that they are petty or frivolous, it seems completely fair to point out that against the backdrop of American history, the General's decision to sue CBS does reflect a new way of thinking. Perhaps George Patton was every bit as stung by media portrayals of him during World War II as William Westmoreland ever was, but Patton did not sue anyone. This observation, however, must be balanced against the other reality of modern times: perhaps American society is more in need today of the "safety valve" of anti-media litigation, for whatever the media did to George Patton, it was probably powerless to change the outcome of World War II, while today the media may indeed influence the outcomes of wars—it undoubtedly influenced the course of events in Vietnam—and with the media's increased power there arguably has come an increase in the need of injured victims to sue the media, not just for themselves, but as representatives of society's interest in keeping the power of the media in check. . . .

. . . The heart of the matter for William Westmoreland, and for sympathetic juries in other libel suits across the United States, may have been that in some circumstances the libel suit provides one of the last hopes for vindicating one's dignity, and for preventing an impersonal corporate media from assuming the big brother role that Americans so often fear from government. We rely on the press to uncover corruption in government, but on whom do we rely to uncover the mistakes of the press? The media's problems in the court today may be to some degree a result of the American public's view that the libel suit is one of the legal system's few useful restraints on the growing concentration of media power. At this juncture the liberal civil libertarian worldview of many fierce defenders of the media ought to provoke a crisis of conscience, for the affirmation of dignity implicit in the civilized, nonviolent forum of the libel suit is arguably just as much a vital "civil liberty" as free expression is. ■

PERSPECTIVES 2 & 3

The Hazelwood Case

In 1988, the U.S. Supreme Court for the first time gave public school officials considerable responsibility over the content of school publications. This case became known as the Hazelwood decision because the case concerned the student newspaper at Hazelwood High School in Hazelwood, Missouri.

The school newspaper staff wanted to publish a story on teenage pregnancy and divorce that included interviews with students. The school principal deleted the stories because he said he felt that the stories were "inappropriate." The Court agreed that the principal had the authority to delete the stories.

What follows are two Perspectives on the Hazelwood case, plus a sampling of opinions from *The New York Times* and the *Washington Post* (see box on page 263).

Consider:

1. Do you agree with Richard M. Schmidt Jr. and N. Frank Wiggins that the decision will have "a pronounced detrimental effect on the educational experience available to student journalists"? Why? Why not?

2. Do you agree with Justice Brennan that "public educators must accommodate some student expression even if it offers views on values that contradict those the school wishes to inculcate"? Why? Why not?

3. Do you agree that "in the rare cases where student journalists and their faculty advisers don't meet reasonable journalistic standards established by school boards . . . the principal [should] have the authority to intervene to assure that those standards are not violated"? Explain.

Censoring Student Papers May Teach a Lesson That Will Return to Haunt the Mainstream Press

RICHARD M. SCHMIDT JR. and N. FRANK WIGGINS

The United States Supreme Court has recently decided a case important in two ways to the determination of the First Amendment rights of students in public secondary schools.

Although the Hazelwood decision will not directly affect the law governing private publications, it is the opinion of many educators that the case will have a pronounced detrimental effect on the educational experience available to student journalists. For this reason, the case may be cause for concern.

The direct holding in *Hazelwood School District* vs. *Kuhlmeier* permits the censorship of student articles in school-sponsored newspapers "so long as (the censorship is) reasonably related to legitimate pedagogical concerns."

More broadly, the court indicated that the same standard would apply to permit censorship of other "school-sponsored expressive activities" such as "theatrical productions, and other expressive activities that students, parents, and members of the public might reasonably perceive to bear the imprimatur of the school."

The three justices who dissented in the case (Justices Brennan, Marshall and Blackmun) char-

acterized this outcome as a significant and unfortunate deviation from previous constitutional adjudications of the First Amendment rights of public school students, particularly the seminal student rights decision in *Tinker* vs. *Des Moines Independent Community School District*.

The student paper in the Hazelwood litigation was produced by students enrolled in a course for which they received credit. The paper had a (more or less) regular schedule of publication, was funded in major part from the school budget and was subject to prepublication review by the principal.

Many journalism educators fear that as a result of this decision high school journalists and students in general will lose valuable experience in the importance of the press and press freedom. And some educators say the decision makes it more important than ever for professional newspaper editors to pay attention to what goes on in high school newspapers.

In a statement issued after the court's decision, the Association for Education in Journalism and Mass Communication said: "The Secondary Education Division of AEJMC deplores the Jan. 13 United States Supreme Court decision in *Hazelwood* vs. *Kuhlmeier*. This decision ignores the value of a vibrant student press and encourages a repressive school environment. . . .

"A vigorous, issue-oriented student press is an effective tool in the citizenship training central to the mission of the public school. . . .

"Many of our nation's finest journalists received their earliest writing encouragement and

Richard M. Schmidt Jr. and N. Frank Wiggins filed a brief *amici curiae* in the Supreme Court in support of the student press in the Hazelwood case on behalf of ASNE, National Association of Broadcasters, Reporters Committee for Freedom of the Press and Sigma Delta Chi. Schmidt is legal counsel for ASNE and he and Wiggins are partners in the Washington, D.C., law firm of Cohn and Marks.

experiences on high school publications. We urge professional journalists to join us in promoting a vigorous student press."

Another group concerned about the ruling is the Journalism Education Association, which is made up of high school journalism teachers and publications advisers.

John Bowen, chair of the JEA scholastic Press Rights Committee, said, "In light of the recent Supreme Court decision on the *Hazelwood School District* vs. *Kuhlmeier* case—that gives public school officials new and broad authority to censor student expression—it is more important than ever for high school journalists to know and practice professional standards of journalism. . . .

"We agree with Justice William Brennan that 'public educators must accommodate some student expression even if it offends them or offers views or values that contradict those the school wishes to inculcate.' "

JEA is urging its state directors to propose changes in state constitutions and state educational codes to guarantee students "the rights provided for them in the U.S. Constitution." California's state education code already has a section on "student exercise of freedom of speech and press" that affirms the importance of free expression for students, sharply limits the grounds for prior restraint, and gives newspaper advisers the responsibility for monitoring what goes into student newspapers.

Some other schools also have policies giving students and their advisers almost complete freedom to assign and edit stories, and specifying that professional journalists be consulted when questions about libel, invasion of privacy or other controversies arise.

The Hazelwood case came to the Supreme Court from the Court of Appeals from the Eighth Circuit, which had found the censorship at issue—the deletion of two articles by the school principal in the course of his customary page proof review of the paper immediately prior to printing—to have been unconstitutional.

The Eighth Circuit panel based that decision on its conclusion that the school had created, through the student newspaper, a "public forum"

comparable to "streets, parks, and other traditional public forums that 'time out of mind, had been used for purposes of assembly, communicating thoughts between citizens, and discussing public questions.' " The government's power to suppress speech in a public forum is limited to extreme and exigent circumstances.

Had the Supreme Court concurred in the characterization of the student paper adopted by the Eighth Circuit, the outcome of the case would almost surely have been different. The Supreme Court found the student paper not to be a public forum, but conceded that this did not end the constitutional inquiry.

Because—unlike the process repeated hourly in newsrooms around the country—the "editing" complained of by the plaintiffs in the Hazelwood case was performed by the government, it remained necessary to determine whether the less rigid but still very considerable limitations on the government's power to suppress speech outside of public forums had been transgressed.

In its introduction to this stage of analysis, the majority opinion formulates a distinction that the dissenting justices characterize as entirely new to student First Amendment analysis:

"The question whether the First Amendment requires a school to tolerate particular student speech—the question that we addressed in Tinker—is different from the question whether the First Amendment requires a school affirmatively to promote particular student speech."

The majority offered the following answer to that question:

"Accordingly, we conclude that the standard articulated in Tinker for determining when a school may punish student expression need not also be the standard for determining when a school may refuse to lend its name and resources to the dissemination of student expression. . . .

"It is only when the decision to censor a school-sponsored publication, theatrical production, or other vehicle of student expression has no valid educational purpose that the First Amendment (will) . . . require judicial intervention to protect students' constitutional rights."

The majority opinion advanced several examples of "valid educational purpose(s)" for the censorship. One of the two articles to which the school principal objected consisted of interviews with three students who had become pregnant while going to school. Pseudonyms were used in the article to identify the young women interviewed. The following excerpts from the majority opinion give a good flavor of the standards for determining "valid educational purpose" sufficient to support censorship:

The principal concluded that the students' anonymity was not adequately protected, however, given the other identifying information in the article and the small number of pregnant students at the school. . . . Reynolds (the principal) therefore could reasonably have feared that the article violated whatever pledge of anonymity had been given to the pregnant students. In addition, he could reasonably have been concerned that the article was not sufficiently sensitive to the privacy interest of the students' boyfriends and parents . . . who were given no opportunity to consent to its publication or to offer a response. . . . The girls did comment in the article . . . concerning their sexual histories and their use or nonuse of birth control. It was not unreasonable for the principal to have concluded that such frank talk was inappropriate in a school-sponsored publication distributed to 14 year-old freshmen and presumably taken home to be read by students' even younger brothers and sisters.

The dissenting justices were not persuaded that the legal standard applied by the majority was correct:

The court offers no more than an obscure tangle of three excuses to afford educators 'greater control' over school-sponsored speech than the Tinker test would permit: the public educator's prerogative to control curriculum; the pedagogical interest in shielding the high school audience from objectionable viewpoints and sensitive topics; and the school's need to dissociate itself from student expression. . . . Tinker fully addresses the first concern; the second is illegitimate; and the third is readily achievable through less oppressive means.

The dissenters agreed that, "the educator may, under Tinker, constitutionally 'censor' poor grammar, writing, or research because to reward such expression would 'materially disrupt' the newspaper's curricular purpose." They diverge from the majority opinion in their assessment of, "censorship designed to shield the audience or dissociate the sponsor from the expression."

"(Such censorship) in no way furthers the curricular purposes of a student newspaper, unless one believes that the purpose of the school newspaper is to teach students that the press ought never report bad news, express unpopular views, or print a thought that might upset its sponsors."

Will the Hazelwood opinion encourage broader school administrator's censorship of student publications? One must wonder why any school administrator would risk community indignation fired by the pronouncements of student journalists when the standards set forth in the Hazelwood case will generally permit withholding publication.

When the principal withheld publication of the articles in question in Hazelwood the students duplicated the censored material and distributed it throughout the school. The *St. Louis Post Dispatch* carried a most interesting article about the censorship "flap" and published the censored articles. In this particular case the student journalists reached a much larger audience by virtue of having been "censored." Being "banned in Boston" may once again become the method of guaranteeing the largest possible audience. ■

'Dirge of Lamentation' Is Unnecessary

IVAN B. GLUCKMAN

The Supreme Court's decision in the case of *Hazelwood* vs. *Kuhlmeier,* upholding the removal of certain articles from a high school newspaper by its principal, has resulted in a dirge of lamentation in many quarters about the future of student journalism.

It is, of course, to be anticipated that professional civil libertarians and student rights activists would decry the decision, since that is their

business, but the general public may not be aware of the disproportionate sympathy these views get on this kind of case through the news media. If there is any subject that reporters view with less than perfect objectivity, it is that of "censorship," by which they mean any limitation of a writer's freedom to publish his views.

Most op-ed columnists, having once been reporters, have also been something less than sympathetic to the plight of school districts and their administrators in dealing with the student press.

The facts of the Hazelwood case were such,

Ivan B. Gluckman is general counsel for the National Association of Secondary School Principals.

however, even to convince some journalists of the wisdom of the Supreme Court's decision. After all, we were not dealing here with the personal, individual expression of student opinion in an unofficial or "underground" newspaper, or even an all-school paper produced as an extra-curricular activity. The paper involved was published by a journalism class, and as a project of that class.

In addition, while the principal admitted to some reservations about the general subject matter of the two articles involved, his primary reason for ordering their removal was a concern with privacy interests of certain students and parents referred to in the articles.

Finally, the specific ruling of the Court of Appeals under review was a finding that the principal could be held liable for damages under the federal Civil Rights Act of 1871 (Section 1983 of Title 42 U.S.C.) for having guessed wrong on the likelihood of the school district's legal liability if sued by parents and students whose privacy interests might have been violated.

For all of these reasons, it was completely appropriate for the Supreme Court to reverse the decision of the Court of Appeals. Even the landmark decision in *Tinker* vs. *Des Moines School District,* which all sides accept as the basic law governing student First Amendment rights, recognizes the invasion of the rights of others as a basis for interfering with a student's right of self-expression. A number of court decisions have also regarded the curriculum as being more subject to administrative control by public school officials than other areas of school activity.

While the specific circumstances of the case would seem to have clearly supported reversal of the Court of Appeals opinion, it is fair to say that Justice White's majority opinion is broader than it needed to be to justify the court's decision. Clearly, the majority wanted to establish some broader authority for school boards and administrators and, perhaps, discourage the continuing flow of federal court suits claiming abuse of student rights under the First Amendment.

Some critics of the decision have claimed that this criterion is so broad as to give a principal virtually unbridled authority to control student expression. However, the kind of situations the court majority in Hazelwood is trying to delineate as being properly within the jurisdiction of public school administrators to control is clearly distinguishable from that it proscribed in Tinker, and Justice White so indicates. Distinguishing between the kind of personal expression involved in Tinker and speech occurring as part of the school curriculum, Justice White states:

"Educators are entitled to exercise greater control over this second form of expression to assure that participants learn whatever lessons the activity is designed to teach, that readers or listeners are not exposed to material that may be inappropriate for their level of maturity, and that views of the individual speakers are not erroneously attributed to the school."

Justice Brennan concludes his dissent with an expression of concern for the kind of civics lesson taught by this decision. It seems likely, however, that prior to this decision many students were getting a far more harmful lesson from their high school journalism experience: that journalists have unlimited freedom to print anything they desire in the newspapers on which they work.

Any adult reporter could tell them how wide of the mark such a conclusion is—and in discussing the decision several have, including Carl Rowan on "Agronsky and Company" (now "Inside Washington"), who summarized his reactions with a statement welcoming students to "the real world." We are pleased, though not surprised, that many newspaper editors also have recognized the merit of the majority decision.

Probably the easiest and best way to understand the Hazelwood decision is to ask, who is the publisher? Clearly, in most cases involving official school publications, the answer is: the school. And the school board and its administrators are accountable to the parents and taxpayers of the district for the products of that school.

Whether this accountability always carries with it the legal obligation of financial damages through litigation should not be the controlling issue—anymore than it is for a private publisher. The school board and its administrators must be concerned for the school's good name and reputation as well; to recognize this responsibility without according these officials and administrators the legal authority to protect those interests violates the most basic principles of law and ethics.

No one can read the future, of course, but in all likelihood, the decision in Hazelwood is likely to have far less sweeping effect than most of its critics fear. High school principals want student publications to be interesting to their intended readers—the students. The principals realize this means that some topics student journalists will want to cover may not be the ones principals would most like to see featured in school publications.

Most also realize, however, that the law will not justify imposing their every whim upon the subject discussed. The accuracy of news stories, and the manner in which they are presented are, however, appropriate concerns of the principal. Most of the issues that might give the principal pause should be resolved by the faculty adviser. And if that adviser is doing his or her job, it will be resolved in a manner that not only satisfies the principal but which increases student understanding of the craft and ethics of journalism.

In the rare case where student journalists and their faculty advisers don't meet reasonable journalistic standards established by school boards, however, the principal will have the authority to intervene to assure that those standards are not violated. This is the proper role of the publisher. It is also good education. ∎

The Definition of Obscenity

Our courts hold the legal responsibility for defining the limits of obscenity. Drawing this line is difficult in a society based on the concept of freedom of expression. Two Supreme Court cases, *Roth* v. *U.S.* and *Miller* v. *California,* established the criteria for obscenity.

Roth v. *U.S.* created what has come to be known as the *Roth* test: "Whether, to the average person, applying contemporary community standards, the dominant theme of the material as a whole appeals to prurient interest." *Miller* v. *California* set a three-part test for obscenity: (1) whether "the average person, applying contemporary standards" would find that the work, taken as a whole, appeals to the prurient interest; (2) whether the work depicts, or describes, in a patently offensive way, sexual conduct specifically defined by applicable state law (3) whether the work, taken as a whole, lacks serious Literary, Artistic, Political, or Scientific value—often called the LAPS test.

In this essay from the *Gannett Center Journal,* communications scholar Frank Beaver describes the difficulty of enforcing proscribed standards of obscenity in today's society.

Consider:

1. According to Beaver, what have been the results of applying guidelines set in the *Miller* case?

2. How does the result in the Kalamazoo case reflect standards of obscenity in today's society, according to Beaver?

3. What new technologies have made the dissemination of pornographic material difficult to enforce, according to Beaver?

4. Will new technologies in fact help to sustain pornography? Why? Why not?

The Awkward Embrace
The Legal Battle Over Obscenity

FRANK BEAVER

From the *Kama Sutra* and the poems of Sappho to *Fanny Hill* and Boswell's *Journal,* men and women of every culture and epoch have been fascinated by sex and its various representations.

"So I began to write tongue-in-cheek, to become outlandish, inventive, and so exaggerated that I thought he would realize I was caricaturing sexuality," wrote Anais Nin in the preface to *Delta of Venus.* "But there was no protest. I spent the day in the library studying the *Kama Sutra,* listened to friends' most extreme adventures.

" 'Less poetry,' said the voice over the telephone. 'Be specific.' "

Where does one draw the line between the bawdy and the socially pernicious tale? Should the line be drawn at all? And if so, by whom? Pornography is perhaps the thorniest problem in the sacred realm of free speech and First Amendment rights, and the perennial dilemma, legally and interpretively, is how to define it. "What is pornography to one man is the laughter of genius to another," said the novelist D. H. Lawrence. "There is no such thing legally as obscenity because obscenity is a matter of individual interpretation," argued Supreme Court Justice Hugo Black. "Obscenity cases are a dangerous hodgepodge," Justice William O. Douglas concurred, "They have no business in the courts."

Federal Precedents

But obscenity and pornography—the two terms are interchangeable for the purposes of this essay—have been very much debated in the courts in America and in other arenas too, especially since 1957, when the Supreme Court decision in *Roth* v. *U.S.* determined that "obscenity is not within the area of constitutionally protected speech."

The *Roth* decision upheld a lower court ruling that convicted a New York man of sending pornographic materials through the mails and of advertising them, and set off a complicated struggle that shows no signs of abating. The main lines of the legal battle have been drawn at the Supreme Court, and the general trend has been away from the nationally applied standards in the liberal-minded Warren Court to locally applied standards in the more conservative Burger court, whose 1973 *Miller* v. *California* decision was a

Frank Beaver chairs the department of communication at the University of Michigan.

second landmark ruling after *Roth*. The pornography battle today is being fought primarily in local settings.

Since 1970, the executive branch has also attempted to clarify the issue with two presidential commissions whose reports have confounded more than informed the debate. The presidential commissions tried to examine obscenity data objectively and scientifically, and at bottom viewed the potential behavioral consequences in terms of the "clear and present danger" test that Justice Holmes once proposed as a reason for limiting free speech.

If a person falsely shouts "Fire!" in a crowded theater, the act of speech presents a clear and present danger of inciting a stampede. While words themselves do not constitute criminal liability, their consequences under certain circumstances can. To change the context while keeping the principle, if pornography should be linked directly to criminal behavior—pedophilia, racketeering, or rape—it could be banned not as speech but as incitement to criminal activity. Stronger laws, beyond those implied by *Roth* and *Miller,* could then be enacted to prohibit it.

The first presidential panel, appointed during the Johnson Administration, reported *no* significant causal relationship between pornography and sex crimes, and recommended the repeal of restrictions against adults buying, reading, and viewing obscene material. The commission's findings received little credence when this first report was presented to President Nixon in 1970, and then-Attorney General John Mitchell, Nixon's top law-and-order man, promptly shelved it. Not surprisingly, Mitchell's counterpart in a more recent Republican Administration decided to revisit the issue.

The Meese Commission report, released in 1986, reached an exactly opposite conclusion. Exposure to pornography *does* contribute to the incidence of sex crimes and to organized crime, this second panel found. Its report urged that censorship efforts be renewed and stepped up through increased prosecution and the buttressing of existing laws. However, many experts questioned the scientific evidence on which the Meese Commission based its findings, and the 11 members in the group were unable to agree on a single definition of what they were investigating.

In the absence of a strong constitutional reason for banning pornography outright, independent critics and government censors have had to work within the legal framework provided by the 1973 *Miller* v. *California* decision. A work can be banned as obscene if it is found, in whole not in part, to have 1) appealed to the prurient interest; 2) depicted or described sexual conduct in a patently offensive manner; and 3) lacked any serious literary, artistic, political, or social value. The "trier of fact" in this three-pronged test, the Court said, should be "the average person, applying contemporary community standards."

Who is the "average person?" What are "contemporary community standards?" The landmark aspect of *Miller* was that it shifted responsibility for interpreting the three criteria to local citizens and judges, instead of presumably more lenient federal ones.

Pornography Law in Middle America

Since 1973, local authorities have had broad leeway to prosecute authors and distributors of pornography, but the results have often been more comic than successful. The right to make "local norms" has proven to be a costly, case-by-case proposition, and, while many state and local ordinances have offered their own definitions, few have lasted long. In 1984, in one of the more inventive efforts, the city of Indianapolis passed a local ordinance that defined and penalized the distribution of sexually explicit material on the grounds that it systematically exploited and violated the civil rights of women. This attempt at censorship would have warmed the hearts of Meese Commission members, but its feminist backers were odd bedfellows alongside right-wing conservatives in the fight against pornography. Other cities, including Minneapolis and Cambridge, joined this effort to move the obscenity issue into this new legal arena, but in early

1986 the Supreme Court struck down the Indian-apolis law. The First Amendment decision, issued without opinion, upheld a lower court ruling that the law discriminated "on the ground of the content of speech" and sought to promote "an 'approved' view of women."

Another local anti-pornography measure that worked more directly within the guidelines of the 1973 Miller decision was signed into law in late 1984 by Governor James Blanchard of Michigan. Senate Bill 899 defined the community standard criterion as the entire state, and sought to "upgrade" the state's obscenity laws through a two-tier legal mechanism. Obscenity in the second degree, with a fine up to $10,000, was defined as the distribution of obscene materials by establishments whose primary business was *other than pornographic trade,* like shopping malls and supermarkets. Michigan State Senator Alan Cropsey, who helped write the bill, told the *Detroit Free Press,* "Our intention was to get rid of adult bookstores and X-rated movie houses and also to get this pornography off the book shelves of the grocery store." The law also provided that individuals or establishments found guilty of distributing pornographic material as a *predominant* part of their business would be charged with obscenity in the first degree, with first-time offenders subject to a fine of up to $100,000 and/ or one year in jail, and second convictions resulting in a minimum fine of $50,000, a maximum fine as high as $5,000,000 and a mandatory one-year jail term. . . .

The "Average Man in Kalamazoo"

. . . [T]he sponsors of the Michigan legislation appear to have over-estimated the public's appetite for striking back at pornography profiteers. In early 1987 an obscenity case came to trial under Senate Bill 899 and put the three criteria of the Supreme Court's *Miller* decision to a direct local test. Terry Whitman Shoultes of the Executive Arts Studio was charged with distributing material described by one reporter who covered the trial as "some of the most vile material available in Kalamazoo."

Was Shoultes' material a prurient and patently offensive representation of sexual conduct? Did it have any redeeming artistic, political, or social value? When the three key obscenity criteria were interpreted by a jury of peers, the "average individual" and "contemporary community standards" were put under a spotlight.

Michigan's law had sought to clarify the meaning of "contemporary community standards" by defining it as "the customary limits of candor and decency in this state at or near the time of the alleged violation of this act." Thus, 33 prospective jurors were questioned about their familiarity with pornography prior to the trial. All but one admitted to personal exposure to obscene material or to having visited an adult bookstore. The Kalamazoo trial attorneys selected three men and three women to sit on the jury. After viewing Shoulte's material and hearing prosecution and defense arguments, the jury found the defendant and his business establishment not guilty.

Was the outcome in Kalamazoo a fluke? Was the jury atypical? Would the same material shown elsewhere in Michigan have brought different results? The Kalamazoo case offered just one legal window onto the obscenity issue but the jury profile and the not guilty verdict suggest that pornography is far more widespread in middle America than would-be censors would want to admit, and that Senate Bill 899 is a weak law that holds up poorly.

Pornography and New Technologies

New technologies, especially home video, are making pornography an accepted part of everyday home life. In a survey of 20 randomly-selected home video rental centers in Michigan conducted by this writer in November, 1987, all admitted to renting sexually-explicit adult videos and discussed this part of their business freely. A consistent pattern of consumption emerged from one store to the next.

Managers of home-entertainment video centers around the state estimated that adult rentals of hard-core pornography videos constitute 15 percent of all rentals, although on Fridays and Saturdays the percentage rises to 40 or 50 percent. One clerk in a suburban video center described late Friday night rentals of adult material as "frenzied."

Who rents? "Everybody rents from time to time," said one manager. A second concurred: "every type, every adult age group, including a lot of senior citizens. Sometimes older women come in with their adult daughters and make a selection together." According to a third, it is common practice for parents and children to come in together, with the parents choosing material from the adult section while the children make a choice elsewhere in the store.

One manager in a large Michigan home entertainment chain emphasized the business importance of its approximately 200 adult tapes among 4,000 possible selections: "If we didn't offer the adult option our movie club subscriptions would suffer significantly: Most subscribers want adult material."

This nonchalant attitude toward the availability and private use of adult materials is more than just a Michigan phenomenon. In its September 1987 issue, *Video Magazine,* a serious, nationally-marketed journal devoted to video technology, art and business, began to include a 12-page sealed cut-out section with advertisements for pornography. The idea behind the section, according to the magazine's publisher, was to preserve the family magazine image while serving general readers who wish to purchase adult entertainment privately through the mail. The November 1987 issue contained articles in the magazine proper on new theatrical releases and technological and business topics, but the sealed section contained ads for videos with titles like "Oriental Orgasms," "Foreskin Foreplay," "Dildo Girls," "Men of Ft. Lauderdale," and "Wanda Whips Wall Street." Publisher Debra Halpert explained: "After new theatrical releases, interest in the adult video market is second highest, well ahead of the educational and instructional areas. Our readership responds enormously to this material."

Another arena where the privatized consumption of adult materials is increasing is in hotels. The *New York Times* reports that adult pay-as-you-view movies are now available in 47 percent of America's hotels with 300 or more rooms, an estimated 40 percent increase since 1980. Within 10 years, it is predicted, nearly all hotels will offer the adult video option. In the hotel industry such service is regarded as simply another amenity. "It's a little thing. But if you don't have it, people will ask for it," says Serge Denis, general manager of the Hotel Parker Meridien in New York.

Many large hotels offer two or more adult channels. Ann McCracken, public relations director for Washington D.C.'s newly-renovated Willard Hotel, says her hotel's pay-as-you-view service provides only one adult option, but will not divulge what percentage of pay-as-you-view revenue it generates. A guest service representative of the Boston Sheraton estimates that one fifth of its pay-as-you-view revenue comes from two adult channels, adding "just about everybody watches the free 10-minute previews."

What impact will this pattern of increased consumption of obscene material have on the future regulation of pornography? The U.S. Supreme Court today is sharply divided on the issue. In May 1987, a 5–4 decision again altered the guidelines for judging sexually explicit materials. On an appeal by two Illinois adult bookstore dealers charged with selling obscene magazines, the Supreme Court dropped the community standard and ruled that judges and juries should assess such material solely from the standpoint of a "reasonable person." In dissent, Justices Stevens, Brennan, and Marshall maintained that the "reasonable person" criterion was too vague and subject to the same questions of constitutionality as the community standards guidelines, and went on to term unconstitutional all laws that "criminalize the sale of magazines to consenting adults who enjoy the constitutional right to read and possess them."

The constitutional right of private use of obscene materials in one's own home, as determined in *Stanley* v. *Georgia* in 1969, has not been followed with the protected right to sell and distribute such materials. Therein resides the division on the current Court. The law seems to be saying, "Read it, watch it, but don't sell it."

What the Future Holds

In *The Secret Museum,* a book which traces the history of pornography in modern culture, author Walter Kendrick maintains that technology may in fact help sustain pornography. "If the smut of 50 or even 20 years ago looks tame by comparison with today's," Kendrick argues, "the reason may have nothing to do with pornography itself. Every mode of representation has become explicit. It has become possible to photograph the earth from outer space, a fetus in the womb, and Vietnamese children in the process of dying. The only difference in the case of pornography is that it faces steady resistance, while other advances in explicitness win praise."

Perhaps the worst fear of obscenity critics is that human nature will combine with new technologies to foster a social and criminal problem blown all out of proportion with the bound of "normal" decency; and their response, predictably, is to mount new campaigns to blunt the viper's thrust.

"This will be a big year for obscenity prosecutions," said William Weld, the head of the Justice Department's criminal division in January 1988. Attorney General Edwin Meese, acting on the findings of his 1986 commission, . . . vowed an "all-out campaign against the distribution of obscene material," relying on a broad interpretation of a 1970 federal anti-racketeering statute.

But some scholars who have studied the pornography "problem" believe that laws expressly written to make this social phenomenon disappear may in fact render it more acute.

"The problem people have with pornography," writes Lee C. Bollinger in his book on the First Amendment, "is in its attraction, or the fear of its attraction. The real social difficulty posed by obscene material, in other words, may lie in the potential for confusion about what toleration would mean. . . . (Those) in the law cannot casually dismiss the claim that sexual instincts . . . lie at the core of an individual's, and presumably a community of individuals', identity."

Where does that leave the defenders—and the censors—of pornography? Locked in an awkward embrace, most probably. If obscenity laws do not work—and the evidence is that they don't—the final irony may be that those who seek to enforce them turn out to be the pornographer's best friend.

As one lawyer in the Michigan Attorney General's office bemusedly said of Senate Bill 899 and the Kalamazoo test case, "The surest way to get rid of a bad law is to try to enforce it." ∎

PERSPECTIVE 5

Rating the Movies

Since 1934, when the motion picture industry adopted the Motion Picture Production Code, the film industry has policed itself. Today's answer is the rating system, which labels movies from G to X, according to movie content. In this article from *The New York Times,* David F. Musto maintains that when the issue is drugs, self-censorship may be a bad idea.

Consider:

1. Why has the motion picture industry historically chosen to censor itself?

2. Is it, as Musto asks, in our best interest to portray drug use not as it is, but as we wish it would be? Why? Why not?

3. Should there be a rating system for films based on the portrayal of drug use, as has been proposed? Why? Why not?

4. Do you agree with Musto that "effective censorship is not the way to protect society from a climate of ignorance favorable to . . . drug use"? Why? Why not?

When It Comes to Drugs, Beware the Censor's Fix

DAVID F. MUSTO

The weight of opinion gathering against drug use indicates that movies and television—which have already responded to the widespread disaffection with cigarettes by diminishing their presence in scripts and on-screen—will follow suit by banishing drugs.

But history also suggests that such an action may be ill-advised.

History raises an important question: Is it in our best interest to portray drug use not as it is but as we wish it would be?

Movies and drugs have a long common history. It embraces depictions of drug use on screen, drug scandals within the industry and an outright ban on depiction of illegal drugs in the Production Code that effectively governed Hollywood for some 20 years beginning in 1934.

"Illegal drug traffic must never be presented," the code said. "Because of its evil consequences, the drug traffic should not be presented in any form. The existence of the trade should not be brought to the attention of audiences."

And so it was that Americans in the 1930's, 40's and 50's—at least those who depended on the movies for keeping posted—grew up largely ignorant of the appeal and consequences of drugs. Censorship, in that sense, was helping to set the stage for acceptance of marijuana, heroin, PCP or angel dust, cocaine and crack.

In view of the surge in opiate and cocaine use in the United States in recent years, it is interesting to note that the last wave of abuse in the country reached its peak in the decade around the turn of the century—just about the time movies arrived. The high level of consumption and its slow decline meant that in early films, depictions of drug use—favorable and unfavorable—were commonplace. Silent films showed opium dens; drugs were a source of humor in Douglas Fairbanks's "Mystery of the Leaping Fish," a 1916 movie in which he played a hyperactive detective named Coke Ennyday. In two 1914 films—"Drug Terror" and "Narcotic Spectre"—drug use was attacked.

David F. Musto is a professor of psychiatry and the history of medicine at Yale University and the author of "The American Disease: Origins of Narcotic Control" (1973), a history of narcotics policy in the United States.

Controversy intensified during the 1920s amid drug scandals within the Hollywood community. The murder of the director William Desmond Taylor in 1922 and the death of the actor Wallace Reid from morphine poisoning in 1923 focused attention on the problem. By then, the vast majority of Americans condemned drug use. Alcohol consumption had already plummeted as a result of Prohibition, another reflection of the broad public antagonism toward drugs. Despite current misconceptions, the 1920s were not one long alcoholic binge. Prohibition initially pleased most Americans, and the number of deaths from liver cirrhosis declined.

Still, "divorce, seduction and the use of drugs were presented in film after film as symbols of the fashionable life," wrote the film historian Arthur Knight in "The Liveliest Art."

In the 1930s, however, tolerance toward films that depicted drug use had evaporated along with support for other forms of behavior that critics perceived as undermining the family, stimulating violence and encouraging bad habits.

Drug use was still in its long cycle of decline, and as it abated, government policy makers shifted from seeking mandatory school instruction on narcotics to a conviction that the situation was now so much improved that it would be best not even to mention the subject.

But Hollywood still had no strictures against depicting drug use. In 1934, the Roman Catholic Church moved to correct the situation. American bishops formed the National Legion of Decency to concentrate their power against Hollywood's laxity, in an action generally favored by other faiths. The motion picture industry reacted to the threat of a boycott by Catholic laity by establishing the Production Code Administration.

The strength of the administration, with its code outlawing depictions of illegal drug traffic, lay in its authority to grant a certificate of approval. For many years, Hollywood accepted the fact that no major motion picture released without the administration's certificate could succeed commercially.

"Reefer Madness," the 1937 exploitation film on marijuana use, received neither a certificate nor a popular audience. Public memory of opiate and cocaine addiction began to fade. Heroin use—a familiar threat in 1915—would be a curiosity when it resurfaced in American society in the early 1950s. When cocaine use in America began to spread some 20 years ago, the epidemic of 1900 barely existed in memory.

A dozen years after the production code was adopted, it was modified. Language adopted in 1946 stated: "The illegal drug traffic must not be portrayed in such a way to stimulate curiosity concerning the use of, or traffic in, such drugs; nor shall scenes be approved which show the use of illegal drugs, or their effects, in detail."

The alteration was adopted to pave the way for "To the Ends of the Earth," a movie about the heroic agents of the Federal Bureau of Narcotics. This admiring tale of the fight against foreign production of drugs and the smugglers who brought them into the United States starred Dick Powell. Not only was the film made with the enthusiastic cooperation of the Federal Bureau of Narcotics; the organization's head, Harry J. Anslinger, even portrayed himself in it.

Mr. Powell's favorable portrayal of an agent may be contrasted with the "narcs" who were depicted as villains or buffoons when drug use was rising during the late 1960s and early 70s. During the upward phase of a drug cycle, agents tend to be portrayed as bluenoses with guns or as criminals as corrupt as their prey. During the downward trend, they are admired as protectors of the health and morality of the nation, as in last year's three-hour television movie "Courage," starring Sophia Loren as a New Yorker whose outrage at the drug problem in her family and neighborhood prompts her to go undercover to help the Drug Enforcement Administration.

In the 1950s the power of the Production Code began to erode. In 1953, Otto Preminger's romantic comedy "The Moon Is Blue," adapted from F. Hugh Herbert's stage success and using the words "pregnant" and "virgin," was denied a certificate but became a box-office hit. In 1955, Mr. Preminger defied the Production Code again—this time with "The Man With the Golden Arm," starring Frank Sinatra as a drug addict.

At the same time, antitrust laws that divested the major studios of ownership of theaters crippled their power to bar unapproved films from their movies houses; and First Amendment rights had been broadened to include motion pictures. The power of the Production Code to ban narcotics from the screen had been broken.

The system that replaced it in 1968—the Motion Picture Association of America ratings system—no longer approved or disapproved a film. Rather, it simply rated a film based on content, using one of the now-familiar letters: G, PG, R or X. It was a period when drug use in the United States was taken as evidence of membership in the avant-garde, of being, as the saying went, "with it."

In such a climate, American moviegoers saw the drug culture advance from the alienated characters of "Easy Rider" (1969) to the mainstream Americans of "Private Benjamin" (1980) and "Poltergeist" (1982).

Although it may seem both paradoxical and arguable, the 60s were also a time when marijuana smokers themselves were laying the groundwork for the present wave of opposition to drugs. It was the marijuana smokers and their lobby who responded to an older generation's fear of cannabis by pointing out the dangers of alcohol—a substance most people had yet to recognize as a drug. This was the first aggressive challenge to alcohol use by young trendsetters since before World War I. And it continued through the 1970s, with youth condemning what they saw as the hypocrisy of accepting alcohol use while penalizing marijuana use.

These days, marijuana has declined in popularity, and the focus of discussion of the drug problem has been tobacco, heroin, angel dust, cocaine and crack. But attitudes in American society are changing; and Hollywood is part of American society. Like the rest of society, it has grown doubtful of the hopes and claims for drugs. The resurgence of drug abuse everywhere has made the accumulation of personal tragedies inevitable. Richard Pryor, for example, nearly burned himself to death while freebasing cocaine. Since his recovery and subsequent detoxi-fication, he has taken an earnest stance against drugs, and conversions like his represent a transitional stage from drug acceptance to abstinence as the national norm.

A poll this year in *The New York Times* found that the number of college freshmen favoring the legalization of marijuana had decreased in the last 10 years from 48.9 percent to 21.3 percent. Among the general public, according to a report last year in *Newsweek,* those favoring criminal penalties for personal possession of small amounts of marijuana increased from 43 percent in 1980 to 67 percent in 1986. Such transitions are spread over decades, and should these trends continue, we will see the nadir of drug use, including alcohol, perhaps in another decade.

Last year, Richard Frank, president of the Academy of Television Arts and Sciences, observed: "You don't see cigarettes on television anymore. Not because anybody passed a law. Writers wrote cigarettes out, directors don't use them as props and actors don't have them as a crutch."

His comments describe what happened to narcotics during the last anti-drug era in the United States. And while the past is no guarantee of the future, it is a useful guide.

So as Hollywood turns against drugs, it is not a matter of the world outside forcing movies to portray drugs differently; it is a reciprocal relationship. Within the film and television industries, groups concerned about drug abuse have formed—among them the Entertainment Industries Council (E.I.C.) and the Creative Coalition Against Drug Abuse. And it is not unreasonable to assume that anti-drug films will grow in box-office popularity.

In 1985, the E.I.C. proposed that the M.P.A.A. expand its rating system to include SA, to be applied to movies showing drug use without negative consequences. Others have recommended an uncompromising X rating for such films. At the same time, appearing at Senate hearings on the problem, Jack Valenti, the president of the M.P.A.A., said, "The rating system is girding itself for sterner treatment of films in whose content is depicted the use of drugs."

In April 1986, the M.P.A.A. and the National Association of Theater Owners, the co-sponsor of its rating system, announced that any depiction of drug use would receive an automatic PG-13 rating, intended to warn parents that "some material may be inappropriate for young children."

The evidence is clear that antagonism to depictions of drug use in the absence of bad consequences is growing. The impulse is laudable, and the hope is that drugs will be banished from America. But history suggests that effective censorship is not the way to protect society from a climate of ignorance favorable to a resurgence of drug use and the tragedies it causes. History suggests that ignorance is not bliss. It is only the illusion of bliss. ■

PERSPECTIVE 6

Effects of Deregulation

Unlike the print media, which are unregulated, the broadcast media are licensed by the government to operate in the "public interest, convenience, and necessity." Overseeing broadcast operators is the five-member Federal Communications Commission (FCC); its commissioners are appointed by the president.

Different presidents have had different ideas about how much control the government should exercise over broadcasters, but since 1981 the commission has adopted a philosophy of deregulation. Such a policy has dismantled many earlier requirements, such as a certain number of hours devoted to public service programming and limits on commercials. In this article, Jane Hall describes how deregulation has affected children's programming.

Consider:

1. Do you agree with Hall that "in the fervor of deregulation, children's television has been a prime casualty"? Why? Why not?

2. Do you agree with the FCC's Bill Johnson that "the federal government is not set up to protect parents from kids nagging their parents for toys"? Why? Why not?

3. What is the danger, according to Hall, of toy-based shows?

4. Do you agree that broadcasters should "develop and present programs which will . . . further the educational and cultural development of America's children"? Or should broadcasters be free to present any programs they choose? Why?

Aladdin's Lamp Goes Dark
The Deregulation of Children's Programming

JANE HALL

When I was a child growing up in West Texas in the 1950s, the rabbit ears of the TV antenna beckoned, first to Howdy Doody's "Peanut Gallery" and then to a wider world beyond: Mary Martin in *Peter Pan,* Leonard Bernstein theatrically conducting the *Young People's Concert,* Walter Cronkite doing voice-over on World War II in *The Twentieth Century.* Today, except for *Pee Wee's Playhouse,* it is difficult to imagine the current generation of youngsters romanticizing in the future about great kids' shows from their childhood. In the fervor of deregulation, children's television has been a prime casualty. Today, award-winning programs are the exception that prove the rule. There is no daily program on commercial TV that compares to *Captain Kangaroo.* Dramatic specials have no regular weekly time slot. TV news for children is practically obsolete. And virtually every cartoon show on independent stations stars He-Man, GoBots, or some other toy in shows that—to an adult eye—look like 30-minute toy commercials. This fall [1987] saw the introduction of the ultimate TV toy tie-in: the controversial interactive toys that allow children to play video games with the television set. Provided, of course, that the child interacts with his parent's pocketbook to buy the new toy.

What's going on here? At the same time that changes in broadcasting have made *pro bono* programming less attractive, the Federal Communications Commission has lifted its require-

ments for public service and its restrictions on commercialism for all audiences, including children. The theory has been "let the marketplace decide," although the Commission's studies have reported that young children, unlike adults, cannot distinguish between a TV sales pitch and a TV show. The marketplace emphasis promises to further a heated debate about the future of children's television that is already almost three decades old.

The Push for Responsible Children's Programming

Recognition of children's programming as a special category by the FCC goes back as far as 1960, when a policy statement listed children's shows as one of 14 "major elements usually necessary to meet" a licensee's public-service obligations as a trustee of the airwaves under the Communications Act of 1934. Children's television became a political cause in the late 1960s, when Peggy Charren, a Boston homemaker, formed Action for Children's Television (ACT), a parents' advocacy group. . . . In the consumerist climate of the time, Charren hit a responsive chord. After Congressional hearings, the Federal Trade Commission set guidelines to prevent deceptive ads aimed at children. The National Association of Broadcasting beefed up its self-regulating code, and the FCC began a wide-ranging inquiry into children's television, with more than 100,000 citizens writing in to express their opinions.

In its 1974 Children's Television Report and Policy Statement, the Commission concluded that

---

Jane Hall reports on TV and media issues for People magazine.

broadcasters "clearly have . . . a responsibility to serve children," not only as part of their community but also because, with "their immaturity and special needs," they "require programming specifically designed for them." As part of a long-standing policy against overcommercialization, the report said, "particular care should be taken to ensure" that children are not exposed to excessive, deceptive advertisements, for "they are far more trusting and vulnerable to commercial 'pitches' than adults, and there is evidence that very young children cannot distinguish conceptually between programming and advertising." The signal to broadcasters was clear: "We expect television broadcasters, as trustees of a valuable public resource, to develop and present programs which will serve the unique needs of the child audience. . . . The use of television to further the educational and cultural development of America's children bears a direct relationship to the licensee's obligations under the Communications Act to operate in the public interest."

Noting that the Communications Act gives the FCC broad powers to regulate broadcasting but prohibits censorship under the First Amendment, the FCC declined ACT's petition to mandate age-specific programming and number of hours required. But, as restated in a later FCC document, the 1974 policy statement specifically asked commercial licensees to: 1) make a 'meaningful effort' to increase the amount of programming for children; 2) air a 'reasonable amount' of programming for children designed to educate and inform and not simply to entertain; 3) air informational programming separately targeted for both preschool and school-age children; and 4) air programming for children scheduled during weekdays as well as weekends. In terms of commercials, broadcasters were expected to: 1) limit the amount of advertising in children's programming; 2) ensure an adequate separation between program content and commercial messages; and 3) eliminate host-selling and tie-in practices.

Although responsible broadcasters already were putting on shows for children, there was a veritable Renaissance of children's programming after the FCC report. "When the heat was turned on in Washington, you could feel it in what broadcasters put on," says Squire Rushnell, ABC's children's programming executive. "And, when the heat was later turned off, you could feel that, too." After the FCC report in 1974 CBS News continued to air its ambitious slate of children's shows, including *In the News,* one-minute spots that ran like commercials within weekend cartoons, special election coverage for kids, and weekly magazines like *Razmatazz* and *30 Minutes,* a *60 Minutes* for small-fry. ABC started its *Afterschool Specials,* ambitious dramatic specials that treated youthful dilemmas, and jazzy one-minute "commercials" for academic subjects like *Multiplication Rock.* NBC began its afterschool specials, called *Special Treat,* and started a topical teen show called *Hot Hero Sandwich.* At the local level, individual stations, station groups, and syndicators produced many ambitious shows. But, still, the FCC was not satisfied. In 1979, a task force on children's programming found that broadcasters, in general, had complied with the advertising guidelines, but not the programming guidelines.

Which Came First: The Toy or the Show?

In 1981, Mark Fowler was appointed chairman of the FCC under Ronald Reagan, and the byword was deregulation. Fowler believed that the free market—not the government—was the best determinant of what was in the public interest. In the process of the FCC's relaxing license-renewal requirements, guidelines on advertising, and other restrictions, children's television lost its special consideration. At times the rulings were about-face from the FCC under previous administrations. In 1969, for example, in a case involving an ABC show based on Mattel's "Hot Wheels" toy, the FCC found that the TV show was "designed primarily to promote the sale of a sponsor's product, rather than serve the public by either entertaining or informing it." Such a product-based show, the ruling said, subordinates "programming in the interest of the public to programming in the interest of its saleability." In 1985, however, the FCC ruled that such commercial tie-ins "did not run afoul" of restrictions against program-length commercials.

As a result of deregulation, you'd be hard pressed to find many quality educational children's series in commercial broadcasting today. CBS News, for example, now programs only five minutes per week of informational spots for children, and they're ahead of ABC News at that. (NBC does the eight-times-a-year *Main Street*.) ABC has continued with *Afterschool Specials* but *Kids are People, Too,* a Sunday magazine, was cancelled. Squire Rushnell lists the cause of death as deregulation. "When we started *Kids Are People* in 1978, we had 75 percent clearance on local stations. By the third season, we had 12 stations carrying it live. There was no outside pressure on stations to carry it." Without FCC encouragement, the true marketplace decides. As Rushnell points out, in order to carry the *Afterschool Specials,* stations usually are preempting the Oprah Winfrey show, which costs them a lot of money in syndication and brings in big ad dollars and ratings. The network compensation for carrying the children's special, as Rushnell wryly notes, is "two pieces of bubblegum and an old sneaker." In-

deed, says one network executive, the whole picture of broadcasting has changed. "In the past, broadcasters put on children's shows because it made them feel good about what they were doing," says the executive. But, in today's newly competitive environment, "Children's television is a low-profit area, and the networks are fighting it out, even on Saturday morning."

Three years after the FCC eliminated its longstanding guidelines, which . . . had limited commercials to nine and one-half minutes an hour on Saturdays and Sundays and 12 minutes an hour on other days, the onslaught of toy-based shows began. . . . Once upon a time, the TV shows created the toy. Now it's the other way round. Today, you invent the toy—then invent the TV show to sell it. According to a count by ACT, no fewer than 72 Saturday morning and afternoon cartoon shows have been toy-based. ABC, NBC, and CBS all have had plenty of shows based on popular toys, from Pound Puppies to Smurfs. But it is on independent stations that the tie-in has been refined as an art, with toy-manufacturers themselves creating the shows and syndicating them. With the right distribution windows, the profits

Distributed by King Features Syndicate

The Miami Herald

Surrogate Mother

can be enormous. Mattel's He-Man—star of stage, screen, tube, and toy shelf—is estimated to have generated $350 million in sales.

"From 20 years of research, we know that children are vulnerable to confusion between what they are seeing for education or entertainment and what they are seeing because they are being sold something." Gerald Lesser, Harvard professor of education and psychology (and co-founder of *Sesame Street*) testified this fall before the House Telecommunications Subcommittee. "To deliberately blur what is program and what is commercials and then leave it to the children to sort it all out for themselves . . . is simply not fair."

Opposing the new interactive toys, Dr. William Dietz, chairman of the children's task force of the American Academy of Pediatrics, says they disturb an important element of child's play. "Games children create for themselves teach mastery of their world, but these toys sap their imaginations," he says. "The term *interactive* should be in quotes. The television sells the toy to the child, and then the *toy* plays with the TV set. This is only the most advanced phase—after 30-second commercials and 30-minute program-length commercials—of using TV to 'teach' kids to buy toys." Yet, despite the protests, the FCC looked into the interactives only on whether they would interfere with the television signal—and found that they did not.

The Outlook for New Commercial Guidelines

After several years in which ACT was on the losing side of regulation, the FCC's statement about commercialism gave them something to stand on. Last spring, the U.S. Court of Appeals in Washington, D.C., in an opinion written by Judge Kenneth W. Starr, a Reagan appointee, found that the FCC had overturned long-standing policy without explanation. "For almost 15 years, the FCC's regulation of children's television was founded on the notion that the television marketplace *does not function* adequately when children make up the audience," wrote Judge Starr. "As the agency has

seen it, kids are different." The court has asked the FCC to explain the change.

In Congress, children's television—long a dormant political issue—is in the spotlight again. [In the fall of 1987] Congressman Ed Markey, chairman of the House Telecommunications Subcommittee, held a day of hearings on overcommercialism in children's TV. Calling children's television "a dumping ground," Markey has introduced a bill that would require the FCC to reinstate the limits on the number of ads in children's shows. Decrying what he calls the "crassly commercial" content of children's TV, Senator Frank Lautenberg has introduced a bill that would require broadcasters to produce at least seven hours of educational children's television. The FCC and the industry "are daring us to take action," fumed Congressman Al Swift during the hearings.

In response to the recent court decision, the FCC has announced an inquiry, but no major change in policy is likely. "The federal government is not set up to protect parents from kids nagging their parents for toys," says Bill Johnson, acting chief of the FCC's mass-media bureau. "How can we determine that the *Sesame Street* toy tie-ins are better than the other ones? If kids don't object to the commercials, it's hard to show what interest it is that we're trying to protect."

That's just the point, of course, to those who want to get the FCC back into the business of regulating children's television. "Broadcasters are a public fiduciary, dealing with a unique audience, our children," says Henry Geller, the former FCC general counsel, who argued ACT's case on commercial guidelines. "Yet, this FCC has said, 'Aw, the hell with them.' If that's how broadcasters are being asked to fulfill their obligations as a public trustee, we should've auctioned off licenses—and used the millions to do shows for kids."

The prospect of Congress mandating seven hours a week of educational programming, however that could be defined, raises the specter of some governmental Big Daddy feeding kids good-for-you, brussels sprouts television and would surely be opposed by broadcasters. But, when it comes to children, it's hard to argue that deregulation has led to greater diversity and more choice. There is choice on public television, with the Nickelodeon and Disney channels, if your parents pay for it. But not on "free" TV.

Although some of her network critics think she's a content-toting nanny who expects television to do what our public schools and fissioned families cannot, Peggy Charren says she's just trying to get the FCC to get broadcasters to do what they do best. "A TV industry that sends its shows around the world knows how to do shows for kids," she says. "Television for children can be an Aladdin's lamp." Or a darkness to curse the light. ■

Regulating Obscenity

Historically, the Federal Communications Commission has been careful not to regulate broadcast content, but in April 1987, faced with some complaints, the FCC announced fines for broadcasters who present "indecent" programming. In October 1988, Congress passed a law that directed the FCC to enforce a 24-hour-a-day ban on indecency. Broadcasters vowed to fight the ban in court. This article from the industry magazine *Broadcasting* provides insight into the controversy.

Consider:

1. Should the FCC decide what is broadcast, or should the audience decide? Why?

2. How is "shock" radio different from what has been broadcast before?

3. Is language that is allowed to be broadcast on radio different from language that is allowed in a movie? Why? Why not?

4. Critics of the ban charge that nothing about indecent or profane language is morally corrupting. Do you agree? Why? Why not?

Indecency: Radio's Sound, FCC's Fury

Commission decision to broaden enforcement of indecency standard, and its subsequent crackdown on three radio stations are seen by some as a threat, by others as salvation; still others wonder whether TV is next target

Over the past several months, a visitor from Mars might have gotten the impression American radio broadcasting had become a swamp where indecency flowered. The FCC, showing that its regulatory muscle had not turned to flab, cracked down on three radio stations, declaring that their programing had violated standards that until then had not been enunciated. Commission officials suggested the action was driven in part by the "20,000 complaints" they said the commission receives annually. Newspapers and magazines did pieces on the subject. Its seriousness was validated when Ted Koppel devoted a *Nightline* to it. The National Decency Forum was triumphant.

There is no doubt that all radio is not for all ears. For many, the humor of some morning personalities is stomach-turning. But has a Gresham's law taken over, with the "bad," at least as perceived by the groups like Morality in Media that make up the National Decency Forum coalition, driving out the "good"? Not really. For instance, those "20,000 complaints"—a statistic first stated publicly by Mass Media Bureau Chief James McKinney and then echoed by General Counsel Diane Killory—involve mostly television and the sex it presents that some in the audience find offensive. In May—after the interest of the public had been stimulated by the publicity given the commission's crackdown—the commission received 272 letters regarding obscenity, indecency and profanity involving AM and FM stations

and a category headed AS (all services). Including television and cable, the total was 357. But many of them dealt with the issue in general, most supporting the commission's policy, some opposing it, and the remainder defending or criticizing the performance of specific stations. Overall, letters supporting the commission's position were running about 7-to-1 ahead of those opposing it.

The mail count, of course, could hold a chilling harbinger for television. The commission, in its forays into indecency regulation in the past, has not called a television licensee to account. But the logic of the commission's new position indicates that television would not be immune in the future. Certainly the policy is not limited to radio—it speaks of "language or material that depicts or describes. . . ." And it seems reasonable that those pleased with the commission's action against three radio stations would be encouraged to turn their attention with renewed vigor to television. Self-interest was undoubtedly one of the factors that led a group of broadcast establishment parties—the television networks, the Motion Picture Association of America and the Radio-Television News Directors Association, among them—to petition the commission for reconsideration of its new standards. the parties said the standards were too vague, too broad and contrary to the public interest. . . .

If nothing else, the commission's order helped focus attention on what some call "shock radio." To critics, it is offensive and obnoxious, not to mention indecent. But in some markets it commands a large and loyal audience. Stern in New York and Philadelphia, Doug (The Greaseman) Tracht on WWDC(FM) Washington, for instance, are powerhouses in their time slots, offering a brand of humor that fans consider creative and inventive and that, at least until the commission's order, depended in part on sexual innuendo. Their humor also strikes some as, at best, insensitive. The Greaseman, for instance, celebrated Martin Luther King Day by suggesting the murder of four more civil rights leaders as a way of giving everyone a week's vacation.

Other morning people may not offer quite the same degree of shock, but there are those who seek and profit from controversy. James (Moby) Carney, on KEGL(FM) Fort Worth, has been quoted as saying, "I pick on ladies, I pick on gays, I pick on fat white guys, rednecks and foreigners." Listeners in the Miami area have complained to the commission that WINZ(FM)'s Neil Rogers "degrades women," "maligns the Pope," "is racist and anti-Semitic." One writer said Rogers called one woman "an old fart." Carolyn Fox on WHJY(FM) Providence, one of the few women in her line of work, has attracted attention with programs on dating and, until she throttled back in the wake of the commission order, on sex and dating. The *Bob and Tom Show,* on WFBQ(FM) Indianapolis has generated complaints from listeners about "degrading" and sexually oriented jokes—although the station manager, Chris Wheat, says the program is "nothing close to anything cited by the FCC." The Northern Florida Council of Boy Scouts of America felt compelled to file several complaints with the commission regarding the jokes of Hoyle Dempsey on WAPE(FM) Jacksonville. One of Dempsey's *bon mots* cited by the Boy Scouts quoted Snow White to the seven dwarfs: "I'm interested in sex, but I wanted seven inches all at once—not one inch at a time."

The "chilling" effect critics have said the commission's order would have seems to affect the talent involved when called by reporters. If they take a telephone call—and many do not—they do no more than refer a caller to the general manager—as Fox did. And sometimes general or station managers decline to discuss the programs that could in the future involve them or their attorneys in correspondence with the commission. "I don't even get into conversations [about the subject]," said Goff Lebhar, the president and general manager of WWDC-AM-FM. "It comes out negatively." (He did, however, volunteer that The Greaseman "is tops in the market in male demographics.") Or, as Norman Rau, vice president and general manager of KEGL, said, "I don't want to comment on it at all. We've had enough publicity. Let someone else have it now."

But Ken Stevens, general manager of WYSP, was not as reticent. He lauded Stern as "a genuine, funny entertainer" who is far and away superior to most of those in the same business. "Most morning talents are mediocre, so they make $250 a week, while Stern makes big bucks," said Stevens. How big? A million dollars? "Could be." Stevens said Stern's morning show had jumped from number 16, when it was introduced into the Philadelphia market in August to number three, as of the last Arbitron book. . . .

Pat Fant, general manager of KLOL(FM) Houston, is one of those broadcasters whose only question when ordered by the commission to jump is, "How high?" "KLOL will always play by the rules," he said last week. His only concern is that he is not absolutely sure what they are. But he is also one of those broadcasters who feel that, in the effort to protect the innocence of children, radio broadcasting is not being treated fairly. He notes that when the lights go up in a movie theater following a performance of "Beverly Hills Cop II," one sees row on row of the "fresh-scrubbed faces" of children who have just heard a heavy dose "of filthy language." The same kids, Fant speculates, watch daytime television with its steamy scenes. Yet there are those who raise questions about KLOL's morning program.

KLOL has probably the hottest morning team in the market, Stevens and Pruett. In the year the team has been performing for it, the station jumped from third to first place in terms of the team's target audience, men between the ages of 18 and 34. And rates have also jumped, from $200 to a minimum of $325 a minute for a live spot; the maximum has reached $400. The team indulges in what Fant describes as "silly," sometimes off-color jokes, "the kind you hear in the office." But Fant insists the team is well this side of shock radio. "These guys reflect what the audience wants to hear," he said. "The ratings prove it." ■

CHAPTER THIRTEEN

For Further Reading

Books

Renata Adler, *Reckless Disregard* (New York: Alfred A. Knopf, 1986).

Ralph L. Holsinger, *Media Law* (New York: Random House, 1987).

Leonard W. Levy, *Emergence of a Free Press* (New York: Oxford University Press, 1986).

National Coalition Against Censorship, *Books on Trial: A Survey of Recent Cases* (New York: National Coalition Against Censorship, 1985).

Don R. Pember, *Mass Media Law,* 4th ed. (Dubuque: Wm. C. Brown Publishers, 1987).

Lucas A. Powe, Jr., *American Broadcasting and the First Amendment* (Berkeley: University of California Press, 1987).

Rodney A. Smolla, *Suing the Press* (New York: Oxford University Press, 1986).

Periodicals

Censorship News, published by the National Coalition Against Censorship

Communications and the Law

Entertainment Law Reporter

Federal Communications Law Journal

News Media and the Law

Ethical Practices

How to Decide What's Right

The word *ethics* derives from the Greek word *ethos,* meaning the traditions and beliefs that guide a culture. In this excerpt from his book *The Messenger's Motives,* Stanford University communications scholar John Hulteng gives an overview of the history of ethical guidelines for the press.

Consider:

1. Do you agree with the statement attributed to William Peter Hamilton of *The Wall Street Journal* that "a newspaper is private enterprise owing nothing whatever to the public, which grants it no franchise"? Why? Why not?

2. How do the authoritarian and libertarian theories of the press differ?

3. What is the concept behind the theory of social responsibility for the press, according to Hulteng?

4. Is it possible, in your opinion, to devise an absolute set of ethical principles by which all media should be governed? Why? Why not?

Searching for the Context

JOHN HULTENG

From Plato to the present the subject of ethics has absorbed the attention of thoughtful persons in all cultures. This has been the case partly because the topic is so fundamental to our simple survival—our ability to get along harmoniously with our fellows in an ever more complex and interdependent society. But it has also been a recurring subject for speculation and analysis partly because it is tantalizingly elusive—difficult to pin down in definitive, concrete terms.

John Hulteng is Professor of Communications at Stanford University.

We all use the words "ethics" or "principles" or "standards" as everyday conversational coinage. But rarely are we confronted with the necessity to go behind the label terms and provide definitions for them; and when such occasions do arise most of us are hard put to come up with anything but the broadest generalities ("Oh, you know what I mean, doing the right thing . . . not breaking the rules . . . being fair . . .").

Yet what is "right"? Whose rules, established by what authority? "Fair" in what context?

If the answers don't come readily to mind, you need not be disconcerted. You have plenty of company.

Through several thousands of years, legions of philosophers have filled libraries with scrolls and books on the topic of ethics. The theories advanced in these volumes range over a wide spectrum, from religious to behavioristic. Some of these theories are vague and mystical; others are infinitely complex; still others coldly mechanical.

Most of the definitions of ethics that have emerged from these centuries of theorizing tend to be laid out first in broad and general strokes, and then painstakingly explained in voluminous, analytical detail that must be considered in totality to be comprehended. If you groped through the volumes in search of simple, one-sentence definitions, you are likely to find yourself back with the label terms.

One twentieth-century philosopher, George E. Moore, observes that "we find that many ethical philosophers are disposed to accept as an adequate definition of 'Ethics' the statement that it deals with the question of what is good or bad in human conduct."

If you turn from the philosophers to the dictionary you won't be much more precisely enlightened. There you will find that the word "ethics" can be used in a general sense to describe the body of moral principles or values governing or distinctive of a particular culture or group (as in "business ethics"). Or it may be used with respect to an individual as a term expressive of the complex of moral principles held, or rules of conduct followed, by an individual.

In all these attempts to set down the meaning of the word, there are open-ended, elastic variables, just as in our own amateur efforts at definition. What, exactly, do "good" and "bad" mean? What is suggested by "moral principles" or "values distinctive of a culture?" Unless you are prepared to undertake a short course in philosophy, however, (and don't expect that from this book or this author), you will probably have to get along as best you can with definitional frames of reference that *are* broad and generalized, even though this will pose problems as we attempt to fit into these frames specific cases drawn from journalistic practice.

Narrowing the Focus

As one explorer in the field of journalistic ethics has pointed out, not many professional journalists have attempted to write about the subject, except to formulate generalized codes. John C. Merrill, author of *The Imperative of Freedom,* observes that:

Perhaps one reason for this is that most editors, publishers, news directors and other journalists simply write the whole subject of ethics off as "relative," giving little or no importance to absolute or universal journalistic principles. A newspaper friend put it succinctly recently when he said that he looked at ethics as "just the individual journalist's way of doing things." Certainly a free journalist has the right to consider ethics in this way, but such a relativistic concept relegates ethics to a kind of "nothingness limbo" where anything any journalist does can be considered ethical.

At another point in his analysis of the philosophical underpinnings of journalistic freedom and integrity, Merrill touches on another reason why the topic of ethics has been one that journalists typically have treated in broad, vague terms rather than detailed specifics:

When we leave the subject of basic orientation and allegiances and enter the area of journalistic ethics, we pass from the more solid ground of sociopsychological empiricism into a swampland of philosophical speculation where eerie mists of judgment hang low over a boggy terrain.

Yet Merrill does not hesitate to strike out into this mist-shrouded countryside, and neither should we. The footing may not be solid, but there is a trail of sorts, so let's follow it as best we can.

In journalism, as in society generally, ethics may be viewed either as a group influence, governing the behavior of all or most who are in this field of activity, or as a set of guidelines unique to an individual practitioner.

In the final analysis, whether an individual journalist behaves ethically depends upon the personal code by which he or she gauges rightness of conduct, that is, determines what *ought* to be done as a journalist.

These personal codes are of course beyond our ability to catalog or anatomize, varying as they do from person to person and reflecting many kinds of input, experience and orientation. What we *can* do, however, is sort through some of the institutionalized influences that may have shaped the personal codes.

Here, as in the earlier general discussion, it is possible to discern central ideas that run far back in time (though not back to Plato, since the press is a relatively recent phenomenon). But the central ideas (for example, the concept that it is the journalist's chief responsibility to report news honestly) have been modified from time to time by the various societal contexts in which the media of mass communication have developed since the invention of movable type.

William L. Rivers, Wilbur Schramm and Clifford G. Christians, in their *Responsibility in Mass Communication,* note several basic theories under which the press has functioned since the time mass communication first became possible.

The first journalists were obliged to operate within an authoritarian society. The rulers of the time were absolute, and the interests of the state—embodied in the ruler—were paramount. All institutions functioned within this context. As Rivers, Schramm and Christians put it:

The basis for communication ethics in such a system is clear. Stated negatively, there should be no publishing which, in the opinion of the authorities, would injure the state and (consequently) its citizens. More positively, all publishing should contribute to the greatness of the beneficent state, which would as a consequence enable man to grow to his fullest usefulness and happiness. Significantly, one need not decide for himself; there is always an authority to serve as umpire.

Authoritarian regimes still hold sway today in some parts of the world, and where they do the press must contend with an imposed ethical system (almost a contradiction in terms). In many nations, however, as absolutist governments were replaced by democratic forms, the authoritarian theory of the press similarly gave way to another concept, that of libertarianism.

This theory rejected the notion that the press must operate to support and benefit the state, and instead encouraged the free expression of ideas without governmental hindrance.

All voices should be free to be heard in the press and, as various viewpoints contended, the public would be able to discern the truth amid the hubbub. There would be an open marketplace of ideas; government must keep hands off, letting the various shades of truth and error contend for the attention of the community. Underlying this theory was the assumption that the public would make rational decisions if it had access to all ideas and viewpoints.

What ethical code figured in this theory? Again from Rivers, Schramm and Christians:

The ethical responsibility of the libertarian communicator might be expressed by John Locke's phrase, "enlightened self-interest." The degree of enlightenment, of course, varies widely with individuals. At one extreme might be a Pulitzer, who wrote that "nothing less than the highest ideals, the most scrupulous anxiety to do right, the most accurate knowledge of the problems it has to meet, and a sincere sense of social responsibility will save journalism." At the other extreme might be placed a statement attributed to William Peter Hamilton of the Wall Street Journal: *"A newspaper is private enterprise owing nothing whatever to the public, which grants it no franchise. It is therefore affected with no public interest. It is emphatically the property of the owner, who is selling a manufactured product at his own risk." Between these extremes are the positions and practices of most publishers, broadcasters and film makers.*

During the last several decades, the libertarian theory has undergone substantial modification. Some writers on the press and society believe that a new theory—that of social responsibility—now influences (or *ought* to influence) the thoughts and behavior of the men and women who work within the media of mass communication.

The social responsibility theory holds that the simple "hands-off" thesis of the libertarians is insufficient as a guideline for the media of today. The libertarian theory was based on the assumption that access to the means of publishing or disseminating information would be available freely to all, or most. Thus it would not matter whether what was published by some journals was distorted or biased, since these would be offset by others slanted in another direction. In the clash of contending viewpoints, the truth would eventually emerge for all to see.

Shrinking Channels

In the period when the libertarian theory was taking form, and particularly at the time that it was embodied in the American Constitution as part of the First Amendment, there may have been at least some plausibility to the assumptions on which it was based. Although there never has been a time when the media were accessible to all, there were in the late eighteenth century relatively numerous channels available, in proportion to the literate population of the time. Newspapers, broadsides and pamphlets came and went on the journalistic scene; neither substantial capital nor complex technology was needed to launch a new communication venture—the proverbial "shirttail full of type" would serve.

But in today's world the means of mass communication are a good deal less accessible to all than they were at the time of the Revolution. Now there are a very few channels, controlled by relatively few persons. In the United States there are approximately 1,700 daily newspapers, 8,000 weeklies, 900 television stations, 8,500 radio stations, nearly 3,000 cable television systems and more than 10,000 magazines of various kinds, most of them highly specialized. And there are about 230 million Americans.

How many of these 230 million have free access to any of the various channels for the dissemination of ideas and information? How many have the wherewithal to hire space or time on those channels? How many have the vast means that would be required to buy or launch their own communication channels to reach large numbers of their fellows?

Today, in virtually all American cities where there are daily newspapers, there is only one such paper, or perhaps one ownership publishing a morning-evening combination. In only 3 percent of our cities does true head-to-head competition between different owners survive. Attempts to revive competition by starting new large-circulation papers have been ruinously costly (with losses running to many millions yearly) and have almost invariably failed. Only in small towns and suburban communities have new papers emerged on the scene and survived.

In most cities there are no more than two or three television stations. And to acquire a TV station is, if anything, even more costly than buying a daily newspaper. Radio stations are more numerous but typically are specialized, reaching only one or two segments of a community with target programming of music and news. The opportunity for the average citizen to find on radio an outlet for his or her views is limited. In time, the realization of the promise of cable systems should provide greater opportunities for public access to the channels of communication, but the full development of multichannel, two-way cable networks may be years away.

So as a practical matter, the assumption on which the libertarian theory of the press once rested does not hold today. And that is why the concept of social responsibility has taken root.

This theory of the press contends that since the channels of communication now are so limited, those who own the channels, and those who gather and process the information that flows out through them, must accept a responsibility to society along with the freedom that they still enjoy from any kind of governmental interference.

In brief, that responsibility is to provide a truthful, balanced and comprehensive account of the news. Under the libertarian theory, it was possible to tolerate biased, distorted or one-sided presentations because there were many channels and many voices were being heard over those channels; the distortions would balance out, and reality would be discernible. But the social responsibility theory recognizes that when there is only one game left in town, it must be an honest one.

Unless those few channels that are available to us provide an accurate, complete flow of news and information, how else can we hope to get a true picture of the world around us, and acquire a basis for making the decisions expected of us in a democratic society?

So the proponents of the social responsibility theory would lay obligations on the journalists, as well as reaffirm their rights. (Among the proponents of the responsibility theory was the Hutchins Commission on Freedom of the Press which issued a landmark report in 1947 after an extensive investigation of the condition of the press at that time.) And from the obligations laid on the press flow ethical implications.

Most observers of the press tend to view these implications as positive. That is, they assume that journalists who subscribe to the theory of social responsibility will direct their efforts toward identifying and then serving the interests of society. The massive power of the media will be employed responsibly, and an accurate picture of reality will be fashioned for the public. Media excesses and abuses will be minimized.

But this is not the only way in which the social responsibility concept is perceived. Some see built into it ominous pitfalls. John C. Merrill warns in *The Imperative of Freedom:*

This "theory" of social responsibility has a good ring to it and has an undeniable attraction for many. . . . Implicit in this trend toward "social responsibility" is the argument that some group (obviously a judicial or governmental one, ultimately) can and must define or decide what is socially responsible. Also, the implication is clear that publishers and journalists acting freely cannot determine what is socially responsible nearly as well as can some "outside" or "impartial" group. If this power elite decides the

press is not responsible, not even the First Amendment will keep the publishers from losing this freedom to government, we are told.

Merrill's point cannot be ignored; it poses a real and valid concern. As far back as 1947 the Hutchins Commission report was hinting darkly at the necessity for the press to discipline itself or face the prospect that some external agency would step in—presumably some agency of government.

Yet most proponents of the concept of social responsibility contend that the press can make its own internal adjustments in time to avoid the prospect of intervention from outside. And they argue that in this period of shrinking channels of information, social responsibility is the only valid and acceptable guiding theory for the press. This appears to be the position of the majority of editors and educators, and of many working journalists as well. That does not mean, however, that there follows a simple step from the social responsibility theory to the definition of an ethical framework logically evolving from it. It is not that easy to pin down the basis for contemporary journalistic ethics.

The principles and standards that are influential in the workings of the mass media today stem from many sources and a variety of theories. The concept of social responsibility does indeed influence many of the men and women who own or work in the media of mass communication. But libertarians abound, too, as well as some crusty individualists who share the nineteenth-century philosophy that a newspaper is a private enterprise "owing nothing whatever to the public."

As a practical matter some ethical concepts— but only some of them—have roots in press theories. Others have grown up as craft attitudes, folkways of the news business. Still others seem to be almost visceral, instinctive in their origin and persistence.

One writer on the standards of journalism, J. Edward Gerald, contends that "the whole of journalism's dependability and usefulness rests in adequate conformance to the articles of faith upon which communication is based and upon rewards and punishments for behavior." And at another point in his overview, *The Social Responsibility of the Press,* Gerald asks: "What are the conventions journalists are taught to respect? What are the rules of their trade? What skills in communication entitle a journalist to the acclaim of his fellows? What errors bring loss of face?"

If we can uncover some answers to these questions we should have a starting point, at least, for the case-by-case exploration of ethical problems that plague the journalist today.

But be warned: the search for these articles of faith, the answers to Gerald's questions, won't be completely productive. The ethical scene in the field of journalism is almost as imprecise and generalized as is the case with the ethics of society as a whole. We can get a view of some wide parameters and some broad principles, but don't expect neat and comprehensive blueprints. ■

PERSPECTIVE 2

Journalists as Propagandists

Restraint is a good journalistic ethic to maintain, but in this article Dan Magil describes how his action as a newspaperman inflamed a community's racial bigotry in 1938.

Consider:

1. In a circumstance such as this, what are a journalist's responsibilities?

2. What mistakes did Magil make in covering the lynchings?

3. What were the consequences of Magil's actions?

4. Do you agree that Magil was "innocent of any wrong-doing"? Why? Why not?

February 1938: Fanning the Flames of Bigotry

DAN MAGIL

Reporters often become propagandists of and for their personal opinions, using the news story as their vehicle.

I have had alternating periods in which I was first a reporter with a detached viewpoint, careful to assemble facts and present them objectively, then as a crusader and propagandist.

It is so easy to become a propagandist rather than a reporter. Almost everyone has opinions of his own. And anyone with more ego than he can handle is likely to let his views color a story or determine the manner in which the story is presented.

I had not been a reporter on the Athens *Herald* very long before I was called upon to write the story of a lynching.

A Negro had been captured in a nearby county, accused of a crime and lynched. I did not attend the lynching and knew nothing of the facts. I was told a few "facts," however, and instructed to write the story.

It was probably the main story in the paper that day. I don't remember. Anyhow, I "went to town" writing that story, used all the adjectives I could remember and explored the dictionary for more. I called the Negro every kind of brute known to Noah Webster.

Not once did it occur to me that the Negro might not have been guilty. It is possible that he was, but I took it for granted that he did just what

he was accused of doing. As I have said, the story was short on facts but long on fancy—and adjectives. I suppose I did what could have been called a good job of lurid writing, but it was unquestionably a bad job of reporting.

My second experience in covering a lynching occurred within a few months of the first. In the second instance, I acted in a dual capacity—that of promoter and reporter. I happened at the time to be desk man as well as reporter. That meant that I handled the headlines. And I also wrote the local stories—at least the "big" stories, such as lynchings.

One morning we received a tip that a woman had been killed in a nearby county, not far from Athens. A young Negro man was suspected of the crime. I published an extra, using the most glaring headlines I could find in the printing shop. I also threw in a few adjectives to whet the appetite of the readers for more of the same, which was soon coming. I think I ran out three extras on the murder during that day and, in the last one, the main headline ran something like this: BLACK BRUTE CAPTURED!

Understand, I had no hatred of Negroes. I was just dumb. But I thought I was a sensation as a newspaperman.

In every extra I put out, I fanned the flames of racial prejudice. I whipped up the emotions of those who read the paper to such an extent it is very likely that I was responsible to a very great degree for what followed. I had no idea what I was doing except that I thought I was getting out a very fine newspaper.

The jail was stormed that afternoon and the

Dan Magil was associate editor of the *Banner-Herald* in Athens, Georgia, when he described these lynchings, which had taken place some 20 years earlier. Magil died in 1951.

Negro taken out. I went to the lynching that night. Everybody else went. But upon approaching the spot where the Negro was tied to a tree—burning—I turned and hastened back to town.

It was not a sense of guilt that drove me back to Athens. The whole occasion was too weird for me. I didn't like the way the Negro kept screaming. And I didn't like the moaning of some of the relatives of the dead woman. So I lammed out of there as quickly as possible.

No one ever knew for certain whether he was guilty. But the stories I had put in the Athens *Herald* left no room for doubting that he was guilty. They were not based on a careful assembling of the facts. It was not reporting I was doing. I accepted things as they appeared to be. I simply didn't know what I was doing. I was just a young fellow playing havoc with human emotions. I had no real sense of responsibility. I had no sense of any kind. I had no knowledge or experience of getting and reporting the facts.

I was innocent of any wrong-doing. The trouble lay in the fact that at a young age and without experience I was placed in a very responsible position on a daily newspaper with too much freedom and I shot the works.

After the lynching, the papers were full of condemnations of lawlessness and a committee of citizens requested both Athens papers—the *Banner* and the *Herald*—to leave out any news of the lynching or its aftermath for a few days until things quieted down. A committee of citizens slept in the jail for several nights to be on guard lest other prisoners be sought by mobs. Pretty soon things righted themselves and all was normal again. It was the last lynching, I believe, I ever covered or promoted. . . . ■

PERSPECTIVES 3 & 4

Privacy Versus Curiosity

Photographs often tell stories better than words, and the issue of the camera's intrusion into everyday life is important in any discussion of ethics. In Perspective 3, written in 1977, columnist Ellen Goodman comments on the nation's preoccupation with photography and its effect on people's privacy. In Perspective 4, ethics scholar Don Fry describes the different approaches two newspapers covering the same story in the same city used to decide which pictures to run with the story.

Consider:

1. Do you agree with Goodman that "we haven't yet developed a clear idea of the ethics of picture-taking"?

2. Do you agree with Goodman that "the right of the public to know, to see and to be affected is considered more important than the right of the individual to mourn, or even die, in privacy"?

3. What were the arguments at the *Journal* and at the *Tribune* for and against running photographs of Sage Volkman? Which newspaper made the right decision? Why?

4. Is it possible, as Fry suggests, that both papers made the right decision? Why? Why not?

5. Given the same situation, what would your decision be? Why?

Protection from the Prying Camera

ELLEN GOODMAN

Maybe it was the year-end picture roundup that finally did it. Maybe it was the double exposure to the same vivid photographs. Or perhaps it was the memory of three amateur photographers carefully standing in the cold last fall, calculating their f-stops and exposures with light meters, trying to find the best angle, pointing their cameras at a drunk in a doorway. Or maybe it was simply my nine-year-old cousin playing Candid Camera at the family gathering.

But whatever the reason, it has finally hit me. We have become a nation of Kodachrome, Nikon, Instamatic addicts. But we haven't yet developed a clear idea of the ethics of picture-taking. We haven't yet determined the parameters of privacy in a world of flash cubes and telescopic lenses.

We "take" pictures. As psychologist Stanley Milgram puts it, "A photographer takes a picture, he does not create it or borrow it." But who has given us the right to "take" those pictures and under what circumstances?

Since the camera first became portable, we have easily and repeatedly aimed it at public people. It has always been open shooting season on them. With new technology, however, those intrusions have intensified. This year [1977], someone with a camera committed the gross indecency of shooting an unaware Gretta Garbo in the nude—and *People* printed it.

This year, again, Ron Galella "took" the image of Jacqueline Onassis and sold it as if it belonged to him. This year, we have pictures of a crumpled Wayne Hays, an indiscreet Nelson Rockefeller, and two presidential candidates in every imaginable pose from the absurd to the embarrassing.

We have accepted the idea that public people are always free targets for the camera—without even a statute of limitations for Jackie or Garbo. We have also accepted the idea that a private person becomes public by being involved in a public event. The earthquake victims of Guatemala, the lynched leftists of Thailand, the terror-stricken of Ireland—their emotions and their bodies become frozen images.

The right of the public to know, to see and to be affected is considered more important than the right of the individual to mourn, or even die, in privacy.

What happens now, however, when cameras proliferate until they are as common as television sets? What happens when the image being "taken" is that of a butcher, a baker, or a derelict, rather than a public figure? Do we all lose our right to privacy simply by stepping into view?

Should we be allowed to point cameras at each other? To regard each other as objects of art? Does the photographer or the photographed own the image?

A widely syndicated columnist for the *Boston Globe,* Ellen Goodman received the Pulitzer Prize for commentary in 1980.

Several years ago, *Time* photographer Steve Northup, who had covered Vietnam, and Watergate, took a group of students around Cambridge shooting pictures. He quietly insisted that they ask every pizza-maker, truck driver and beautician for permission. His attitude toward private citizens was one of careful respect for the power of "exposure." In contrast to this, the average camera bug—like the average tourist—too often goes about snapping "quaint" people, along with "quaint" scenes: See the natives smile, see the natives carrying baskets of fruit, see the native children begging, see the drunk in the doorway. As Milgram wrote, "I find it hard to understand wherein the photographer has derived the right to keep for his own purposes the image of the peasant's face."

Where do we get the right to bring other people home in a canister? Where did we lose the right to control our image?

In a study that Milgram conducted last year, a full 65 percent of the people to whom his students talked in midtown Manhattan refused to have their pictures taken, refused to be photographed. I don't think they were camera shy, in the sense of being vain. Rather they were reluctant to have their pictures "taken."

The Navahos long believed that the photographer took a piece of them away in his film. Like them, we are coming to understand the power of these frozen images. Photographs can help us to hold onto the truth of our past, to make our history and identity more real. Or they can rip something away from us as precious as the privacy which once clothed Greta Garbo. ∎

The Shocking Pictures of Sage
Two Newpapers, Two Answers

DON FRY

On October 24, 1986, as Sage Volkman slept, a spark from a wood stove set her father's camper on fire. The flames burned the five-year-old girl over 45 percent of her body, destroyed her eyelids, nose, and left ear, fused her toes together, and melted the skin on her legs, arms, chest, and face. Later, doctors had to amputate her fingers.

Two local newspapers, the Albuquerque *Journal* and *Tribune,* faced a series of decisions on printing photographs of the scarred girl as she struggled through operations, therapy, and her return to public view. One paper eventually decided not to risk offending its readers with shocking pictures, while the other printed gruesome photographs large in a special section. Why would two newspapers, edited for the same city, published in the same building under a joint operating agreement, reach such opposite conclusions on essentially the same materials?

The *Journal*

The *Journal* initially ran three stories, illustrated only with a school photo of Sage *before* her accident. Then, six weeks after the fire, it sent re-

Don Fry, associate director of The Poynter Institute for Media Studies in St. Petersburg, Florida, teaches newswriting and ethics.

porter Steve Reynolds and photographer Gene Burton to the Shriners Burn Institute in Galveston, Texas, to report on Sage's treatment. Initially, Burton had some problems with feeling intrusive in the therapy sessions, but he began to think, "What wonderful pictures." He soon came to regard the Volkmans as "one of the strongest and most courageous families I've ever been involved with," the universal reaction among people who have met them.

For the December 25th issue, Reynolds wrote a story on the Volkman's emotional struggles. Asked how the Volkmans felt about the paper's coverage, he told his editors that the family was "open to publicity." Indeed, counselors at the Burn Institute had told the Volkmans that Sage would face major problems with public reactions. The institute's former nursing director, James Winkler, had said, as reported in Reynolds's story, "She's going back into the street for the first time as an entirely different person. . . . Society is going to be very cruel to her and it's going to, not intentionally, stop and stare and she's going to be ostracized." He recommended preparing Sage's schoolmates for her new appearance.

Burton offered a portfolio of pictures, which his photo editor took to higher editors for consultation. Eventually they settled for a color picture of the parents with Sage wrapped up in her Jobst suit, an elasticized body covering. A mask covered her face. This picture ran on page A-1, accompanied on A-13 by a black-and-white of the family without Sage. Reporter Reynolds, who did not participate in the photo deliberations, called the color picture "the least offensive photo we had [of her], and the safest."

This decision matched the style of the *Journal,* a statewide paper with a morning circulation of 117,000 daily and 153,000 on Sunday. The *Journal* considers itself a paper of record, and favors hard-news treatments. Its editor, Jerry Crawford, a short, neat, cautious man, has won wide respect for his courageous stands against corrupt politicians. He consults often and broadly, and runs an aggressive paper. Crawford characterizes the *Journal* as "very careful with pictures," always cautious about its "responsibility to anticipate what the public can deal with."

Sage returned to Albuquerque on February 20, 1987, and the *Journal* ran a large picture on the front page. Totally covered up by her Jobst suit and mask, Sage reaches toward her brother, who smiles back. Crawford called it "the most appealing picture we had taken . . . with the greatest impact in terms of tugging the heart." The editors had rejected all the other pictures as "much too graphic."

During this period, the *Journal* discussed the pictures in editors' meetings, and Crawford often took them upstairs to Tom Lang, publisher of the *Journal.* Lang manages the joint operating agreement between the *Journal* and the *Tribune.* He also heads the Albuquerque Publishing Company, which owns the building and prints the two papers. Lang rejected some of the pictures as "too graphic."

The photographer got complete cooperation from the Volkmans, who were willing to unbandage and disrobe Sage in the hospital. Although the family had preferred photos in Texas with Sage's mask on, after her return they began taking her out in public without it, as the Galveston counselors had advised. Reporter Reynolds told his editors that the family did not mind the coverage, indeed welcomed it.

The Shriners agreed to cover most of Sage's medical costs until her 18th birthday, estimated to run as high as $1 million. But the Volkmans faced other expenses far beyond Michael's means as a tree planter and Denise's salary as a kindergarten teacher. A whole series of fund-raising events helped build a trust fund for Sage.

Five of the stories in the *Journal* ended with a detailed notice on where to send contributions. Editor Crawford and Publisher Lang had several discussions about the family's need for publicity. Lang worried that the Volkmans were trying to make the paper into their advertising agency: "We didn't want to be their solicitor of funds." Crawford also suspected that the family wanted more explicit pictures in the paper.

By the summer of 1987, Sage improved remarkably, learning to walk again and even riding her bike with training wheels. The family wanted to prepare Sage and her classmates for her return to school.

On July 27, the *Journal* made a decision that affected the coverage of Sage in unexpected ways. Although staff members remember the sequence of events with slight variations, a picture of the key meeting emerges.

Burton shot a new series of photographs, mostly at a therapy clinic. He brought both black-and-white and color pictures to Dan Ritchey, the Metro Plus section editor, while reporter Reynolds worked on a long story about the many people who voluntarily helped Sage and her parents.

Dan Ritchey found the pictures shocking, but "very warm, as warm as you could shoot." He and the photographer spread the prints on a slant table outside the office of Frankie McCarty, the managing editor for news, and asked her opinion. McCarty looked them over and said, "They're pretty shocking, but we might be able to get by with this one," indicating one of the black-and-whites. She found the other pictures "gruesome," likely to offend readers, even outrage them. But she decided to consult the editor, Jerry Crawford.

Crawford came out and immediately rejected the color photos. He looked over the others, and said: "I see only one picture we can publish," paused, and said, "No, not even that one." Crawford pronounced all the pictures "too graphic." He took the pictures to his assistant editor, Kent

Walz, for a second opinion, returned, and said, "Not even this one." Managing Editor McCarty left.

Crawford felt amazed that the staff had proposed such photos, because he had turned down "less gruesome" ones before. He "thought the family wanted the paper to run shocking photos to educate potential classmates." He worried about the paper's reputation, as he always does, and "didn't want to be considered reckless." But he stayed and debated the issue with Ritchey and Burton.

Crawford brought up a page-one photo in the *Journal* several weeks before, showing an injured cyclist lying in the street. Paramedics had slit the rider's pants to treat his wounds, and Crawford had to field calls about revealing the underpants. He said, "I could tell the news value overrode the shock value *there,* but what is the news value *here?*" Section editor Ritchey argued that the family wanted people prepared for what Sage looked like; with the start of school coming up, they needed the pictures to break the ice. Photographer Burton argued: "Here's a story about a little girl. We should publish a picture. If it's okay with the family, why not with us?" Both stressed their desire to help the Volkmans. Crawford countered: "No, we've done that. . . . there's a fine line between our responsibility to our readers and helping this little girl."

The discussion ended.

Crawford did not think he had made a hard decision, "no big deal." But he sympathized with the disappointment he anticipated: "The staff was so close to it, so they felt let down. I felt sorry for Gene [Burton] and the writer because they wanted their work out." Managing Editor McCarty also worried about her staff's reaction, but she approved of the decision, although she felt that "any story about a person is better with a picture of that person."

Crawford saw his decision as simple: "we would not run *those* photographs on *that* story." But as the decision began to reverberate through the newsroom, staff members separately interpreted its implications for their own work. Burton, the photographer, thought the decision meant that "we can never publish another picture of that girl in this newspaper." He received no further assignments on the Volkmans in 1987, and generated none himself.

Ritchey, the section editor, felt upset by the decision, but he thinks he got a fair hearing. Like the photographer, he took the finding to mean that the *Journal* would run no further pictures of the girl. He thought "To have stories [on Sage], we have to have photos." Ritchey concluded: "It seemed dishonest to write stories about the child being accepted while saying the child's face is too gruesome to run in the newspaper." He assigned no further stories on Sage Volkman.

Reynolds, the reporter, learned of the debate, and thought: "If you're not going to use those pictures, you're not going to use any." As a writer, he worried that describing Sage's disfigurement would seem "exploitive and sensational." Only pictures could capture "the way she is in public." He felt disillusioned, and lost interest in the Volkman story. Apparently no one in the newsroom thought a policy on Sage had been announced, but many other staffers were upset by the implications.

The next day, July 28, Reynolds's story appeared in a zoned section, with no pictures. In a later edition, the main section of the *Journal* picked it up and ran it with the old file photo taken before the fire. Section editor Ritchey angrily sealed the library copy of the mug shot in an envelope so it could never run again. He thought it was "insensitive to remind people how cute and beautiful she was." Despite a series of fundraising events, the *Journal* published no further stories on Sage until December 4, seven weeks after the *Tribune*'s special section came out.

The *Tribune*

Meanwhile, the *Tribune* had published nothing on Sage beyond a few city briefs. Vickie Lewis, a staff photographer, began shooting pictures with the Volkman family on her own time. One day in February or March (no one seems to remember), she tossed a half-dozen difficult photos onto Editor Tim Gallagher's desk and proposed a pictorial

essay. Tim says he made no formal decision on what would become a major project involving controversial photographs; he just told Vickie "to take all the time you need." The casual style of this interchange tells a lot about the contrast between the two papers and their editors.

The *Tribune,* an afternoon daily owned by Scripps-Howard, has a circulation of 43,000, about one-third of the *Journal*'s, with only 15 percent overlap in readership. The *Journal*'s editor, Jerry Crawford, characterizes the rival paper as "less cautious . . . more likely to rush into print." He thinks "the *Tribune* has to gain attention. They're number two, so they try harder."

The *Tribune*'s managing editor, Jack McElroy, agrees with that assessment, praising the rival *Journal* as complete, thorough, methodical, and tenacious as a government watchdog. But he adds: "They're a tortoise; we're a hare."

The two papers differ markedly in their handling of photographs. In January 1987, when Pennsylvania state treasurer Bud Dwyer committed suicide at a press conference, the *Journal* ran two AP wirephotos inside on page A-3, one with Dwyer reaching into an envelope for his gun, and the other, waving the pistol. But the *Tribune* ran the two most disturbing wirephotos on page one above the fold, of Dwyer with the weapon in his mouth, and just after he pulled the trigger. Managing Editor McElroy says he "would like to take that one back," but concedes that it shows "the direction we tend to err in."

The *Tribune*'s Tim Gallagher looks nothing like his rival editor, Jerry Crawford. Tall and rumpled, he hunches his shoulders and looks at you out of the top of his eyes. He shouts comic remarks across the newsroom and laughs a lot. In January 1987, Scripps-Howard sent him to Albuquerque to revive a stagnant and boring paper, suffering disastrously from bad advice and falling circulation.

Gallagher recalls his older brother Charlie, who suffered from Down's Syndrome. Like the Volkmans, his parents braved the reactions of others, taking Charlie out with them in public. Other children mocked his brother, and Gallagher felt "a deep desire to have people understand Charlie, to explain why staring hurt my brother's feelings." Later, as a reporter, he wrote a highly regarded series on mainstreaming the handicapped. This concern stayed in the front of his mind throughout the Volkman project.

Managing Editor McElroy says the "question never arose of *not* publishing the photographs." Indeed, all the discussions seemed to concern packaging the pictures and the story in ways to make them acceptable and powerful for the reader. Mike Davis, the photo editor, says the *Tribune*'s style is to ask *how* photos and text should run. The staff tends to make decisions in casual and mostly technical discussions among the players, rather than in editors' meetings. Generally, Gallagher says go and leaves them alone. Managing Editor McElroy had little direct involvement in the project, and none in the photo screening.

Through the year, the team kept adding players as Gallagher hired his new staff. Vickie Lewis, the photographer, privately recruited Julie Klein, a new reporter whose style she liked. Klein gathered materials for Sage's story on her own time, before she got the formal assignment. Eventually the team decided on a special tabloid section with no advertisements, designed to ease the reader into accepting very difficult pictures. The package included a letter from the parents printed twice, an emotional editorial, excerpts from the mother's diary, and a careful sequencing of photographs.

One night late in the process, reporter Klein sat around the kitchen table with the Volkmans and took dictation while they composed a letter to the public (see box, right).

Printed on page A-1 of the main paper and reprinted on page two of the special section, accompanied by an appealing photograph of Sage before her accident, the letter obviated all arguments about privacy and exploitation. Kent Walz, the *Journal*'s assistant editor, believes the letter muted potential negative reaction, because criticizing the paper would amount to criticizing the family.

The photographs and the text each follow their own logic, and seldom correspond on individual pages. The staff designed the photo sequence to ease the reader in toward the middle. On the cover, Sage's mother smiles and snuggles her. The reader sees Sage smiling and getting along with her schoolmates before coming to the harshest picture in the double truck. The *Journal*'s editor, Jerry Crawford, would later praise the *Tribune* for their "extraordinary pains to diminish the impact" on readers.

Two weeks before publication, Vickie Lewis took one final photograph that provoked the strongest reaction and the most debate, both before and after publication. This photograph will become a classic case in photo ethics debates for years to come. The double truck depicts Sage and her mother after her painful nightly bath. The naked, scarred girl sobs while her mother comforts her (see page [298]).

Tim Gallagher confesses he had "an anxiety attack" over this picture, "so graphic you couldn't help but feel her pain." But it reminded him of his parents' struggles with his disabled brother, and he knew he had to use it. He thought: "This is the private side of Sage. People have to

> *The following is the letter Sage's parents wrote for the October 16* Tribune:
>
> Dear Readers:
>
> We wanted this article written to make our daughter Sage's adjustment to her new life as easy as possible.
>
> We would like you to be aware of her struggle from when she was first burned and almost through death's door to her return to us as a 6-year-old girl with feelings who sees life in terms of Barbie dolls and her Brownie troop.
>
> When you come upon Sage unexpectedly in a store or restaurant, your first reaction may be one of sadness.
>
> But if you do run into her, we hope you will see her as we do—as a brave little girl.
>
> Thank you.
>
> From Sage's family: Michael, Denise and Avery Volkman.
>
> P.S. We would like you to share these thoughts with your children.

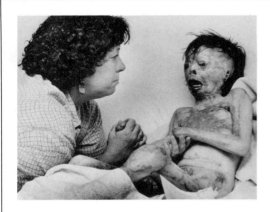

The picture [above] accompanied this story by Julie Klein which appeared in the Tribune's *special section on Sage on October 16:*

Bath time for Sage is a time-consuming ritual that begins daily at 7 p.m. For months, a typical bath took three hours. Now it's down to an hour and a half, and friends of the family sometimes schedule their evenings to help Sage with her bath.

Scabs consume the evening. They're a welcome sign that her skin is healing. But each scab must be picked with forceps. Then, the open wounds are scrubbed with anti-infection soap.

"Michael picks and I scrub," Denise said. "I'm a pretty good scrubber."

After bathing, Sage is propped up in her hospital bed in her bedroom. Her parents break pustules and cleanse them with hydrogen peroxide.

The peroxide stings more than usual. Her skin feels as if it is on fire and Sage cries about the excruciating pain.

"We don't mean to do things that make you cry," Denise said.

She reminds Sage about another burned little girl whose parents stopped giving her home therapy because she wept too much. Now that little girl can't walk.

Sage stops sobbing. Minutes later, her sullenness is followed by uncontrollable tears.

"I wish I could give my body or anything so that little girl could walk again," Sage said through her tears.

know it." Lewis feared she had lost her objectivity as a photographer, and worried about exploitation of private grief. But the mother convinced her, and Lewis decided that "this photo tells so much from the woman's face about how she accepts her daughter." The graphics editor, Randall Roberts, held out, worried that the picture was "too strong," but he finally gave in. He then decided it "was the strongest picture, so we ran it big." But he paired it with a smaller photo of Denise cuddling Sage in her Jobst suit.

Two days before the section ran on October 16, the values of the two organizations collided in the backshop. Persistent rumors say that two engravers, Dennis Gardner and Jeff Micono, tried to stop the pictures, even in one version taking their case directly to Tom Lang, owner of the press and a man of legendary inaccessibility. Technicians in production do not normally question editorial

judgments, especially in organizations involved in a joint operating agreement. In an interview, with his production director present, Gardner insisted that he merely pointed out "excessive grain" to his supervisor.

Tom Lang gives this official explanation: the engravers called attention to a technical problem, which was then solved. That problem came to the attention of Hugh Sarrels, operations director of the Albuquerque Publishing Company, who expressed misgivings about the pictures to Tim Gallagher, and suggested he run them by Lang.

Gallagher and Lang discussed Lang's worries about the family exploiting the newspapers, the proximity of publication to Halloween, and the very graphic double truck. Lang spoke of the balance between "offending the reader versus tugging the heart." Gallagher described the various efforts to soften the impact for the readers, concluding: "This is a story about a little kid who has more courage than any of us will ever have." Lang said, as he usually does, "It's your call."

The presses rolled, and all the players braced themselves for phone calls and cancellations. To everyone's surprise and relief, the *Tribune* got no negative reactions at all; in fact, quite the opposite. Readers deluged the newspaper with praise. Contributions poured into Sage's trust fund. The section sparked a whole new series of fund-raising events. And parents showed the pictures to their children and discussed them, as the Volkmans' letter suggested. Even Sage liked the pictures.

The *Tribune* newsroom responded joyously. George Baldwin, a columnist, called it "the best thing in my 52 years with this newspaper." On the other side of the building, the *Journal* staff reacted variously, some with surprise and fascination, some with anger, and some with dismay. Assistant editor Kent Walz thought: "I'm glad we didn't do that."

Which paper made the right choice? Both editors stand by their decisions, and neither would have done what the other did. In my opinion, both newspapers chose correctly, in that each remained true to its own identity and values. Journalism school classes and professional seminars debate photo choices like these at length and in rather high-flown ethical terms, but the two staffs made quick operational decisions, more on grounds of credibility than ethics.

But how could they come to such opposite conclusions? We can see some obvious reasons in the story above:

▲ The traditionally feisty P.M. chasing the traditionally gray A.M.,
▲ a newsroom culture of risk versus a newsroom culture of restraint, and
▲ two editors as different as two editors could be.

This list leaves out what I consider the most important difference: the way the two papers frame questions. The *Journal* tends to talk in images of a balancing act, or of drawing lines. State editor Bruce Daniels, for example, spoke of the "fine line between arresting photos and pornography." They try to judge whether a decision would cross those fine lines or upset a balance. They ask "yes or no" questions, and they settle for "yes or no" answers. The *Tribune*, on the other hand, tends to ask process questions, not "*should* we put this in the paper?" but "*how* can we present this to the reader?"

"Yes or no" questions serve a restrained newsroom culture well, because in sticky situations, the answer usually turns out "no." But answering "no" repeatedly tends to stifle creativity and injure morale. Process questions serve a more adventurous newsroom culture well, because they get the staff deep into a project before anyone asks hard questions that might stop the project. Unfortunately, the players tend not to ask the hard questions at all, or too late. As the *Tribune*'s Jack McElroy puts it: "We're more aware today of how the ice can get thin out where we skate." ■

Creating News

By covering an event, the media often change the character of that event. Three events sparked this column by *Los Angeles Times* media critic Howard Rosenberg: the on-air threat by a man named Gary Stollman to KNBC-TV personality David Horowitz, the broadcast of a videotape of hostage Charles Glass, and the promotion of Iran-Contra hearings figure Fawn Hall.

Consider:

1. What does Rosenberg mean when he says, "The symbiosis connecting news medium and news-maker automatically become operative"?

2. Do you agree that in the hostage case, broadcast of the videotape served "the captors, not the captive," as Glass maintains? Why not?

3. What is the role of the media in promoting Fawn Hall's celebrity? Is it proper? Why? Why not?

4. Why, according to Rosenberg, is the gap narrowing between message and messenger? Do you agree? Why? Why not?

Media Held Hostage by Its Own News
Good Guys and Bad Guys Alike Get a Chance to Air Their Views on the Tube

HOWARD ROSENBERG

TV has become society's electronic turnstile, a gangplank, a passage, the start of something big.

That something may be access or entree, the means to instantly communicate with thousands, sometimes millions of viewers. The red light comes on, and you are immediately reaching the world.

Howard Rosenberg is the *Los Angeles Times'* television columnist.

Or the payoff may be personal fame, wherein the messenger becomes the message.

The terrorist kidnapping and the escape (or release) last week of journalist Charles Glass and the exploding celebrity of Iran-Contra figure Fawn Hall apply.

So does last week's bizarre and frightening incident on KNBC-TV in Los Angeles that received national coverage. It also reflects anew the mutually exploitative relationship—one that is sometimes unavoidable—linking news media and news-makers.

KNBC consumer specialist David Horowitz was just getting into his report at 4:42 P.M. Wednesday when a man—later identified as Gary Stollman—appeared behind him holding what seemed to be a handgun and ordered him to read a long, rambling statement on the air or be shot. With outward cool, Horowitz complied as co-anchors John Beard and Kirstie Wilde sat frozen a few feet from Horowitz and Stollman and news director Tom Capra in another room ordered the program to go black.

Stollman was on the air live for only 28 seconds, KNBC said later. For the next seven minutes, KNBC broadcast an NBC logo and program promos while Horowitz read the statement, with Stollman apparently believing the newscast was still on the air.

When Horowitz had finished, Stollman put down his weapon, which turned out to be a toy replica, and was taken into custody. Then the newscast resumed, with Beard and Wilde explaining what had happened.

By evening's end, in fact, more than one thing had happened.

First there was the tense, nightmarish incident itself (Wilde could be heard gasping upon seeing Stollman's plastic .45-caliber pistol replica). Next came exhaustive coverage of the incident that night on KNBC and other Los Angeles stations and in subsequent days' newspapers.

Who came out a winner? In a curious, yet predictable way, everyone. Although he was cut off the air, Stollman did achieve some of what he wanted. At least a portion of his unclear and befuddling statement—which alluded in part to his father, former KNBC pharmaceutical reporter Max Stollman; the CIA and a plot to overthrow the government—was aired and reported in newspapers as part of the coverage.

And along with a scare, KNBC got a terrific story, albeit not one it sought.

The symbiosis connecting news medium and news-maker automatically became operative. No matter how mentally disturbed he may have been, Stollman had a message. The desperate way he chose to deliver that message became a news story. And the media are in the business of reporting news stories.

KNBC naturally led its later newscasts with the story. Its coverage was exemplary and unsensational. Horowitz was interviewed. Beard and Wilde were interviewed.

The story was also prominently featured on other TV stations. As it turned out, Stollman got quite a lot for his trouble.

"We took him off the air, because we cannot allow people like this to take television stations hostage," Capra said afterward. In effect, though, Stollman did indeed take KNBC hostage, and the other media as well, by becoming a news story they could not ignore.

As recent history shows, there are other ways to do it without walking into a TV studio and brandishing a weapon.

Glass, the reporter on leave from ABC, was on TV Wednesday, too, being interviewed in London about his flight from Moslem fundamentalist kidnappers in Lebanon after more than two months' captivity.

While a hostage, Glass made a videotaped confession that he had worked with the CIA, a statement that he read—trying in the process to drop hints that he was under duress—with a revolver aimed at his head.

The statement got wide TV exposure in the United States, and Glass now thinks that was a mistake. Such tapes—which seem to be an inevitable propaganda spinoff in hostage cases—serve "the captors, not the captive," he said.

Glass' remarks "hit me like a bolt," said CNN reporter Jeremy Levin, who spent 11 months as a hostage in Lebanon. Levin said on CNN that he was not sure he agreed with Glass' views about broadcasting hostage tapes and that he'd have to think about it.

In any event, they will continue to be broadcast, you can be sure of that. This is yet another case of terrorists holding the media hostage along with their captives and manipulating TV from across the seas.

Any information about unseen, unheard-from hostages—whether its purpose is propaganda or distortion—is almost always news. Hence, TV continues to be the terrorist's currency and entree to global millions.

TV is nothing if not eclectic, so superagent Norman Brokaw of the famed William Morris agency got his shot on TV Wednesday, too.

The agency's newest client is none other than Hall, former secretary to Lt. Col. Oliver L. North, former witness in the Iran-Contra hearings and—according to Brokaw—future star.

He said he sees a book ahead for Hall, and then a movie based on the book, followed by a "career in broadcasting because she showed she has the ability to hold an audience."

Brokaw had the evidence—booming ratings for the hearings on CNN when Hall appeared.

Credit Hall with loyalty, great looks and great shredding, and she may also be a crackerjack secretary. But a book and movie about her?

Hall seemed the reluctant witness at the hearings, frequently dour and defensive, perhaps not cognizant of the payoff ahead. Look how this has mushroomed. We used to wonder who would play Fawn—Kim Basinger?—in Ollie's story. Now it is the reverse.

All because she can hold a TV audience.

The scenario is set. After the book and movie will come the inevitable exercise cassette, followed by that broadcasting career Brokaw predicted. Well, there are some newscasts that could use some help. "Good evening, this is the 'CBS Evening News' with Dan Rather and Fawn Hall."

Message and messenger. On TV, the gap narrows. ■

PERSPECTIVES 6 & 7

An Advertising Industry Survey on Ethics

In this survey, 256 members of the advertising industry were asked to describe how they would react to twelve specific advertising business scenarios. First, decide whether the action described in each situation is ethical. Then compare your answers with the industry responses.

Consider:

1. What does the overall pattern of responses reveal about the advertising industry members who were surveyed?
2. Do you believe their answers are typical of their profession?
3. How do your answers compare with the industry members' responses?
4. Would you call yourself "ethical"? Why? Why not?

Twelve Ethical Dilemmas: What Would You Do?

1. You are competing with three other agencies for the Magnasonic Consumer Electronics business. Its chief competitor is Rolavision, handled by XYZ Advertising. XYZ's account supervisor on Rolavision has interviewed with you recently for a job. You hire him, specifically to help with the Magnasonic pitch.

	Ethical	Unethical
Agency	75%	25%
Advertiser	74%	26%
Media	78%	22%
Other	64%	36%

2. A good friend of yours calls and says an associate of his is looking for a new advertising agency. His associate knows little about advertising and has asked for his advice. He offers to recommend your company provided he will be paid a finder's fee of $20,000 if you land the business. You agree.

	Ethical	Unethical
Agency	35%	65%
Advertiser	26%	74%
Media	26%	74%
Other	39%	61%

3. Same as Question 2, but your friend is in the business of consulting for clients looking for new advertising agencies, and he is being paid a fee by his client.

	Ethical	Unethical
Agency	44%	56%
Advertiser	22%	78%
Media	35%	65%
Other	52%	48%

4. Your agency is one of four semifinalists asked to participate in a competition for a new-product assignment from a major toy marketer. While the agency has had experience in marketing to children, this assignment would be your agency's first in the toy category—and with a leading manufacturer. During a final briefing your prospective client discloses that the "new product" is a compatible set of war toys complete with pseudo-ammunition, guns, etc. Your agency decides that it will accept the assignment if it is awarded to them.

	Ethical	Unethical
Agency	75%	25%
Advertiser	86%	14%
Media	73%	27%
Other	88%	12%

5. You and two other agencies are in the final stages of a competition. Part of your pitch has to do with recommending and supporting a new marketing strategy. Late one evening, a few days before the scheduled presentation, you are proofing your slides at a slide supply house. By accident, you are handed a fairly complete set of slides put together for one of your competitors. You have enough time to examine and get the gist of it before returning the set to the supplier, who is embarrassed at his mistake. When you return to the office, you make significant changes in the way your agency presents itself so as to attack your competitor's recommended strategy in a direct and forceful manner without, of course, revealing to anyone that you have information on your competitor's actual recommendations.

	Ethical	Unethical
Agency	46%	54%
Advertiser	44%	56%
Media	48%	52%
Other	37%	63%

6. Same as Question 5, except your competitor's slides are in a file folder on the worktable next to you. You have to wait for the supplier to leave the room before you peek at them.

	Ethical	Unethical
Agency	4%	96%
Advertiser	6%	94%
Media	13%	87%
Other	11%	89%

7. You've been invited to compete for the business of a retail chain that has headquarters in the Southeast. The chain is run autocratically by its 75-year-old founder. Every member of his senior management team is white, male and more than 40 years old. In past discussions, you've come away with a clear impression that they are narrow-minded, too. As it happens, a few months ago your agency lost the business of a large New York retail chain. You did excellent work for the chain, and the account supervisor who knows all about the business still works for you but has been without an assignment for more than three months. The problem is, the account supervisor is a 35-year-old woman. You decide not to use her in your presentation.

	Ethical	Unethical
Agency	40%	60%
Advertiser	51%	49%
Media	41%	59%
Other	36%	54%

8. Same as Question 7, except that your account supervisor is male, 45 years old and black. You decide not to include him in the presentation.

	Ethical	Unethical
Agency	38%	62%
Advertiser	49%	51%
Media	45%	55%
Other	31%	69%

9. Your agency is looking to hire a senior account management person. You interview a management supervisor who promises to bring with him one of the accounts he is responsible for at his current agency if you hire him at the salary he is asking. You hire him, and the account comes to you.

	Ethical	Unethical
Agency	84%	16%
Advertiser	63%	37%
Media	87%	13%
Other	73%	27%

10. You and three other agencies are in a competition for a major airline account. As luck would have it, a good friend of yours is sleeping with the secretary for the airline's marketing VP. She's very indiscreet and tells your friend all about the exciting things going back and forth at her company during the review, including the individual views of the members of the airline's agency selection committee. Your friend gives you feedback on all your meetings with the airline.

	Ethical	Unethical
Agency	56%	44%
Advertiser	50%	50%
Media	65%	35%
Other	54%	46%

11. Same as Question 10, except your friend asks for a consulting fee, with a bonus if you get the business.

	Ethical	Unethical
Agency	7%	93%
Advertiser	0%	100%
Media	4%	96%
Other	9%	91%

12. Your agency is being considered by a group of restaurants that offers "good tasting" food at low prices. They ask your company to develop a better "price" story since they will soon be cutting their prices even further. When the agency delves into the reasons why the company can continue to serve the same "good tasting" food at even lower prices, it learns that the group has found a supplier of slightly "off" food. While the food is not yet spoiled, it is close to that stage and requires significant additional seasonings and preservatives. Your agency accepts the assignment.

	Ethical	Unethical
Agency	15%	85%
Advertiser	12%	88%
Media	13%	87%
Other	27%	73%

This questionnaire was created for the Center for Communications, a New York-based group that brings together students and professors with professionals in the communications fields to share practical information rather than theory. ■

Industry Ethics Are Alive, Says Advertising Age

When the Advertising Club of New York asked its members to complete a survey on the ethics of certain business practices, *Advertising Age,* with the adclub's permission, asked its readers the same questions.

The idea was to compare advertiser, agency, media and "other" responses from the East, Midwest, South and West on issues that ranged from stealing clients to giving payoffs. The 256 replies, tabulated [in Perspective 6] demonstrated that no geographic area is uniquely unethical. Nor was any particular segment of the advertising business noteworthy for its variation from the ethical norm.

Still, there were some interesting differences.

For instance, of all the categories of responses, Eastern advertisers considered more of the business practices to be unethical than any other group (a whopping 68%).

By region, 59% of the Midwest respondents repudiated the scenarios (such as hiring away an account supervisor and his account) as unethical, while 54% in the South condemned them. The disapproval rate in the East was 57%, in the West 58%.

When the results were averaged by profession, 41% of advertisers overall found the scenarios to be ethical.

Forty-four percent of media respondents said the situations were ethical. Ad agencies and "others" fell in between at 43%.

How to explain the position of advertisers? Is it that they simply enjoy the easy high-mindedness that comes from being the boss?

That's impossible to say, but keep in mind that while advertisers don't have to compete for agency dollars, agencies, the media and everyone else must compete for advertiser dollars.

Many business practices, however, such as the ones described in Question #1, received fairly universal acceptance.

Most readers agreed that it's ethical to hire away the "Rolavision" account supervisor from XYZ Advertising to help pitch Rolavision's competitor.

Meanwhile, most readers found the practice in Question #2 unethical: They wouldn't pay a $20,000 finder's fee to a friend who recommended their agency to someone seeking an agency.

What if that friend is a consultant being paid by a client and he still asked for a finder's fee? Unethical, said everyone, with advertisers (75%) and respondents from the West (69%) the most against it.

Question #4, which basically wondered whether it's ethical to advertise realistic war toys, received a general go right ahead—though several respondents noted that they personally wouldn't do it.

Westerners and Southerners polarized on this issue, with 63% of Western region respondents approving the war toy pitch, compared with 93% in the South.

Question #12, however, which asked whether it's ethical to advertise food that's cheap because it's "slightly off," got a repulsed and resounding no from almost everyone.

Voicing the minority opinion, one reader wrote, "Why not—if the food's not unlawful?"

The majority agreed that the actions in Question #5—examining the competition's materials when received accidently—aren't ethical—and even less ethical in Question #6, in which the materials are viewed on the sly. The South was the region most offended by this behavior, with only 3% condoning the action.

Questions #7 and #8 revealed at least as much about sexism as they did about ethics. The first asked whether, when pitching a very narrow-minded client, it was ethical to exclude the most competent account supervisor simply because she's a young woman. Only advertisers found this an ethical decision, with 51% giving it their OK. "Others" found it least (36%) ethical.

Question #8 set forth exactly the same scenario—except that this time the excluded account supervisor was a middle-age black man. Advertisers, agencies and "others" found this scenario even more objectionable.

Only the media (59%) found it more unethical to bypass a woman than a black man (55%).

This pair of questions also highlighted a big regional difference. Southerners were far more likely to find the exclusion of a woman or a black man to be ethical (54%) than their Eastern counterparts, who thoroughly condemned these practices.

Only 34% of the Eastern respondents found excluding a woman ethical, and even fewer (31%) approved of excluding the black executive.

Most respondents didn't object to Question #9, where a new agency employee brings along one of his accounts, though advertisers were the least enthusiastic about this decision.

And, as expected, advertisers were the most upset by the seamy scenario in Question #10, where a friend is sleeping with the secretary of the marketing VP at the airline you're pitching. Half found it ethical, half didn't. The other professions found it less objectionable, and in the East, 59% of the respondents approved.

But almost everyone agreed that the even seamier circumstances in Question #11, where the friend wanted a consulting fee, made the situation completely unethical. It was unanimously condemned among advertisers and Southerners.

Several readers noted that though they might consider certain practices to be ethical, they personally wouldn't follow them—for business reasons.

For instance, one Midwestern agency respondent wrote that he wouldn't hire away another agency's account supervisor who promised to bring along his account because "If he did it to them he might do it to me."

A Pennsylvania graphics agency owner wrote, "As for romancing 'narrow-minded' clients and those who sell 'off food,' the decisions aren't so much unethical as just plain poor business practice. Those clients are quite likely to treat an agency with an equal lack of respect. Why ask for trouble?" ■

PERSPECTIVE 8

News Ethics and the Radio-Television News Directors

In this survey, journalism professors K. Tim Wulfemeyer and Lori L. McFadden of San Diego State University questioned 220 news directors about a proposed revision to the Radio-Television News Directors Association (RTNDA) Code of Broadcast News Ethics. The new code was adopted in 1987.

Consider:

1. Do you agree with the majority of radio-television news directors that "freebies" are acceptable? Why? Why not?

2. Less than a majority (37 percent) of news directors said there was too much sensationalism in TV news, and about the same number (34 percent) said there was too much "fluff" in TV news broadcasts. Do you agree or disagree? Why?

3. Less than a majority (31 percent) said hidden cameras and microphones should not be used to gather news. Do you agree or disagree? Why?

4. About one-fourth of the news directors (26 percent) said that the RTNDA or some other journalistic organization should have the authority to fine, suspend, or otherwise sanction TV journalists who violate accepted ethics guidelines. Do you agree or disagree? Why?

Broadcast News Ethics and the RTNDA's Code of Ethics: Perceptions of Local Television News Directors

K. TIM WULFEMEYER and LORI L. McFADDEN

Ethics in journalism, like beauty, is often in the eye of the beholder. Actions that some call "ethical" are called "unethical" by others. Actions that under certain circumstances are judged ethical, under other circumstances might be judged unethical.

The vagaries of journalistic ethics have prompted many news professionals and news consumers to "give up" on trying to arrive at any uniform conduct standards for journalists, but this hasn't stopped the Radio-Television News Directors Association from developing a new "Code of Broadcast News Ethics." The new code will be offered to RTNDA members for their approval at the 1987 RTNDA International Conference.

The proposed code was written by members

K. Tim Wulfemeyer and Lori L. McFadden are members of the Journalism Department at San Diego State University.

of the RTNDA's ethics committee and has been approved by the RTNDA's Board of Directors. Like most codes of ethics in journalism, the new RTNDA code is fairly general and there are no provisions for penalizing broadcast journalists who violate any of the guidelines. Still, the new code does attempt to establish some baselines of "professional" behavior and it is about half as long as the current RTNDA "Code of Broadcast News Ethics" that was originally adopted in 1966 and amended in 1973.

A code of ethics, if it is going to have any utility at all, must have the support of at least a significant number of the people for whom it is written. This is especially true for codes, like all of those in journalism, that do not contain provisions for sanctions against those who violate code guidelines. The purpose of this study is to report the findings of a survey of television news directors to determine their views concerning ethics and to see how much support there is for the RTNDAs new code.*

The ethics of journalists has received a great deal of attention in recent years. Most of the attention has focused on an alleged "credibility" problem and even though research is mixed on the subject, it seems clear that a reasonably large number of people in the United States do not think very highly of journalists.

Journalists have tried a variety of ways to improve their tarnished image. Seminars and workshops have been held, panel discussions at conventions and meetings have been conducted, articles have been written and more rigid code guidelines, including provisions for punishing offenders, have been suggested.

It could be that a great deal of the hand-wringing and soul-searching by journalists and their critics over the perceived declining moral fiber of radio and television journalists might be "sound and fury signifying nothing." According to a study by Vernon Stone, very few radio and television stations fire anyone for violation of ethics codes or standards. Only about 6% of the TV stations and 1% of the radio stations responding to this survey in 1986 reported that a staffer had been fired for reasons of ethics during the preceding 12 months. Stone reported that his research suggests ethics is *NOT* a major problem in broadcast journalism, because whatever violations might be occurring have not been severe enough to warrant firings.

Stone's research might be interpreted in another way, however. It might very well be that radio and television journalists are doing a great many things that are "unethical," but the people in charge of hiring and firing—usually news directors—do not feel that such behavior is "unethical." In other words, if a news director doesn't think it's unethical for a journalist to accept a free Rolex watch from a grateful news source and a staffer does just that, the staffer is not going to be

fired for the action. Does this mean there are "no problems" with ethics?

If the "judges" of what is and what is not "ethical" are not very ethical themselves, they are not going to demand very high standards of moral conduct from their staffers. As a result, *THEY* report few problems with ethics, but that doesn't mean, in reality, there really are "no problems."

Obviously, it's a question of definition. Just what is "ethical" behavior and what isn't? Do we allow individuals to decide for themselves what is ethical or do we band together, form associations and organizations, and develop guidelines for determining what is ethical? Clearly, the RTNDA believes the latter course of action is best. This study is designed to help determine if local television news directors will likely accept what the RTNDA defines as "ethical" behavior.

Methods

Based on interviews with 25 journalists and journalism educators, a comprehensive literature review and approximately 12 years of professional journalistic experience, the authors developed a 117-question survey dealing with ethics in local television. The survey was pre-tested with 10 local television news directors and journalism educators. Some minor revision in wording and question order were made as a result of the pretest.

Surveys were sent to 538 news directors of network-affiliated television stations in the United States. The first mailing was done in May, 1985. A second mailing was done in November, 1985. The results reported in this study are based on the responses of 220 news directors. The return rate was 41%.

Findings

About 41% of the stations followed formal codes of ethics. About 50% of the NBC affiliates, 43% of the CBS affiliates and 29% of the ABC affiliates had adopted codes. There were no differences among large, medium or small stations.

*Author's Note: The code as finally adopted appears at the end of this Perspective on page 311.

The RTNDA code was the most frequently adopted (15%). A station or company code was adopted by about 9% of the stations, followed by a combination of codes (6%), a network code (4%), the SPJ,SDX code (4%) and the NAB code (4%).

About 90% of the news directors said television journalists should follow the guidelines suggested in formal codes of ethics. Among the advantages of such codes, "having a list of standards for all, especially new, staffers" was the most frequently listed (71%). "Improves the ethics of staffers" (21%), "improves the 'social responsibility' of staffers" (13%), "reduces unethical behavior" (9%) and "improves credibility and public trust" (5%) were the other advantages most frequently mentioned.

The news directors also saw some disadvantages of adopting a formal code of ethics. "Creates a loss of flexibility" was most often mentioned (41%), followed by "too vague/too general" (34%), "removes individual judgment" (23%) and "could be used against station in court" (9%). This last concern appears to be especially well-founded according to a recent study by Robert Drechsel.

Now, an examination of the RTNDA's proposed code—guideline by guideline.

Guideline #1 states:

RTNDA members will conduct themselves in a manner that protects them from conflicts of interest, real or perceived. They will decline gifts or favors which would influence or appear to influence their judgments.

In the survey, 51% of the news directors reported that at least some "freebies" were acceptable. Free tickets to cover news, sports and entertainment events were judged most acceptable, but free food and non-alcoholic beverages at news and non-news events were also given the okay. When asked to set a "maximum value" for an acceptable freebie, 40% of the news directors said NOTHING OF VALUE should be accepted and 96% suggested dollar values of $25 or less.

About 78% of the news directors reported that at least some moonlighting opportunities were acceptable. Non-journalistic work that does not compromise journalistic integrity or objectivity was judged most acceptable, but sports event announcing for radio stations was judged okay, too. Low salaries in radio-TV news was often mentioned as a justification for allowing moonlighting.

About 91% of the news directors thought it was all right for TV journalists to belong to community groups and about 65% thought it was all right to hold office in such groups. About 24% thought the self-interests of TV journalists too often affect the content of news programs.

Guideline #2 states:

RTNDA members will not misrepresent the source or nature of broadcast news material. They will guard against using audio or video material in a way that deceives the audience. They will not mislead the public by presenting as spontaneous any material which is staged or rehearsed.

In the survey, 82% of the news directors reported it was okay for TV journalists to go "undercover" to gather news. About 21% said the grammar mistakes made by sources should be corrected before broadcast. About 44% said factual mistakes made by sources should be corrected before broadcast and about 49% said profane language used by sources should be cleaned up before broadcast.

About 89% of the news directors believed "checkbook journalism" was NOT acceptable. About 68% said it was okay to enter journalistic contests sponsored by commercial organizations, but 100% said it was okay to enter such contests if they are sponsored by journalistic organizations.

Guideline #3 states:

RTNDA members will evaluate information solely on its merit as news, rejecting sensationalism or misleading emphasis in any form.

In the survey, about 37% of the news directors said there was too much sensationalism in TV news. About 34% said there was too much "fluff" in TV newscasts and about 19% said "visuals" were emphasized too much in TV news. About 31% said live shots for their own sake were okay.

About 31% said that in reports of dangerous or illegal "stunts," the names and affiliations of the "daredevils" or publicity seekers should NOT be aired. About 10% said in reports of acts of terrorism, the names and affiliations of the terrorists should NOT be aired.

Guideline #4 states:

RTNDA members will respect the dignity, privacy and well-being of people with whom they deal.

In the survey, about 31% of the news directors said hidden cameras and microphones should NOT be used to gather news. About 72% said TV journalists should NOT intrude on the private grief of people in times of tragedy. About 19% said the private lives of public people should NOT be reported any differently from the private lives of private people. About 76% said developments in the private lives of public people should NOT be reported unless it is clear that such developments affect the public lives of such people.

About 53% of the news directors thought "ambush interviews" were okay. About 67% thought TV journalists should NOT read memos or look through folders they find on the desks of news sources without first obtaining permission. About 88% said rape victims should NOT be named or shown. About 98% said the names of people who have been killed or seriously injured in accidents should NOT be aired until the victims' families have been notified.

About 86% of the news directors reported that information about suicides should NOT be aired unless public people are involved. About 30% said TV journalists should "hold" stories when asked to do so by government or law enforcement officials. About 55% thought TV journalists should try to help the victims in news events whenever possible.

Guideline #5 states:

RTNDA members will identify people by race, creed, nationality or prior status only when it is relevant.

Guideline #6 states:

RTNDA members will clearly label opinion and commentary.

Guideline #7 states:

RTNDA members will promptly acknowledge and correct errors.

The survey did not contain any questions/statements relevant for guidelines 5, 6, or 7.

Guideline #8 states:

RTNDA members will recognize the need to protect confidential information and sources.

In the survey, about 94% of the news directors reported that it was all right to grant confidentiality to news sources. About 72% said stories that contain anonymous attribution should NOT air unless the news director and/or producer knows the name of the source. About 59% thought there was too much quoting of unnamed sources in TV journalism.

Guideline #9 states:

RTNDA members will respect the right of an individual to a fair trial.

In the survey, about 59% of the news directors believed there should be NO restrictions on who or what can be videotaped/recorded in courtrooms. About 78% thought TV journalists should "pool" equipment when asked to do so by judges and other government officials.

Guideline #10 states:

RTNDA members will not broadcast without permission the private transmissions of other broadcasters.

In the survey, about 91% of the news directors said TV journalists should NOT play such "dirty tricks" on competitors as monitoring radio calls, unplugging microphone or electrical cords, providing misinformation, etc.

Guideline #11 states:

RTNDA members will actively encourage observance of these standards by all journalists, whether members of the Radio-Television News Directors Association or not.

In the survey, about 11% of the news directors believed TV journalists should have to take a prescribed course of academic study and be licensed before they are permitted to practice their craft (much like doctors and lawyers). About 26% of the news directors said the RTNDA or some other journalistic organization should have the power to fine, suspend or otherwise sanction TV journalists who violate accepted ethics guidelines.

A Cautionary Note

Some caution should be used before attempting to generalize the findings of this study to the total population of local TV news directors in the United States. Even though the news directors who responded to the survey are a reasonably representative group, it's likely that they have stronger feelings about ethics than do non-respondents.

This study is part of a continuing effort to examine ethics in journalism in order to develop reasonable, practical, enforceable guidelines for journalistic codes of ethics. The hope is that if journalists follow such guidelines and the public is aware of the effort and the content of the guidelines, public confidence in and appreciation of journalism and journalists will improve. ■

Code of Broadcast News Ethics
Radio-Television News Directors Association

The responsibility of radio and television journalists is to gather and report information of importance and interest to the public accurately, honestly and impartially.

The members of the Radio-Television News Directors Association accept these standards and will:

1. Strive to present the source or nature of broadcast news material in a way that is balanced, accurate and fair.

A. They will evaluate information solely on its merits as news, rejecting sensationalism or misleading emphasis in any form.

B. They will guard against using audio or video material in a way that deceives the audience.

C. They will not mislead the public by presenting as spontaneous news any material which is staged or rehearsed.

D. They will identify people by race, creed, nationality or prior status only when it is relevant.

E. They will clearly label opinion and commentary.

F. They will promptly acknowledge and correct errors.

2. Strive to conduct themselves in a manner that protects them from conflicts of interest, real or perceived. They will decline gifts or favors which would influence or appear to influence their judgments.

3. Respect the dignity, privacy and well-being of people with whom they deal.

4. Recognize the need to protect confidential sources. They will promise confidentiality only with the intention of keeping that promise.

5. Respect everyone's right to a fair trial.

6. Broadcast the private transmissions of other broadcasters only with permission.

7. Actively encourage observance of this Code by all journalists, whether members of the Radio-Television News Directors Association or not.

CHAPTER FOURTEEN

For Further Reading

Books

Clifford G. Christians, Kim B. Rotzoll, and Mark Fackler, *Media Ethics,* 2nd ed. (New York: Longman, 1987).

Tom Goldstein, *The News At Any Cost* (New York: Simon & Schuster, 1985).

Stephen Klaidman and Tom L. Beauchamp, *The Virtuous Journalist* (New York: Oxford University Press, 1987).

Philip Meyer, *Ethical Journalism: A Guide for Students, Practitioners, and Consumers* (New York: Longman, 1987).

Periodicals

Columbia Journalism Review

Editor & Publisher

Journal of Mass Media Ethics

Washington Journalism Review

International Media

PART V

World Media Systems

CHAPTER FIFTEEN

Understanding World Media Systems

In this article written especially for this collection, international communications scholar L. John Martin offers an overview of world media systems and some reasons why it is important to understand how the media in other countries operate.

Consider:

1. Which media functions are universal, according to Martin?

2. How do the world media differ?

3. What is the difference between the media's purposive role and the media's informational role?

4. How does the role of the news media in Western democracies differ from the role of the news media in Communist countries? In Third World countries?

5. What role do the Big Five news agencies play in gathering international news?

6. How does ownership of the media affect what is disseminated?

World Media

L. JOHN MARTIN

If you were to take a trip around the world, you would certainly be struck by how similar newspapers and magazines look everywhere, how familiar television programs are, and how radio sounds almost exactly the way it sounds at home. Sure, the languages are different and you may not be able to read or understand what you see and hear in the media, but you would have no difficulty recognizing a newspaper, a magazine, or a television or radio program. In fact, much of the content of the media would be so recognizable that in spite of language differences, you would feel quite at home with them.

This shouldn't come as very much of a surprise, of course. You wouldn't expect cars to look different in other countries, or even houses, since they serve the same functions as those you are familiar with. In the same way, at least superficially, mass media serve many of the same functions everywhere in the world. Among the functions that appear to be universal is the development of a community consensus. Be-

L. John Martin is professor of journalism at the University of Maryland.

cause people are exposed to the same media in a given location, they have a common fund of information that causes them to focus on the same elements of an issue. Mass media, along with the family and schools, also help to pass on society's social heritage. Mass media multipy life's experiences while at the same time simplifying them. They add to the economic and social well-being of the community by spreading knowledge about what is available, creating a demand for new products, and helping to raise the standard of living. This is so by definition. Mass media make possible what would not otherwise be possible in mass society, which is that large numbers of people acquire a common fund of knowledge and give common meaning to their experiences. As people multiplied, mass communication became a necessity and its most efficient manifestations were either invented or borrowed universally.

Differences in World Media

Differences do exist, however, in the world's mass media in spite of these universal roles. The reason is that mass media also have other roles that are not spontaneous but are defined by the culture in which the media exist. One of the oldest of these defined or purposive roles of mass media is that of bulletin board. This is a function that in primitive or traditional societies used to be and often still is carried out by the town crier, who walked about town and announced forthcoming events as well as news of general interest to the community. Mass media are being used in this way in the modern world both in developing and developed countries. It certainly is the quickest way to let people know about meetings, new regulations, the closing or opening of roads and bridges, and other such matters of general interest to the community.

Another purposive role is that of informing the public about advances in science and technology; developments in the health field, business and finance, and commercial ventures and activities; discoveries and inventions; and a host of other things that people are willing to pay to

be informed about. Mass media in all countries provide such information. In the Western or capitalist world (which includes parts of what is generally referred to as the Third World) they sell it to the public, which is more than willing to pay for the service either directly through subscriptions or indirectly through advertising. In the Communist world and in some socialist and authoritarian Third World countries, it is selectively provided as a service in the interest of education or indoctrinating the community. This does not mean that readers, viewers, and listeners do not pay for their media. It merely means that the selection of media content is more studiedly utilitarian.

Related to the informational role is the purposive role of indoctrination or persuasion. The media in all countries attempt to do this, whether through conscious or unconscious selection of details in the news, through the juxtaposition of facts (often referred to as interpretation), or through outright advocacy (which in the United States is generally called editorializing). We in the United States prefer not to call this "indoctrination" or "propaganda" but rather the presentation of a point of view. Lenin, on the other hand, taught that Communist media must be "not only a collective propagandist and a collective agitator, [but] also a collective organizer." Third World spokesmen have said that the principal role of the mass media should be to advance national development by educating the public.

Mass media universally have yet another purposive role: that of entertainment. Speaking of his once great people, the Roman poet Juvenal in the first century A.D. said they now long eagerly "for just two things, bread and circus games," in other words, food and entertainment. Mass media, especially electronic media, of all countries can and do make entertainment available to their publics cheaply and very successfully. Entertainment, of course, is subject to definition. The print media in many European and Communist countries carry little that may be considered entertaining, although they do take literary, theater, and art criticism seriously and have regular columns devoted to the arts and culture. Some daily and weekly newspapers, more frequently than in the United States, print short stories and serialized novels.

Finally, the media in most Western democracies consider it their responsibility to serve as a watchdog over government and even big business. This is not so in Communist countries, where the media are owned and operated by the government. Nor is it true in many Third World countries, especially those that have a military or other type of authoritarian government. Such countries cannot afford to permit a private individual or organization to second-guess them on how to run the government.

Would we find mass media content to be fairly similar worldwide, or do different cultures consider different things suitable for inclusion in their pages, programs, or on their screens? Here there is a difference between what leaders in some countries say is appropriate media content and what the media actually carry. In general, Western countries have a policy of including "all the news that's fit to print" in their newspapers, by which they mean all the news they can sell, since news is treated as a salable commodity. They also squeeze in as much headline news and commentary into their electronic media as the public can take; the rest is educational, cultural and entertainment programming.

In Communist countries news must serve a purpose. Negative news, unless it serves as an object lesson, serves little purpose and should normally, therefore, not be reported. This is the view of Soviet journalists and Communist theoreticians. Entertainment, too, must have a moral. This, in theory, is what guides the Communist media gatekeeper. But in recent years, especially since Secretary Mikhail Gorbachev came into power in the Soviet Union, there has been a relaxing of these rules. Negative news has been reported in increasing frequency and detail because it is now felt by leaders in the Soviet Union that keeping people in the dark is counterproductive.

Many Third World leaders and writers have held that the role of the mass media should be mainly to educate the public in the interest of national development. They feel that developing countries have much catching up to do and can't afford to trivialize their mass media. Yet, numerous studies that have been done on the content of Third World media find little that can be called developmental journalism and much that falls under the heading of negative news—crime, corruption, war, and disaster. Furthermore, even much of the entertainment programming on television, which, of course, is very costly to produce, is largely of Western, especially of U.S., origin.

How about the treatment of news—the way it is written, what kinds of facts are included or excluded, the importance of timeliness, the focus on the individual as opposed to the group? Actually, there is more difference between, say, German and British news treatment than there is between the Western media as a whole and Third World media. German media are more similar to other Central European and even Communist media than they are to American media, at least so far as the treatment of news is concerned.

There are many reasons why news treatments differ or why they are very similar in some countries. In many Third World countries that were colonies until the 1960s, the journalists were trained by nationals of the colonizing power. The media in these countries were often founded, owned, and staffed by Europeans who brought with them their journalistic training. Printed and electronic media in former French colonies, therefore, look very much like those in mother France; the British, similarly, have left their mark on their former colonies.

But equally important when it comes to similarities in news treatment is the fact that most of the world's news is collected by five international wire services. These are the Associated Press and United Press International, both of the United States; Reuters of Britain; Agence France-Presse of France; and TASS of the Soviet Union. While most countries and even some regions comprising several countries have their own local wire services, for their international news these smaller press agencies turn to the big five. This means that unless a medium wants to (or can afford to) rewrite everything in its own style, the treatment of news—at least foreign news—is going to look very similar worldwide. The same goes for entertainment—especially television entertainment—that is syndicated globally. Sweden, for example, found that it costs an average of eight times as much to produce television programs locally as to import them. Until the late 1970s, the United States had a near monopoly in the syndication of television programs. But in recent years, many major countries, even in the Third World, have begun to export some of their programs. Among important exporters today, besides the United States, are Britain, France, West Germany, Canada, Egypt, India, Japan, Taiwan, Spain, and Australia.

Local news, however, and locally written commentary can differ markedly from country to country. One major reason for such differences is how a country views the role of the individual in society. In the United States, Britain, and other countries that emphasize individualism as opposed to collective interests, news tends to focus on the individual. Central European papers, on the other hand, are less likely to devote much space to non-elite individuals, while Communist countries focus almost exclusively on the collective—workers at a factory, members of a union, a protest meeting, or a government's actions.

Differences in news treatment also stem from a culture's attitude toward time. In highly industrialized, free enterprise systems, time plays a much more important role than in agricultural, technologically less advanced, authoritarian systems. Thus in most of the Western world and in Japan, news not only ages fast, but news stories emphasize the up-to-the-minute angle, and even the tomorrow angle. This is far less important in the Communist and Third World countries.

News content in the world's media also differs in terms of how the privacy of the individual is viewed. The English-language press, for example, tends to consider society's right to know as being superior to the individual's right to privacy. French- and German-language media, on the other hand, though no more concerned about individual privacy, are simply less interested in non-elite individuals and, therefore, carry less news about the general public. Details about a person's life are, therefore, more likely to appear in English-language media. The Japanese press is very similar to the Anglo-American press in this regard.

One very noticeable difference in the world's media concerns coverage of government news and whether the government is the source or the subject of the news. Communist countries and many Third World countries tend to report government news in bulletin board fashion. The reports are in the form of announcements from government departments. In the Western world, on the other hand, government news frequently originates with a reporter who has "dug up" the news through personal enterprise.

Finally, the appearance of newspapers and magazines probably varies more within a given country than it does between countries. Printing technology has made tremendous strides in recent years, and most countries today can afford to produce very attractive publications. Illustrations, which used to be prohibitively expensive in the past, are widely used. If a newspaper looks gray, it is probably because it chooses not to use illustrations which it feels might tend to "popularize" or cheapen the paper. The *Neue Zürcher Zeitung* of Switzerland, for example, is one of the holdouts that still uses very few pictures on inside pages.

Ownership and Influence

About half of the world's radio and television stations are government-owned. Another fifth are owned by public corporations which are not under direct government supervision but which nevertheless are chartered by the goverment as non-profit, public organizations. Some 15 to 20 percent are operated by private, commercial companies, and the remaining 10 to 15 percent are under a combination of these types of ownership. In Communist and authoritarian Third World countries, direct control of broadcasting systems by the government is universal. But even in some Western democracies, the government controls broadcasting, while the printed media are privately owned and operated.

Wherever the government holds a monopoly over communication media, it exercises a great deal of influence, maybe not over what people think, but certainly over what people think about. The government, in effect, sets people's agenda of public issues. And yet, one might ask, are there no great newspapers in such countries? John C. Merrill, in *The World's Great Dailies,* argues that "in every major country one newspaper, and often two or three, stands out as a journal of elite opinion" with a tremendous influence not only within the country but in other countries as well. He defines as great a newspaper that is well-informed on government matters, has a reputation for reliability, and provides an accurate image of governmental thinking. Using these criteria, he lists in his book 50 newspapers that may be termed "quality," "prestige," or world-class newspapers. He contends that although many in the West would deny the description of greatness to *Pravda,* the official organ of the Soviet Union's Communist Party, or to *Renmin Ribao* (People's Daily), the voice of the Central Committee of the Chinese Communist Party, they qualify as quality papers because they appeal to opinion leaders everywhere. People recognize their importance and take them seriously because they represent the views of those who have a say in the running of their countries.

Merrill lists several dailies in the United States as quality papers, including, of course, the *New York Times,* the *Washington Post,* and the *Christian Science Monitor.* Among other great newspapers of the world, one should include the *Neue Zürcher Zeitung* of Switzerland; *The Times, Daily Telegraph* and *The Guardian* of Britain; *Frankfurter Allgemeine, Süddeutsche Zeitung* and *Die Welt* of West Germany; *Le Figaro* and *Le Monde* of France; *Corriere della Sera* and *La Stampa* of Italy; *ABC* and *El Pais* of Spain; *Al Ahram* of Egypt; *Asahi Shimbun* of Japan; *The Statesman, The Times of India* and *The Hindu* of India; and *Izvestia* (not mentioned earlier) of the Soviet Union.

This is not necessarily a comprehensive list of the world's great newspaper. But it represents the dailies that are frequently cited by opinion leaders around the world. These papers give a large proportion of their space to world affairs, tend to have well-educated staffs, are well-written and edited (at least by the standards of their own country), de-emphasize sensational news, and have a good grasp and coverage of national news.

In looking at the world's press at the end of the 1980s, the impact of the jet age, of satellites, of modern printing and broadcast technology is abundantly evident. Similarities in content and style are greater than ever. At least in mass communication, Marshall McLuhan's global village is close to becoming a reality. ∎

PERSPECTIVE 2

Overseas Investment in U.S. Media

This article describes Mark Wössner of the German company Bertelsmann, the world's largest media company. Bertelsmann owns Doubleday, Bantam Books, and RCA Records.

Consider:

1. What are the advantages to a worldwide media company of establishing a presence in the United States?

2. What steps did the company take after buying RCA Records to make it profitable?

3. How will the company use the profits from RCA and Doubleday?

4. The United States places few limits on overseas buyers of publicly held U.S. corporations. Do you think there should be limits? What would be the advantages? Disadvantages?

The Latest U.S. Media Giant Isn't Even American

RICHARD C. MORAIS

Asked to name the world's largest media company, most Americans would probably guess $4.4 billion Capital Cities/ABC or perhaps $4.2 billion Time Inc. The right answer is a media giant situated in the small (pop. 80,000) city of Gütersloh in northern West Germany, where $6.4 billion (1987 revenues, at 1.67 deutsche marks to the dollar) Bertelsmann A.G. hangs its hat.

Bertelsmann is the world's largest book club operator and mass market book publisher. It's also one of the world's largest record companies.

Richard C. Morais is a reporter for *Forbes* magazine.

The 152-year-old company is 90% owned by Reinhard Mohn and his family. Currently near the top of *Forbes'* list of 145 billionaires (with a fortune estimated at $2.5 billion), Mohn has just announced that the entire fortune is going to charity after his death.

How did a privately owned German company grow so large in media? Much of the credit goes to Bertelsmann's risk-taking current chief executive, Mark Wössner. Wössner took the helm in 1983. Late in 1986 he took a pair of back-to-back risks when he paid $330 million for then ailing RCA Records and another $475 million for troubled Doubleday.

"I agree Doubleday was too expensive for what we got," says Wössner, lounging at his Gütersloh conference table in a camel-colored sweater. "But when we bought it, we had a vision of what we could turn it into. We had a strategic plan of how to integrate the business. Judging the acquisition after the restructuring, the price now seems okay."

Wössner attacked RCA Records' and Doubleday's problems with a formula Bertelsmann has used many times before when making acquisitions: Give local management elbowroom for creativity but hold them accountable to the ferocious Gütersloh accountants.

When Wössner bought RCA Records, Bertelsmann's $630 million sales music group—which also includes the Ariola, Arista and Red Seal labels—was losing $30 million a year at the operating level. (Bertelsmann has its own unique method of calculating operating profit.) Board director Michael Dornemann was put in charge of music and told to convert the $30 million loss into a $30 million profit within a year. Dornemann gave RCA Records' creative people more leash and doubled spending on classical and pop artists. But he also chopped some $15 million, or 17%, out of U.S. overhead the first year. As revenues began pouring in from hot artists like Whitney Houston and British teen heartthrob Rick Astley, more of it flowed to the bottom line. Music division operating income should come to about $55 million [in 1988].

Already big and experienced in book clubs, Bertelsmann is now pushing its record clubs. "We're number two in the U.S. now," says Dornemann. "I think we'll be catching CBS [Records] very soon."

Bertelsmann has owned Bantam Books since 1977. Soon after buying Doubleday, which included Dell/Delacorte, Wössner carved it into book clubs, stores, printing and publishing divisions. They, in turn, were folded into existing Bertelsmann divisions. Bantam's head, Alberto Vitale, was put in charge of merging the U.S. publishing outfits.

Vitale consolidated the groups' warehousing, accounting and computer systems. Although he merged the sales organizations, editorial and publishing departments were kept separate to maintain the identity of each imprint. Dell Publishing's trade magazines, other than its crossword puzzle publications, where it was number one, were closed. All in all, Doubleday's titles have been cut by a third, and the group's total staff is down 30%, to around 1,200 employees. Vitale, says William Goldstein, trade news editor at *Publishers Weekly,* "has a good eye for moving personnel."

"There's a lot of pressure now," says Vitale. "What we have to do is build up the list. In this business, if you have the right books, you're successful. If you don't, you're not."

By the 1990 fiscal year Bertelsmann should have an operating profit of around $600 million and net income of around $270 million, according to Wössner. "By then we expect to have the same quality business as we had before the acquisitions, and to be comparable in profitability to Daimler-Benz," he says. Of that $600 million operating profit, RCA Records and Doubleday should together contribute at least $120 million, and perhaps as much as $180 million—less than one-fifth what Wössner paid for them. This will help finance Wössner's intended plunge into the Far East, where Bertelsmann has virtually no presence.

Wössner, 49, also says he is preparing an attack on the U.S. magazine business. It will be Bertelsmann's second attempt. In the early 1980s Bertelsmann failed spectacularly when it lost an estimated $45 million on a U.S. version of *Geo,* Europe's *National Geographic*-style magazine. But for Wössner, failure is something that is to be learned from, not to be discouraged by.

"It was an expensive lesson," Wössner concedes. "We never had such tough competition, and we were just not prepared. We learned a lot of respect for the American media market." Which he is about to start applying. ■

'Round the World with TV and Video

In this survey of the world media, *Channels* magazine describes developments and advancements in television and video in other countries.

Consider:

1. In which nation(s) do the media seem to be greatly different from those in the United States?

2. In which nation(s) do the media seem to be closely similar to those in the United States?

3. How do the media in China, Japan, and the Soviet Union compare with those in Western European countries?

4. How do the media in Brazil, Mexico, and India compare with the U.S. media?

Beyond the American Screen

ADAM SNYDER

Australia Last summer's [1986] media-ownership-and-control law, which allows a company to own TV stations up to a 60 percent maximum national audience reach and forbids anyone from owning a major TV station and newspaper in the same city, sparked a wave of buying and selling that has changed the makeup of the Australian television scene. Alan Bond, a company called Northern Star Holdings and Christopher Skase have replaced Rupert Murdoch, Kerry Packer and John Fairfax Ltd. as the three largest players. Dominance of the airwaves is particularly important since free TV is pretty much the only game in town. Cable television is not expected before 1990.

Adam Snyder is a free-lance writer.

Brazil Brazil is unable to pay the interest on its massive debt, so it's no surprise that there are few dollars available to purchase foreign programming. This, combined with a strong sense of nationalism, means that most of the country's television is produced domestically. For example, 95 percent of Brazilian network TV Globo's 5:30 to 11 P.M. schedule is created internally. All stations can take advantage of low labor costs and the best production know-how in Latin America to export shows around the world. Led by its expansion-minded founder, Roberto Marinho Sr., TV Globo continues to dominate the scene, recording as much as 80 percent of the country's TV ad revenue. TV Globo has entered the U.S. market with The Portuguese Channel, watched by some 220,000 subscribers in Massachusetts and Rhode

Island. Home video is on the rise in Brazil, but an estimated 75 to 80 percent of the prerecorded cassette business is controlled by pirates.

Canada The state-run Canadian Broadcasting Corp., although operating at a deficit, maintains its status as the most accessible Canadian television service, boasting a 99 percent market reach. Large numbers of viewers still turn to its competitors, however: CTV, Global TV and TV Ontario, along with a variety of cable networks. Yankee programs continue to dominate Canadian viewing, and the government continues to try and stem the influx. In a switch, the U.S. industry has developed a growing dependency on Canada. Chiefly because of the favorable dollar-to-dollar exchange rate, numerous U.S. network and syndicated shows are being shot there. The attempt now will be to export Canadian programming, which could be aided by technological innovations such as the world's first miniseries to be shot in high-definition video: *Chasing Rainbows,* a 14-hour series about two World War I soldiers, aired in 1988. Canadian broadcasters face pressure to increase domestically produced prime time drama by the 1991–92 season, but budget increases are far below the inflation rate. Meanwhile, competing entertainment sources are growing rapidly: VCR penetration levels rose from 23.4 percent in '85 to 35 percent in '86, and cable systems have increased from 562 in '81 to 950.

China China Central Television runs the show, supplemented by local, government-owned channels in large cities. About half of all airtime is devoted to political programming—often consisting of longwinded speeches. As part of the preparations for the nationwide sixth annual National Games, held in the southern Chinese province of Guangdong in November, authorities dismantled hundreds of thousands of TV antennas tuned to Hong Kong and the nearby Portuguese colony of Macao. Western programs are beginning to air legitimately, however. Worldvision sold 24 episodes of *Little House on the Prairie* to CCTV, which in turn contracted IBS, an

American firm, to sell advertising time in the series to multinational companies. Thirty-second spots went for $10,000 apiece. *Little House* was seen by more than 100 million Chinese, and negotiations are underway for a second season of the show (for which Worldvision reportedly would sell the advertising time itself). Lorimar-Telepictures also has made a significant sale of programs to China.

France In just three years France has deregulated its TV industry, doubling its networks from three to six and placing four of them under private ownership. The question now is whether ad revenues can rise fast enough to support the four. The expected launch of the satellite TDF-1 could add another four private channels as early as spring [1988], although given the history of European DBS, further postponement is likely. Canal Plus, an over-the-air pay-TV service that relies heavily on theatrical films, is the industry's most impressive success. Losses totalled $100 million during its first two years, but in its third fiscal year it could boast 1.9 million subscribers and profits of about $32 million on revenues of $555 million. TF-1 has begun airing two U.S. soap operas, *General Hospital* and *One Life to Live.* And *La Roue de la Fortune,* the French version of King World's American hit *Wheel of Fortune,* has become the country's top game show. The lifting of a 33 percent tax on VCRs has helped the French video market. About 3 million videocassettes were sold in 1987, compared to only 850,000 in 1986. Cable wiring continues to move slowly, however. Fewer than 20 percent of French households will have cable during the next ten years.

India The Indian people are in the midst of a love affair with television since the arrival of commercial broadcasting. TV sets and VCRs have become popular dowry items. And since *The Lucy Show* debuted in India, hundreds of baby girls have been named Lucy—not exactly a traditional Indian name. On Tuesday and Saturday evenings, when the wildly popular soap opera *Buniyaad* airs, the country's frenzied pace slows to a virtual stop. In just three years the number of TV sets has jumped from 6 million to more than 10 million. By 1990, the number of evening viewers is expected to jump from 45 million to 260 million people. The government strictly controls TV fare, particularly news, so viewers don't see the latest violent clashes between Hindus and Muslims. A special by U.S. columnist Jack Anderson, *Rajiv Gandhi's India,* made with government approval, was canceled one hour before transmission. There are 872 languages and dialects in India but most shows are in Hindi, leading many to urge that more broadcast time be turned over to the states to produce television programs in their local tongues.

Italy   Another year [1987] has gone by without the passage of an Italian broadcasting bill, and after all this time there's little reason to think legislation will be enacted any time soon. In this regulatory vacuum, the state-financed RAI continues to be the only network allowed to broadcast live, although competitor Rete A recently challenged the law by going on the air with a national news report. If a new law *is* ever enacted, rumor has it that Silvio Berlusconi might drop one of his three non-interconnected networks in exchange for the right to broadcast live nationwide. Berlusconi, who recently raided RAI's top talent pool, is also the chief beneficiary of Italy's rising ad revenues. Italian TV has given a huge boost to the recently ailing Italian film industry, financing, at least in part, 80 percent of Italy's film productions. Increased talks on both sides of the ocean continue concerning coproductions. American syndicator Harmony Gold, for instance, has coproductions underway with both RAI and Berlusconi's ReteEuropa.

Japan   The rapidly changing European environment contrasts dramatically with the calm of Japanese television. The number of TV network stations that could operate per market had been limited to two, though that is changing and more are being allowed. Cable growth is slow at best. Shows from the U.S., which in recent years have not done well, seem to be making a comeback in prime time. *Dallas,* a huge international success,

originally flopped in Japan but is doing better after scheduling changes. In October the Tokyo Broadcasting Company began airing *The CBS Evening News with Dan Rather,* scheduling the newscast Tuesdays through Saturdays between 12:30 A.M. and 1:30 A.M. The show can be heard in either Japanese or English through dual audio channels, which many Japanese TV sets are equipped to receive.

Mexico   The four private stations (two national, two regional) owned by the media powerhouse Televisa continue to dwarf the seldom-watched state-run stations. Televisa controls many other areas of entertainment as well and is said to receive about 70 percent of all advertising money in Mexico. It also owns the cable TV outlet in Mexico City, although revenue is limited since advertisements on cable are prohibited. All broadcasters are well aware that nearly 60 percent of Mexico's 83 million people are 25 or younger. A wave of new miniseries focusing on Mexico's past are aimed at acquainting young people with the country's revolutionary and historic leaders. Forty-five percent of all programming, however, is imported, with the most popular shows—*Falcon Crest, Dynasty* and *Hill Street Blues*—hailing from the U.S.

Spain   New legislation in 1987 has paved the way for three private channels although government regulations make many wonder if the Socialist government, which at present controls the two state-run channels, is really interested in any change. The new law mandates that at least 40 percent of a new station's programming be produced in Spain, and that half of its feature films be produced in Common Market countries; commercials may not exceed 10 percent of airtime. The most controversial provision is that no one may own more than 25 percent of any network—or 15 percent if the person or company owns as much as 15 percent of another Spanish media outlet. Ironically, this gives foreigners like Robert Maxwell and Silvio Berlusconi an advantage over Spanish media barons because the foreigners don't have other media properties in Spain. As the owner of a major Madrid studio, Berlusconi already has a foothold here, and Maxwell personally met with King Juan Carlos to lobby for the 25 percent rule.

Sweden Four subsidiaries of the Swedish Broadcasting Corporation control television, national and local radio and educational radio. The two television channels have been restructured and renamed SVT/Channel-1 and SVT/Channel-2. A rivalry has already sprung up between the smaller second channel, nicknamed "the peasant channel," and its better-financed sister, dubbed "the Stockholm channel." Both stations will have international acquisition budgets. The legalization of individual reception of satellite channels at the beginning of 1985, the lack of movement on a much talked about commercial station and the country's high percentage of English-speaking citizens have combined to make Sweden one of Europe's hottest markets for backyard satellite dishes and videocassette sales. TV advertising is not expected unless the Social Democratic Party loses power. That's not considered likely anytime soon, although Swedish advertising agencies are preparing for the eventuality by perfecting their skills producing public service announcements.

United Kingdom The Tory government has directed both the BBC and the commercial ITV to turn over one quarter of their production to independent producers, or risk legislation that will mandate the transfer. The percentage is being challenged by both networks, which want to maintain control of their programming, but it is certain that British broadcasters will be commissioning more from outside suppliers. ITV has been under attack for its reluctance to open the network to outside producers, as well as for its advertising monopoly that has allowed profits to soar without providing an incentive to produce more quality programs. A move to allow advertising on the BBC has failed; it will continue to be financed (to the tune of about $1 billion a year) by annual receiver-license fees. Meanwhile, Rupert Murdoch has lost some $30 million over the last five years operating Sky Channel, his pan-European satellite network, and he reportedly plans to bring in investors or a partner. Sky Channel currently reaches about 92 percent of cable subscribers in Europe, and its next great challenge lies in easing restrictions on advertising in several of its major markets. MTV launched in August; Superchannel continues to encounter problems.

USSR *Glasnost* has come to Soviet television in the form of more straightforward reporting of domestic problems, although information on Western events and philosophy is still heavily censored. There are two national channels, one reaching 90 percent of the population, the other, 48 percent. The annual budget for TV and radio combined is more than $3 billion, with over two-thirds of the total going to television. Airtime on the channel with the greatest reach is split primarily between films (20–25 percent), news (15 percent), music programs (15 percent), stage productions (12 percent) and children's shows (10 percent). About 170 films are produced each year. Soviet TV purchases some programs from the West, mostly classic dramas, but has a self-imposed ceiling for what it will pay—$15,000 per show or series. Nonetheless, it is slowly becoming a viable market. The national television network has to contend with the logistical nightmare of broadcasting in 45 languages to ten time zones.

West Germany The two established non-private channels, ARD and ZDF, allow only 20 minutes of advertising per day, but new private cable operations, such as SAT 1 and Luxembourg's German-language RTL Plus, are under no such restrictions. They have other problems, however, mainly weak signals, low ad revenues and meager budgets, compared with their wealthy, state-financed competitors. Thanks to a talk/entertainment program launched late last year by RTL Plus, Germans can now watch early morning television for the first time. ARD and ZDF may soon launch an early morning competitor. Silvio Berlusconi has expanded his media empire into West Germany with a 45 percent stake in Kabel Media Programm Gesellschaft, operator of Musicbox, the 24-hour satellite-to-cable music-video service. ∎

Worldwide Advertising Sales

This chart from *Advertising Age* details the top 10 advertisers in the major advertising markets throughout the world in 1986. Which company names do you recognize?

Top 10 Ad Spenders Around the Globe

Ranked in the following 34 tables are the largest advertisers in the world, representing spending in 41 countries.

Marketers ranked in the Arabian Peninsula's top ten represent ad dollars spent in Saudi Arabia, Kuwait, United Arab Emirates, Bahrain, Qatar, Oman and Jordan. Belgium's top ten includes ad spending in Luxembourg.

Sources and exchange rates are listed beneath tables. For more information on this report, see *Where Ad Age Got Its Data,* page [333].

AFRICA

South Africa

| Advertiser | Ad spending | |
	1986	1985
Unilever	9,860	8,999
O.K. Bazaars	8,121	7,813
Checkers	7,143	3,838
Pick & Pay	7,059	6,443
S.A. Breweries	6,166	5,491
Toyota Motor Corp.	6,157	6,085
United Tobacco S.A.	4,498	3,680
Oudemeester	3,583	4,027
SFW	3,527	3,603
Ford Motor Co.	3,469	3,722

Source: Market Research Africa Adindex. Notes: Dollars are in thousands and include measured media only. Conversion rate: 0.4284 dollars to the Rand.

ASIA

Arabian Peninsula

| Advertiser | Ad spending | |
	1986	1985
Philip Morris Cos.	6,652	N/A
Rothmans International	3,567	N/A
Toyota Motor Corp.	3,454	N/A
Nissan Motor Co. Ltd.	3,401	N/A
Hattori Seiko Corp.	1,773	N/A
Rado	1,557	N/A
Loews Corp.	1,447	N/A

Source: Pan Arab Research Centre, Kuwait. Notes: Dollars are in thousands. Includes Saudi Arabia, United Arab Emirates, Kuwait, Bahrain, Qatar, Oman and Jordan for year-ending April 1986.

Hong Kong

Advertiser	Ad spending	
	1986	1985
Philip Morris Cos.	7,065	N/A
Hong Tai Travel	4,634	N/A
Wing On Group	4,497	N/A
Vita Drinks	3,835	N/A
Matsushita Electric Industrial Co.	3,643	N/A
Loews Corp.	3,509	N/A
Morning Star Travel	3,371	N/A
RJR Nabisco	3,132	N/A
Hattori-Seiko Co. Ltd.	3,119	N/A
Mild Seven	2,813	N/A

Source: Hong Kong Abex, a subsidiary of AGB McNair.
Note: Dollars are in thousands.

India

Advertiser	Ad spending	
	1986	1985
Unilever	16,809	12,308
Colgate-Palmolive Co.	4,137	3,952
McDowell & Co. Ltd.	3,893	2,378
Peico Electronics & Electricals	3,561	2,663
ITC Ltd.	3,236	2,826
Claxo Laboratories	2,758	1,948
Escorts Ltd.	2,701	2,374
Bombay Dyeing Ltd.	2,646	1,974
Bata India Ltd.	2,221	1,474
Tata Oils Mills	2,173	1,401

Source: Economic Times Research Bureau, New Delhi.
Notes: Dollars are in thousands for years-ending March 1986 and 1985. Conversion rate: 0.0805 dollars to the Rupee.

Indonesia

Advertiser	Ad spending	
	1986	1985
Unilever	3,129	N/A
Suzuki Motor Co.	1,473	N/A
Toyota Motor Corp.	1,388	N/A
Daihatsu Cars	1,169	N/A
Lux Soap	774	N/A
Baygon Insecticide	765	N/A
Citra Lotion	740	N/A
Dancow Milk Powder	732	N/A

Source: Advertising Age. Notes: Dollars are in thousands. Conversion rate: 0.000841 dollars to the Rupiah.

Japan

Advertiser	Ad spending	
	1986	1985
Kao Corp.	184,758	177,311
Honda Motor Co. Ltd.	184,470	149,006
Toyota Motor Corp.	173,428	175,890
Nissan Motor Co. Ltd.	163,136	158,007
Matsushita Electric Industrial Co.	160,211	158,939
Hitachi Ltd.	158,117	152,328
Mazda Motor Corp.	155,584	120,795
NEC Corp.	148,425	115,596
Sony Corp.	142,471	106,960
Toshiba Corp.	140,741	151,988

Source: MOF Portfolio Reports, Tokyo. Notes: Dollars are in thousands for years-ending March 1986 and 1985. Figures do not include foreign company ad spending. Conversion rate: 0.005769 dollars to the Yen.

Malaysia

Advertiser	Ad spending	
	1986	1985
Rothmans International	14,819	7,623
Malaysian Tobacco Co.	11,334	8,869
Nupro	7,516	8,031
Unilever	4,514	3,085
Colgate-Palmolive	4,325	3,352
RJR Nabisco	3,463	3,641
Matsushita Electric Industrial Co.	1,825	3,324
Ederan Otomobil Nasional Sdn. Bhd.	1,528	849
Guinness	1,289	N/A
Toyota Motor Corp.	1,229	2,304

Source: Survey Research Malaysia. Notes: Dollars are in thousands and include TV, radio, newspaper, magazine and video. Conversion rate: 0.433 dollars to the Mdollar.

New Zealand

Advertiser	Ad spending	
	1986	1985
FTC Farmers	4,839	N/A
F.W. Woolworth Co.	3,538	N/A
New World Supermarkets	3,330	N/A
Smith & Brown	1,680	N/A
McDonald's Corp.	1,349	N/A
Four Square	1,329	N/A
United Building Society	1,275	N/A

(continued)

New Zealand

Advertiser	Ad spending 1986	1985
NZ Listener	1,240	N/A
Foodtown	1,194	N/A
PepsiCo Inc.	1,139	N/A

Source: Hunter: AGB Ltd., Auckland. Notes: Dollars are in thousands and include TV and print only. Conversion rate: 0.5252 dollars to the NZdollar.

Philippines

Advertiser	Ad spending 1986	1985
San Miguel Corp.	767	N/A
Nestle SA	639	N/A
Colgate-Palmolive Co.	613	N/A
Philippine Refining	613	N/A
Procter & Gamble Co.	409	N/A
California Manufacturing	153	N/A
Warner-Lambert Co.	102	N/A
Philip Morris Cos.	77	N/A
Johnson & Johnson	61	N/A
RJR Nabisco	41	N/A

Source: J. Walter Thompson Co., Manila. Notes: Dollars are in thousands and include measured and unmeasured media. Conversion rate: 0.0511 dollars to the Peso.

Singapore

Advertiser	Ad spending 1986	1985
Yaohan Stores	1,623	N/A
American Express Co.	1,577	N/A
McDonald's Corp.	1,438	N/A
PepsiCo Inc.	1,113	N/A
Federal Publication	1,020	N/A
Metro Stores	881	N/A
Singapore International Airlines	881	N/A
Guinness	835	N/A
Citicorp	696	N/A
Matsushita Electric Industrial Co.	696	N/A

Source: Survey Research Singapore Ltd. Notes: Dollars are in thousands. Conversion rate: 0.4638 dollars to the Sdollar.

South Korea

Advertiser	Ad spending 1986	1985
Goldstar & Lucky Ltd.	29,232	23,446
Samsung Electronics & Jeil Sugar	27,932	25,981
Daewoo Electronics & Motors	17,883	12,810
Pacific Chemical	14,800	12,934
Lotte Confectionary	8,794	6,676
Nhong Shim	8,619	8,817
Yuhan Corp.	7,785	7,134
Samyang Foods	7,743	5,916
Dong-A Pharmaceuticals	7,544	6,834
Hai-Tai Confectionary	7,483	6,874

Source: Korea First Advertising. Notes: Dollars are in thousands. Conversion rate: 0.001131 dollars to the Won.

Taiwan

Advertiser	Ad spending 1986	1985
China Airlines	8,967	N/A
Peiuf Enterprises	8,533	N/A
President Enterprises Corp.	6,693	N/A
Matsushita Electric Industrial Co.	5,663	N/A
Anping Distributors Ltd.	4,376	N/A
Weichuan Foods Corp.	3,919	N/A
Sanyo Electric Co. Ltd.	3,802	N/A
Taiwan Kao Corp.	3,500	N/A
Hey-Song Corp.	3,383	N/A
Formosa United Industrial Corp.	3,349	N/A

Source: Advertising Age. Notes: Dollars are in thousands. Figures were reported in U.S. dollars.

AUSTRALIA

Australia

Advertiser	Ad spending 1986	1985
G.J. Coles & Co. Ltd.	63,813	53,382
Mars Inc.	27,067	21,932
Unilever	19,441	17,094
Australian Gov't	18,936	11,704
Telecom Australia	17,445	13,478

(continued)

Advertiser	Ad spending 1986	1985
F.W. Woolworth Co.	15,842	16,292
Cadbury Schweppes PLC	14,797	16,311
Reckitt & Colman PLC	14,480	12,926
Nissan Motor Co. Ltd.	12,969	10,085
Amatil Ltd.	12,861	12,478

Source: Tart Research, Brookvale, Australia. Notes: Dollars are in thousands and include all measured media. Conversion rate: 0.6769 dollars to the Adollar.

EUROPE

Austria

Advertiser	Ad spending 1986	1985
Unilever	9,383	17,541
Henkel	7,301	7,484
Creditanstalt Bankverein	3,956	2,726
Drogeriemarkt	3,754	3,022
Procter & Gamble Co.	3,527	4,638
Kastner & Orhler	3,515	2,461
BAWAG	3,269	3,048
Kika Moebelhandel	2,934	2,751
Billa Konzern	2,814	2,398
Kleider-Bauer	2,650	2,335

Source: A.C. Nielsen & Co. and MMO Media and Market Observer. Notes: Dollars are in thousands. Conversion rate: 0.0631 dollars to the Schilling.

Belgium

Advertiser	Ad spending 1986	1985
Procter & Gamble Co.	7,848	8,342
GB-Inno-BM	7,224	8,063
BSN-Gervais Danone	7,160	5,805
Henkel	6,493	5,913
D'Ieteren	6,192	6,515
Peugeot	5,848	5,440
Ford Motor Co.	5,784	4,429
Delhaize Le Lion	5,698	5,612
Unilever	5,676	4,085
Mars Inc.	5,633	4,924

Source: Advertising Marketing Services, Brussels. Notes: Dollars are in thousands and include all public measured media in Belgium and Luxembourg. Conversion rate: 0.0215 dollars to the Bfrancs.

Finland

Advertiser	Ad spending 1986	1985
Valio	10,938	6,457
Kesko	7,620	6,282
SYP	7,039	N/A
Korpivaara	6,515	5,449
Saastopankit + SKOP	6,360	5,662
Verikkaus	5,604	N/A
Aro-yhtyma	5,410	N/A
Osuuspankit + OKO	5,197	4,789
Ford Motor Co.	4,654	4,363
OP-Kiinteistokeskus	4,266	4,324

Source: Markkinatutlimus OY, Helsinki. Notes: Dollars are in thousands and include measured media only. Conversion rate: 0.1939 dollars to the Markka.

France

Advertiser	Ad spending 1986	1985
Renault	83,927	73,096
Loterie Nationale	48,333	34,009
Nestle SA	41,192	35,384
Ford Motor Co.	40,911	36,085
Procter & Gamble Co.	36,310	41,978
Peugeot	36,225	27,513
Colgate-Palmolive Co.	35,945	26,517
Citroen	30,094	26,517
Intermarche Magasins	29,786	21,564
General Motors Corp.	28,481	26,180

Source: SECODIP, Paris. Notes: Dollars are in thousands. Conversion rate: 0.1403 dollars to the Franc.

Ireland

Advertiser	Ad spending 1986	1985
Procter & Gamble Co.	85,751	47,374
Guinness	54,092	52,160
Kellogg Co.	39,294	32,870
Mars Inc.	32,398	30,988
Rowntree Mackintosh	28,851	30,988
Unilever	27,524	47,374
Cadbury Schweppes PLC	27,477	24,545
Coca-Cola Co.	26,340	12,371
Ford Motor Co.	24,979	19,134
P.J. Carroll	22,475	16,177

Source: Advertising Statistics Ireland. Notes: Dollars are in thousands and include measured media only. Conversion rate: 1.313 dollars to the Pound.

Italy

Advertiser	Ad spending 1986	1985
Procter & Gamble Co	116,210	62,085
Unilever	100,560	39,299
Fiat SpA	94,344	101,529
Barilla Pasta	64,945	43,418
Renault	56,241	36,460
Sagit	51,447	32,755
Alfa Lancia	50,161	31,052
Fater	48,323	32,940
Colgate-Palmolive Co.	47,463	25,123
Mattel Inc.	44,018	36,119

Source: AGB Italia SpA, Milan. Notes: Dollars are in thousands and represent gross ad expenditures. It is custom in Italy to take a 40% to 60% discount. Conversion rate: 0.000648 dollars to the Lira.

Netherlands

Advertiser	Ad spending 1986	1985
Unilever	19,268	N/A
Mars Inc.	8,032	N/A
Heineken B.V.	7,159	N/A
Vendex	6,880	N/A
NV Philips	6,767	N/A
Postbank NV	6,652	N/A
Akzo Adv. Coord. Groep	6,427	N/A
Rijksvoorlichtingsdienst	6,132	N/A
Henkel	5,343	N/A
Ned. Zuivelburo	5,275	N/A

Source: VEA. Notes: Dollars are in thousands and do not include regional advertisers or direct mail. Conversion rate: 0.3934 dollars to the Guilder.

Portugal

Advertiser	Ad spending 1986	1985
Unilever	4,461	2,199
Central Cerverjas	2,109	1,129
Nestle SA	2,036	1,537
Santa Casa de Misericordia	1,838	2,312
	1,510	855
Colgate-Palmolive Co.	1,509	909
Renault	1,334	1,029
FIMA	1,314	1,039

Advertiser	Ad spending 1986	1985
S.C. Johnson & Son	1,007	789
Unicer	972	N/A
Knorr Portuguesa		

Source: Lintas: Worldwide, Lisbon.
Notes: Dollars are in thousands. Conversion rate: 0.006683 dollars to the Escudo.

Spain

Advertiser	Ad spending 1986	1985
El Corte Ingles Group	28,115	23,823
Peugeot	26,014	20,919
Volkswagen AG	25,205	24,207
Renault	24,451	19,328
Nestle SA	23,913	14,937
Unilever	23,851	15,496
Ministry of Economy	22,036	21,813
Henkel	22,015	13,758
Ford Motor Co.	16,536	12,669
BSN-Gervais Danone	14,798	13,094

Source: Annual Report on Advertising Expenditures by J. Walter Thompson Co., based on Repress/Nielsen data. Notes: Dollars are in thousands and include measured media, direct marketing, point of sale, promotions, trade fairs, annual reports and brochures. Conversion rate: 0.00698 dollars to the Peseta.

Sweden

Advertiser	Ad spending 1986	1985
Kooperativa Forbundet	53,528	51,277
ICA	47,534	46,609
Ahlens	14,735	12,139
B & W Stormarknader	11,172	6,988
Hennes & Mauritz	9,170	8,203
Kapp Ahl	6,808	5,234
Samhallsinformations Kommun/Landsting	6,781	6,380
Volvo AB	6,463	7,457
Favor-Butikerna	6,394	5,648
Televerket	5,759	5,524

Source: Reklamstatistik. Notes: Dollars are in thousands and include daily newspapers only. Conversion rate: 0.1381 dollars to the Kroner.

Switzerland

Advertiser	Ad spending 1986	1985
Migros	36,165	36,767
Co-op	26,251	22,936
Denner	10,737	10,057
General Motors Corp.	10,006	9,657
Toyota Motor Corp.	9,928	8,911
Pfister Moebel	7,276	5,988
Maus Brothers	7,169	6,954
Mars Inc.	6,763	4,992
Volkswagen AG	6,491	6,451
Nissan Motor Co. Ltd.	6,404	5,212

Source: A.C. Nielsen & Co. Notes: Dollars are in thousands. Conversion rate: 0.5371 dollars to the Sfranc.

United Kingdom

Advertiser	Ad spending 1986	1985
Unilever	156,171	179,192
British Government	119,414	46,631
Mars Inc.	68,690	82,647
Hanson Trust PLC	66,412	N/A
Allied-Lyons	59,139	53,410
Asda MFI Group	56,201	55,311
Nestle SA	53,279	59,437
British Telecom	52,968	60,582
Procter & Gamble Co.	51,763	70,029
British Gas	48,323	8,166

Source: Campaign magazine, from Haymarket Publishing: The Top 100 Spenders, June 13, 1986. Notes: Dollars are in thousands. Conversion rate: 1.4679 dollars to the Pound.

West Germany

Advertiser	Ad spending 1986	1985
Siemens	208,936	N/A
Unilever NV	102,915	88,276
C&A Brenninkmeyer	95,596	94,487
Volkswagen AG	60,951	59,886
Henkel	60,773	54,563
General Motors Corp.	51,458	36,375
Karstadt	47,554	47,909
Mars Inc.	43,162	33,714
Ford Motor Co.	41,787	34,157
Deutsche Bundespost	39,480	32,826

Source: Schmidt & Pohlmann, a subsidiary of A.C. Nielsen & Co. Notes: Dollars are in thousands. Conversion rate: 0.4436 dollars to the Mark.

N. AMERICA

Canada

Advertiser	Ad spending 1986	1985
Canadian Government	45,912	51,443
Procter & Gamble Co.	36,858	33,344
John Labatt Ltd.	27,097	24,694
Unilever	23,102	22,421
Molson Breweries	23,075	21,347
Philip Morris Cos.	22,522	21,321
General Motors Corp.	19,714	22,404
Gov't of Ontario	18,759	25,117
Thomson Group	17,300	12,645
RJR Nabisco	16,162	18,416

Source: Media Measurement Services, Toronto. Notes: Dollars are in thousands. Conversion rate: 0.721 dollars to the Cdollar.

Mexico

Advertiser	Ad spending 1986	1985
Pedro Domecq	12,740	N/A
Procter & Gamble Co.	12,740	N/A
Bacardi Corp.	11,830	N/A
Grupo Cuauhtemoc	9,828	N/A
Colgate-Palmolive Co.	9,646	N/A
Nestle SA	9,464	N/A
Organisacion Bimbo	9,100	N/A
PepsiCo	6,552	N/A
Gamesa	6,188	N/A
Kellogg Co.	5,824	N/A

Source: PMP Group, Mexico City. Notes: Dollars are in thousands and include TV ad expenditures only. Conversion rate: 0.00182 dollars to the Peso.

Puerto Rico

Advertiser	Ad spending 1986	1985
Colgate-Palmolive Co.	7,952	6,540
Procter & Gamble Co.	7,220	6,793
Sears, Roebuck & Co.	6,684	4,398
Unilever	6,465	6,092
Bacardi Corp.	4,672	N/A
Banco Popular Puerto Rico	4,273	1,575
Schaefer Brewing	3,318	1,901

(continued)

Puerto Rico

Advertiser	Ad spending 1986	1985
Mars Inc.	2,536	538
Gillette Co.	2,434	1,533
Anheuser-Busch Cos.	2,225	1,430

Source: Publish Records Service, San Juan. Notes: Dollars are in thousands and include TV and print media spending only.

United States

Advertiser	Ad spending 1986	1985
Procter & Gamble Co.	1,435	1,600
Philip Morris Cos.	1,364	1,400
Sears, Roebuck & Co.	1,005	800
RJR Nabisco	935	1,093
General Motors Corp.	839	779
Ford Motor Co.	649	615
Anheuser-Busch Cos.	644	523
McDonald's Corp.	592	550
K mart Corp.	590	567
PepsiCo	581	478

Source: Advertising Age 100 Leading National Advertisers, September 24, 1987, including data from BAR/LNA reports. Media Records, Radio Expenditure Reports, Rome Reports and AGRICOM. Notes: Dollars are in millions and include measured and unmeasured media.

S. AMERICA

Argentina

Advertiser	Ad spending 1986	1985
Aurora	12,092	2,788
Philip Morris Cos.	9,034	2,981
Batus Industries	8,123	3,717
NV Philips	7,379	3,007
Unilever	6,004	3,291
S.C. Johnson & Son	5,567	N/A
Kenia Saic	5,022	1,122
Jacobs Suchard	4,730	2,321
Loterie Chaquena	4,627	3,156
Drean	4,544	1,059

Source: Fuentes & CIA, Buenos Aires. Notes: Dollars are in thousands and include TV ad spending only. Conversion rate: 1.184 dollars to the Austral.

Brazil

Advertiser	Ad spending 1986	1985
Grupo Dorsay	25,287	13,338
Grupo Pao de Acucar	18,070	10,772
Unilever	13,520	6,295
Nestle SA	11,884	5,735
Lopes Cons Imoveis	11,484	2,042
Mesbla	10,867	7,080
Lundgren	10,234	4,870
NV Philips	10,220	4,884
CX Economica Federal	10,052	2,973
B.A.T. Industries	9,725	6,433

Source: Advertising Age. Notes: Dollars are in thousands and include measured media only. Conversion rate: 0.072686 dollars to the Cruzado.

Chile

Advertiser	Ad spending 1986	1985
Unilever	12,547	N/A
Nestle SA	6,368	N/A
Coca-Cola Co.	3,359	N/A
Bayer AG	3,196	N/A
Corona	2,783	N/A
CCU	2,698	N/A
Comercial Eccsa	2,530	N/A
El Mercurio	2,459	N/A
Editorial Portada	2,310	N/A
La Tercera	2,142	N/A

Source: Megatec, Santiago. Notes: Dollars are in thousands. Conversion rate: 0.0054 dollars to the Peso.

Colombia

Advertiser	Ad spending 1986	1985
Colgate-Palmolive Co.	7,663	N/A
Unilever	6,642	N/A
Postobon	5,017	N/A
Nestle SA	4,293	N/A
Technoquimicas	2,711	N/A
Varela	2,624	N/A
Gillette Co.	2,603	N/A
Disa	2,446	N/A
Cine Colombia	1,998	N/A
Federacion Natl. de Cafeteros	1,814	N/A

Source: A.C. Nielsen & Co. Notes: Dollars are in thousands and include measured media only. Conversion rate: 0.0054 dollars to the Peso.

Where Ad Age *Got Its Data*

KEVIN BROWN

Advertising Age in this special section takes a look at worldwide advertising from both the media and advertiser side.

In its first ranking of the 50 largest non-U.S. advertisers, *Ad Age* pooled ad totals from its international reporting network and sources around the world.

Rankings of advertisers from 34 regions on six continents were compiled, including the Arabian Peninsula, Hong Kong, India, Indonesia, Japan, Malaysia, New Zealand, Philippines, Singapore, South Korea, Taiwan, Argentina, Brazil, Chile, Colombia, Australia, Austria, Belgium, Finland, France, West Germany, Ireland, Italy, the Netherlands, Portugal, Spain, Sweden, Switzerland, the U.K., Canada, Mexico, Puerto Rico, South Africa and the U.S.

The Arabian Peninsula includes Saudi Arabia, United Arab Emirates, Kuwait, Bahrain, Qatar, Oman and Jordan. Belgium includes spending in Luxembourg.

Although every effort was made to compile advertising expenditures by these companies in all countries, only rankings of the top 10 advertisers were available in some countries.

Data from several countries was reported by brand, rather than by advertiser. Brand spending was added into parent company spending wherever possible. Also, in some instances, local

Kevin Brown is a reporter for *Advertising Age.*

sources compiled parent company spending by monitoring brand spending—but only including brands closely associated with the parent company. This resulted in some low local parent total spending figures.

Local sources and media information are listed beneath the top ten advertisers by country.

Data from the U.S. is based on AA's 100 Leading National Advertisers, Sept. 4, 1987, and Second 100 Leading National Advertisers, Nov. 23, 1987.

BAR/LNA reports supplies the bulk of U.S. measured media information. Magazine and newspaper supplements are supplied to Leading National Advertisers by Publishers Information Bureau. Outdoor is supplied to LNA by the Outdoor Advertising Association of America and Institute of Outdoor Advertisers. Network TV, spot TV, network radio and cable TV networks are supplied by Broadcast Advertisers Reports.

Other U.S. monitored media include newspapers from Media Records, business publications from Rome Reports, farm publications from AGRICOM and spot radio from Radio Expenditure Reports.

U.S. advertising expenditures include estimated unmeasured media depending for direct mail, promotion, co-op and couponing, to name a few, unless otherwise noted.

The worldwide ranking includes all advertisers monitored by *Ad Age,* regardless of whether any foreign advertising expenditures were reported. ■

World Media Issues

CHAPTER SIXTEEN

The World as Media Marketplace

In this overview of the media's role, Communications Professor George Gerbner examines how decisions about the media in the United States hold implications for media throughout the world. Technology is creating a mass culture, says Gerbner, with many hazards.

Consider:

1. Do you agree with Gerbner that "the mechanisms that govern the mass media marketplace are those of property and money"? Why? Why not?

2. What would be the results of "concentration and conglomeration that tend toward the creation of an electronically based global empire"?

3. What is the danger, according to Gerbner, of "a centralized mass ritual like television . . . that reaches nearly every home in widespread and otherwise heterogeneous communities with the same system of messages"?

4. What does Gerbner mean when he says, "Consumers choose from what is made available to them in the cultural cafeteria. Citizens must choose the cafeteria"?

Ministry of Culture, the USA, and the "Free Marketplace of Ideas"

GEORGE GERBNER

A confluence of technological, institutional, and cultural currents, with television as their mainstream, is sweeping away the historical bases of democratic assumptions about the role of religion, politics, and the press in self-government. The situation calls for a new diagnosis of our predicament.

George Gerbner is professor of Communications and dean of the Annenberg School of Communications, University of Pennsylvania.

State and church ruled in the Middle Ages in a symbiotic relationship of mutual dependence and tension. State was the economic and political order; Church, its sometimes unruly cultural arm.

Capitalist revolutions separated the three orders. The political order became the public government; the economic order, a privately run government; and the mass media, the cultural arms of the economic order. The First Amendment to the Constitution of the United States tried to protect freedom of religion by forbidding its establishment; and freedom of speech and the press, by forbidding its abridgement by public government. The Founding Fathers did not foresee the rise of large conglomerates acting as private governments. Nor did they envision their cultural arms, the mass media, but especially television, forming a virtual private Ministry of Culture and Established Church rolled into one, influencing the socialization of all Americans. In licensing broadcasters and then letting the marketplace take its course, Congress has made law respecting the establishment of the modern equivalent of religion and has given a few giant conglomerates the right to abridge freedom of speech, something the elected public government is forbidden to do.

A book to be published next year by Sue Curry Jansen says: "There are no free markets, only markets controlled by capitalists, kings, communists or pirates, for markets are complex human organizations which cannot exist without order, hierarchy, power, and control." To put it bluntly, the market is plutocracy, not democracy. Markets are run by establishments that safeguard their own freedoms but do not confer them on others unless forced. Market-driven mass media like to speak in the name of the public but shun, marginalize, or criminalize public views not saleable to large groups of paying customers.

Freedom is the invention of outlaws, rebels, blasphemers, and others who challenge order, hierarchy, and control. They are more likely to be a nuisance or menace than profitable commodities to be supplied on demand. Their value for the survival of self-government is not set by the laws of supply and demand.

The mechanisms that govern the mass media marketplace are those of property and money. Such mechanisms include technology, capital investment needed to enter the communications marketplace, reliance on corporate sponsors, and relative insulation from democratic (public) participation in policymaking. These mechanisms generate the dynamics of concentration and conglomeration that tend toward the creation of an electronically based global empire. New communication technologies such as cable, cassettes, and VCRs, far from eroding the old, sharpen the aim and deepen the penetration of concentrated culture-power into new areas of life. Cable companies are on the way to becoming the usual Big Five or Big Three ruling the market with programs less diverse than those available through either network programming or the print media they replace. VCRs are used to see fewer network programs at more convenient times or to substitute for moviegoing and reading—but with fewer choices. "Free markets" in the telecommunicatons age achieve ideological homogeneity and deflect serious challenge to their hegemony more efficiently (and less conspicuously) than any laws publicly enacted.

Rulers always define freedom as what *they* do. Control of communications is necessary for the freedom of action of any establishment. Their freedom is the freedom to censor. Censorship is the rule, not the exception, in all societies. Democratic theory counters that imperative with the requirements of self-government in a society of conflicting interests.

Application of democratic theory is difficult, often painful, and always incomplete. It requires that we accept the subversive challenge, the occasional disruption, the periodic and unpleasant but vital shock of recognition.

The First Amendment permits the creation of the dynamics of social survival but does not secure them. In fact, current interpretations of the First Amendment provide a shield for their evasion.

Every modern political theory includes some conception of the role of the "press" in governance. A secular press of politics and commerce was instrumental to the rise of diverse mass publics independent of church and nobility. The press was (and is) a relatively specific and selectively used organ of the more literate of every class. Its hard-won freedom to express and advocate competing and conflicting ideologies and class, group, and political party interests was supposed to sustain the diversity necessary for self-government in a complex society.

The demise of the party press in the nineteenth century, and the subsequent decline of political parties themselves in the twentieth, made commercial mass media the primary means of communication with voters. Parties exist today mainly to raise money for television, allocate patronage, and maintain the illusion of choice. The principal challenge to democratic theory and practice today is the rise to dominance of a single, market-driven, advertiser-sponsored, and ideologically coherent media system claiming to represent diverse publics and invoking constitutional protection to preempt challenge to its controls.

Many studies document the trend toward media concentration. Two wire services, one near bankruptcy, supply most world and national news. Chains dominate the daily and weekly press, with the top ten controlling more than one-third of circulation. Only 4 percent of cities have competing newspapers. A strike can leave a city like Philadelphia without a daily paper for weeks. Magazines and books provide the most-varied fare, but electronically based conglomerates own the biggest publishing houses. Broadcasting is, of course, the most concentrated. The top one hundred advertisers pay for two-thirds of all network television. Three networks, increasingly allied to giant transnational corporate entities, what I call our private Ministry of Culture, control over 70 percent of the market. More importantly, they control programming for all people. "The greatest threat to journalistic independence and integrity is not the Jesse Helmses," a network news executive was reported saying, "and it's not the libel suit—it's red ink."

Entertainment—the universal source of information for those who seek no information—is even more constrained. Some fifty weekly series are cancelled every year, many without being given a fair chance to build a public. Many programs and films are made but never shown. A handful of huge conglomerates, probably not many more than forty, manage the bulk of mass media output. With the current "merger mania," their numbers are shrinking and their reach is expanding every year. Other interests, minority views, the potential to challenge dominant perspectives, lose ground with every merger.

There is not much ground to lose. The high point of ideological ferment following Allied victory in World War II provoked furious reaction: loyalty oaths, witch hunts, and intimidation were associated with the name of the late Senator McCarthy but were aided and abetted by timid and self-serving media. Their "free marketplace of ideas" had to be "saved from communism." But it did not save unions from being "purged"; radicals from being blacklisted or jailed; academic, political, and other leaders from being silenced.

The civil rights, women's, anti-war, gay, and environmental movements broke the chill of the fifties but provoked, by the seventies, the new virulence of fundamentalist and other orthodox attacks on minority rights, science, textbooks, education, and academic freedom. By then, however, the cultural mainstream itself had undergone a sea change. To appreciate its magnitude, we shall take a whirlwind tour of history from a communications perspective.

"If I were permitted to write all the ballads I need not care who makes the laws of the nation." Scotch patriot Andrew Fletcher made that comment in 1704. He may have been the first to recognize the governing power of a centralized system of "ballads"—the songs, legends, and stories that convey both information and what we call entertainment. Today we have such a system. It forms a compelling mythology reaching into every home, conferring power that kings, emperors, and popes could only dream about. To understand how this system came about, we need to recall what we are and how we reached our present predicament.

Humans interpret experience in a symbolic context. Most of what we know, or think we know, comes not from direct (i.e., nonsymbolic) experience but from the stories with which we grow up and through which we live in a world far beyond the reach of our senses.

There are three types of stories performing different (though often overlapping) functions. The first are stories of *how things work*. Usually called fiction or drama, they make the all-important but invisible structure of social relationships and the hidden dynamics of life visible and understandable.

Second are stories of *what things are*. These are the facts, the legends, the news selected to relate to social values and powers. They give credibility to each society's fantasies and alert it to threats and opportunities.

Third are stories of *what to do*. These are stories of value and choice. They present some behavior or style of life as desirable (or undesirable) and propose ways to attain (or avoid) it. These are sermons, instructions, laws. Today most of them are commercial messages in the media.

These three types of stories (or story functions) mingle in the process that weaves the fabric of culture. That is the symbolic environment in which humans grow, learn, and live like humans. They compose, in different combinations, what we call art, science, religion, education.

Until the invention of printing, all three types of stories were told face-to-face. A community was defined by the rituals and mythologies held in common. Stories memorized and recited or read and interpreted from rare manuscripts united the tribe or community into a coherent structure.

Then came printing. It was the industrial revolution in storytelling, a prerequisite for all the other upheavals to come. Printing broke up the ritual, challenged sacred interpretations, extended communities beyond previous boundaries of time and space. Printing ushered in the Reformation. Religious plurality paved the way for the rise of other pluralities. Consciousness of different religious, class, ethnic, and other interests, cultivated through the right (won after much struggle, but now again in doubt) to tell stories from competing and conflicting points of view, gave rise to modern mass publics. These publics are loose aggregations of people who never meet face-to-face and yet have much in common through the stories they share via media they can use for their own purposes. Modern theories of public policy formation assign the "press" the role of maintaining a diversity of publics reflect-ing and preserving a diversity of interests essential for self-government.

The latest transformation in storytelling is electronic. As print broke up the central mythology and ritual of the pre-industrial age, so television short-circuits the selective potentials of previous media. It is watched relatively nonselectively, by the clock rather than the program. It is the central mass-ritual of the telecommunications age. It abolishes isolation and parochialism and erodes pluralism. It reaches the previously unreachable with its streamlined and compelling centralized mythology. It tells "all the ballads" Andrew Fletcher wrote about, to all the children, parents, and grandparents at the same time. For the first time in history, children are born into a mass-produced, symbolic environment, which pervades the average home for more than seven hours a day. It is no longer the parent, the school, or the church but a distant corporation that tells most of the stories to most of the people most of the time, bringing to them the message and perspective of its sponsors.

We have studied that process for nearly two decades and found that television satisfies many previously felt religious needs for participating in a common ritual and for sharing beliefs about the meaning of life and the modes of right conduct. It is, therefore, not an exaggeration to suggest that the licensing of television represents the modern functional equivalent of government establishment of religion.

The essence of a centralized mass ritual like television is that it reaches nearly every home in widespread and otherwise heterogeneous communities with the same system of messages, bypassing family and other local channels and previous requirements for communication like mobility and literacy. This process tends to blur traditional social distinctions and class or minority interests, blend them into a more integrated perspective, and bend them to its own institutional interests.

The cultural tidal wave that is television alters viewers' conceptions of reality, shifts political orientations, and—vocal claims to the contrary—cultivates conformity and intolerance of differences. Provisions that had attempted to preserve fairness, plurality, and public participation in broadcast policy crumble under the impact of a shift of controls to ever-larger industrial combinations. This process is called deregulation and is justified by an appeal to the free marketplace. The trade paper *Variety* announced in its September 11, 1985, issue: "Diversity in the entertainment business, for decades the cornerstone of government policy and congressional oversight, seemingly has melted overnight into something akin to benign neglect." The last feeble remnant of broadcast fairness, the so-called Fairness Doctrine, was attacked by broadcasters as an infringement on their right to program as they (and their sponsors) please. The agency that was supposed to enforce the Doctrine decided to dismantle it because it "chills and coerces speech"—that is, the speech of sponsors. When Florida enacted a tax on advertising, those champions of the free marketplace of ideas proposed to blank out that state for national advertising,

further confounding the distinction between free speech and the possible most-profitable speech.

We have drifted into a historic dilemma from which there is no easy way out. Many democratic countries face this dilemma and try to resolve it in ways from which we can learn. An analytical and critical approach to the mass media is an essential requirement for making the choices consumers have to make, and even more, the choices citizens have to make. Consumers choose from what is made available to them in the cultural cafeteria. Citizens must choose the cafeteria.

Television is a mass and not a class act; the task is not to make it into an elite pastime. It is to begin the long process of public discussion about the resources, ideas, and actions needed to liberate this great medium from the constraints imposed on it by the mechanisms misnamed the "free marketplace." The task is to extend the First Amendment's prohibition of an establishment of religion and abridgement of free speech and press to private as well as public government. ∎

PERSPECTIVE 2

Western Videos Challenge State Control

When Western video meets Eastern European audiences, the result can be true culture shock. This article describes what is happening in Eastern bloc countries as a result of the importation of videos like "Rambo" and "Dallas."
   Consider:

1. What view of the United States are Eastern European audiences likely to form from the U.S. videos they see?

2. How has the VCR expanded access to Western culture in Eastern bloc nations?

3. How has the VCR expanded the access of Poles to their own culture?

East Europe on Cultural Fast Forward

JACKSON DIEHL

Warsaw—Like a gaudy cultural taunt, the M.W. video shop stands with bright yellow signs and flashing lights on a hill overlooking the Soviet embassy here. On the wall are posters advertising "Dallas" and "The Terminator," and on the shelves are thousands of video cassettes of mostly American films, ranging from "Citizen Kane" to "Rambo."

Although the cashier's window boasts a decal of the U.S. flag, this neatly kept converted garage has no ties to American business or diplomacy. Rather, M-W is simply one of dozens of private shops in this communist capital catering to a booming video market—and Poles' seemingly insatiable appetite for western entertainment.

"A VCR is a very useful gadget capable of serving various purposes," the state weekly *Polityka* noted recently. "But in Poland's situation . . . the first round has been won by 'Rocky.'"

In fact, Poland is the leader of a boom of video ownership in Eastern Europe that has significantly weakened state control over culture and information. In Poland, Hungary, Czechoslovakia and even Bulgaria, VCRs have become a mass phenomenon that has given millions of people access to long-taboo western products, ranging from pornography and adventure films to uncensored political news and documentaries.

Although their average yearly income barely equals the price of a video recorder, Poles have managed to acquire at least 700,000 western-built VCRs since 1981, or one for every 20 households in the country, official figures show. Hungary is estimated to have about 300,000 units, and Czechoslovakia at least 150,000.

In all three countries, millions of video cassettes with thousands of different programs are circulating through shops, clubs and hand-to-hand trade, in many cases without censorship or sanction by state authorities. And although a few East Bloc films are marketed on cassettes, almost all of the material available is western.

The story of how this explosion of independent culture came to pass is a classic example of how East Bloc states have fallen victim to their own technological backwardness and slowness to respond to innovations in communications.

It suggests that new policies of political and cultural *glasnost,* or openness, adopted by governments in Eastern Europe are in part a response to the breakdown of the state's ablity to control information.

Above all, the video phenomenon in Eastern Europe is a remarkable testament to what East Bloc societies can now accomplish through their own private enterprise. The massive spread of VCRs and cassettes through the region not only has overwhelmed state efforts at control but also has occurred in spite of the almost complete lack of locally produced VCRs and tapes.

"The video market has managed to escape any control by the state and perhaps this is the reason why it is flourishing," said Poland's *Polityka* weekly. "The video movement has been a genuine grass-roots initiative and cannot and should not be interfered with."

Jackson Diehl is a reporter for the *Washington Post.*

According to accounts by state media and western experts, video machines began to appear in Eastern European countries in 1980–81, carried or smuggled in by tourists or workers returning from western trips. So rare were VCRs in the early 1980s that many owners earned extra income by turning their living rooms into informal theaters on weekends and charging admission to see films.

In the following years, government authorities in most East European countries allowed the private importation of western VCRs, and Poland permitted private entrepreneurs to establish rental shops.

At the same time, East Bloc governments failed to produce their own supplies of video recorders and tapes, meaning that the spread of the new technology became an exclusively private, western-oriented movement. Even now, state industries in Eastern Europe are unable to produce significant supplies of video recorders. Poland and Czechoslovakia claim production of between 10,000 and 20,000 VCRs last year, but the machines are almost never seen in stores. Hungary has entered into joint ventures with two Japanese and one Western European firm to build recorders, but most of the relatively small production has been exported.

The supply of tapes is an even more serious problem for cultural authorities. While Poland's market is swamped with thousands of western films, state video libraries offer only 134 different cassettes, of which 100 represent Polish or other East Bloc productions. Although the supply of state films is somewhat better in Hungary and Czechoslovakia, the VCR retains the image in those countries of a ticket to western culture.

The treats that East Bloc consumers have sought through videos have tended to be neither sophisticated nor overtly political. A chief popular enthusiasm in the medium's first years, in fact, has been for pornography, which was unknown in Eastern Europe before the advent of the video.

A recent survey in Poland showed that the most popular films included tapes of American soap operas such as "Dallas" and "Dynasty," movies by Sylvester Stallone and Tom Cruise, the "Police Academy" series and sexually explicit movies featuring Kim Basinger. At the same time, opposition political groups in both Poland and Czechoslovakia have begun to use video to defeat censorship. The Polish underground publisher Nowa has issued more than a dozen video tapes in the past two years, including banned Polish films spirited from the censor's closet, clandestinely produced documentaries and the western productions "1984" and "Sophie's Choice," for which it obtained legal rights.

Nowa's latest offering, a documentary entitled "Witnesses" about the 1946 pogrom in the city of Kielce, has been one of the most talked-about films in Poland this year, despite never having been released or even mentioned by official media.

In Czechoslovakia, a series of "video magazines" produced on cassette by Karel Kyncl, an emigré Czechoslovak journalist in London, have been circulating around the country, copied and recopied by students and intellectuals eager to see its assemblage of western news reports and interviews with Czechoslovak cultural and political figures.

"People eventually get tired of watching porno and start to see the video as an access to more serious things," says Jiri Dienstbier, a journalist and prominent Czechoslovak opposition activist. "Then video becomes a perfect medium for alternative expression."

The technological simplicity of video and its spread through private hands has undermined most government efforts to control the medium until now. Most Eastern European governments have attempted in recent years to censor cassettes passing into the country or appearing on private shop shelves. But the easy-to-hide tapes have eluded controls even in the most repressive countries.

Bulgaria, for example, requires the registration of all imported video recorders and the review by censors of all imported tapes. Persons who sell or show banned tapes risk a jail term of three years or more. Nevertheless, western diplomats say a wide range of films circulate privately among Sofia's estimated 50,000 VCR owners. The U.S. Embassy alone lends 20 to 25 tapes of American films a day to Bulgarians, and many are copied and passed on, officials say.

In Poland, authorities implemented new regulations at the beginning of this year to tighten controls over private video shops, nominally in an effort to curtail trafficking of pirated western films that make up the majority of the shops' stocks. Yet, while the new policy nominally limits the Polish cassette market to the 134 state-approved titles, private video shops in Warsaw have exploited loopholes in the law to continue lending other tapes.

Articles in the state media have ridiculed the official effort to control a market so clearly beyond the government's reach. "Most of these endeavors must end in fiasco," said *Polityka*. "The basic principle of the state's policy toward the video market," it said, "should read, 'Disturb as little as possible.'" ■

PERSPECTIVE 3

Reporting on Apartheid

In late 1985, the government of South Africa placed a ban on reporting of anti-apartheid protest activities within the country. Analysts predicted that without worldwide coverage of the actions of the South African government, the issue of apartheid would quickly disappear from the public agenda.

Consider:

1. How does press coverage of the South African government today differ from press coverage in the mid-1980s, according to Brown?

2. Do you agree with Edward Hoagland's assessment of the American press that they are "a press that travels only belatedly and as a thundering herd, so that as a nation we are perpetually astonished after the fact at whatever goes on in the world"? Why? Why not?

3. How much did the ban on press coverage of protests affect international attention to the issue of apartheid, according to Brown?

4. What is the main reason, according to Brown, that the actions in South Africa continue today "largely out of the international spotlight"? Do you agree? Disagree? Explain.

Why Has the U.S. Media Spotlight Turned Away from South Africa?

TREVOR BROWN

Americans' questions to a native South African have changed. From the 1960s through the early 1980s they used to ask, "When do you think the revolution will occur?" Now they ask, "What's really happening there?" Guided by the information and images of the press, Americans have shifted from prediction to confusion, from "apocalypse now" through "the fire next time" to "engage or disinvest?" Even that question may have been tabled. South Africa was on the nation's agenda in 1985–86. It is not now, not unless the Rev. Jesse Jackson can lure it back by insisting that the Democratic Party define South Africa as a terrorist state. The apartheid story, it seems, has almost disappeared.

The sad irony is that the press is better prepared in 1988 to help the public tackle the South African issue than it was when South Africa exploded into American consciousness in March 1960 with the shooting at Sharpeville. Edward Hoagland's later judgment on the American press may have applied for the period 1960–1976. A stay-at-home intellectual community, he wrote, "has resulted in a stay-at-home journalism, a press that travels only belatedly and as a thundering herd, so that as a nation we are perpetually astonished after the fact at whatever goes on in the world."

Sharpeville did not so much astonish attentive citizens as confirm their expectations. "For

Trevor Brown is dean of the School of Journalism at Indiana University. Born in Cape Town, South Africa, he worked for the *Cape Times* in the mid-1960s before coming to the United States in 1968.

years it had been predicted," Newsweek wrote on April 4, 1960, "last week it happened." The magazine did not define "it," but the apocalyptic tone left little doubt as to what "it" was. Two weeks later Newsweek wrote, "South Africa may be headed for massive racial war, flaring up sporadically in the middle '60s, setting the whole continent alight in the '70s."

During those weeks journalists from all over the world thundered to South Africa, trying after the fact to understand how initiative for protest had passed from the hands of the African National Congress led by Albert Luthuli, "a typical embodiment of moderate African nationalism," as the New York Times described him in 1959.

"With the responsible leaders regarded as moderates banned or banished," the Times wrote in March 1960, "the extremist elements are left to whip up anti-white sentiment through organizations such as the Pan African Congress, headed by Robert Mangaliso Sobukwe."

The labels "moderate," "responsible," and "extremist" were not only serviceable shorthand for reporters suddenly projected into another foreign crisis. They were the currency of white South African liberals on whom American reporters relied for analysis of Sharpeville and later, at least for the first few weeks, of the Soweto uprising in 1976.

Novelist Alan Paton, in fact, almost single-handedly interpreted South Africa to the United States for 16 years. Only on June 24, 1976, did Paton acknowledge in the Times that he was "not writing for all the people in South Africa. I am writing for its white people. White people cannot write for black people any more."

Sharing that awareness, American reporters significantly matured in their analysis of South Africa. In 1976 they had once again thundered late to the scene, no more informed about Steven Biko's black consciousness movement in the late 1960s and early 1970s than they had been about Sobukwe's PAC in 1960.

In August 1976 Anthony Lewis expressed the puzzle for American reporters this way: "In the past, the common pattern has been a single incident, met by unyielding repression. But the trouble that began with the riots in Soweto last June 16 has not stopped. . . . For protest to continue so long is extraordinary under the conditions of black life in South Africa."

American reporters worked after 1976 to describe and understand those conditions, no longer relying on white South African liberals who had intelligent and moral understanding of apartheid but virtually no experience of the lives South African blacks lived. Such reporting was to win Pulitzer Prizes for Joseph Lelyveld's 1985 book, "Move Your Shadow," and for Michael Parks of the Los Angeles Times for his "comprehensive and balanced coverage of South Africa" in 1986.

So why has the apartheid story seemingly disappeared? In a study published in 1987 sociologist Eleanor Singer and statistician Jacob Ludwig hypothesized that the South African government's ban in November 1985 on photographic and sound recordings of protest activities would reduce American media coverage of protest-related stories, the overall volume of coverage, and the prominence of the South Africa story.

They found that coverage had already begun to decline before the ban, which turned out not to have had the effects they predicted during the period studied. As the South African government tightened press restrictions in 1986 and 1987, however, American journalists persuaded Singer and Ludwig that these later restrictions had reduced coverage.

Here is another hypothesis. Media coverage after 1976 informed attentive American citizens of the complexity of the South African story and contributed with very newsworthy domestic activism to establishing apartheid as an issue on the national agenda. South Africa became a problem requiring more vigorous bipartisan response than the Reagan administration's benign diplomacy of constructive engagement.

Through its representatives in Congress and against the wishes of its president, the concerned American public made its statement on South Africa with the passage of the Comprehensive Anti-Apartheid Act of 1986. Its conscience was essentially salved. South Africa had been dealt with and other items crowded the agenda.

At the same time the South African government made life awkward for the thundering herd and, by brutal oppression as in the past, painful for newsworthy protest. South Africa is not the photo opportunity in 1988 that it was in 1960, 1976 and 1984.

So what is really happening there? One fears that Newsweek in 1960 may have had it right: "In South Africa, a land so lovely even those who hate it can hardly bear to leave it, masses of black men chanting 'kill, kill, kill,' clashed with white men shouting 'Back you black b———s!' " Newsweek's melodrama of hate may not be that lurid in contemporary South Africa. Nevertheless the violence that attracted the American press to the scene continues now largely out of the international spotlight. South Africa threatens still to fulfill this nation's dismal predictions, but our attention is elsewhere. ■

The Film Industry in the U.S.S.R.

This view from filmmaker Elem Klimov provides valuable insight into the Soviet film industry.

Consider:

1. How are all Soviet movies financed? What does this mean to the Soviet film industry?

2. What dangers does Klimov see if the Soviet cinema become commercialized?

3. Will the new *glasnost* policy change the Soviet film industry?

4. Under the new system, who ultimately will hold censorship power in the Soviet Union, according to Klimov?

Back in the USSR

ELEM KLIMOV

I suppose it was the fact that it was the last thing I wanted to do that got me elected first secretary of the Soviet Filmmakers Union [in 1986]. There had always been elections, but it was only an automatic process: People were given a list of candidates and were not only afraid to vote against them, they were afraid even to abstain. This time—at the Fifth Congress of the Filmmakers Union—there was an enormous list of people who were nominated. It was passed round, and everybody crossed off the names they didn't want. And the ones who were left were the ones who were voted in.

The only producer in the Soviet Union is the state committee for cinematography—Goskino—and it finances all the films. It's an enormous apparatus of people whose main job has been to stick their noses into the creative process. The pressure from this organization had become so strong, so overwhelming, that in the end the filmmakers at the congress just revolted.

I think the people of my generation, my circle, were all very much aware that this congress was really a turning point, not only for Soviet cinema, but for Soviet society as a whole. It was a moment we had to grasp, because who knew if it would ever come again? But, of course, the reason why this new type of congress was possible was because of the changes taking place in the country as a whole: We'd just had the Twenty-Seventh Party Congress, which, again, was very critical, very different from previous ones.

After the filmmaking congress, we started fighting for reforms throughout the cinema in-

---

Elem Klimov is first secretary of the Soviet Filmmakers Union. His films include *Rasputin* (1975, released in the U.S. in 1986), *Come and See* (1985, released in the U.S. in 1987), and *Farewell* (1983, released in the U.S. in 1987).

dustry, to completely change its structure so that the creative personnel would be the ones with the deciding voice on what was going to happen. We started by looking at the criteria for judging a film, which were completely dislocated, completely deformed. Something would be obviously black, and you'd open the newspaper and read "It's obviously very white. A great film by a great master." The film would be getting the state prize, while in fact the cinemas were empty.

There was a whole series of filmmakers who were what we called "The Untouchables" because the critics weren't allowed to touch them. So we decided to start with the critics, with cinema magazines. Six months or so before the congress, there'd been a lot of very strong criticism in the newspapers about the cinema. Very strong—and there was absolutely zero reaction from the cinema magazines, the cinema establishment. Because, of course, they were under the thumb of Goskino. So we understood we had to change the magazines, and change the people running the magazines. Now the editors are new, and the screen magazines are suddenly interesting.

The Goskino leadership has also changed. And the situation is already very different in the studios: New ones are going to be set up all over the Soviet Union, with new art directors, new screenplay writers, new directors, new everything. And the creative intelligentsia will have a much more important role to play.

We're no longer going to have people sitting there on salaries—they're all going to be freelancers. Here, too, the social consequences will tell: There will be people who are suddenly not going to be getting work. It would be nice if we could just kick them all out onto the streets, but again, we have our responsibilities. We'll try to do it in a humane way—to find jobs for the people who aren't getting work in the cinema. That's another complication of this transitional era. But you can already see how much easier it is. A lot of the senseless old rules and regulations have already gone out the window.

The studios themselves are going to be giving the go-ahead to screenplays and will be pass-

ing on the films once they're made. The government will give each studio a certain amount of credit to start with; everybody will get the same amount. Then over the next few years, the studios will be expected to create their own capital and invest it in any way they see fit—and either expand or go bust. The distribution system will also be completely different—the studios and the distribution organizations will now be directly linked.

We do understand that there's a real danger of our cinema being commercialized. So we're thinking of all the defense mechanisms that, perhaps, we ought to be putting into place to defend the talented people making art cinema, to defend those who are taking risks in their work, to defend the young cinema people. A fund has been set up in the hands of the Filmmakers Union so that we can support both the studios and young filmmakers, talented filmmakers, and those good people who may happen to be in a difficult position for the moment.

Of course, the first and quickest to react to all these changes were the documentary makers. Several extremely critical, extremely truthful films have already appeared—about the people who go to work in the far north or in Siberia, and about the Chernobyl tragedy. And big changes in films for children are coming about, as well. Because we make quite a lot of children's films—but, as somebody was saying, they all seem to be about the sort of children that don't exist, and made for the sort of children that don't exist. Children are worthy of better than that, aren't they? You know, they always say you should make films for children the way you make films for grown-ups, only better.

We also set up a group called the Commission for Conflict in Creative Issues. Basically, its job was to review all the films which had previously been banned or partly banned, and decide what was to be done with them. And to read all the screenplays which had never been allowed to be made into films, and, again, to decide what to do with them. We thought it would be a very quick job.

The commission is insisting on leaving nothing out: full-length feature films, documentary films, television films, even cartoons and shorts. It wants to see every banned film. And restore justice. Some of them are very good films. Some of them are mediocre. Some of them are basically bad. But those films, too, we said, have got to be given their due. They must be entered into the filmographies of those who made them. And let the filmmakers have a look at them again and decide whether they want to have them released.

There are some filmmakers for whom it was such a terrible trauma when their film was banned that they would just rather not hear about it now. But some of the banned films are already being issued: Gleb Panfilov's *Theme,* for instance [shown in the United States at last year's New York Film Festival]. And an [anti-Stalinist] Georgian film, Tenghiz Abuladze's *Repentance,* which is an enormous success. It wasn't banned—they were afraid to even *show* it to the censors. *Repentance* is really an enormous turning point, not only in Soviet cinema, but in Soviet society.

It was first shown in just three or four Georgian cinemas because they only had three or four copies. And then they showed it—admittedly rather late in the evening—on Georgian television. Then, in January 1987, they started to show it in Moscow—but in enormous cinemas, the sort that have three thousand seats. They were stuffed full to overflowing; there was a time when the tickets were all sold for two months ahead. You can't imagine what went on in the auditorium. People were clapping, shouting, crying, embracing, hugging each other. Discussions were raging all around the cinemas. If I've got my figures right, three million people saw it in Moscow alone in two months. (I figure English distributors' hearts would be warmed to hear figures like that!) Then new copies were made, and now the film is going around to the rest of the Soviet Union. (Although someone told me that in the provinces the reaction is a little bit different. There some young people say, "That time—Stalin, Stalin, Stalin—has nothing to do with us. We're bored by it." So there are varying opinions.)

I also have the feeling that we haven't seen the end of films about the last [world] war. It's a subject that's in our very lifeblood. People just can't forget the war. They see it as the most terrible, the most significant thing that has ever happened in the history of our nation. New young directors are emerging who all want to have their say about the war.

But as you know, a film takes two or two and a half years to make, so, unfortunately, the studios are still bumbling on under the old momentum. It's a difficult thing to stop a film that's already in production: Money has already been spent. Or the director comes and says, "You know, if you stop my film, I'll pour petrol on myself and set fire to myself in public." So you'll only really see the changes by 1989 or 1990.

The other point is a more ethical thing. We know that perhaps the director is lousy, or the screenplay is bad—but we can't start banning anything now ourselves. People will start saying, "Aha, yes. A new set of censors." So we're trying to do something positive, to push forward the talented and honest filmmakers.

Also, we've already bought, or are negotiating for, several excellent Western films—up until recently, we've only been buying bad Western films! As for Western directors—of course, like anybody else, I am open to influences. I suppose some of the main influences on me have been Jean Vigo, Orson Welles—especially *Citizen Kane*. Kurosawa, of course. And in my cutting room, I've always had, and will always have, a portrait of Fellini hanging on the wall. As for Russians, Eisenstein has influenced every filmmaker. He's so vast; he even influences people who hate his work. Just like Tarkovsky, who has influenced people who can't stand him.

As for myself, I'm trying to teach myself not to admire any of my work. I think it's necessary for self-preservation. As soon as you start liking one of your films, that's the end of you as a filmmaker. It's better to like other people's films. ∎

The U.S. Press and Foreign Policy

This article by Journalism Professor William A. Dorman discusses the role that the media play in shaping our view of parts of the world that we cannot experience firsthand.

Consider:

1. According to Dorman, how is it that the U.S. press "creates a general mood about how the United States is doing in the world"?

2. Why does Dorman call the simultaneous creation of the Nuclear Age and the Television Age a "disastrous technological coincidence"?

3. Define what Dorman calls the "journalism of deference"; what is its effect on U.S. foreign policy?

4. Do you agree with Dorman that "the nature of the national security state has come to dominate our institutions and our thinking because of the introduction of nuclear weapons into the calculus of world affairs"? Why? Why not?

Mass Media and Public Discourse in the Nuclear Age

WILLIAM A. DORMAN

Given the unhappy history of the Cold War, there may be no more important subject to examine systematically than how the modern media shape our second-hand world, as the sociologist C. Wright Mills termed it. He was

William A. Dorman teaches journalism at California State University, Sacramento, and is an associate of the Center for War, Peace, and the News Media at New York University. He is co-author with Mansour Farhang of a recently published book from the University of California Press, *The U.S. Press and Iran: Foreign Policy and the Journalism of Deference*.

speaking, of course, of the fact that as humans we react to symbols that are given us for the most part by others. And in the modern world, of course, these symbols are often the product of the news media.

In some fundamental ways, the press creates a general mood about how the United States is doing in the world. On a day-to-day, situation-to-situation basis, the press gives us a highly generalized sense of things. The press, with its labels and stereotypes, tells us who is enemy and who is friend, who deserves our support and who deserves our contempt. The press tells us who threatens us and who does not. The press can alarm us greatly—or calm us down.

I am concerned about public discourse on these issues because how we come to discuss public matters—the vocabulary we use, the labels we employ—determines how we think about such matters. And how we think about such matters, in turn, influences the policies we choose or allow to be chosen in our name. I am not optimistic about the quality of public discourse in this country on the issues of war and peace, particularly where the news media are concerned.

Two possible explanations may convey the reasons why an open and robust debate on national defense is not being carried out in today's mass media. The first way in which the mass media may weaken public discourse involves the fact that a disastrous technological coincidence has occurred: the Nuclear Age and the Television Age have evolved practically at the same time.

At precisely the most critical moment in human history, our public discourse is dominated by a medium that discourages, if not actively defeats, serious thought. There is no better expression of this possibility than the recent book by Neil Postman entitled *Amusing Ourselves to Death: Public Discourse in the Age of Show Business.* Postman argues that television has conditioned us to tolerate only visually entertaining material measured out in spoonfuls of time, to the detriment of rational public discourse and rational handling of public affairs. He argues persuasively that we have become a television (visual) rather than a print culture and that we have, in many profound ways, changed our ways of thinking just as the coming of a print culture in the mid-1400's caused us to abandon the oral culture and Socrates' way of thinking:

From this country's beginning well into the nineteenth century, America was as dominated by the printed word and an oratory based on the printed word as any society we know of. As Richard Hofstadter reminds us, America was founded by intellectuals, a rare occurrence in the history of modern nations. "The Founding Fathers," he writes, "were sages, scientists, men of broad cultivation, many of them apt in classical learning, who used their wide reading in history, politics, and law to solve the exigent problems of their time."

Now a much different communication environment exists, one in which our political leaders quote lines from movies and television programs to make their debating points.

Politics, in many ways, has become show business. Vital issues are trivialized. Our public debate is characterized by a singular failure of imagination. Even the Cold War is reduced to a miniseries adventure film, as we saw... with ABC's presentation of "Amerika," which, judging from public comments, some people came to confuse with a documentary.

The second explanation for why the media may be doing serious damage to the quality of public discourse on defense and foreign policy has its roots in what might be termed the permanent state of emergency in which this country has found itself for the past forty or so years since the beginning of the Cold War. I believe that foreign affairs come to us from a system of news gathering deeply flawed by the subtle influence of a worldview that favors policymakers. The result is what I call a journalism of deference to the national security state.

This journalism of deference involves a willingness by the press in most situations most of the time to defer to Washington's perspective on the world scene, particularly where the Soviet Union and international conflict are concerned. To be certain, every news system in every nation-state has a bias when it comes to matters of foreign policy. Yet American journalists, so far as I know, are alone in their insistence that they are not subject to the effects of a worldview. Somehow, through toughminded training and a commitment to objectivity, they believe they have managed to transcend the human condition. Their work, in other words, has no significant subjective dimension.

The unwillingness or inability of American journalists to recognize the effects of worldview on their work may result from two factors. First, American journalism has established a fairly effective system to eliminate *personal* reportorial bias from stories about most domestic affairs. The problem with news about the Cold War, however, stem from *collective,* rather than individual bias. Because bias toward the Soviet Union, for instance, is so widely shared, it appears to journalists to be no bias at all. Yet American journalism has devised no set of safeguards against widely shared prejudice.

A second factor may be that American journalists assume they are nonideological because there is no tightly knit doctrine determining the shape of their work, unlike Soviet journalists who are guided by Marxism-Leninism. Yet any coherent system of ideas can comprise an ideology, whether these ideas are in the form of closely reasoned doctrine or not. Indeed, so strong is the clash of ideas between the two superpowers that what is called ego threat occurs, perhaps the most powerful factor contributing to enemy formation. Because of ego threat, Americans too frequently mistake threats to their deeply held values for physical danger.

The deference of the mainstream press is directly rooted in the establishment in this country of a sense of continuing crisis, especially since World War II. Consider what has happened during the Cold War. First, for the only time in two hundred years, the United States acquired a permanent enemy, the Soviet Union. Second, never before in our history have Americans had to endure perpetual anxiety. Third, we face for the first time in history what I call species threat, a threat made possible by the ultimate siege weapon— the nuclear bomb or missile. Such a threat does not just spell possible military defeat, but also the defeat of the species.

If the American press has always served the state during time of hot war, why should we be surprised when the press serves the state during a cold war, particularly one that (if things go wrong) promises total warfare against the homeland and devastation of the species. In short, the problems with press coverage of the Cold War are bound up in some forty years of antagonism, fear,

and anxiety. Journalism, like other major institutions, is operating on a wartime footing. And while the behavior of journalists is largely reflexive rather than deliberate, more the result of Cold War conditioning than the result of a conspiracy, the quality of public debate over the course of American policy suffers just the same.

Beyond anything else, the nature of the national security state has come to dominate our institutions and our thinking because of the introduction of nuclear weapons into the calculus of world affairs. The very technology of nuclear weapons demands that decision-making power in the realm of defense policy be concentrated at the top. Gradually, we have come to accept the notion that living on the nuclear edge demands that the fate of the many must rest in the hands of the few. Moreover, we sense there is no way to unlink the possibility of nuclear war with conventional conflicts, and we end up deferring to the president and his top decision makers in matters involving conventional conflicts as well.

The role I see for the press is quite simple: we need a reality check on decision making in high places. Those of us who are politically aware and politically active need to have a view of world conditions that is independent of Washington, no matter who sits in the White House.

To be sure, the press is not always deferential. That the press can still play a vital role is made abundantly clear by the recent events known as Irangate. Consider for a moment what Americans have learned from the press since last November: the administration of a president whose reputation in world affairs was built largely on his campaign against world terrorism has been selling arms to a country he has routinely vilified as being in the first ranks of terrorist nations. As a result, journalists have responded to the story much as they would if Nancy Reagan's staff, in the midst of her campaign against drugs, were caught peddling cocaine out the back door of the White House.

Perhaps even worse, we discover that the plan to sell arms to Iran was adopted by the president against the best advice of his highest policy advisers, and that the plan seems to have been conceived by a Marine Lieutenant Colonel with an Action Comic Book for a Mind.

Recent media revelations about the Iran-Contra affair aside, the problem remains that the press only seems to rouse itself under the most extreme circumstances. And that was as much the case with the Bay of Pigs adventure under Kennedy as it has been the case of Irangate with Reagan.

Richard Falk, a Princeton professor of international law, has pointed out that no tyrant in history has ever possessed such unconditional ultimate power as the President of the United States or the supreme leader of the Soviet Union. This power, of course, stems from nuclear weapons. At least in this country, such a concentration of power is the very antithesis of an open society in which politics ought to be played out in the public forum by citizens who have the right to participate fully in debate over national policy. Yet since World War II, we have gradually allowed ourselves to drift into allowing a patently undemocratic system of decision making to evolve. In a very fundamental sense in the nuclear age, even those who are lucky enough to live in free societies have been demoted from being citizens; they have become mere subjects. In this regard,

the concept of an "Imperial Presidency" seems entirely accurate.

If we think for a moment about a subject living in a nuclear kingdom and a citizen living in a democratic society, we see many differences. A citizen is given to robust criticism of the state. A citizen takes pride in active participation in public dialogue. A citizen considers it a duty to question authority.

By stark contrast, the subject is docile. The subject is quite willing to follow. The subject is fearful of questioning those who rule. The subject is willing to trade political freedom for a life of material security.

If we are ever to begin the long march through the nuclear wilderness, we must first begin to question seriously the assumptions that make our path so difficult to see. The challenge seems to be simply this: those of us who have somehow managed to hold on to our citizenship must work to preserve it. Those of us who have lost our citizenship must work to regain it.

It will be no easy task in either case; but it will be an impossible task without a vigorous press willing to challenge the givens of the Nuclear Kingdom. ■

CHAPTERS FIFTEEN AND SIXTEEN

For Further Reading

Books

William C. Adams, (ed.), *Television Coverage of International Affairs* (Norwood: Ablex Publishing Corp., 1982).

William A. Dorman and Mansour Farhang, *The U.S. Press and Iran* (Berkeley: University of California Press, 1987).

Sydney W. Head, *World Broadcasting Systems: A Comparative Analysis* (Belmont: Wadsworth, 1985).

George Thomas Kurian, *World Press Encyclopedia* (New York: Facts on File, 1982).

L. John Martin and Anju Grover Chaudhary, *Comparative Mass Media Systems* (New York: Longman, 1983).

John C. Merrill, *Global Journalism* (New York: Longman, 1983).

Hamid Mowlana, *Global Information and World Communication: New Frontiers in International Relations* (New York: Longman, 1985).

Edward Said, *Covering Islam: How the Media and the Experts Determine How We See the Rest of the World* (New York: Pantheon Books, 1981).

Anthony Smith, *The Geopolitics of Information: How Western Culture Dominates the World* (London: Faber & Faber, 1980).

Jeremy Turnstall, *The Media Are American: Anglo-American Media in the World* (New York: Columbia University Press, 1977).

Periodicals

Foreign Affairs

Foreign Policy

Public Opinion Quarterly

Television/Radio International

World Broadcast News

World Policy

Article
Citations

Chapter One (pp. 2–23)

1. "Roles, Rights, and Responsibilities: Whom Should the Media Serve?," by Ray Newton, *National Forum,* Vol. LXVIII, No. 4, Fall 1987, pp. 2–4. Used with permission of *National Forum.*

2. "An Introduction to Mass Communication," by Jay Black and Frederick C. Whitney. Excerpted from *Introduction to Mass Communication,* 2nd ed. Dubuque, Iowa: Wm. C. Brown, 1988, pp. 18–29. Copyright © 1988 by Wm. C. Brown Publishers. All rights reserved. Used with permission of Wm. C. Brown Publishers.

3. "Trivializing America: Entertainment," by Norman Corwin. Excerpted from *Trivializing America: The Triumph of Mediocrity,* Secaucus, N.J.: Lyle Stuart, 1986, pp. 19–32. Copyright © 1986. Used with permission of Lyle Stuart, Inc.

4. "A Coming of Age: Sea Changes for the Mass Media," by Everette E. Dennis. Excerpted from a speech given to the Council for Advancement and Support of Education, annual meeting, San Antonio, Tex., July 1986. Used with permission of Everette E. Dennis.

Chapter Two (pp. 26–47)

1. "Miami, It's Murder," by Edna Buchanan, Excerpted from *The Corpse Had a Familiar Face: Covering Miami, America's Hottest Beat,* New York: Random House, 1987, pp. 3–6. Copyright © 1987 by Edna Buchanan. Used with permission of Random House, Inc.

    Photograph of Edna Buchanan © by Mary Lou Foy. Used with permission of Random House, Inc.

2. "Tabloid Circulation Falls as the Rude Replaces the Lewd," by Jon Nordheimer, as reprinted in *The Sacramento Bee,* Feb. 18, 1988. From "Mild Mannered Buyers Tame Wild Tabloids," *The New York Times,* Feb. 4, 1988. Copyright © 1988 by The New York Times Company. Used with permission of The New York Times Company.

    Born Loser cartoon. Used with permission of UFS, Inc./United Media.

3. "Owning Your Own Weekly," by Bill Bishop. *Washington Journalism Review,* Vol. 10, May 1988. Used with permission of *Washington Journalism Review.*

4. How (and Why) One Small Daily Hired Five Minority Journalists in Just Six Months," by Mike Hengel. *ASNE Bulletin,* No. 703, March 1988. Used with permission of Mike Hengel.

5. "1987 Publishers/General Managers on All U.S. Daily and Sunday Newspapers by Gender." Table from *ASNE Bulletin,* No. 701, January 1988, p. 14.

6. "Reporter-Start Rates Average $378 U.S., $472 Canada." *The Guild Reporter,* Jan. 15, 1988, p. 1. Used with permission of *The Guild Reporter.*

7. "Paul Conrad's Work Uses Dramatic Images and Packs a Wallop," by Eileen White. *The Wall Street Journal,* Sept. 22, 1986, p. 1. © Dow Jones & Company, Inc. 1986. All rights reserved. Used with permission of *The Wall Street Journal.*

    "Commercial TV Fare," cartoon by Paul Conrad. © *Los Angeles Times.* Used with permission of the Los Angeles Times Syndicate.

Chapter Three (pp. 48–67)

1. "Understanding Magazines," by Shirley Biagi. Adapted from *How to Write and Sell Magazine Articles,* 2nd ed., Englewood Cliffs, N.J.: Prentice-Hall, 1989. Used with permission of Shirley Biagi.

2. "When Frank Sinatra Had a Cold," by Gay Talese. *Esquire,* Vol. 108, No. 5, November 1987, pp. 161–66. Adapted from *The Best American Essays 1987,* New York: Ticknor & Fields, 1987. Used with permission of Gay Talese.

3. "Readership Figures for Periodicals Stir Debate in Publishing Industry," by Joanne Lipman. *The Wall Street Journal,* Sept. 2, 1987, p. 25. © Dow Jones & Company, Inc. 1987. All rights reserved. Used with permission of *The Wall Street Journal.*

4. "Magazine Cover Roulette," by Mary W. Quigley. *Washington Journalism Review,* Vol. 10, No. 6, July/August 1988, pp. 18 + . Used with permission of *Washington Journalism Review.*

Chapter Four (pp. 68–85)

1. "Radio Romance," by John Updike. *Esquire,* Vol. 107, No. 6, June 1987, pp. 117–18. Used with permission of John Updike.

2. *The War of the Worlds,* by Orson Welles, as broadcast on the CBS radio network, October 30, 1938.

3. "Mr. Welles and Mass Delusion," by Dorothy Thompson. *New York Herald Tribune,* Nov. 2, 1938.

4. "Yuppie Radio: New Age Makes WAVE," by Robert Goldberg. *The Wall Street Journal,* June 18, 1987, p. 24. Used with permission of Robert Goldberg.

5. "The Sultan of 'Sportstalk'," by Frederick C. Klein. *The Wall Street Journal,* Sept. 26, 1986. p. 26. ©

Dow Jones & Company, Inc. 1986. All rights reserved. Used with permission of *The Wall Street Journal*.

6. "Radio Daze: Tuning Out the News," by John Motavalli. *Columbia Journalism Review*, Vol. XXVI, No. 4, November/December 1987, pp. 4–6. Used with permission of *Columbia Journalism Review* and John Motavalli.

7. "Radio's Unique Ability to Target and Deliver Specific Audience Segments," by Charles D. Peebler. *Television/Radio Age*, Vol. 33, No. 28, July 7, 1986, p. 87. © 1986. All rights reserved. Used with permission of Television Editorial Corporation.

Chapter Five (pp. 86–106)

1. "The Great Ratings Flap," by Charles Fountain. *Columbia Journalism Review*, Vol. XXVI, No. 4, November/December 1987, pp. 46–52. Used with permission of Charles Fountain.

   Jack Ohman cartoon from *The Oregonian*. Used with permission of Tribune Media Services.

2. "How Network Viewership Declined." Data from CBS; A. C. Nielsen.

3. "TV Is Going Tabloid as Shows Seek Sleaze and Find Profits, Too," by Dennis Kneale. *The Wall Street Journal*, May 18, 1988, p. 1. © Dow Jones & Company, Inc. 1988. All rights reserved. Used with permission of *The Wall Street Journal*.

4. "The Color of Laughter," by David Ehrenstein. *American Film*, Vol. XIII, No. 10, September 1988, pp. 8 + . Copyright 1988 by Billboard Publications, Inc. Used with permission of Billboard.

5. "As Milestones Fall, Cable Carries Weight," by Len Strazewski. *Advertising Age*, Nov. 30, 1987, p. 57. Copyright 1987 Crain Communications, Inc. Used with permission of Crain Communications, Inc.

   "Cable TV Gross Revenue Estimates." Table from *Cable TV Advertising*, Carmel, Calif.: Paul Kagan Associates, November 30, 1987.

Chapter Six (pp. 107–125)

1. "Now Playing: The New Hollywood," by Aljean Harmetz. *The New York Times*, Jan. 10, 1988, p. H-1. Copyright © 1988 by The New York Times Company. Used with permission of The New York Times Company.

2. "Color Bars: A Panel Discussion." *American Film*, Vol. XIII, No. 6, April 1988, pp. 37–42. Excerpted from the panel "Blacks on Film," presented by the Center for American Culture Studies, New York: Columbia University, Feb. 11, 1987. Used with permission.

3. "Hollywood Weekend: Word-Working Time," by David T. Friendly. *Los Angeles Times*, Jan. 29, 1987, p. VI-1. Copyright 1987 *Los Angeles Times*. Used with permission of *Los Angeles Times*.

4. "In Defense of Artists' Rights: 'The Beginning of the Battle to Preserve Our Humanity,' " by George Lucas. *Washington Post*, Feb. 28, 1988, p. G1. Used with permission of George Lucas.

   Photograph of George Lucas © 1988 by Lucasfilm.

5. "In Defense of Artists' Rights: 'The Creation of Art Is Not a Democratic Process,' " by Steven Spielberg. *Washington Post*, Feb. 28, 1988, p. G1. Used with permission of Amblin Entertainment.

   Photograph of Steven Spielberg © 1987 by Universal City Studios, Inc. Used with permission.

Chapter Seven (pp. 126–135)

1. "Music Is Alive with the Sound of High Tech," by Terri Thompson, Carlo Wolff, and Dan Cook. *Business Week*, No. 3023, Oct. 26, 1987. Copyright © 1987 by McGraw-Hill, Inc. Used with permission of *Business Week*.

   Graph: "The Electronic Keyboard Crescendo," as reprinted in *Business Week*, No. 3023, Oct. 26, 1987. Copyright © 1987 by McGraw-Hill, Inc. Used with permission of *Business Week*.

2. "Records: Growing Again . . . But Fewer Bright Spots." Data from Recording Industry Association of America.

3. "A New and Awful Silence," by Bernard Holland. *Harper's*, Vol. 275, No. 1646, July 1987. Copyright © 1987 by *Harper's Magazine*. All rights reserved. Used with special permission of *Harper's Magazine*.

4. "The Beat Goes On, But It Costs Lots More," by William K. Knoedelseder Jr. From "Memo: Recording Studios," *Los Angeles Times*, July 4, 1988. Copyright 1988 *Los Angeles Times*. Used with permission of *Los Angeles Times*.

Chapter Eight (pp. 136–149)

1. "The Wages of Writing," by Paul William Kingston and Jonathan R. Cole. Excerpted from *The Wages of Writing*, New York: Columbia University Press, 1986, pp. 1–19. Copyright © 1986 Columbia Uni-

versity Press. Used with permission of Columbia University Press.

Drawing by Weber. © 1988 The New Yorker Magazine, Inc. Used with permission.

2. "Hype House," by Gerri Hirshey. Excerpted from an article in *Manhattan inc.,* Vol. 4, No. 3, March 1987, pp. 99–108. Used with permission of Gerri Hirshey.

3. "The Art of Serious Fiction," by Milan Kundera. Excerpted from *The Art of the Novel,* New York: Grove Press, 1988, pp. 16–18. Used with permission of Grove Press.

4. " 'Ever Et Raw Meat?' and Other Weird Questions," by Stephen King. *The New York Times Book Review,* Dec. 6, 1987, p. 7. Used with permission of the author's agent, Kirby McCauley Ltd.

Chapter Nine (pp. 152–167)

1. "Where the Money Goes," by Alex Ben Block. *Forbes,* Vol. 140, No. 6, Sept. 21, 1987, pp. 178–180. © Forbes Inc. 1988. Used with permission of *Forbes* magazine.

2. "Single-Source Ad Research Heralds Detailed Look at Household Habits," by Joanne Lipman. *The Wall Street Journal,* Feb. 16, 1988, p. 35. © 1988 Dow Jones & Company, Inc. All rights reserved. Used with permission of *The Wall Street Journal.*

"Learning About Grape-Nuts in Denver," by Joanne Lipman. *The Wall Street Journal,* Feb. 16, 1988, p. 35. © 1988 Dow Jones & Company, Inc. All rights reserved. Used with permission of *The Wall Street Journal.*

3. "Psychological Appeal in TV Ads Found Effective," by Kim Foltz. *Adweek's Marketing Week,* Vol. XXVIII, No. 4, Aug. 31, 1987, p. 38. Used with permission of *Adweek.*

"Emotional Pitches Do Sell Well." Graph from "Psychological Appeal in TV Ads Found Effective," by Kim Foltz. *Adweek's Marketing Week,* Vol. XXVIII, No. 4, Aug. 31, 1987, p. 38. Used with permission of *Adweek.*

4. "Smart Move: Caps, Gowns, Chicks," by Debbie Seaman. *Adweek,* Vol. XXVII, No. 42, Sept. 8, 1986, p. 30. Used with permission of *Adweek.*

5. "Marketing to Hispanics," by Ed Fitch. *Advertising Age,* Feb. 8, 1988, p. S-1. Copyright 1988 Crain Communications, Inc. Used with permission of Crain Communications, Inc.

"Hispanic Market Ad Expenditures." Data from *Hispanic Business.* In "Marketing to Hispan-

ics," by Ed Fitch. *Advertising Age,* Feb. 8, 1988, p. S-1. Copyright 1988 Crain Communications, Inc. Used with permission of Crain Communications, Inc.

"Top 15 Advertisers in the Hispanic Market." Data from *Hispanic Business.* In "Marketing to Hispanics," by Ed Fitch. *Advertising Age,* Feb. 8, 1988, p. S-1. Copyright 1988 Crain Communications, Inc. Used with permission of Crain Communications, Inc.

Chapter Ten (pp. 168–191)

1. "PR—What Is It?," by Doug Newsom and Alan Scott. Excerpted from *This Is PR,* 3rd ed. Belmont, Calif.: Wadsworth, 1985, pp. 5–22. Used with permission of Wadsworth Publishing Company.

2. "Father of PR Analyzes Its History," by Edward L. Bernays. *Communication World,* April 1984, pp. 38–39. Excerpted from a speech to a public relations symposium at the University of Florida, Gainesville. Used with permission of the International Association of Business Communicators.

3. "How Political Public Relations Shapes the News," by Jeff Blyskal and Marie Blyskal. Excerpted from *PR: How the Public Relations Industry Writes the News,* New York: William Morrow, 1985, pp. 190–94. Copyright © 1985 by Jeff and Marie Blyskal. Used with permission of William Morrow and Company, Inc.

4. "Public Relations: How to Make the Best Use of Contacts with Editors and Reporters," by Frederick Buchstein. Reprinted from *Vital Speeches,* Vol. LIV, No. 17, June 15, 1988, pp. 535–39. From a speech delivered before the Internal Revenue Service, Continuing Education Series, Cleveland, Ohio, April 20, 1988. Used with permission of Frederick Buchstein.

5. "Hail to the Image," by Steven W. Colford. *Advertising Age,* Vol. 59, No. 27, June 27, 1988, p. 3. Copyright 1988 Crain Communications, Inc. Used with permission of Crain Communications, Inc.

Ziggy, by Tom Wilson. Copyright 1987 Universal Press Syndicate. Reprinted with permission. All rights reserved.

Chapter Eleven (pp. 194–227)

1. "Citizens Rich," by William P. Barrett. *Forbes.* Vol. 140, No. 13, Dec. 14, 1987, pp. 141–48. © Forbes Inc. 1987. Used with permission of *Forbes* magazine.

"Hearst Corp.: The Empire at 100." Table from

Forbes, Vol. 140, No. 13, Dec. 14, 1987, pp. 141–48. © Forbes Inc. 1987. Used with permission of *Forbes* magazine.

2. "Who Makes What?," by Robert Pack. Excerpted from *Washingtonian,* May 1988, pp. 192–93. Used with permission of the *Washingtonian.*

3. "Can Elephants Learn to Waltz?" by Merrill Brown. From a speech delivered to the Association of Journalism School Administrators, March 1988. Used with permission of Merrill Brown.

4. "Let's Look Much Harder at Mergers," by Irwin Karp. *Publishers Weekly,* Vol. 231, No. 15, Apr. 17, 1987, p. 46. Used with permission of *Publishers Weekly.*

5. "How Politicians and the Press Interrelate," by Mario M. Cuomo. *Editor & Publisher,* Vol. 118, No. 19, May 11, 1985. Excerpted from a speech presented to the American Society of Newspaper Editors' annual convention, Washington, D.C., April 1985. Used with permission of the Governor's Office.

6. "The Question Hart Asked For," by Paul Taylor. *The New York Times,* May 28, 1987, as reprinted in *The Sacramento Bee,* May 28, 1987, p. B-7. Used with permission of Paul Taylor.

   Cartoon: "The New Journalism," reprinted by permission of King Features Syndicate, Inc.

7. "AIDS Coverage: A Mirror of Society," by Ron Dorfman. *The Quill,* Vol. 75, No. 10, Dec. 1987, pp. 16–18. Used with permission of Ron Dorfman.

8. "We Don't Need a Scandal to Make Religion an Important News Beat," by Richard A. Oppel. *ASNE Bulletin,* No. 701, Jan. 1988, pp. 4–11. Used with permission of Richard A. Oppel.

Chapter Twelve (pp. 228–253)

1. "Is Television Shortening Our Attention Span?," by Robert MacNeil. *National Forum,* Vol. LXVIII, No. 4, Fall 1987, pp. 21–23. Used with permission of *National Forum.*

2. "Don't Blame TV," by Jeff Greenfield. *TV Guide,* Vol. 34, No. 3, Jan. 18, 1986, pp. 4–6. Copyright © 1986 by Triangle Publications, Inc., Radnor, Pennsylvania. Used with permission of Triangle Publications, Inc. and Jeff Greenfield.

3. "Money and Class in America," by Lewis H. Lapham. Excerpted from *Money and Class in America,* New York: Weidenfeld & Nicolson, 1988, pp. 60, 67–68, 149–50, 187–88, 227, 235. © 1988 by

Lewis H. Lapham. Used with permission of Weidenfeld & Nicolson, a division of the Wheatland Corporation.

4. "Making Sense of Sex Stereotypes in Advertising," by Karlene Ferrante. Abbreviated version of a paper presented at the 1988 annual convention of the Association for Education in Journalism and Mass Communication in Portland, Oregon. Used with permission of Karlene Ferrante.

5. "Coming Out Stories: The Creation of Lesbian Images on Prime Time TV," by Marguerite J. Moritz. Abbreviated version of a paper presented at the 1988 annual convention of the Association for Education in Journalism and Mass Communication in Portland, Oregon. Used with permission of Marguerite J. Moritz.

6. "All It Takes to Be a Hero Today Is Fame," by Bob Greene. *Chicago Tribune,* Jan. 1, 1987. Used with permission of Tribune Media Services.

7. "A Conversation with Sam Donaldson About the Media and Politics," by Shirley Biagi. Excerpted from *NewsTalk II: State-of-the-Art Conversations with Today's Broadcast Journalists,* Belmont, Calif.: Wadsworth, 1987, pp. 85–100. Used with permission of Wadsworth Publishing Company.

   Photo of Sam Donaldson courtesy of ABC News.

Chapter Thirteen (pp. 254–282)

1. "The Thinning American Skin," by Rodney A. Smolla. From *Suing the Press,* New York: Oxford University Press, 1986, pp. 3–24. Copyright 1986 by Oxford University Press, Inc. Used with permission of Oxford University Press.

2. "Censoring Student Papers May Teach a Lesson That Will Return to Haunt the Mainstream Press," by Richard M. Schmidt Jr. and N. Frank Wiggins. *ASNE Bulletin,* No. 702, Feb. 1988, pp. 4–11. Used with permission of Richard M. Schmidt Jr. and N. Frank Wiggins.

   "Some Views on the Hazelwood Ruling." *ASNE Bulletin,* No. 702, Feb. 1988, pp. 4–11.

3. "'Dirge of Lamentation' Is Unnecessary," by Ivan B. Gluckman. *ASNE Bulletin,* No. 702, Feb. 1988, pp. 4–11. Used with permission of Ivan B. Gluckman.

4. "The Awkward Embrace," by Frank Beaver. *Gannett Center Journal,* Vol. 2, No. 1, Winter 1988, pp. 81–90. Used with permission of Frank Beaver.

5. "When It Comes to Drugs, Beware the Censor's Fix," by David F. Musto. *The New York Times,* June 28, 1987, p. H-17. Copyright © 1987 by The New York Times Company. Used with permission of The New York Times Company.

6. "Aladdin's Lamp Goes Dark," by Jane Hall. *Gannett Center Journal,* Vol. 2, No. 1, Winter 1988, pp. 17–23. Used with permission of Jane Hall.

    "Surrogate Mother," cartoon by Jim Morin— *The Miami Herald*/King Features Syndicate. Used with permission.

7. "Indecency: Radio's Sound, FCC's Fury." *Broadcasting,* Vol. 112, No. 25, June 22, 1987, pp. 46–49. Used with permission of *Broadcasting.*

Chapter Fourteen (pp. 283–312)

1. "Searching for the Context," by John Hulteng. Excerpted from *The Messenger's Motives: Ethical Problems of the News Media,* 2nd ed., Englewood Cliffs, N.J.: Prentice-Hall, 1985, pp. 5–13. © 1985. Used with permission of Prentice-Hall, Inc.

2. "February 1938: Fanning the Flames of Bigotry," by Dan Magil. *The Quill,* Vol. 75, No. 11, Nov. 1987, pp. 32–33. Used with permission of The Society of Professional Journalists.

3. "Protection from the Prying Camera," by Ellen Goodman. *Washington Post,* Jan. 4, 1977, p. 34. Copyright © 1977 The Boston Globe Newspaper Company/Washington Post Writers Group. Used with permission of the Washington Post Writers Group.

4. "The Shocking Pictures of Sage: Two Newspapers, Two Answers," by Don Fry. *The Washington Journalism Review,* Vol. 10, No. 3, Apr. 1988, pp. 35–41. Used with permission of *Washington Journalism Review.*

    Sage Volkman (before). Photo by Vickie Lewis. Copyright © by the *Albuquerque Tribune.* Used with permission.

    Sage Volkman (after). Photo by Vickie Lewis. Copyright © by the *Albuquerque Tribune.* Used with permission.

5. "Media Held Hostage by Its Own News," by Howard Rosenberg. *Los Angeles Times,* as reprinted in *The Sacramento Bee,* Aug. 24, 1987, p. B-7. Copyright 1987 *Los Angeles Times.* Used with permission.

6. "Twelve Ethical Dilemmas." Table created for the Center for Communications. *Advertising Age,* Apr. 18, 1988, p. 88. Copyright 1988 Crain Communica-

tions, Inc. Used with permission of Crain Communications, Inc.

7. "Industry Ethics Are Alive, Says *Advertising Age,*" *Advertising Age,* Apr. 18, 1988, p. 88. Copyright 1988 Crain Communications, Inc. Used with permission of Crain Communications, Inc.

8. "Broadcast News Ethics and the RTNDA's Code of Ethics: Perceptions of Local Television News Directors," by K. Tim Wulfemeyer and Lori L. McFadden. Research presented to the Association for Education in Journalism and Mass Communication, annual convention, San Antonio, Texas, August 1987. The research was supported by a grant from the Carol Burnett Fund for Responsible Journalism, University of Hawaii-Manoa, Honolulu, Hawaii. Used here with permission of K. Tim Wulfemeyer and Lori L. McFadden.

Chapter Fifteen (pp. 314–333)

1. "World Media," by L. John Martin. Copyright © 1989 by L. John Martin. Article written expressly for this text.

2. "The Latest U.S. Media Giant Isn't Even American," by Richard C. Morais. *Forbes,* Vol. 141, No. 9, Apr. 25, 1988, pp. 70–71. © Forbes Inc. 1988. Used with permission of *Forbes* magazine.

3. "Beyond the American Screen," by Adam Snyder. *Channels: The Business of Communications,* Vol. 7, No. 11, Dec. 1987, pp. 24–25. Copyright 1987 Channels Magazine. Used with permission of *Channels.*

4. "Top 10 Ad Spenders Around the Globe." Table from *Advertising Age,* Dec. 14, 1987, pp. 62–63. Copyright 1987 by Crain Communications, Inc. Used with permission of Crain Communications, Inc.

    "Where *Ad Age* Got Its Data," by Kevin Brown. *Advertising Age,* Dec. 14, 1987, p. 65. Copyright 1987 by Crain Communications, Inc. Used with permission of Crain Communications, Inc.

Chapter Sixteen (pp. 334–352)

1. "Ministry of Culture, the USA, and the 'Free Marketplace of Ideas,'" by George Gerbner. *National Forum,* Vol. LXVIII, No. 4, Fall 1987, pp. 15–17. Used with permission of *National Forum.*

2. "East Europe on Cultural Fast Forward," by Jackson Diehl. *The Washington Post National Weekly Edition,* May 2–8, 1988, p. 10. Used with permission of *The Washington Post.*

3.   "Why Has the U.S. Media Spotlight Turned Away from South Africa?" by Trevor Brown. *ASNE Bulletin,* No. 106, July/Aug. 1988, pp. 34–36. Used with permission of Trevor Brown.

4.   "Back in the USSR," by Elem Klimov. Remarks excerpted from his April 1987 Guardian Lecture at the British Film Institute's National Film Theatre. *American Film,* Vol. XIII, No. 5, Mar. 1988, pp. 45–58. Used with permission of the American-Soviet Film Initiative.

5.   "Mass Media and Public Discourse in the Nuclear Age," by William A. Dorman. *National Forum,* Vol. XIII, No. 5, Fall 1987, pp. 28–29. Used with permission of William A. Dorman.

Index

Obst, David, 119
Oppel, Richard A., 222–226
Orion, 112
Ornelas, Victor, 165–166

Pack, Robert, 202–204
Parade
    Nixon and, 178
Parker, Dorothy, 49
Paton, Alan, 343–344
Peebler, Charles D., 83–84
People
    covers, 62, 63
Pero, John, 164
Peter, John, 61
Petrillo, James C., 70
Philip Morris Co., 164
Playboy, covers, 64
Plimpton, George, 19
Politics
    media and, 12, 249–253
Polityka, 340, 342
Postaer, Larry, 154
Postman, Neil, 349
Pravda, 319
Preminger, Otto, 272
Prince, Charles, 222–223
Printing press, 3
Privacy issues, 292–299
Pryor, Richard, 101–102
Public Broadcasting Service (PBS), 11
Public relations, 169–173
    advertising, 172
    function, 171
    futurists, 173
    history, 174–175
    marketing, 172–173
    merchandising, 173
    phone interview, 184
    political, 176–178
    press agents, 171
    press and the public, 250–251
    press conference, 183–184
    press relations, 182–184
    press release, 183
    promotional campaigns, 171
    public affairs, 171–172
    publicity, 172
Publishing. *See specific media*
Pulse, 77

Quigley, Mary W., 61–66

Race
    comedic treatment of, 99–102
    in film, discussion, 113–117
Race relations
    minority hiring by media, 38–40
Radecki, Thomas E., 97
Radio
    advertising, 12, 83–84
        newspaper clients, 84

audiences, 11
circulation, 4
employment decline, 81
indecency standard, 280–282
music, 69–71
New Age, 76–78
ownership turnover, 82
programming requirements, 81
public service requirements, 82
sports, 78–80
television compared to, 11
"The War of the Worlds," 72–75
Radio-Television News Directors
        Association (RTNDA), 280, 307,
        309–311
Rather, Dan, 92
    salary, 202
RAW, 101
RCA Records, 321
Reader's Digest, 179
    readership figures, 58
Reagan, President Ronald, 247
    marketing approach, 187–190
    political cartoons and, 44
Recording. *See* Music
Recording Industry Association of
        America, 134
Redbook, 61
"Reefer Madness," 272
Religion
    media treatment of, 222–226
Renmin Ribao, 319
Repentance, 347
*Responsibility in Mass
        Communication,* 286
Reynolds, Steve, 294–296
Rice, Donna, 6, 31, 216
Ritchey, Dan, 295–296
Rivera, Geraldo, 98
Rivers, William L., 286
Roberts, Randall, 298
Rogers, Neil, 281
Roman Catholic Church, drug problem
        elimination and, 272
Roosevelt, Theodore, 175
Root, Jane, 240
Rosenberg, Howard, 300
Rosser, Jeff, 91
Roth vs. United States, 266
Rowan, Carl, 264
Rowe, Jeff, 81
Royko, Mike, 6
Rushnell, Squire, 277
Rust, Jr., Art, 78–79

Sabato, Larry, 189–190
Salaries
    of journalists, 202–204
"Saturday Night Live," 101
Sayles, John, 115–117
Schanzer, Karl, 118
Schmidt, Richard M., 260–263

Schramm, Wilbur, 286
Schultz, Ernie, 82
Science and Sanity, 13
Scott, Alan, 169–173
Scott, Ron, 62, 63
Scott, Willard, 202
Scruples, 142–144
Seaman, Debbie, 162–163
Seattle Post–Intelligencer, 199
Seattle Times, 199
Seeff, Norman, 153–154
Sex role orientation
    media depiction of, 243–246
Sex stereotypes
    in advertising, 239–242
Sex Stereotyping in Advertising, 239
Seymour, Horatio, 214
She's Gotta Have It, 116
Shoultes, Terry Whitman, 268–269
Simmons Market Research Bureau
        Inc., 58–60
Sinatra, Frank, 45
    interview with, 53–57
60 Minutes, 177–178
Smith, Albert, 36
Smolla, Rodney A., 255–259
Snyder, Adam, 322–325
Soul Man, 99
South Africa, media changes, 343–344
Speakes, Larry, 187–189
Spielberg, Steven, 123–124
Stanley vs. Georgia, 269–270
Stanton, Frank, 58
Star, 31
Starr, Judge Kenneth W., 278
Stauderman, Al, 154
Stern, Howard, 281
Stolley, Richard, 62, 66
Stollman, Gary, 301
Stone, Chris, 135
Stone, Radford, 103–104
Stone, Vernon, 308
Stone, Vernon A., 81
Strazewski, Len, 103–106
Streep, Meryl, 248
Sun, 30
Sweet Sweetback's Baadasssss, 117
Swift, Al, 278
Swift, Richard, 88
Symbol, 14–15

Tabloid
    circulation, 30–32
    television. *See* Television, tabloid
    topic changes, 30–32
Talese, Gay, 52–57
Tarbell, Ida, 49
Taylor, Paul, 216
Technology. *See* Media, technology
Television
    advertising, 12
        psychological appeal, 159–161

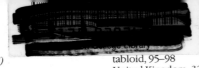

/ 111

ABS – 5496